Germania Illustrata

Habent sua fata libelli

Volume XVIII
of
Sixteenth Century Essays & Studies
Charles G. Nauert, Jr., General Editor

Composed by NMSU typographer, Gwen Blotevogel, Kirksville, Missouri
Cover Design by Teresa Wheeler, NMSU Designer
Printed by Edwards Brothers, Ann Arbor, Michigan
Text is set in Bembo II 10/12

Germania Illustrata

Essays on Early Modern Germany
Presented to Gerald Strauss

edited by
Andrew C. Fix *and*
Susan C. Karant-Nunn

Volume XVIII
Sixteenth Century Essays & Studies

This book has been brought to publication with the
generous support of
Northeast Missouri State University

Library of Congress Cataloging-in-Publication Data

Germania illustrata : essays on early modern Germany presented to Gerald Strauss
/ edited by Andrew C. Fix and Susan C. Karant-Nunn.

    p.   cm. – (Sixteenth century essays & studies ; v. 18)

Includes bibliographical references and index.

ISBN 0-940474-19-0 (alk. paper)

    1. Reformation – Germany. 2. Germany – History – 1517-1871. I. Fix, Andrew
C. (Andrew Cooper), 1955– . II. Karant-Nunn, Susan C. III. Strauss, Gerald,
1922– . IV. Series.

    BR309.038   1992

    943'.03–dc20   92-3256

                                                      CIP

Contents

POLITICS

Illustrations

Editors' Preface

GERALD STRAUSS DID NOT DESIRE A *FESTSCHRIFT*. We can assure him that we were aware of that fact when we took the decision to prepare one. The principal reason why we have enjoined all participants in this enterprise to keep it secret was so that he would make no effort to hinder it. All contributors, as well as those who were invited to take part but could not, were in agreement that Strauss deserved this tribute from his peers and his students. By common consent, even among scholars whose perspective on sixteenth-century Germany is at odds with his, Strauss's work up to now has had an effect on the subdiscipline of Reformation history that will persist for many years to come. He is surely one of the leading experts on early modern Germany of his generation. And we, his students, have frequently been made aware how very far beyond that time and that language area his knowledge extends. With this volume we salute not just a teacher, mentor, and friend, but also a true intellectual and a Renaissance man. We offer no apologies, Gerald.

We have incurred many debts: to the authors, who have patiently borne the editors' requests for the names of publishers, the closing page numbers of citations, and translations of German and Latin quotations; to those who have helped defray the costs of publication, whose names repose only *in* Robert V. Schnucker's *pectore;* to Schnucker himself, whose continual gifts of labor and love to his profession will never be adequately sung; to Lafayette College for a grant in support of typing the manuscript on disks; to the Department of History, Indiana University, for its cooperation; and to Mrs. Hilda Cooper for typing.

After reading through the essays in manuscript form, we realized that for several compelling reasons we could not achieve uniformity in the style of citing sixteenth-century books and passages quoted from them. We decided that insofar as possible, we would leave these as presented by each author. We editors have shared all tasks equally. Our names are in alphabetical order.

Andrew C. Fix

Susan Karant-Nunn

Autumn 1991

Gerald Strauss

Gerald Strauss: Historian

"HISTORY, HE KNOWS, IS A STAGE on which 'good and bad men, praise – and blame – worthy deeds . . . noble virtues and bad vices' display themselves so that we may draw our object lessons."[1] Thus wrote Gerald Strauss, quoting the Swiss historian Johann Stumpf to illustrate the wide scope of interest and curiosity that motivated the writers of the sixteenth-century topographical-historical literature that was the subject of Strauss's first book, *Sixteenth-Century Germany: Its Topography and Topographers* (1959). Just as the great humanist Conrad Celtis stimulated the interests of an entire generation of German historians with the ideals of his project to collect and write a *Germania illustrata* – a geographical and historical description of Germany set against its development from ancient tribal society to modern urban civilization – so, too, has Gerald Strauss inspired a generation of students and colleagues with his many important works surveying the intellectual, social, and political geography of sixteenth-century Germany.

With an eye no less discriminating and interests no less universal than those of the humanists, historians, and topographers that he described, Strauss has written about the land, its people and institutions, with a generosity of spirit and a genuine passion for his subjects, a passion that he communicates to his readers with a vivid, warm, and personal style of writing. His works invite, indeed impel, his readers to share his own sense of excitement and wonder at the works and lives of the past. In describing the lucid and inspired narrative style of the Bavarian humanist and historian Johann Aventinus, Strauss wrote, ". . . without the vehemence of passion, history was only chronicle."[2] The many students in whom Strauss's eloquent and sensitive study of Aventinus and his work has kindled both a passion for the study of history and an understanding of the nature and work of the historian would certainly agree with this assertion.

After receiving his Ph.D. in history from Columbia University in 1957 and teaching briefly at the University of Alabama, Strauss joined the faculty of Indiana University in Bloomington in 1959, thus beginning a long and distinguished career at that institution. That same year he published his first book. *Sixteenth-Century Germany* was the first account of the topographical interests of the German humanists of that century, surveying the works of such figures as Sebastian Münster, Joachim Vadian, Sebastian Brant, Johann

---

[1]Gerald Strauss, *Sixteenth-Century Germany: Its Topography and Topographers* (Madison: University of Wisconsin Press, 1959), 106.

[2]Gerald Strauss, *Historian in an Age of Crisis: The Life and Work of Johannes Aventinus* (Cambridge, Mass.: Harvard University Press, 1963), 247.

Cuspinian, Sebastian Franck, Johannes Stumpf, Johann Rauw, and others. Building upon the tradition of classical geographers such as Ptolemy and Strabo, the German humanists developed a descriptive geographical genre that served as a patriotic study of Germany and its people, providing readers with a knowledge of their heritage and a sense of their country's destiny. In describing this literature Strauss showed a genius for verbal portraiture equaling that of the authors he focused on. Taking their inspiration in part from the ideas of Celtis, these writers set out to illustrate Germany by narrating its history from earliest times and by describing the living, changing Germany of the sixteenth century.

With great care Strauss described regional chorographies focusing on Alsace, Swabia, Bavaria, Austria, and Switzerland, as well as the larger cosmologies of Franck, Münster, and Rauw, which took as their subjects all of Germany. The strong civic patriotism of Switzerland helped to make that region one of the most surveyed in sixteenth-century greater Germany. Strauss examined especially the works of Vadian and Stumpf. The latter's *Description of the Confederation* was the only account of all of Switzerland, a narrative filled with republican fervor and Protestant zeal that described the region canton by canton, city by city.[3] The colorful descriptions of the countryside made by Stumpf and Vadian as well as by other regional topographers were lucidly reproduced by Strauss in such a way that the reader can follow along behind the authors and see the region as they saw it. "These German humanists were not only patient scholars, but great travelers and storytellers as well," Strauss wrote, and the same could be said of his brilliant description of these men and their work.[4]

The great cosmologies of Franck, Münster, and Rauw occupied much of Strauss's attention. Münster worked for eighteen years on his *Cosmographia,* which surveyed all of Germany and concentrated on geography and local color. The cosmography was to be a receptacle for everything worth learning about a country, an encyclopedia of knowledge of the world and man, of the marvels of nature and human inventiveness, Strauss explained.[5] Such works were very popular with sixteenth-century readers despite their lack of any sophisticated political analysis. The humanists' optimism about the increase of learning and the advance of the human spirit filled their pages, Strauss related, and their authors believed that the achievements of the mind held the key to solving vital human problems. Strauss concluded: "Beyond the excitement of all this, beyond the color and variety which chorographic

[3]Strauss, *Sixteenth-Century Germany,* 45-59.
[4]Ibid., 106.
[5]Ibid., 116-17.

form held, these books breathe an assertive spirit and speak with such buoyancy that they are a joy to the heart as they are a pleasure to the mind."[6]

From his general treatment of the topographical-historical literature of sixteenth-century Germany, Strauss moved on to concentrate on one of these historians and his work – Johann Aventinus of Bavaria. In *Historian in an Age of Crisis: The Life and Work of Johannes Aventinus (1477-1534)*, published in 1963, Strauss provided a vivid portrait of this important humanist and historiographer who blended medieval universalism with the new perspectives of the Italian Renaissance and Erasmian reformism. Strauss emphasized the intellectual milieu within which Aventinus's intellectual development took place, including the atmosphere in the German universities of the late fifteenth and early sixteenth centuries. Aventinus's strengths as a historian – his patient search for primary sources – as well as his weaknesses – his lack of a critical approach to his sources, and poor organization – emerge from Strauss's portrait to create a balanced understanding of the man and his work. In the life and writings of Aventinus many of the important themes of pre-Reformation culture are evident. It was with these themes as much as with the man himself that Strauss was concerned.

At the University of Ingolstadt Aventinus came under the influence of Celtis, whom he followed to Vienna in 1497. Soon Aventinus had become Celtis's favorite disciple and received close personal instruction. From Celtis, Aventinus took shape and direction for his interest in history, Strauss explained. Celtis saw the need for an expansion of historical studies in Germany, and he enlisted Aventinus and others in his project to produce a *Germania illustrata*. Aventinus soon developed into a more perceptive historian than his mentor, and as a humanist he took as his models the great moral historians of antiquity. He moved on to the University of Paris in 1503, where he was influenced by Jacques Lefevre d'Etaples. After receiving his M.A. at Paris in 1504, Aventinus returned to Vienna, where he came to know Vadian and others.[7]

In 1517 Aventinus was commissioned by the dukes of Bavaria to write an official history of the duchy. This was to be his major work, and thus Strauss devoted much attention to the composition of its Latin and German versions. Compared to older chronicles, Aventinus's work "breathed a new spirit nourished on the classical historians" and was "infused with meaning," Strauss asserted.[8] Aventinus saw history as "a broad stream of related incidents reaching from the past to the present," and he combined past and present by "endowing the present with historically induced sensations collected in

---

[6]Ibid., 147.

[7]Strauss, *Historian in an Age of Crisis,* 10-41.

[8]Ibid., 70-78.

the passage: recollection and anticipation, remorse and confidence, despair and hope."[9]

By 1521 the Latin version of the Bavarian history was complete, but Aventinus worked over ten more years on the German edition. Strauss depicted these as years of disillusionment and disappointment for Aventinus, as the turmoil of Germany in the 1520s made its mark on the historian and led to an increasingly pessimistic outlook on history. Strauss saw this pessimism as central to Aventinus's later works and as symptomatic of the times. The German version of the Bavarian history became "a moralistic confession of Aventinus's own historical faith" infused with his own personal passion and criticisms of society. Aventinus intended his history:

> to document the instability of countries and men, 'so that each of us may guard against placing his trust in earthly things.' History shows us that 'just as men die and snow melts, so countries and peoples, even towns and villages, cannot exceed their given time, but they vanish and are obliterated so thoroughly that neither name nor location remains to mark their moment in time.'[10]

Although Aventinus's work lacked unity of concept and composition and failed to integrate history and geography very well, Strauss found it to have a powerful message nonetheless. Aventinus saw history as driven by the two great forces of divine providence and human free will. Free will acts in history, he declared, and God's purpose operates under the surface of history. "Only the historian as a man of conscience and custodian of faith could perceive the calm flow of purpose under the eddies of individual lives and actions," Strauss wrote, expressing Aventinus's view. Like the classical historians, Aventinus saw history as cyclical, and he also believed that time was running out and that the world was losing its strength and becoming exhausted as the end of time neared.[11]

At the end of his life Aventinus returned to Celtis's dream of a *Germania illustrata* and began working on his own geographical-historical description of all Germany. After consulting with Beatus Rhenanus and Vadian, he began to write in 1531, but when he died in 1534 the work was unfinished. Even so, Aventinus left readers with much to read and ponder. Like his mentor, Celtis, he believed that history was "queen among the arts . . . [standing] with poetry at the apex of disciplines" because it answered so many questions of that troubled age. For Aventinus history had a divine charge to keep a balance sheet of human deeds, and it furnished examples of good and bad actions to educate mankind. Indeed, history was mankind's indispensable

[9]Ibid., 80.
[10]Ibid., 107.
[11]Ibid., 206-9.

repository of collective knowledge and experience, and it was with great personal commitment and narrative verve that Aventinus wrote the history of his land and people.[12] The extent to which the historian identifies with his subject varies according to individual personality, but it would be unusual if we could read this account of Aventinus's conception of the nature and purposes of historical study without reflecting upon the personal commitment and depth of understanding that have marked Gerald Strauss's own career as a historian. That he admired his subject's vision is clear from the concluding words of the book, with which he reached a final judgment on Aventinus and his work: "Historical judgment is rendered independently of achievement. There were successful men and influential men in Aventinus's time, and even men of genius. Many were greater than he, but few better."[13]

The year 1966 saw the publication of Strauss's third book, *Nuremberg in the Sixteenth Century,* a work that marked a turning point in his career. From the optimistic humanism of the topographers Strauss had passed to the pessimistic historiography of Aventinus; and in this account of the people, institutions, and economic life of the great south German city he moved away from his interest in humanism and intellectual history altogether and began to concentrate instead on an analysis of social and political life and on a description of the activities and ideas of average people, an emphasis that would characterize his later work. Spurred by the growing interest of the 1960s in the role of towns in the great historical developments of sixteenth-century Germany, Strauss provided a complete picture of life in Nuremberg during its golden age. He discussed the patrician class and its control over political life and commerce, the wide extent of the city's trade and the skill of its artisans, the influence and impact of government institutions and regulations on the city and its people, and the various social classes and their roles in political and economic life. He provided a fascinating account of the everyday life and work of the people, stressing the wide gap between the lives of rich and poor and the impact of Roman law in Nuremberg after 1477.[14] He discussed the associations formed by city merchants and the flourishing trade that made Nuremberg foremost among south German mercantile cities up to 1550. Strauss also analyzed the important connections between business success and political power in a city with such far-flung trade routes, and the ways in which economic goals were adjusted to moral and political standards.[15]

Strauss also examined the religious and intellectual life of the city. Religion was part of civic life and never got caught up in the passions of the Reformation,

---

[12]Ibid., 230-32.

[13]Ibid., 259.

[14]Gerald Strauss, *Nuremberg in the Sixteenth Century* (New York: John Wiley, 1966), 219-25. Reissued in 1976 (Bloomington: Indiana University Press).

[15]Ibid., 117-53.

Strauss maintained. The city government had nearly complete control of church administration and clergy, but Lutheranism spread among the leading citizens of the city for purely religious reasons, Strauss argued, somewhat in contrast to the findings of Bernd Moeller.[16] In 1525 the city council held a debate that resulted in the adoption of Lutheranism as the official religion of Nuremberg, and thereafter the city followed the typical pattern of the urban Reformation: the council assumed control of the new territorial church and the monasteries were dissolved.[17]

Nuremberg was not a great center of intellectual life, Strauss continued, despite the presence of such figures as the Schedels, Willibald Pirckheimer, and Albrecht Dürer. Strauss examined intellectual life by looking at humanism, the schools, libraries, legal studies and jurists, and the artistic community, but he concluded that the penny-pinching attitude of many burghers prevented Nuremberg from gaining prominence as an intellectual center. "Burghers and artisans saw no use in stuffing brains and books with recondite matter in dead languages," Strauss concluded.[18]

Strauss continued his examination of the social, political, and intellectual life of Germany during the late fifteenth and early sixteenth centuries with two edited volumes, *Manifestations of Discontent in Germany on the Eve of the Reformation* (1971), a selection of primary source documents that Strauss introduced and translated, and *Pre-Reformation Germany* (1972), a volume in the Stratum series of reprints from scholarly journals.[19] *Manifestations of Discontent* made an immediate impact on the field of Reformation studies and became a standard text in undergraduate courses on early modern Germany. Its thirty-five documents illustrated the complex and uneasy social, political, and cultural atmosphere in Germany during the late fifteenth and early sixteenth centuries. Grievances against the papacy, social unrest, economic exploitation, imperial weakness, wounded national pride, and millenarian fervor all emerge from the documents to portray the period 1490-1525 as one of turmoil and ferment. Peasant protest, urban discontent, the grievances of the imperial knights, protests over the spread of Roman law, and a feeling that time and society were somehow out of joint combined to provide the background against which Luther's message appeared and spread. The grievance literature of the period was a dense and undifferentiated compound of theories, ideals, convictions, and attitudes mixing Augustinian historical schemes with

[16]Bernd Moeller, *Imperial Cities and the Reformation: Three Essays* (Durham, N.C.: Labyrinth Press, 1972).

[17]Ibid., 154-86.

[18]Ibid., 249.

[19]Gerald Strauss, ed., *Manifestations of Discontent in Germany on the Eve of the Reformation* (Bloomington: Indiana University Press, 1971). Gerald Strauss, ed., *Pre-Reformation Germany* (London and Basingstoke: The Macmillan Press, 1972); American paperback edition (New York: Harper and Row, 1972).

classical ideas of the progressive decay of the world's energies and the millenarian preachings of Joachim of Fiore. In his introduction Strauss commented, "Hopes for an improvement in man's condition clashed with the belief that human nature was incapable of self-correction, and these in turn competed with reveries of a blessed golden age and the fervent wish for its restoration. . . . A fresh interest in the data and process of human history rivaled an obsessive fascination with cosmic schemes as given in astrology, revelation and sooth-saying."[20] This combination of religious, political, and poetic traditions formed the temper of a troubled and expectant society, and it was in this milieu that Luther emerged.[21]

With his work on *Manifestations of Discontent* and *Pre-Reformation Germany,* a selection of edited and translated articles by eminent scholars on various aspects of German society on the eve of the Reformation, Strauss prepared for what was to become perhaps his most important, and certainly his most controversial work, *Luther's House of Learning: Indoctrination of the Young in the German Reformation.*[22]

In *Luther's House of Learning* Strauss took up three major themes. He first examined the concepts of the child and of childhood held by Lutheran educators during the Reformation era. He proceeded to the pedagogical program of the reformers themselves, and he concluded with an estimation of their success in realizing their goals. His multiple and multifaceted sources included the long-familiar school ordinances and less consulted treatises on education and childhood, as well as the usually unfamiliar parish visitation protocols from throughout the century that are plentiful in many German archives. Strauss determined to view not only the ideal type, modeled by the reformer in his study, but also the actual result as revealed in the records of scribe-participants, men who took down what the visitors dictated all over Germany.

Outside of the major cities of Germany, schools were so few that it is impossible to think of a burgeoning *class* of educators engaged both in instruction and in rethinking the ideals underlying their tasks. Instead, by *educators* Strauss meant religious innovators, particularly Martin Luther, Philip Melanchthon, and their followers; city fathers, themselves introduced to a learning tinged with humanist principles, who were long the very group most committed to seeing their own children educated and who were long charged with the oversight of city classrooms; and representatives of the territorial state, who in the service of various princes' aggrandizing ends promoted learning and discipline as an aid to the docility of their subjects.

---

[20]Strauss, *Manifestations of Discontent,* xxi-xxii.

[21]Ibid.

[22]Gerald Strauss, *Luther's House of Learning: Indoctrination of the Young in the German Reformation* (Baltimore: Johns Hopkins University Press, 1978).

The relative importance of these three participants in the shaping of the new education fluctuated over the course of the sixteenth century, but early in the period Lutheran leaders inserted themselves with the vigor of new conviction into the educational arena. Strauss showed in 1978, before "confessionalization" had become a scholarly preoccupation, that the Reformation was not directed merely at the Catholic church and the practice of religion but at all of society, including ineluctably every single body and soul. Reform was not to be chiefly doctrinal or intellectual or political – it was to be moral. Through the indoctrination of the child, the cultivation of the tender young shoot until it grew into the "new man," all society would be transformed in compliance with God's wishes.

Before 1525 Luther envisioned the family home as the site of indoctrination and transformation. After the Peasants' War, however, he was no longer confident that parents had the capacity or even the will to tend the spiritual gardens entrusted to them. As the superior agencies of moral transformation, schools had to be created everywhere, not just in the towns. "If people's behavior were to be conformed at least outwardly to Christian standards of conduct, government intervention seemed the only answer."[23] Rulers and reformers alike acknowledged that schools were to be an instrument of this intervention. All children, no matter how intellectually dull, had the capacity to be trained.

Strauss perceived in Lutheran thinkers a growing interest in childhood as a distinct phase of life, with experiences that left their imprint on the adult. Theorists, including Luther, reflected on whether infants were indeed innocent or, as Augustine had observed, sinful from the start. Should they be corporally punished? The reformers tended to see puberty and irrepressible sexuality as the end of docility, a condition for which early marriage might be a partial cure. In the curricula being drawn up it was of the utmost importance to present to children edifying biblical models.

The post-Reformation decades witnessed a flurry of discussion about education and the founding of numerous schools – many of them vernacular schools despite the reformers' frequent condemnation of these (except the ones for girls) as damaging competitors of the much-touted Latin schools. Despite a noticeable continuity between humanist and reformed curricula, Lutheran pedagogues introduced a few new works.

Perhaps the single most indispensable Protestant addition (and shortly afterward a Catholic addition, too) was the catechism. Strauss devoted a chapter to this genre that quickly became ubiquitous. This was the instrument by means of which Lutheran authorities made "a conscious, systematic, and vigorous effort . . . to change the human personality through pedagogical

[23]Ibid., 44.

conditioning."[24] In schools as well as in separate catechism classes, the catechism was drilled into all those children, and the few adults, who appeared before their pastors and teachers for this purpose. It was thought essential to have every child commit a shorter catechism to memory so that its lessons might act as an omnipresent brake on base human impulses. Hymns and hymnals served a similar purpose; melodies became mnemonic devices, engraving the messages of pious lyrics upon the brain. Pupils had to confront their sinfulness before they could struggle against it, yet Reformation and post-Reformation pedagogues did not want to dishearten their charges unduly with an overly pessimistic refrain. They sought a balance between admonition and encouragement, between theological doctrines of human helplessness and the societal necessity of upright behavior.

Strauss noted that "religion as an independent subject of instruction was a new departure in the history of education, a creation of the Reformation's endeavor to nurture and mold the maturing young person in a learning environment imbued with evangelical associations."[25] The reformers' confidence in children's malleability may be a major point of contact between humanist and Reformation pedagogy. In some sense, the reformers, too, can be said to have looked to a golden age of upright living based on schooling even as, in another part of themselves, they anticipated the millennium. In the end, they could not exorcise the devil from Lutheran society. Their best efforts "to make people – all people – think, feel, and act as Christians, to imbue them with a Christian mind-set, motivational drive, and way of life" failed.[26] Drawing on the dispirited testimony of the reformers' letters and other commentary and on the voluminous and often dejected visitors' reports throughout sixteenth-century Germany, Strauss concluded that one of the West's major educational campaigns met defeat. Literacy continued to spread, but Strauss remarked elsewhere, "For our explanation of how literacy came to grow in the sixteenth century we must look to mundane pragmatic causes, not to the Lutheran Reformation."[27]

In contrast to Strauss's earlier work, *Luther's House of Learning* gave rise to over a decade of controversy among Reformation historians. While Joachim Whaley could state in a review in the *Times Literary Supplement*, "This is undoubtedly one of the most important books to have been published on the Reformation for some time,"[28] a number of scholars, including, among others, Lewis Spitz, James Kittelson, Scott Hendrix, and Steven Ozment,

[24]Ibid., 175.
[25]Ibid., 226, 230.
[26]Ibid., 307.
[27]"Lutheransim and Literacy: A Reassessment," in Kaspar von Greyerz, ed., *Religion and Society in Early Modern Europe 1500-1800* (London: Allen and Unwin, 1984), 119.
[28]*Times Literary Supplement,* 21 March 1980, 336.

objected to Strauss's conclusions.[29] Without paying much attention to the first two sections of the book, they concentrated instead on the final section, in which Strauss concluded that Lutheran pedagogical efforts had failed to achieve the goals set for them by the reformers themselves. Strauss's critics often seemed to interpret this conclusion as a charge of failure directed at the Reformation per se. Simultaneously, however, a body of scholarship was taking shape that started from the perception that the sixteenth century witnessed the concerted and often successful efforts of the state to place itself in control of all aspects of citizens' lives. Historians examining the period from this perspective emphasized that the German princes fully exploited religion as a means of achieving political quiescence, or "discipline," among their subjects.[30] From this perspective, Strauss's findings were accurate. Confessional reservations notwithstanding, since the appearance of *Luther's House of Learning,* its theses have been solidly integrated into the historiography on early modern Germany.

After having been the object of both praise and criticism since 1978, Strauss may have been relieved by the calm and uniformly favorable reception that met *Law, Resistance, and the State: The Opposition to Roman Law in Reformation Germany.*[31] Still, this book continued to develop a main theme of *Luther's House of Learning:* the rising power of the state and the extension of the state's means of controlling its citizens. Indeed, this interest is visible in Strauss's work as early as the publication of *Pre-Reformation Germany,* with its two articles on Roman law in the Holy Roman Empire.[32]

In contrast with the vast body of literature on the subject of Roman law in Germany, Strauss examined not the laws themselves and how from a juridical point of view they meshed or did not mesh with Germanic laws. Instead, he took up as a whole the underlying nature of Roman law, what

[29]Lewis Spitz, review of *Luther's House of Learning,* in *American Historical Review* 85 (1980): 143; James M. Kittelson, "Successes and Failures in the German Reformation: The Report from Strasbourg," *Archive for Reformation History* 73 (1982): 153-75; Kittelson, "Visitations and Popular Religious Culture: Further Reports from Strasbourg," in Philip N. Bebb and Kyle C. Sessions, eds., *Pietas et Societas: New Trends in Reformation Social History* (Kirksville, Mo.: Sixteenth Century Journal Publishers, 1985), 89-101; Scott H. Hendrix, "Luther's Impact on the Sixteenth Century," *Sixteenth Century Journal* 16 (1985): 3-14; Steven Ozment, review of *Luther's House of Learning,* in *Journal of Modern History* 51 (1979): 837-39. Cf. Mark Edwards, Jr., "Lutheran Pedagogy in Reformation Germany," *History of Education Quarterly 21 (1981):* 471-77.

[30]The literature related to the subjects of "confessionalization" and "social disciplining" has become vast. R. Po-chia Hsia has recently summarized it in *Social Discipline in the Reformation: Central Europe 1550-1750* (London: Routledge, 1989), esp. his annotated bibliography, 188-212. Heinz Schilling has played a prominent role in the formulation of theory as well as the gathering of evidence, as his contribution to this volume, including the notes, shows.

[31]Gerald Straus, *Law, Resistance, and the State: The Opposition to Roman Law in Reformation Germany* (Princeton, N.J.: Princeton University Press, 1986).

[32]Wolfgang Kunkel, "The Reception of Roman Law in Germany: An Interpretation," 225-62; George Dahm, "On the Reception of Roman and Italian Law in Germany," 282-316.

it represented to those who championed it, and why the German people viewed it as an interloper and energetically resisted it.

To explain the growing influence of Roman law in Germany, Strauss pointed to the role of lawyers. Germanic law had lain within the purview of the laity, not nobles alone but also city magistrates and even peasants. From Italy came the idea that only those trained specifically in the law could know it well and administer it expertly. As the German humanists complained, Germany stood in Italy's shadow; legal training in Italy carried with it great prestige. As early as the thirteenth century, German scholars brought knowledge of Roman law back with them from Italy. Some were attracted to Roman law through their occupation with canon law, which was heavily derived from the Roman. Whatever the jurists' motives, both city governments and princes during the fifteenth century, the age of "the reception of Roman law," were irresistibly attracted to it. Roman law met their urban and commercial requirements in a way that German customary law did not, and it facilitated the creation of centralized authority. Yet Strauss pointed out that "scarcely a segment of German society failed to be drawn, at one time or another, to the utility of the Roman law." It should thus not be regarded as imposed from above, at least not initially.[33]

The enthusiasm with which rulers espoused Roman law as they sought to concentrate power in their hands produced a reaction, according to Strauss. As professional jurists took over the laymen's function in the administration of the law, as the numbers of lawyers and courts grew, and as both, as agents of the state, encroached inexorably upon every traditional sphere, the popular hackles rose. What we may view as an aspect of modernization threatened to undo that status quo in which peasants, artisans, and nobles alike found security. All segments of the opposition vilified lawyers. Strauss summarized:

> The high visibility of jurists and their "semi-learned" colleagues resulted from the centrality of law in public affairs, and this, in turn, was a product of new institutions and untraditional practices associated with the shift from a pre-modern to a modern organization of society. To the extent that this transition caused anxiety and distress, law and lawyers were objects of ill will. Held responsible for the disappearance of old ways and the imposition of unwanted new ones, they became targets for society's resentment, anger, fear, and suspicion. More than mere symptoms of what was viewed with alarm, law and lawyers were representative figures standing for an accelerated pace toward untried objectives and the seeming loss of control suffered by individuals over their own destinies.[34]

[33]Strauss, *Law, Resistance, and the State,* 73.
[34]Ibid., 191.

In a particularly illuminating chapter on the Reformation, Strauss explained why the rebellious peasants sought refuge behind the divine, or "godly" law.[35] The will of God as revealed in Scripture was surely the only implement with enough force to repel the devastating intrusion of Roman law, borne by the state, into village institutions. Not even the emperor could refute divine law. Martin Luther himself was inconsistent when it came to the question of the civil law. While he insisted on absolute obedience to princes and magistrates, he also detested members of the legal profession for disregarding truth and justice in arguing their cases; to lawyers, winning was paramount. Luther was in general an exponent of what Otto Brunner has called the "medieval" view that law must accord with principles of righteousness and equity.[36] By contrast, Melanchthon represented the "modern" position, one strongly reinforced by Roman law, that the will of the state determines what is legal. Luther's close associate regarded the law as a force for good.[37] His influential opinion marked a "redirection of the [Reformation] movement's basic thrust," according to Strauss.[38] Lutheran governments, and Catholic ones too, grappled the territorial church and religion to themselves and wielded them as an arm of the state, all with the sanction of Roman law. The Lutheran Reformation, by giving princes an opportunity to take over the sphere and the resources of organized religion, promoted the expansion of the early modern state.

The nearly universal resistance to the new law was most boldly articulated throughout the sixteenth century in the assemblies of estates. These debates were in vain. Knights, city fathers, and peasants endlessly presented lists of grievances at the opening of these diets, and rulers just as endlessly received them – and made no substantive concessions. According to Strauss, this exchange increasingly assumed the aspect of a ritual from which all the earlier significance had departed.

*   *   *

EACH OF GERALD STRAUSS'S BOOKS is built upon a massive and varied foundation of contemporary and modern sources. Taken singly, each has constituted a rich addition to the field of historical study focusing on sixteenth-century Germany. Viewed collectively, these books reveal a great deal about their author. They depict a man of rare intellectual range and insatiable curiosity about disparate themes. Many highly respected scholars have spent their careers mining the archives of one city or exploring a single topic further

---

[35]Ibid., 191-239.

[36]Otto Brunner, *Land und Herrschaft. Grundfragen der territorialen Verfassungsgeschichte Östereichs im Mittelalter*, 5th ed. (Vienna: Institut für Geschichtsforschung und Archivwissenschaft, 1965), 133-46. Discussed by Strauss, *Law, Resistance, and the State*, 244.

[37]Ibid., 227-31.

[38]Ibid., 229.

and further. Strauss has not been content to do this, although it would have saved him traveling repeatedly from archive to archive. With the completion of each book-length project, he has taken up an entirely new aspect of the history of Germany in this crucial stage of its development. The result has not just been a series of valuable and original monographs, but a many-sided contribution to scholarship and a seldom-encountered breadth of knowledge and understanding of the society and culture of early modern Germany.

The classical education that Strauss received as a youth added an intimate familiarity with those very ancient works that formed the backbone of early modern intellectual life. Whether or not, as he has casually remarked, that curriculum was meaningless to him at the time he first encountered it, it has provided its own ingredient to his profound grasp of the world of the sixteenth century. In conveying this understanding to his readers, Strauss has made use of what many reviewers have remarked upon as a felicitous and compelling use of the English language. This is more admirable, indeed remarkable, when we recall that English is not his mother tongue.

Gerald Strauss is one of the first scholars of the sixteenth century to integrate religious history into its broad context. Partly as a result of his career, the Reformation can no longer be seen strictly in confessional or theological terms; its interpreters must take into account causes including the mundane, motives including the self-serving, processes including the inglorious, and consequences including failure.

Strauss gives his readers a glimpse of the rare combination in one man of exceptional mental acuity and versatility, an unquenchable desire to expand his expertise and add new elements to his grasp of early modern European history, a close acquaintance with classical literature, an exemplary facility in several languages, and ceaseless assiduity. All of these characteristics taken together justify the comparison of Gerald Strauss to the best of Renaissance humanists. To the humanists' qualities he adds another perhaps more valuable and more greatly needed in the late twentieth century than in the sixteenth century: a sensitive and humane outlook on human affairs. His own "illustrations" of Germany, although different from Celtis's, will prove to have left a mark every bit as indelible on the field of sixteenth-century German history.

Saint Jerome in his study

Intellectual Life

The Antichrist in the Early German Reformation: Reflections on Theology and Propaganda

Hans J. Hillerbrand

This essay argues that the concept of the Antichrist, derived from the Book of Daniel and the Book of Revelation, played an important role in the early Reformation as both a theological concept and a propaganda tool. It surveys the extensive uses of and references to the Antichrist in the early years of the Reformation, notes the use of art to convey the idea of the Antichrist, and explores how the concept of the Antichrist was of decisive importance in turning a movement for reform within the Catholic church into one of change from without.

IT IS NOT SURPRISING, given the restive turbulence of the early years of the Reformation of the sixteenth century, that the Antichrist made a prompt appearance in the Reformation controversy.[1] And a dramatic appearance it was, coming as it did in Martin Luther's response to the papal bull *Exsurge Domine*, which had threatened him with excommunication. Luther's poignant declaration *Adversus Execrabilem Antichristi Bullam (Against the Damned Bull of the Antichrist)* made a swift and categorical identification of pope with Antichrist.[2] Whatever the biblical and theological justification Luther adduced for this identification, the reality was clear enough. Luther responded to the most dramatic pronouncement of which the papacy was capable, namely excommunication – and its concomitant, the loss of eternal salvation – with the most dramatic pronouncement of his own, namely the "counter-excommunication" of the pope as Antichrist.

Luther's defiant declaration can be better understood when it is placed into its proper historical context. After all, the notion of the Antichrist had a lengthy history. Biblical passages such as Daniel 8, I John 2:18 and 4:3, and Revelation 13-19, to cite just a few, had incited theological reflection ever since the early days of Christianity. These passages affirmed the reality

---

[1] See, for a useful introduction, F. Lepp, *Schlagwörter des Reformationszeitalters* (Leipzig: M. Heinsius, 1908) and the routinely cited work by H. Preuss, *Die Vorstellungen vom Antichrist im späteren Mittelalter, bei Luther und in der konfessionellen Polemik* (Leipzig: J. C. Hinrichs, 1906).

[2] See *D. Martin Luthers Werke* (Weimar: Böhlau, 1883-1987), 6:597-612, esp. 598. Hereafter abbreviated WA.

of the Antichrist, and identified him, moreover, as the eschatological counterpart of Christ and the church. The Antichrist was thus a major figure, dramatically labeled "Son of Satan" by Hippolytus.

The theological consensus was that, prior to the Second Coming of Christ, the Antichrist would appear and rule for a brief period of time, but eventually be subdued by Christ. The exegetical and theological tradition focused on the Antichrist's characteristics – his blasphemy, his arrogant self-esteem, his persecution of the saints of God – particularly in decided contrast to the simplicity, humility, and truthfulness of Jews. Prominent among these characteristics was his theological error – so much so, as a matter of fact, that Origen saw the Antichrist as a synonym for heresy.

Uncertainty and disagreement remained, however, on a key point. Some theologians held that the Antichrist was not yet present on earth, even though his precursors were, while others argued that he was already here.[3] The Donatist theologian Tyconius developed the thesis that the Antichrist was not only already present, but was – horror of horrors! – in the church. The argument, while startling, was not surprising. Tyconius, after all, had to come to grips with the reality that the church had declared the Donatist understanding of Christianity heretical, and he therefore had to find a way to describe the church that had done so. The fact that his perspective proved to be influential in subsequent centuries suggests that the issue – how dissenters should characterize the church that had condemned them – did not go away. By the same token, Tyconius's exegesis made it possible to give the Book of Revelation a mystical interpretation above and beyond the literal sense, and it allowed one to come to the conclusion that one's own theological opponents, within or without the church, were the Antichrist.[4]

The Antichrist was part and parcel of the larger scheme of salvation history. Although enigmatic and not part of the central credal affirmations, he was crucially important nonetheless. He was the "gauge" for the imminence of Christ's return, a reality promptly experienced whenever biblical or secular chronology seemed to intimate the end. After all, the Antichrist epitomized the end, the Second Coming of Jesus, the Last Judgment.[5] Those who read the Scriptures with an eye to the chronology of the end were bound to see

---

[3]Bernard of Clairvaux wondered if Anakletus II was the Antichrist, while Emperor Frederick II declared that Gregory IX was the Antichrist.

[4]For a thorough treatment of Tyconius see H. D. Rauh, *Das Bild des Antichrist im Mittelalter: Von Tyconius zum deutschen Symbolismus* (Münster: Aschendorff, 1979), 102-20. Joachim of Fiore also observed that the established church persecuted the true Christian; thus its identification with the Antichrist was made possible. See here the other, still useful works of E. Benz, *Ecclesia Spiritualis. Kirchenidee und Geschichtstheologie der franziskanischen Reformation* (Stuttgart: Kohlhammer, 1934), 48.

[5]See the informative articles on the Antichrist in Religion in *Geschichte und Gegenwart* and, esp., in the *Theologische Realenzyklopädie* (Berlin: de Gruyter, 1977–).

him as important. The Antichrist thus became crucial for the understanding of history.

Even though the disappearance of persecution had caused the eschatological fervor of early Christianity by and large to disappear in the medieval church, with the Antichrist declining in importance, intermittent interest continued throughout the Middle Ages. Adso of Montier-en-Der, a tenth-century monk, produced one of the earliest medieval treatments of the Antichrist in a work known as *Libellus de Antichristo*.[6] Giovanni Nanni published his *De futuris Christianorum Triumphis in Sarcenos* (or, *Glossa sive Expositio Super Apocalypsim*) in 1481. He identified Mohammed with the Antichrist and envisioned a Christian conquest of Constantinople. His book was astoundingly successful, as is evidenced by no less than ten editions, including one by Martin Luther.[7] John Purvey's commentary on Revelation, completed in 1390, identified the pope with the Antichrist, whose power would soon end.[8] Not surprisingly, it was in medieval dissent, and especially within the Wycliffite and Hussite traditions, that the identification of the pope with Antichrist was most stridently propounded.[9] While this identification at times was with a particular pope whose life was seen as profoundly perverted, it was also with the entire church. The fourteenth and fifteenth centuries were replete with premonitions of the coming of the Antichrist, with numerous specific dates suggested for his appearance.[10] Books on the Antichrist appeared right up to the outbreak of the Reformation, even as more literary and less theological expositions and portrayals – such as Antichrist plays, homilies, poems, and histories – grew into a widespread tradition.[11] On the eve of the Reformation, the Antichrist was a most important figure in salvation history.[12] The contours of his image were still very much as they had been delineated as early as the twelfth century by Hildegard of Bingen. The Antichrist would come from within the church. Prior to his appearance a restitution would take place –

[6]See here Rauh, *Das Bild,* 153-64, as well as R. K. Emmerson, "The Coming of Antichrist: An Apocalyptic Tradition in Medieval Literature" (doctoral dissertation, Stanford University, 1977), 107-41; K. Aickele, *Das Antichristdrama des Mittelalters, der Reformation und Gegenreformation* (The Hague: Martinus Nijhoff, 1976).

[7]WA 50:98ff.

[8]Luther published the commentary in 1528 (WA 26:122-24) with the observation "ut orbi notum faceremus, nos non esse primos, qui Papatum pro Antichristum regno interpretentur."

[9]See G. Leff, *Heresy in the Later Middle Ages: The Relation of Heterodoxy to Dissent, ca. 1250-1450* (New York: Barnes and Noble, 1967), esp. 2:520.

[10]See F. Saxl, "A Spiritual Encyclopedia of the Later Middle Ages," *Journal of the Warburg and Courtauld Institutes* 5 (1942):85-86.

[11]Dis büchlin sagt von des Endchrists Leben vnnd regierung (Strasbourg, 1505). It was reprinted in 1516.

[12]R. K. Emmerson, "The Coming," 440.

that is, the true Gospel would be restored – but this would be followed in turn by gross heresies.[13]

By the early sixteenth century, then, there existed a rich tradition which was the common lore of theologians and churchmen. Martin Luther's early reflections on the matter cautiously followed this tradition and identified the Antichrist simply as the enemy of the Gospel. His notion was not related to the pope. Quite consistently, in those early days of exegetical exploration Luther used the future tense when talking about the Antichrist. In other words, Luther appropriated the consensus about the dualism of Christ and Antichrist and expected the Antichrist to appear at some undefined future date.

Once the indulgence controversy had gotten under way, however, new elements quickly made their appearance in Luther's thinking. In his response to the papal theologian Sylvester Prierias, Luther noted (hypothetically, or, as he put it, "quod non spero") that if Rome taught perverted doctrine, then it must be concluded that the Antichrist ruled there.[14] In March 1519, in preparation for his Leipzig disputation with John Eck, Luther confided to a friend, "I am not at all sure if the pope is the Antichrist or an apostle."[15] The uncertainty was well taken. Luther was groping because he was ambivalent about the consequences of papal hostility toward what he perceived to be the true Gospel. Soon, however, ambivalence turned into certainty. The pope was the Antichrist.[16]

The reason for Luther's conclusion was that, while his evangelical discovery had given him a new understanding of the Gospel, the increasingly strident opposition of the papacy caused him to decide (since only one side could be right) that the pope and the papacy were enemies of the true Gospel. The legacy of medieval denunciations of heresy, put into Luther's lap by Eck's charge that he was nothing but a damned Hussite, called forth the reformer's identification of pope and Antichrist as an obvious countercharge.

The decisive year 1520 brought the culmination of Luther's pronouncements. In the *Babylonian Captivity,* the equation of pope and Antichrist became categorical.[17] Luther knew that the decision about his excommunication was about to be made, and he rose to launch a vehement and determined counterattack.

---

[13]Rauh, *Das Bild,* 513.

[14]WA 6:328, *Quid est Antichristus, si talis Papa non est Antichristus?"*

[15]WA *Briefwechsel* (hereafter *BR*) 1:359, "Nescio an papa sit Antichristus ipse vel Apostolus." The sentence continues, "adeo misere corrumpitur et crucifigitur Christus (idest veritas) ab eo in decretis." For detailed studies of Luther's development during that time, see E. Bizer, *Luther und der Papst* (Munich: Kaiser, 1958); E. Wolf, *Peregrinatio* I (Munich: Kaiser, 1954); U. Asendorf, *Eschatologie bei Luther* (Göttingen: Vandenhoeck and Ruprecht, 1967), 173ff.

[16]WA *BR* 2:48, "Ego sic augor, ut prope non dubitem papam esse proprie Antichristum illum, quem vulgata opinione expectat mundus."

[17]WA 6:498, "Papatum esse regnum Babylonis."

There were, of course, theological issues, not only about indulgences and grace, but also about ecclesiastical authority. But one may argue that at this point the key question for Luther was a strategic one – how to respond most effectively to the increasingly categorical pronouncements from Rome. This question raised such related questions as, Who did hold power in the church? How was it possible to rally support for his cause?

Luther pursued all avenues. He attacked the pope and the theologians, but he also declared filial loyalty to the pope. He explored ties with other theologians, rallied German anti-Roman sentiment, and, above all, turned the cause of religious reform into one of broad societal renewal. Luther's ambivalences prior to 1520 find their explanation in the ambivalence of the situation he faced at that time.[18] Was the papacy going to excommunicate him – which would have been not only a strident repudiation of the "Gospel," which he thought he had rediscovered, but also, in all probability, his own demise, plain and simple? Was he going to be tolerated?

Not surprisingly, Luther's sentiment prior to his burning of the papal bull *Exsurge Domine* on 10 December 1520, lacked crispness. Two months earlier Luther had written that he was certain that the pope was the Antichrist, but in the same breath he had assured Pope Leo X of his support and loyalty.[19] He had called his *Babylonian Captivity* a sharp and formidable trumpet sound against the tyranny of the Roman Antichrist, but he also assured the pope that he wanted his best.[20] Luther's appeal to a general council, issued when he received the papal bull, referred to the pope as "a damned heretic and schismatic." Interestingly enough, the Latin version of the appeal used the term *Antichrist.*[21] The German version did not.

The lines of argumentation were clear. Luther angrily pursued the pope as the Antichrist. And it was not just a transitory tirade either. If anything, the passing of time made Luther's polemic more vehement, more poignant, and more pronounced.[22] The range of his polemic widened. It did so appropriately, for the paramount issue from 1520 onward was to convey to the world that the break with the Roman church was categorical. The stories of Revelation 13-19 (the beast from the sea and from the earth, and the seven plagues) were directly applied to the papacy.[23] Luther routinely referred to the "imperial

[18]This is R. Baumer's term; see his *Martin Luther und der Papst* (Münster: Aschendorff, 1985).

[19]WA BR 2:195. Earlier Luther had called the Babylonian Captivity a "sharp and formidable trumpet sound against the tyranny of the Roman Antichrist." WA BR 2:168.

[20]WA 7:6. Rome is now, however, "eyn weyt auffgesperrter rache der helle."

[21]WA 7:75, 89.

[22]See M. Edwards, *Luther's Last Battles. Politics and Polemics 1531-1546* (Ithaca: Cornell University Press, 1983).

[23]WA *Deutsche Bibel* (hereafter *DB*), 7:12. This despite Luther's well-known aversion to the book, which was, in his opinion, "neither apostolic nor prophetic."

papacy" *(kaiserliche Bapstum)* to denote the worldly and secular character of the papal office. It was anything but a spiritual entity. In his 1524 translation of "The Revelation of the Antichrist in the Prophet Daniel," Luther confirmed his earlier verdict: "And the conclusion is that the pope is the Antichrist."[24] What Luther said here was that the Antichrist is not a specific person, but an institution. Still, in his *Response to Catharinus,* Luther argued that the pope was the Antichrist not only because of his perversion of the Gospel, but also because of the perversion of his life.

A publication of a popular sort became the spectacular vehicle for communicating Luther's notion that the pope was the Antichrist. The new propaganda tool was the pictorial broadside – and the figure of the Antichrist appeared as a weapon in the reformer's propaganda arsenal. The publication was *The Passional of Christ and Antichrist,* of 1521. It was a dramatic appeal to the common people, not to theologians. To be sure, one can read into the twelve pairs of woodcuts that comprised *The Passional* some underlying theological perspectives.[25] But what was indicted in the work was the pope's life and demeanor, not his teaching. And the indictment was a visual one. The primacy of the aural modality in the movement of reform was replaced here, clearly for propaganda purposes, by the primacy of visual modality. Image was to reign over word.

Twenty reprints attest to the popularity of *The Passional.* Its appeal rests on its pictures. The text is sparse, limited, and expository. It rounds out and complements the message of the woodcuts, rather than vice versa. The twelve sequences of woodcuts highlight familiar Gospel stories and episodes: Jesus' flight when he was to be crowned king (John 6); the crown of thorns (John 19); Jesus washing his disciples' feet (John 13); Jesus paying taxes (Matthew 17); Jesus' humility (Philipinans 2); the tired Jesus (John 4); Jesus preaching to the common people (Luke 4); his humble birth (Luke 2); Jesus on the donkey (Matthew 21); Jesus' simplicity of life (Matthew 10; Luke 17); and the expulsion from the temple (John 2).

The style throughout the pamphlet is one of simplicity, pointedness, and loneliness. It is a portrayal of the passion in the twofold sense of the word – passion as suffering and as empathy for the simple folk. "Passion" is the manger scene: the stable, simple and decrepit; devout parents worshiping the Christ Child, as do ox and donkey. "Passion" also is Jesus preaching under a tree to a group of ordinary men and women, the latter with infants on their knees.

The pictures with scenes from the life of Jesus offer reflections on Jesus. But they also exude, in their various settings, the quiet piety of the ordinary

---

[24]"Offenbarung des Endchrists aus dem Propheten Daniel," in WA 7:708.

[25]*The Passional* is in WA 9:676ff. See also R. Wohlfeil, "Lutherische Bildtheologie," in *Martin Luther. Probleme seiner Zeit* (Stuttgart: Klett-Cotta, 1986), 283ff.; and S. Scharfe, *Religiöse Bildpropaganda der Reformationszeit* (Göttingen: Vandenhoeck and Ruprecht, 1951).

life. In a striking way, the contrasts drawn between Jesus and the pope go far beyond the pope. They are contrasts between weakness and power – between the "we," the simple and familiar, and the "they," the important and powerful. The woodcuts graphically depict the contrast between the simplicity of the common folk and the luxury of the high and mighty.

Thus, there is a subtle but distinct antiauthoritarian and antiestablishment element in the woodcuts of *The Passional*. Even devoid of their text, minimal as it is, the pictures convey their message. This is particularly the case with the portrayals of the pope as Antichrist – the elegant banquet, the luxurious carriage, and the pomp of the kissing of the pope's feet. While we must not see the pictures as antiauthoritarian in a political sense, their strident criticism of authority and power in the church was bound to be received as an unsettling, antiestablishment statement. In other words, it was easy to read a political agenda into the nonpolitical pictures.

This is graphically expressed in the picture showing the pope's feet being kissed (in contrast to Jesus kissing his disciples' feet). The pope is the attention-getting center of the woodcut. But there is more. The scene depicts two secular rulers and other laymen waiting in the wings, while overweight ecclesiastical dignitaries – cardinals, bishops, and monks – keep the pope company. The message conveyed is both political and religious, and it is simple. Such luxurious living is not in harmony with the Christian faith, even as the pope's disparagement of secular authority is deemed offensive.

The Passional raises, in its own way, a fundamental question for the consideration of the transmission of ideas and popular culture, and for the role of the cultured elites in this process. That is, did *The Passional* shape or did it reflect prevailing ideology and culture?[26] In other words, did *The Passional* incorporate existing sentiment regarding the church and the papacy, offering a pointed expression of anticlericalism in the early Reformation, or did it mold, create, and shape popular thinking and culture? With respect to the specific topic of the Antichrist, the answer seems fairly easy. There is no evidence that, in the setting of the *causa Lutheri,* this identification was proffered by anyone but Luther. More difficult to answer is the question of whether Luther, in drawing on what was, after all, a distinct medieval tradition, merely voiced latent anticlericalism, to which he added the explicit identification of pope and Antichrist for good measure.

The Passional did not remain the only instance of Luther's pictorial propaganda. There were additional expressions, notably the *Papstesel* and the *Mönchskalb* of 1523; the illustrations of the September Bible; the tract, *The Papacy with Its Members, Painted and Described,* of 1526; and, many years later, the tract, *Against the Papacy in Rome, Founded by the Devil,* of 1545.

[26] See the stimulating monograph of R. W. Scribner, *For the Sake of Simple Folk: Popular Propaganda for the German Reformation* (Cambridge: Cambridge University Press, 1981).

Luther's 1526 tract, *The Papacy with Its Members,* is fairly restrained. In sixty-five highly stylized woodcuts, the pope, representatives of the hierarchy, and those of the monastic orders are introduced and described. Each woodcut includes an eight-line rhyme, characterized by neither literary eloquence nor much factual information. For example, the rhyme about cardinals simply informs the reader that the pope needs many helpers in his realm. Cardinals serve that purpose, and (so *The Papacy* informs the reader) they dress in purple. The pope himself, again depicted as heavily overweight, is referred to as "pope and Antichrist."[27]

The extensive use of visual means to convey the message must be noted. It pointedly proclaimed the polemic use to which this particular argument was to be put. The objective was to arouse popular sentiment and support. Luther's 1545 pronouncement about the pope as the Antichrist reiterated the stridency of earlier years and, once more, relied heavily on illustrations. The pamphlet consisted of a series of woodcuts provided by Lucas Cranach.[28] The intense crudity of the illustrations is notorious. Some of the woodcuts are offensive; others are outright obscene. One of them shows Pope Clement IV decapitating Emperor Conrad IV, another depicts the hangings of pope and cardinals, and yet another has two peasants using the papal tiara as a chamber pot and latrine.

The notoriety of this publication prompted Johann Mathesius, in his famous sermons on the life of Luther, to view the pamphlet as the finale of Luther's struggle against the papacy. As far as he was concerned, these pictures were meant "for lay people unable to read about the essence and the abomination of the Antichrist."[29] Mathesius made no comment, though, on the need for vulgarity to make the point.

The parallels to *The Passional* of 1521 must be noted. Both publications have a minimum of text, even though in *Against the Papacy . . .* it is more extensive than in *The Passional.* The message to be conveyed is in the pictures, an indication that the intended audience of the publication is the common people, very much along the lines of *The Passional.*

Needless to say, Martin Luther represents only a small part of the picture of the early Reformation. We must broaden our purview and ask about other notions of the Antichrist in the early Reformation. The evidence, however, seems disappointing. Not much was said, and what was said proved an echo

[27] See H. Grisar, *Luthers Kampfbilder* (Freiburg: Herder, 1921-1923), 94ff.
[28] WA 54:348ff.
[29] J. Mathesius, *Luthers Leben in Predigten* (Prague: Joseph Koch, 1906), 349.

of Luther.[30] One may surmise that the point had been made so categorically and extensively by Luther that nothing needed to be added.

This is not surprising. In the Germany of the 1520s, the papacy, the epitome of the Catholic Church, was the one major enemy for the advocates of reform. The pope was the personification of what the church was and stood for. Luther's argument to identify this personification with the Antichrist was plausible indeed; and there was not much that the other advocates of reform could add.

The same held true, *mutatis mutandis,* for the proponents of the emerging radical reform. Theirs was a dilemma. For one thing, they were preoccupied with the nature of their dissent from Luther, in addition to their opposition to Rome. The identification of the Antichrist was a minor issue for them. The problem was that the radicals had two major opponents – pope and Luther – and yet there was only one Antichrist to be assigned. They may have preferred to remain silent.

A good example of this was Thomas Müntzer. His first reference to the Antichrist came in a letter of June 1521, in which he noted that his was the time of the Antichrist, whose forerunner was Pope Julius II. The Antichrist would be discovered when the true Gospel was preached.[31] Müntzer repudiated the notion, expressed by none other than Martin Luther (who, in turn, had echoed Tertullian), that the Antichrist would come at the time of the Last Judgment. In his Prague Manifesto of 1521, Müntzer followed Luther's precedent by identifying the pope as the Antichrist. He noted that, after the judgment of Christendom brought on by the Turks, the "Antichrist will rule, the very antithesis of Christ, who will after a short time, however, give the kingdom of this world to his elect forever and ever."[32] In his "Sermon to the Saxon Princes," that famous exposition of the second chapter of the Book of Daniel, Müntzer introduced five empires (instead of the traditional four) from the biblical text – the first one the "earthen" one, and the present one "before our eyes," a "time rent asunder."[33] It was, in truth, the time of the Antichrist.

After the debacle of Frankenhausen and the defeat of the peasants, Müntzer acknowledged that he had erred in assuming that the end was at hand. The

[30]That Catholic opponents of Luther were eager to repay in kind is suggested by Erasmus's musing, at the time of Luther's marriage, that according to tradition the Antichrist would emanate from the union between a monk and a nun. See E. Kroker, *Katharina von Bora, Martin Luthers Frau* (Berlin: Evangelische Verlagsanstalt, 1972), 70. See also n. 51 below.

[31]Thomas Müntzer, *Schriften und Briefe,* ed. G. Franz (Gütersloh: Gerd Mohn, 1968), 373, "Jam est tempus Antichristi . . . . Errant omnes, qui papam superiorem Antichristum dicunt. Ipse enim verus preco eiusdem est, sed quarta bestia dominabitur universae terrae et regnum eius maius omnibus erit."

[32] Ibid., 493, where Müntzer speaks of the "entchrists knechten." This is in the German version of the "Manifesto," *Schriften und Briefe,* 504.

[33]Ibid., 256, 243.

peasants and his followers had not sought God, but "each one his own advantage more than Christian justice" ("eyn yder seyn eygen nutz mehr gesucht dan die rechtfertigung der christenheyt").[34] Accordingly, it is clear that Müntzer had to revise his notion about the Antichrist. The implications from his acknowledgment are clear: the Antichrist is here, but the end of all things has not yet come.

The Antichrist figured prominently among the early Anabaptists as well. The South German Hans Hut, echoing Thomas Müntzer, argued that according to Revelation 13:5 the rule of the Antichrist would last three and a half years, and he identified the peasants' uprising as the beginning of that rule.[35] Melchior Rinck observed that "even though Luther initially possessed the spirit of God, he has now become a devil and true Antichrist."[36]

Melchior Hofmann put his conception of Antichrist into the broader setting of history. There had been eight kingdoms of the Antichrist – the last one, the Holy Roman Empire, being the most vicious because of its union of pope and emperor. Hofmann shared the conviction that his were the last days, marked by the clash between the rule of the Antichrist and the Spirit.[37] In Hofmann's writings the familiar theme recurred – the pope is the Antichrist.[38] The pope had placed himself above the Word of God; he had "murdered, choked, tortured, and punished" God's faithful; and he had also "darkened the sun of Christ."[39]

In Pilgram Marpeck, who wrote slightly later, the notion of the Antichrist is interpreted differently. The Antichrist is the embodiment of antichristian elements. To be sure, Marpeck affirmed that "the pope and his camp represent the Antichrist," thus echoing Luther's fundamental identification of the two. He also rendered the judgment that the Antichrist had invaded the church of God.[40] But Marpeck's basic notion was a different one, and it went far beyond a blunt (or glib) identification of pope and Antichrist.[41]

Marpeck wrote prolifically of the Antichrist, in fact, more so than any other reformer, including Luther. Marpeck made it clear that the Antichrist

---

[34]Ibid., 473.

[35]G. Seebass, "Müntzers Erbe. Werk, Leben und Theologie des Hans Hut," Theological Habilitation, University of Erlangen, 1972, 2:72.

[36]G. Franz, ed., *Urkundliche Quellen zur hessischen Reformationsgeschichte*, vol. 4, *Wiedertäuferadten 1527-1626* (Marburg: N. G. Elwert, 1951), 4.

[37]J. M. Stayer, *Anabaptists and the Sword* (Lawrence, Kan.: Coronado Press, 1972), 217.

[38]K. Deppermann, *Melchior Hofmann, soziale Unruhen und apokalyptische Visionen* (Göttingen: Vandenhoeck and Ruprecht, 1979), 65. The reference is to *Offenbarung Joannis*, E 7 b.

[39]Melchior Hofmann, *Offenbarung Joannis*, 85.

[40]Pilgram Marpeck, "Vermanung," N v, in W. Klassen, ed., *The Writings of Pilgram Marpeck* (Scottsdale, Pa.: Herald, 1978), 297, "the Antichrist's troops have come and have grown in the church of Christ."

[41]Pilgram Marpeck, "Vermanung," K v, in Klassen, *The Writings,* 265.

was not at all peripheral, but fundamental to the Christian faith.[42] The very use of the plural when speaking of the Antichrist – "Antichrists and their breed" – denotes that more was at stake than the pope.[43] At issue was a fundamental understanding of the meaning of history. Gone was the intense eschatological urgency of the early 1520s, in which the Antichrist was, as a specific person, a necessary element as the harbinger of the imminent end. For Pilgram Marpeck a different notion emerged. The Antichrist as a specific person was no longer significant. The issue was the world, in which everything had gone awry. In this world the Antichrist ruled. The Antichrist was thus the epitome of the evil world, where God and his Gospel were forlorn and persecuted, where the children of darkness ruled and the children of light suffered pain. Luther's notion of the "two kingdoms" was turned upside down. "In life, however, one has the feeling that the Antichrist or Christ's opponent is everywhere present."[44] Marpeck spoke of the "realm of the Antichrist," into which one is initiated by infant baptism.[45]

The theme of a world divided into two realms is also found in the writings of the Münster Anabaptists, notably in the works of their theologian, Bernhard Rothmann. For Rothmann, the Antichrist and the last days went together.[46] He acknowledged that Luther restored the Gospel and identified the Antichrist.[47] The pope was the Antichrist in that he obscured the Gospel.[48] Seeking to avoid the dilemma faced by other radicals, Rothmann was quite prepared to identify all opponents of the Münster Anabaptists as Antichrist.[49]

Two anonymous tracts also deserve mention. One appeared in both a Latin and a vernacular version. Entitled *Prognosticon Antichristi,* it was written in 1521/22 and was published in 1524.[50] It was a vehement attack on the new heresies, an indication that, even in the early years of the Reformation

[42]Ibid., 64, 90, 202, 207, etc.

[43]Pilgram Marpeck, "Clare Verantwortung," A vii, in Klassen, *The Writings,* 50; cf. also 54. Since the "Verantwortung" was written against the Spiritualists, who eschewed external ceremonies, it should be evident that the Antichrist was, according to Marpeck, also found among them.

[44]Pilgram Marpeck, "Vermanung," D v, in Klassen, *The Writings,* 202. In a similar fashion, 314, 29r, "Many Antichrists have now appeared who deny both the divinity and the humanity of Christ."

[45]"Vermanung," K ij, in Klassen, *The Writings,"* 259.

[46]Bernhard Rothmann, "Von der Verborgenheit der Schrift," in *Die Schriften der münsterischen Täufer,* ed. R. Stupperich (Münster: Aschendorff, 1970), l:337.

[47]Bernhard Rothmann, "Restitution," in Stupperich, *Die Schriften,* 219, "Wy seggen, de Restitution hebbe begonnen by Luthers tyden, do hefft vns godt den gruwel vnnde den Antichrist tho lernen gegeuen."

[48]Stupperich, *Die Schriften,* 220, "durch den Antichrist gantz verdGstert vnnde verdoruen."

[49]Ibid., 408.

[50]See Anon., *Der deventer Endechrist von 1524. Ein reformationsgeschichtliches Zeugnis,* ed. H. Niebaum, R. Peters, E. Schütz, T. Sodmann (Cologne: Böhlau, 1984), esp. xxvii ff.

controversy, the Catholics were capable of responding vigorously (if not always eloquently and persuasively) to the challenges of the advocates of reform. The accusation was now reversed: Martin Luther and his followers were called the "precursors and messengers of the Antichrist" ("endechristes vorlopers vnde boden").[51]

The *Prognosticon* makes it clear that the Protestant reformers' use of the Antichrist in their religious polemics could backfire. Exegesis was determined by politics. Martin Luther and the other reformers were themselves not exempt from receiving the same charges they had leveled against the Catholic Church and the pope.

A second anonymous tract, *Auffdeckung der Babylonischen Hurn und Antichrist,* from the late 1520s, is probably of Anabaptist origin.[52] The "discovered whore" was, of course, the Roman church and the discovery that the church had fallen. The Antichrist, in turn, was the result of the liaison of the "whore" with the temporal authorities. The pamphlet acknowledged that Luther had exposed and "discovered" this, but he had promptly fallen into the same morass.[53] He, too, was the Antichrist because he had made common cause with the secular powers to further his goals.

The Antichrist played a surprisingly important role in the early years of the Reformation. Martin Luther led the way, affording this figure dramatic prominence by identifying him with the pope, even though Luther did not engage in speculation concerning the timing and circumstances of the last days. Unlike some medieval pronouncements, Luther's did not identify the Antichrist with a specific pope.[54] Pope Leo X was the Antichrist only as paradigm. The institution of the papacy – that is, the claims of authority advanced by that office, rather than an individual representative – was so labeled.[55] The Antichrist ceased being a specific person and became a category. The synonym of "Antichrist" was antichristian.[56]

The Antichrist signified total and comprehensive abuse of the Gospel. *Omnes enim abutuntur.* Luther's list of abuses was lengthy and comprehensive:

[51]Ibid., xxvii.

[52]H. Hillerbrand, "An Early Anabaptist Treatise on the Christian and the State," *Mennonite Quarterly Review* 32 (1958): 28-47. Recently, W. Klassen has sought to identify Pilgram Marpeck as the author; see his "Investigation into the Authorship and the Historical Background of the Anabaptist Tract, 'Auffdeckung der Babylonischen Hurn'," *Mennonite Quarterly Review* 61 (1987): 251-61.

[53]Hillerbrand, "An Early Anabaptist Treatise," 44.

[54]By H. Preuss, *Die Vorstellungen vom Antichrist.*

[55]E. Kohlmeyer, "Zu Luthers Anschauung vom Antichristus und von weltlicher Obrigkeit," *Archiv für Reformationsgeschichte* 24 (1927): 142ff.

[56]See, for example, WA 7:728-29, "stabit autem non uma personam, sed totum regnum et successum regum" which is expressed in vestibus, cibis, personis, domibus, gestibus. Perspecuum ergo est, hunc regem fore Antichristum. See also ibid., 723, the Antichrist is "ille totum corpus et chaos hominum impiorum totamque."

God, Christ, Holy Spirit, church, righteousness, truth, good works, merit –
all had been perverted by the Roman Antichrist.[57] The pope had distorted
true Christian teaching. The pope led people astray from the good news of
the Gospel.[58] In essence, the issue was that papal authority was placed over
the authority of the Word of God.[59]

Luther's understanding of the pope as Antichrist meshed neatly with his
understanding of the theology of the cross (*theologia crucis*). Luther was
convinced that God always worked *sub contrarie*, contrary to appearance,
expectation, and presumption. This theme meant that the Antichrist was
found precisely where one did not expect him. The pope claimed to be the
vicar of Christ on earth and the successor to the Apostle Peter. The reality
was the exact opposite: the pope was the Antichrist. What a transvaluation!
But this is how things worked. Evil always appeared to come from good,
Luther observed. Lucifer descended from the angels; sin came from the
Garden of Eden; Jesus was crucified in the Holy City; Judas was one of the
apostles; Rome was now the place of the Antichrist.[60] The pope allowed
what Christ prohibited, and vice versa. He was the true Antichrist.[61] "The
Antichrist does not sit in a devil's barn, in a pigsty, or among a group of
unbelievers, but at the noblest and holiest of places, namely the temple of
God."[62] The Antichrist pretended that "whatever he does against the pious
takes place by the command and in the name of God."[63]

Finally, Luther's identification of pope and Antichrist allowed him to
delineate a broader philosophy of history.[64] In the context of the intense
eschatological spirit of the time, the identification of the pope as the Antichrist
intimated the beginning of the end. The revelation of pope as Antichrist was
the unmistakable sign that the end had come.[65] Luther observed that the end
would begin with the reign of the Antichrist.[66] *Antichristi regnum finiri
incipit.*[67] At times Luther saw the end in the not-too-distant future; at others

[57]WA 7:728; see also WA 30:2, 483.

[58]In 1537 Luther used rather harsh words for such misleading, WA 50:88, "das sie erhenckt,
ertrencket, gekoepfft, verbrennet wuerden, welchs jnen zu wundschen were."

[59]WA 10:2, 141, "Das keyn groesser unglueck auff erden komen solt denn des Endchrists
vnd letztis ubel."

[60]WA 7:178.

[61]WA 18:259.

[62]WA 40:1, 7l; 5, 349.

[63]WA 5:349.

[64]WA 8:678.

[65]For example, Job Fincel's *Wunderzeichen*, "der juengste tag nunmehr vor der thuer sey,"
as quoted by H. Schilling, "Job Fincel und die Zeichen der Endzeit," in Wolfgang Brückner,
ed., *Volkerszählung und Reformation* (Berlin: E. Schmidt, 1974), 362.

[66]WA 8:678.

[67]WA BR 2:211.

he saw it as just around the corner. When Philip Melanchthon, who was given to astrology, observed in 1532 that the emperor would live to be forty-eight years of age, Luther responded that the world would not last that long, according to the book of Ezekiel.[68]

Two considerations converged in Luther's polemic. One was the notion that the perversion of the Catholic Church was fundamental. No mere tinkering on the periphery could set things straight; abuse touched the core of things. Secondly, there was the connection between the pope and the end time. The German word *Endchrist* appeared frequently in place of *Antichrist*, indicating that even linguistically the connection was made between the Antichrist and the Second Coming.

Alongside these theological considerations, the propaganda aspect of the identification of pope and Antichrist must be noted. To make his case, Luther took to popular agitation, dramatically expressed in *The Passional of Christ and Antichrist*. The explanation for this is to be sought in the time just prior to Luther's excommunication, when he first hurled his identification of pope and Antichrist into the public arena. Luther thereby introduced a new element into the controversy. Previously, his pronouncements had moved along two separable, if intertwining, avenues – theological exposition and spiritual exhortation. The former were for his fellow theologians and the papacy, while the latter were addressed to the common people. We are only beginning to understand that the latter writings, which found so many reprints in an amazingly short time, provide the explanation for Luther's increasing popularity in 1519 and beyond.

Yet it would be difficult to posit a categorical difference between Luther's tracts and those of his predecessors. The new theological perspective, while present, paled in the face of the continuities. Luther's tract on the proper preparation for dying, for example, differed only in degree from the late medieval "art of dying" literature. Luther's vernacular tracts of 1518-1520 sought to persuade, to challenge, to reorient. Had it not been for Luther's concurrent theological controversy, which involved increasing indications of his divergence from the theological consensus, neither his early tracts nor his public demeanor would have given any indication that his readers were challenged to make a categorical break with their past.

Luther's blunt identification of pope and Antichrist constituted the watershed in the early Reformation controversy. His challenge to readers and followers became categorical. It was a challenge to take a position apart from (and even opposed to) that of the church. The traditional way of understanding the Christian religion was to be abandoned. A change had to take place. Luther demanded nothing less from his readers than a break with the past, a different way of thinking, a conversion, a turning around. More than anything else, the claim that the pope was the Antichrist did that.

Accordingly, the identification of pope and Antichrist was an important propaganda tool for the advocates of reform. It was a retort, a counterattack. It did not come slowly, but Martin Luther jumped the gun, as it were. On the heels of the papal threat of excommunication came the indictment of the pope as Antichrist. The purported heretic stood against the purported Antichrist.

The concept of the Antichrist was thus, whatever else it was theologically, a propaganda tool employed to repudiate the papacy in the strongest way possible. The use of the idea of the Antichrist as propaganda is borne out by its speedy translation into common parlance, as witnessed by *The Passional of Christ and Antichrist*. The point was obvious: the case for the break with the Catholic Church and the pope was made publicly, among the people. The objective was to make the case before a wider public. The issue was clear-cut, straightforward, and, above all, simple. The declaration of the categorical dichotomy between appearance and reality spoke to people with a yearning to believe, whatever their status in society. What they saw before their eyes could not be ultimate reality.

The Antichrist, by Lucas Cranach the Younger

Discovery of Hebrew and Discrimination against the Jews: The *Veritas Hebraica* as Double-Edged Sword in Renaissance and Reformation

Heiko A. Oberman

In this essay Oberman investigates the impact of humanist Hebrew studies and scholarship on the Hebrew scriptures, on early modern attitudes toward Jews in general, and on the rise of anti-Semitism in particular. Far from acting as a counter to anti-Semitism, Hebrew studies reinforced old attitudes toward Jews and actually contributed to the growth of negative stereotypes during the Reformation.

IT IS TIME THAT WE RECOUP THE ELEMENT OF TRUTH in the "glorious" view of the Renaissance as the key period for the pursuit of the dignity of man and religious toleration. Though increasingly discredited by historians sensitive to the gap between ideology and reality,[1] this idea is properly part of every course on the history of Western culture because it is a crucial part of that powerful dream of political equity and social justice which gives rise to discontent,[2] inspires resistance, and, where it is repressed, causes revolution. This lofty but potent realm of what can perhaps best be described as "human aspirations" has been the traditional domain of the old-style intellectual historian. In the central period for our theme, roughly 1300 through 1600, the leading scholars have usually been students of philosophy or theology who privileged literary sources, preferably the most sophisticated and innovative treatises on the presumed foci of these aspirations – justice and freedom, self-determination and self-realization, private happiness and public benefit (*bonum commune*).

I. The Fate of Failure

The word *lofty* in this characterization has been chosen advisedly to denote the usually concomitant disregard for the social matrix of these favored sources and a lack of interest in the textual community thereby intended or actually served. Here the "ideas" not only have legs, but giant boots that

[1]"The humanist attitude toward history was emphatically selective, elitist, self-congratulatory, and fixed to a criterion of worldly success. The humanists were drawn irresistibly to the ranks of winners, except when victory went to 'barbarism.'" Lauro Martines, *Power and Imagination. City-States in Renaissance Italy* (Baltimore: Johns Hopkins University Press, 1988 [1979]), 198.

[2]Made accessible and documented for our period by Gerald Strauss, *Manifestations of Discontent in Germany on the Eve of the Reformation* (Bloomington: Indiana University Press, 1971).

allow for jumping over the crests of time by homing in on the "great minds." When these ideas are placed in artful succession, they suggest a perennial philosophy, testifying to the unfailing engine of progress or documenting the ultimate superiority of mind over matter. In this view, the history of human aspirations does not know failures, but only occasional and temporary setbacks.[3]

The agenda of the modern social historian reads as a necessary corrective: the view from the mountaintop is redirected to the daily life in rural valleys and urban alleys. Now the social matrix is analyzed with a particular interest in the common man, whose life and thought are drawn out of the shadow of the great thinkers by decoding the archival records, thus liberating him from marginalization by the ruling elite and its text-producing hegemony. What seemed to the intellectual historian to be merely temporary setbacks now appear as failures in molding interests "from above," often understood as the manipulation of the real interest of the common man in the service of the aspirations of the dominant classes. Cooperation between these two camps of historians will be achieved to the extent that the participants become aware that even at times of rapid social change, crises only explode into revolutionary mass movements when the hiatus between the "lofty" ideals and aspirations – pursued by the intellectual historian – and the daily reality – as privileged by the social historian – is found and articulated to be unjust and, therefore, unbearable.

The ringleaders of provocation and masters of crisis management prove to be those who could legitimize collective action by translating the once lofty ideals into a religious, political, social, and economic program of change. There is a consensus in our field that in the period of the Middle Ages, Renaissance, and Reformation such legitimation could only be provided by the Holy Scriptures, quite apart from the question of how its relation to the unwritten traditions of the medieval church might be conceived. It is clear that in this context the time-honored technical term *Veritas Hebraica* takes on crucial significance as the true voice of the Hebrew scriptures for all who had not reduced the Holy Scriptures to the Christian New Testament. In the following discussion we want to recapture the challenge to established truth created by the increasing recovery of the Hebrew Bible. In the final part of the paper we proceed to ask whether the new respect for the language of the Jews in any way changed the perception of the Jews at a time of a multifarious increase in anti-Semitism.

---

[3] In this context, it is understandable that the substantial work of Gerald Strauss, *Luther's House of Learning. The Indoctrination of the Young in the German Reformation* (Baltimore: Johns Hopkins University Press, 1978) evoked more smoke than the fire warranted.

II. Hebrew as a New Network of Meaning

The pursuit of the *Veritas Hebraica* was by no means new in the fifteenth and sixteenth centuries.[4] On October 16, 1333, Nicolas of Lyra published his treatise on the differences between the Vulgate and the Hebrew original, *Tractatus differentiarum Novi ac Veteris Testamenti cum explicatione nominum hebreorum*.[5] Lyra, a French Franciscan (1270-1349), summarized here his life's work. In his *Postillae,* or commentaries on all of scripture, he heavily relied on the work of the learned French Rabbi Rashi, born in Troyes in 1030 (†1105). Though Lyra's *Postillae* found a wide distribution throughout Christian Europe, his reliance on Jewish learning must have seemed less than dramatic or shocking because it was his consistent procedure first to quote Rashi and then to prove him wrong. Furthermore, once Lyra was printed, his work was usually published together with the *Additiones* of Paul of Burgos (†1435), who protected the reader's orthodox sensitivities by his sharp criticism of Lyra's reliance on Rashi.[6] Beryl Smalley, criticizing the traditional thesis of a thirteen-century decline in biblical studies as "over-simplification,"[7] has documented the intense interest of the friars in the literal sense of scripture and in the original Hebrew meaning, particularly of passages in the Psalms. Biblical studies as such were not in decline, but the monastic *lectura,* with its quest for the spiritual food under the external literal sense, was increasingly neglected. The commentaries of the friars resound with expressions like "the Hebrew text reads" – *Hebreus habet* and *in Hebreo habetur.* Ms. Smalley's conclusion is therefore convincing: "Lyra represents the culmination of a

[4] The quest for the original text of scripture had been legally sanctioned in the *Decretum Gratiani:* "Ut veterum librorum fides de Hebraicis voluminibus examinanda, ita novorum Veritas Graeci sermonis normam desiderat." *Corpus Iuris Canonici* I, dist. IX, 6. The words here assigned to Augustine were actually drawn from Jerome, Ep. 71, 5; *CSEL* 55, 6. This passage is understandably highlighted in times of suspicion. The later (1539) Royal Printer and Bookseller in Hebrew and Latin, Robert Estienne (1503?-1559), laid the groundwork for his future daring Bible editions in Paris and Geneva by invoking this passage in the preface of his first folio edition of the Vulgate (1528). See Eugene F. Rice, Jr., ed., *The Prefatory Epistles of Jacques Lefèvre d'Étaples and Related Texts* (New York: Columbia University Press, 1972), 495. This did not prevent the Sorbonne from proscribing the earlier Vulgate Bible as well as the later original versions. See Elizabeth Armstrong, *Robert Estienne: Royal Printer. An Historical Study of the Elder Stephanus* (Cambridge: Harvard University Press, 1954), app. A, 174. R. Estienne even printed a translation of the Geneva Catechism into Hebrew (1554), ibid., 230.

[5] See Herman Hailperin, *Rashi and the Christian Scholars* (Pittsburgh: University of Pittsburgh Press, 1963), 283-84.

[6] Lyra is by no means an innovator, but because of the power of the printed word, a new beginning. See Gilbert Dahan, "Les interprétations juives dans les commentaires du Pentateuque de Pierre le Chantre," in *The Bible in the Medieval World. Essays in Memory of Beryl Smalley,* ed., Katherine Walsh and Diana Wood (Oxford: Blackwell, 1985), 131-55; and the rich literature quoted here.

[7] Beryl Smalley, *The Study of the Bible in the Middle Ages* (Oxford: Blackwell, 1952), 265.

movement for the study of Hebrew and rabbinics. He owed much to the past."[8]

The next century, however, would not just see a culmination of the work of Lyra. For the new pursuit of what was increasingly called the *Veritas Hebraica,* knowledge of Hebrew no longer served merely the incidental purpose of correcting single words in the Vulgate, but became part of the general programmatic search for the original meaning in all historical documents, a meaning supposed to have been lost under the thick layers of later interpretations and medieval accretions. As is well known, in the classical century of the rediscovery of eloquence, *rhetorica* was not an abstract ideal but a matter of hands-on application in the lecture hall, pulpit, parliament, and courtroom; in each case, what was at stake was the need to reach and move an audience (*fidem facere*).

What is neglected in modern studies, however, is that at the same time an underlying problem was uncovered: that such communication – be it in oral or written form – must bridge the meaning gap between author and recipient, and therefore demands far more than learning a list of single words. It demands the understanding of word systems or networks of meaning.[9] The fifteenth-century pursuit of the *Veritas Hebraica* became a challenge for established truth in church and university when the claim was made that beyond those incidental corrections of the twelfth and thirteenth centuries, the Hebrew original, if only properly decoded, could reveal a comprehensive and authentic network of meaning.

Lorenzo Valla (†1457) articulated the crucial importance of such a comprehensive interpretation when he expressed the desire to really grasp the "Hebrew Truth" of the Psalms – and this not only in the service of text-emendation in the scholar's study, but also to achieve true devotion while reciting the Psalms in church services.[10] Valla thus incorporated the quest for the *Hebraica Veritas* in his general – and generally hair-raising – avalanche of historical studies. His return *ad fontes* had already yielded the triple shocker of establishing the Donation of Constantine as a forgery, the Apostles' Creed as not the product of the twelve apostles, and Dionysius the Areopagite as

[8]Ibid., 355.

[9]See the treatise of Leonardo Bruni, "On the Correct Way to Translate" (1424-26), newly edited in *The Humanism of Leonardo Bruni. Selected Texts,* ed. Gordon Griffiths, James Hankins, and David Thomson. Medieval and Renaissance Texts and Studies, vol. 46 (Binghamton, New York: Renaissance Society of America, 1987), 217-34; esp. 218-19.

[10]". . . utinam hebraicam linguam plane noscerem, ut secundum hebraicam veritatem et vocem psalmos edicerem, et quidem in aedibus sacris," *Recriminationes* IV, in *Opera* (Basel, 1540), 626; quoted by A. Morisi Guerra, "Cultura ebraica ed esegesi biblica cristiana tra Umanesimo e Riforma," in *Ebrei e Cristiani Nell'italia Medievale e Moderna: Conversioni, Scambi, Contrasti. Atti del VI Congresso internazionale dell'AISG S. Miniato, 4-6 novembre 1986, Associazione Italiana per lo Studio del Giudaismo. Testi e Studi 6* (Rome: Carruci, 1988), 209-23; 211, n. 8. See here also for extensive references to contemporary scholarship.

not the convert of St. Paul. His insistence on the knowledge of Hebrew could not but appear to be yet another threat to established religious thought and practice.

For all who have profited from the research of Paul Oskar Kristeller, it is not surprising that Valla does not represent the view of Renaissance humanism on the importance of Hebrew. There are, indeed, three trends or lines of argument discernible that prevented Hebrew from reaching that place of coequality with Latin and Greek which would later be institutionalized in the *Collegium Trilingue* in Louvain.[11] Different in importance and motivation, they vie with one another in containing the fervor for Hebrew studies.[12] There is first of all the argument of Leonardo Bruni, who pointed to the vast difference between the *eruditio* of the Greeks and the *ruditas* of the Jews. The Jews' language and alphabet is so shockingly deviant "that they even write in a contrary way [i.e. "abnormal," from right to left] . . . no one in his right mind will deny that Latin and Greek will serve much more the improvement of morals than the *Judaeorum barbaries.*"[13] In the European humanistic school system, Bruni's view of the unique resources of Greek and Latin literature would prove to be victorious; here Hebrew never gained much more status than that of an optional field of studies.

The second trend or factor that prevented the full emancipation of Hebrew studies can be traced to the aftermath of the expulsion of Jews from Spain in 1492. The ensuing suspicion against the Marranos as disguised and subversive pseudo-Christians fed so strongly into the more general fear of Judaism as an external and legalistic religion that it could even encourage the reduction of the scriptures to the Christian New Testament.

The third and related limiting factor is associated with the fact that two early protagonists of Hebrew studies, Pico della Mirandola in Italy and Johannes Reuchlin in Germany, combined their respect for rabbinic studies with the conviction that the Kabbalah (Cabala) would afford access to the

[11]In March 1518 the Louvain (Leuven) printer Dirk Martens published the *Alphabeticum Hebraicum,* a Hebrew alphabet with Latin explanations – probably intended for the first Hebrew course offered by Matthaeus Adriani in 1518. See *Erasmus en Leuven. Catalogus,* preface by J. K. Steppe (Louvain: Stedelijk Museum, 1969), 398. The early history of Hebrew teaching in Louvain was tenuous. But also at other "professive" universities it proved to be difficult to find a capable Hebraist who was not "judaising" from the perspective of the established academic community. Almost simultaneously with Adriani, Johannes Böschenstein published his *Hebraicae Grammaticae institutiones* for his lectures at Wittenberg, with Luther's early printer Johannes Grunenberg, in Wittenberg in 1518. See Gerhard Hammer, *Archiv zur Weimarer Ausgabe* II (Luther, *Operationes in Psalmos* [Cologne: Böhlau, 1981]), 6, n. 17.

[12]Cf. the findings of Jeremy Cohen, "Scholarship and Intolerance in the Medieval Academy: The Study and Evaluation of Judaism in European Christendom," *American Historical Review* 9 (1986): 592-613.

[13]See the edition of his *Epistolarum Libri,* ed. L. Mehus (Florence, 1742), 2:160-64; quoted by A. Morisi Guerra, 213, n. 12.

mysteries behind the literal meaning of the text.[14] Even before the publication of his Hebrew primer, the *De Rudimentis* of 1506, Reuchlin had already pointed to this in *De verbo mirifico* (1492), following it up with a programmatic plea for the Cabala in *De arte cabalistica* in 1517. Reuchlin gives the Cabala a Christian interpretation by regarding it as the tool to unveil the Old Testament prophecy of Jesus as the messiah. Though Reuchlin with his Christian Cabala silences the talmudic tradition as artfully as Pfefferkorn designed to do it forcefully,[15] the defense of Hebrew studies was severely compromised.

Johannes – formerly Joseph – Pfefferkorn exploits this when he assails Reuchlin in his *Sturmglock* of 1514 as "the new Hus who threatens to subvert the Church with his Judaising sect."[16] It was all the more necessary for Luther to insist on the distinction between Cabala and Hebrew. The Wittenburg reformer studied Hebrew intensively, in the beginning years (1513-1515) with Reuchlin's grammar in hand. But after an initial positive reference to the Cabala, in 1519[17] he designates the supporters of the Cabala as *curiosi et ociosi* and the Cabala as superstition, since it demands faith in single letters rather than in the Word of God expressed therein.[18] Yet this severe critique did not in the slightest diminish his respect for the Hebrew language. To the contrary, Hebrew is *omnium optima . . . ac purissima* with its unspeculative clarity, so unlike Greek.[19] Erasmus of Rotterdam, on the other hand, did not make the same clear distinction. The whole wave of interest in Hebrew studies seemed to him as dangerous by advancing the cause of Judaism as the adoration of the Italian Renaissance furthered the cause of paganism.[20]

---

[14]On the meaning of the Christian Cabala (Kabbalah) and the difference between Pico and Reuchlin, see Hans-Martin Kirn, *Das Bild vom Juden im Deutschland des frühen 16. Jahrhunderts, dargestellt an den Schriften Johannes Pfefferkorns,* Texts and Studies in Medieval and Early Modern Judaism 3, ed. Maurice R. Hayoun, Ivan G. Marcus, and Peter Schäfer (Tübingen: J. C. B. Mohr, 1989), 156-72.

[15]"Darumb, nemet in den weg der bucher, verbernet [verbrennet] sy, so syn sie dan dester lichtlicher zo bewegen auf den weg der warheit." Kirn, *Das Bild vom Juden,* 225, 68.

[16]Ibid., 172, n. 208.

[17]See my *Die Reformation von Wittenberg nach Genf* (Göttingen: Vandenhoeck and Ruprecht, 1986), 51, n. 17.

[18]*WA TR* (Weimarer Ausgabe, Abteilung Tischreden) 5:384, 12. See the clear analysis of Siegfried Raeder, *Grammatica Theologica. Studien zu Luthers Operationes in Psalmos,* Beiträge zur historischen Theologie, vol. 51 (Tübingen: J. C. B. Mohr, 1977), 59-80, 79.

[19]*WA TR* 1:no. 1041, p. 525, 42-44; Sept.-Nov. 1532. *WA TR* 2: no. 2771a; cf. no. 2779a.

[20]See my *Wurzeln des Antisemitismus. Christenangst und Judenplage im Zeitalter von Humanismus und Reformation* (Berlin: Siedler, 1981), 51. (*The Roots of Anti-Semitism* [Philadelphia: Fortress Press, 1984], 40).

The Cabala and rabbinic studies are for him less than alluring: "mihi sane neque Cabala neque Talmud unquam arrisit."[21]

Hence also in the field of Hebrew studies, the voices of Luther and Erasmus were in contention to sway the mind of the succeeding generations. Yet interestingly, it is through the former disciples of Erasmus, Capito in Strasbourg and Zwingli in Zürich, that the vision of Luther would prevail in biblical studies. In a letter of March 13, 1518, to Wolfgang Capito, Erasmus documents the fluent transition from a lack of enthusiasm for the Hebrew language to that kind of evaluation of the Jewish race which I find difficult to distinguish from anti-Semitism:

> I could wish you were more inclined to Greek than to that Hebrew of yours, about which you are so uncritical. I see them [the Jews] as a nation given to the most egregious fabrications, who spread a kind of fog over everything: Talmud, Cabala, Tetragrammaton, *Gates of Light,* words, words, words. I would rather accept a mixture of Christ with Scotus than with that rubbish of theirs. Italy is full of Jews, in Spain there are hardly any Christians. I fear this [the new Hebrew language studies] may give that pestilence, so long ago suppressed, a chance to rear its ugly head.[22]

To this transition from the scholarly pursuit of the *Veritas Hebraica* to the history of anti-Semitism we shall return in Section IV. Here it suffices to conclude that the conventional ideal of the humanist as *trilinguis* stands to be corrected. Exactly because the study of languages should and could convey (*fidem facere*) networks of forgotten meaning (*veritas*), the tradition we encountered with Valla and Luther had to contend with the reservations of Bruni and Erasmus. Christian society could handle the glorious achievements of Greeks and Romans long dead, but it was at a loss when it came to dealing with the "stubborn Jews," who – as they once killed Christ – continued to kill his Spirit with their Hebrew letter.

III. The *Veritas Hebraica* as Challenge to Orthodoxy

Not only in the realm of the church, but also in the domain of historical scholarship, we encounter the phenomenon of "ceremony" in the form of reverential reference to authorities established and canonized by decades of ritualized expressions of respect. In our field this has been the fate of the

---

[21]P. S. Allen, *Opus epistolarum Des. Erasmi Roterodami* (Oxford: Oxford University Press, 1913), 3:589 with n. 967. Cf. *The Correspondence of Erasmus* in Complete Works of Erasmus, vol. 6 (Toronto: Toronto University Press, 1982), 368, 79-80. The same parallel already in the letter to Capito of February 26, 1517. Allen, *Opus epistolarum* (Oxford: Oxford University Press, 1910), vol. 2, no. 541, p. 491, 133-39.

[22]Adapted from *The Correspondence of Erasmus, Complete Works of Erasmus* 5, 347, 20-26; Allen, *Opus epistolarum* 3:798. I cannot accept the mitigating interpretation of the editors in their introduction to *Opus epistolarum* 3:694.

slight volume of Ludwig Geiger – the great authority on the life and writings
of Johannes Reuchlin[23] – who published his study of Hebrew in Germany
from the end of the fifteenth to the middle of the sixteenth century in Breslau
in 1870.[24] A personal anecdote may illustrate the ambivalent yield of the
scholarly rites of adoration. My copy had to be ordered through interlibrary
loan, and it arrived with the explicit condition that it could only be consulted
in the Rare Book Reading Room – a proper expression of respect for a classic
from 1870. Upon inspection, however, the protection of this precious book
proved to have been so successful that the pages were still uncut and had to
be opened for the first time after 120 years.

This work of Ludwig Geiger deserves its renown, insofar as it is an
eminent scholarly achievement in the context of the state of scholarship in
the third quarter of the nineteenth century. Though more often quoted than
read, it is on all central points still influential by presenting Reuchlin as the
watershed in the history of the Christian reception of Hebrew. This view is
in keeping with Reuchlin's self-understanding, but, as in the case of similar
claims made by Erasmus for Greek and Latin studies, it stands to be corrected.

Under the heading "The Forerunners of Reuchlin," Geiger dedicates
one passage to Wessel Gansfort (1400-1489). Here Gansfort is presented as
an early and enthusiastic student of Hebrew who, Geiger claims, unfortunately
did not leave any written evidence of his Hebrew studies but who influenced
the next generation of humanists by teaching them Hebrew.[25] This assessment
of Wessel Gansfort contains a positive and a negative assertion, each of which
has an uncertain footing in the sources. Undocumented is the view of Wessel
as the Hebrew teacher of his time and particularly as the teacher of both the
young Johannes Reuchlin (1455-1522) in Paris and the young Rudolf Agricola
(1444-1485) in Basel and Groningen.[26] The cradle of this legend is the
over-interpretation of an oration written by Philip Melanchthon in 1539 on
the life of Rudolph Agricola, which indeed reports reliable oral tradition
about Wessel's enthusiasm for Hebrew and instruction of Hebrew, but it
does not at all say that Wessel initiated either Reuchlin or Agricola into the

---

[23]Ludwig Geiger, *Johann Reuchlin. Sein Leben und seine Werke* (Leipzig, 1871).

[24]Idem., *Das Studium der Hebräischen Sprache in Deutschland. Von Ende des XV. bis zur Mitte des XVI. Jahrhunderts* (Breslau: Schletter'sche Buchhandlung, H. Skutsch, 1870).

[25]"Schriftliche Denkmale seiner Beschäftigung mit dieser Sprache hat er nicht hinterlassen; den Rudolf Agrikola hat er darin unterrichtet, vielleicht auch Andere," Geiger, *Studium*, 23.

[26]See Maarten van Rhijn, *Wessel Gansfort* ('s-Gravenhage: Martinus Nijhoff, 1917), appendix A, x-xi. Further literature and source references here.

world of Hebrew studies.[27] As Geiger has shown, Reuchlin did not learn Hebrew as a young man at the feet of Wessel either in Paris or Basel but rather late in his forties, in 1491 in Linz, from Jakob Jehiel Loans, the personal physician of the Emperor Frederick III, and from Jakob Ben Obadja Sfurno in 1498 in Rome.[28] And if Wessel taught Agricola, he was not overly successful; Agricola achieved eminence not as a Hebraist but as a Greek scholar who, in the words of Joseph Ijsewijn, succeeded in "transferring ancient Greek wisdom and literature from Greece to the Latin West. . . ."[29]

Yet Wessel Gansfort is crucial for our story. As a teacher of Hebrew he may be overrated, but his works amply document the extent to which he actually used the *Veritas Hebraica* to call key assumptions of the ecclesiastical and scholastic traditions into question. In turning now to this as yet unwritten chapter in the recovery of Hebrew, I want to concentrate on two samples of the revolutionary reinterpretation of the Vulgate on the basis of the *Veritas Hebraica*. They document the challenge of this philological renaissance to both dogma and piety, to be mentioned in one breath with the shaking of the foundations of the New Testament by Erasmus's *Novum Instrumentum* of 1516.

As far as the early praise for Wessel Gansfort as a connoisseur of both biblical languages is concerned, one cannot say much more than that he knew some key Greek words. From the precious letter written to him sometime between 1483 and 1489 by Erasmus's teacher, Alexander Hegius, we know

[27]"In Theologia quid desideraverit, memini huc scribere Iosquinum Groningensem senem, pietate et gravitate excellentem, se adolescentem interfuisse sermonibus Rodolphi et Wesseli, in quibus deplorarint Ecclesiae tenebras, et reprehenderint prophanationem in Missis, et coelibatum: Item disputaverint de iusticia fidei, quid sit quod Paulus toties inculcat homines fide iustos esse, non operibus. Scribebat Iosquinus, aperte reiecisse eos Monachorum opinionem, quae fingit homines operibus iustos esse: Item sensisse eos de humanis traditionibus, errare eos, qui affingunt illis opinionem cultus, et non posse violari iudicant. Nihil fingo, nam haec fere ad verbum huc scripsit Iosquinus. Ac satis credibile est, eum diligenter disputasse de doctrina Christiana, praesertim cum esset familiaris Wesselo, cuius fuit summum ingenium: ad quod amplissimam eruditionem in omnibus disciplinis adiunxit, et Graecae et Ebraicae linguae cognitionem. Ad haec exercitatus fuit in certaminibus religionis. Lutetia pulsus propter taxatas superstitiones, venit Basileam: ibi pro Wesselo dixerunt Basilium Groningum; narrabatque Capnion eum Theologiam, Graecas et Ebraicas literas eodem tempore tradidisse studiosis, si qui eum audire cupierant. Inde cum in Belgicum rediisset, saepe adiit senem Rodolphus natu minor, sed in literis Latinis et Graecis eruditior, et flagrans studio Christianae doctrinae. Idque ipse saepe de se praedicat, se quod reliquum esset aetatis, collocaturum esse in sacras literas: qui si vixisset, haud dubie egregiam operam Ecclesiae navasset." *Corpus Reformatorum*, vol. 11, *Philippi Melanthonis Opera quae supersunt omnia*, ed. Carolus G. Bretschneider (Halle/Saale: C. A. Schwetschke et Fil, 1843), col. 444. By "Iosquinus" is meant Goswinus of Halen (1468-1530), for many years the "famulus" or private secretary of Wessel. See Maarten van Rhijn, *Studien over Wessel Gansfort en zijn tijd* (Utrecht: Kemink en Zoon N.V., 1933), 137-59.

[28]*Johann Reuchlins Briefwechsel* (Tübingen, 1875), 8. Quoted and discussed by van Rhijn, *Wessel Gansfort*, x-xi.

[29]Joseph Ijsewijn, "Agricola as a Greek scholar," in *Rodolphus Agricola Phrisius (1444-1485). Proceedings of the International Conference at the University of Groningen October 28-30, 1985*, ed. F. Akkerman and A. J. Vanderjagt (Leiden: Brill, 1988), 21-37; 37.

that Alexander was delighted to have found for Wessel the Greek homilies of Chrysostom and that he asked to borrow Wessel's copy of the New Testament in Greek.[30] Yet I cannot but confirm the conclusion of Maarten van Rhijn that Wessel's Greek knowledge was perhaps noteworthy for his time but nevertheless mediocre from the perspective of an Agricola or a Melanchthon.[31] Whatever his level of competence, Wessel was not able to use his Greek in such a way that he could come to a new interpretation of any text in the New Testament.

Quite the opposite was the case with Wessel's command of Hebrew. Some twenty years before Reuchlin designed his Hebrew grammar (1506), Wessel acquired such a profound knowledge of Hebrew that at a number of crucial points he dared to proffer critical deviations from the Vulgate version. In his reinterpretation of the Lord's Prayer, Wessel points to Psalm 15:6, where the psalmist prays that God remember his *rechem* (Rahem) as well as his *chesed* (Hased). Wessel criticizes the fact that the Latin interpreters have passed over the difference between these two forms of love by translating both as "mercy" (*miserationes/misericordiae*). But the Hebrew original makes it quite clear that *rechem* refers to the mother womb and means the concern of "motherly love," whereas *chesed* stands for male affection and fatherly care.[32] This observation has far-reaching consequences: one should not just pray to God as Father, but with the same biblical validity to God as Mother:

---

[30]*M. Wesseli Gansfortii Groningensis, rarae et reconditae doctrinae viri, qui olim Lux Mundi vulgo dictus fuit, Opera.* (Groningen, 1614), fol.***4v.

[31]See van Rhijn, *Wessel Gansfort,* 65.

[32]"Quando ergo Propheta 'Rahem' et 'Hased' conjungit (Ps. 25:6), et 'Rahem' naturalem, quia aeternum patris affectum ad filios vere ostendit, quia sicut Deus nobis pater, sic mater est. Sed hoc levius interpretes transierunt, semper 'misericordiam' interpretati." *Opera,* fol. 60. Cf. Augustine, for whom *miseratio* and *misericordia* are synonyms. E.g., *Enarratio* in Ps. 24:6; *C. Chr.* 38, 138. This "equality in diversity" Wessel notes in *Proverbs* and the *Song of Songs:* "Solomon in Proverbiis aeque matris ut patris meminit ad filium. Et sponsa in *Canticis Opera,*" fol. 60. Wessel draws up an impressive verb list of "female" and "male" care to show that both mother love and father love go into the formation of all true Christians: "Universos enim illius civitatis futuros aliquando cives matrice sua concepit, confovit, coagulavit, coaluit, plasmavit, figuravit, formavit, vivificavit, auxit, praegnavit, gravidavit, portavit, parturivit, laboravit, peperit, involvit, reclinavit, gestavit, lactavit, balneavit, nutrivit, educavit, duxit, erudivit, instituit, docuit, traxit, incitavit, desiderio ignivit, superincendit, amore inflammavit. Quos et paterne, quia pater misericordiarum, amavit condendo, educando, sufferendo, parcendo, exspectando, revocando, ignoscendo, reconciliando, recipiendo, consolando, conforando, promittendo, exaudiendo, defendendo, protegendo, suggerendo, dirigendo, medendo, ducendo." *Opera,* fol. 60. This leads Wessel in turn to construct – or rather to observe – an *ordo scalaris* in which the *pietas materna* precedes the *pietas paterna:* "Sunt enim quaedam operativa nostrae salutis ex parte nostri: scilicet fides, spes, et charitas, quo ad nos exercendos. Alia sunt ex parte Dei, ipsum scilicet inducentia quo ad nos salvandos, quorum is est ordo scalaris: Misericordia, et est qua nostra miseria Deum movet ad miserendum nostra mala (om.: ad obaudiendum). Gratia, qua nos benevole vult gratificare sibi (add.: ad obaudiendum). Viscera, seu pietas materna, qua sicut mater super puero uteri sui, ita super nobis afficitur. Pietas paterna, qua non solum adoptione contentus, sed ingenuos et nobiles filios esse volet. Cor sponsi, quo prorsus se dignos esse volet." *Opera,* fol. 61. Cf. fol. 403, 453, 479, 721.

". . . *sicut Deus nobis pater, sic mater est.*"[33] Wessel applies this finding to all three Persons of the Trinity: "God is my loving father and my loving mother; the Incarnate Word is my brother and my sister; and the Holy Spirit is my bridegroom and my bride, my *amicus* and my *amica.*"[34] As Caroline Bynum has shown, the earlier mystical tradition had – at times and hesitantly – already dared to look upon "Jesus as Mother."[35] But now for the first time this experience was given biblical authentication: ignorance of Hebrew had engendered male supremacy *in* God through "male-fication" *of* God.

This emphasis on "God as Mother" and "Jesus as Sister" may go a long way in explaining why the Virgin Mary, who plays such a central and ever-increasing role in late medieval piety and theology, is so markedly absent from the works of Wessel. But at this point it must remain a matter of speculation what the range of implications of this revolutionary view are. Suffice it to say that I have found no imitators of the view of Wessel Gansfort. Apparently it was so aberrant that it was immediately isolated and remained without echo even among those who revered his name and protected his heritage by publishing his works.

Though Wessel Gansfort would protest against any contrast between piety and dogma, another of his Hebrew discoveries was relatively more at odds with established doctrine than with forms of piety. This second daring shift concerns the divine self-revelation to Moses when God, according to the Vulgate, reveals his name as "*Ego sum qui sum*" (Exodus 3:14). An immense superstructure of scholastic speculation was based on the ontological analysis of this "I am"; it was invoked as the proof text for the common ground of being of all existence. Hence Wessel is again shaking the foundations when he argues that God in the Hebrew original does not at all say "I am" ("*Ego sum qui sum*") but rather "shall be" ("*Ero qui ero*").[36] Wessel goes a step further when he not only questions the proper translation of the name of God, but also the traditional claim to a definable knowledge of God based on this interpretation of His name. When God is not "I am who I am" but "shall be who shall be," it means that He is always "ahead" and always

[33]*Opera,* fol. 60.

[34]*Opera,* fol. 721.

[35]Caroline Bynum, *Jesus As Mother* (Berkeley: University of California Press, 1982).

[36]"Expedit ergo nunc veritatem innotescere, ut dicamus nomen Dei esse *Ero qui ero,* de futuro, et absque pronomine *Ego.*" *Opera,* fol. 419. Cf. fol. 78l! The *Hebraica Veritas* enables Wessel to criticize even the authority of Bernard of Clairvaux, fol. 484. Without mentioning any names, Wessel is here probably relying on Rashi. David Berger kindly pointed me to Rashi's interpretation of Exodus 3:14: "I will be" with them in this tribulation "who will be" or "as I will be" with them in the subjugation to other kingdoms. Moses said before God, "Master of the Universe, why should I mention another tribulation? This one is enough." He replied to him, "You have spoken well. 'This shall you say etc.'" (The "etc." represents the phrase "to the children of Israel, 'I will be' has sent me to you." Thus, this is why "I will be" is then said only once.) Rashi's comment is based on Babylonian Talmud *Berakhot* 9b. *Rashi al ha Torah,* ed. Abraham Berliner, 2nd ed. (Frankfurt: J. Kauffmann, 1905), 106.

"beyond" human knowledge. Even the blessed ones in heaven (*beati*) will grasp God only partially, since there will "always be some dimension of God they do not understand."[37] It is all the more true that the earthly pilgrim (*viator*), however exalted and elevated his meditation may be, will always "undershoot" God by far . . . .[38]

It does not take much imagination to see how this emphasis on the transcendent character of the knowledge of God lays the foundation for a critique of the so-called "labyrinth" of scholasticism that will prove to be fertile soil for criticism on the part of both Renaissance and Reformation authors. In the hands of Wessel Gansfort, the search for the *Veritas Hebraica* has become far more than the incidental fourteenth-century correction of single words in the Vulgate. He ventured to advance a reformulation of key texts for traditional dogma and piety, a reformulation which gave the word *veritas* its ideological connotation of challenging truth. Wessel Gansfort was not merely a "forerunner" of Reuchlin, he was a watershed in his own right. Notwithstanding the immense merit of Reuchlin for Hebrew studies, the novelty and challenge of the Hebrew truth could only be blunted through the pious sublimation by the Christian "Cabala."[39] The Christian Hebraists of the sixteenth century would continue to revere the name of Reuchlin but follow unknowingly in the footsteps of Wessel Gansfort.

IV. The *Veritas Hebraica* and the Assessment of the Jews

In his last and indeed formidable book, *Pest-Geissler-Judenmorde. Das 14. Jahrhundert als Krisenzeit,* Frantisek Graus placed the history of late medieval anti-Semitism in the wider social context of the catastrophes and crises of the times.[40] Apart from the rich documentation and quotation of numerous single sources, this book's lasting significance may well prove to be its theoretical analysis of the late medieval sense of disorientation and loss of meaning. It is with this wider setting in mind that I now turn to the increasing

---

[37]"Omnibus ergo beatis erit haec vicissitudo Dei: ut quantumlibet norint et videant, semper erit quod non comprehendant. Et hoc puto dictum, *Ero qui ero.* Quia quantum adscenderit homo ad cor altum, semper exaltabitur Deus, et ambulabit super pennas eius, et erit semper super eum quod erit, et ita transiens ministrabit ministris suis." *Opera,* fol. 421. See also fol. 51; cf. fol. 97-98.

[38]". . . quia quantumlibet bonum et bene cogitaveris, longe semper infra remanebis, etiam si Cherubico volatu, Seraphico contuitu contenderis. Unde ridiculum est altissimum quaerere in his quae infra cogitatum hominis, quantacunque sublimiter cogitantis." *Opera,* fol. 75. Instead of "infra" I suggest we read "supra cogitatum hominis. . . ." Cf. n. 30 above.

[39]See Joseph Leon Blau, *The Christian Interpretation of the Cabala in the Renaissance* (Port Washington, N.Y.: Kennikat Press, 1965 [1944]), esp. 41-64. Cf. Moshe Idel, "Universalization and Integration: Two Conceptions of Mystical Union in Jewish Mysticism," in *Mystical Union and Monotheistic Faith: An Ecumenical Dialogue,* ed. Moshe Idel and Bernard McGinn (New York: Macmillan, 1989), 270-57, 196-203.

[40]I use the second revised edition (Göttingen: Vandenhoeck and Ruprecht, 1988 [1987]). Here also is found the most extensive modern bibliography, 568-600.

recovery of the *Veritas Hebraica* as one of the noteworthy factors in the late medieval intensification of anti-Semitism.

Whereas Frantisek Graus properly discussed the late medieval persecution of the Jews in the larger societal context of efforts to cope with real or perceived catastrophes, such catastrophes only become crises when what was formerly regarded as an "act of God" comes to be identified as the willful sin of man.[41] As indicated in the introduction, it is the eminent function of intellectual history to study the opinion makers who become crucial agents in this process of transformation, be it as legitimizers or as plotters and planners. It is this perspective which today should orient our search for the roots of modern anti-Semitism in the age of Renaissance and Reformation.[42]

Yet we are still groping to determine the exact ingredients that went into the escalation of late medieval anti-Jewish propaganda. We can agree, I suggest, on the fact that there was a noticeable shift away from the accusation against the Jews as "blind" to that of being "stubborn"; instead of being regarded as destitute of light and therefore in need of illumination, the Jew was now presented as unwilling to accept the obvious, the Gospel Truth.[43] A number of factors have already been identified. Amos Funkenstein has convincingly pointed to the fact that the newly gained knowledge about Talmud and Torah made for an intensification of the traditional polemics by contrasting postbiblical Judaism with biblical or classical Judaism.[44] This distinction underlies a whole series of aggressive actions, which range from forced disputations to the burning of Talmudic books.

Jeremy Cohen has called attention to the particular role that the mendicant friars played in the intensification of anti-Jewish propaganda. The new study of the Talmudic books allowed the friars to argue that the Jews were not at all ignorant, but well informed and therefore willingly heretical in their rejection of the Gospel. At once complementing and correcting Beryl Smalley's observation that Nicolas of Lyra "represents the culmination of a movement for the study of Hebrew and rabbinics," Jeremy Cohen established that Lyra's anti-Jewish writings were "the natural outgrowth of the polemical trend begun by the friars . . . ."[45] I am inclined to regard Jacobus Perez of Valencia (c. 1408-1490) as the fifteenth-century climax of this phalanx of the friars,

[41]"Jede Gemeinschaft hat ein System von 'Ventilen'. . . . In der Zeit der Pest waren es die großen Judenpogrome und die Geißlerzüge . . . ." *Pest-Geissler-Judenmorde*, 37; cf. 458. The German word *Ventilen* has its equivalent in the original meaning of the English expression "to air" or "to ventilate" grievances.

[42]See my *Wurzeln des Antisemitismus*.

[43]See my article, "The Stubborn Jews. Timing the Escalation of Anti-Semitism in Late Medieval Europe," *Leo Baeck Institute Yearbook* 34 (1989), xi-xxv.

[44]Amos Funkenstein, "Basic Types of Christian Anti-Jewish Polemics in the Later Middle Ages," *Viator* 2 (1971): 373-82.

[45]Jeremy Cohen, *The Friars and the Jews. The Evolution of Medieval Anti-Judaism* (Ithaca: Cornell University Press, 1982), 190.

since this Spanish inquisitor declares in this treatise against the Jews (*Tractatus contra Judaeos*) that the whole campaign of the church directed towards the conversion of the Jews has to be called off because the Jews are stubborn "beyond repair."[46]

Ever since Ludwig Geiger, modern scholarship has tended to see in the recovery of the *Veritas Hebraica* a courageous countermovement climaxing in Johannes Reuchlin, opposing the trend of the times with a new concern for protecting the Jews.[47] And indeed, when Wessel Gansfort corrected existing views in the domains of doctrine and piety, he documented the extent to which the church herself had been unable to find access to the sources of the Gospel: the ignorance, formerly the mark of the Jew, apparently also applied to the Christian. This new access to the "Hebrew Truth" could indeed very well have become an antidote against the poison of anti-Semitism. In fact it did not; to the contrary!

To start with the case of Wessel Gansfort, we note that he did not translate his respect for Hebrew into terms of a new appreciation of the Jews, but rather continued to characterize them as "enemies of our faith," *hostes fidei nostrae.*[48] When Wessel turned to the parable of Matthew 20:1-16 and (probably in keeping with the original intention of the text) identified the Jews as those who protested against equal payment with the late-coming Christians, his point was not Jewish equality but Jewish hostility. He found this hatred so deeply rooted in Jewish nature that the Divine Promises had to be written under the disguise of a *tropus* to prevent the Jews from eradicating the truth from their own books: "*Oportuit igitur vetus testamentum tali tropo conscribi, quo non hostes veritatis abiicerent.*"[49] From here it is only a short step to the so-called "old" Luther of the 1540s who accused the rabbis of willingly distorting the truth of their own scriptures.

The great "watershed" Johannes Reuchlin did not defend the Talmudic books because of concern for the Jews or reverence for the Talmudic tradition as an expression of Jewish faith. He wanted to save these books from Pfefferkorn's fire as crucial linguistic resources for the understanding of the Old Testament. They had therefore to be preserved for posterity, not in Jewish hands but

---

[46]See my article "The Stubborn Jews . . .," xxiv. Jeremy Cohen has pointed to the thirteenth-century beginnings of this view in "high theology." See his "Robert Chazan's 'Medieval Anti-Semitism': A Note on the Impact of Theology," in *History and Hate: The Dimensions of Anti-Semitism,* ed. David Berger (Philadelphia: Jewish Publication Society, 1986), 67-72, 70. Cf. Tarald Rasmussen, *Inimici Ecclesiae. Studies in Medieval and Reformation Thought* (Leiden: Brill, 1989), 134-39.

[47]James H. Overfield has shown convincingly that the Reuchlin Affair did not pitch humanists against scholastics; however, he retained the view that Reuchlin was motivated by "concern for protecting the Jews." See his *Humanism and Scholasticism in Late Medieval Germany* (Princeton: Princeton University Press, 1984), 290.

[48]Gansfort, *Opera,* fol. 557.

[49]Ibid., fol. 57.

preferably in episcopal libraries.[50] The same conclusion applies to Conrad Pellican (†1556), Reuchlin's predecessor and instructor. This former Franciscan became the leading Christian Hebraist of the sixteenth century as a collector, transcriber, and translator of *rabbinica*. It is erroneously assumed that he was the disciple of Reuchlin and dependent on the latter's 1506 grammar. Actually, he had already published his Hebrew primer in 1504, and – two years later – he helped Reuchlin to design and index the *Rudimenta*.[51] Pellican's auto-biography, the *Hauschronik,* is not only a precise record of a life dedicated to the acquisition and transcription of rabbinical commentaries; it is also a testimony to a deep-seated disdain for the "usurious" and "ignorant Jews" who extorted exorbitant prices for a Hebrew manuscript even though they could not understand a word of it.[52]

Pellican was indeed convinced that it was impossible to understand the scriptures without the rabbinical books. It is no surprise, therefore, that Pellican's five-volume biblical commentary on the Hebrew scriptures, published by Froschauer in Zürich between 1523 and 1537, was placed on the Index – first on the Index of Louvain in 1546, and then on the Paris Index of 1549.[53] Pellican was prepared to invest his last penny to get the most recent printed treasures from the Venetian press, such as the works of David Kimhi, Abram Ibn Ezra, or Salomon Ben Isaac. He acquired with particular avidity the beautiful complete Talmud of 1517 or its reprint of 1524-1525. Yet, as a recently discovered letter reveals, he was up in arms when his good friend Capito, co-pastor with Martin Bucer in Strasbourg, crossed the demarcation line between a high regard for Hebrew studies and a respect for the Jews as Jews.[54] Pellican instructs Capito not to rely on the Jewish rabbis any more than on the Sorbonne doctors: all of them are *novicii* (beginners).[55] Capito is wrong in thinking that God promised that the Jews will establish a state in Israel: ". . . quasi regnum corporale permittis futurum eis . . . ." The bottom line of the admonition was that the Jews were good for grammar

[50]See my *Roots of Anti-Semitism,* 30-31.

[51]Pellican's primer was entitled *De modo legendi et intelligendi Hebraeum* (Strasbourg, 1504). Reprint 1877, ed. Eberhard Nestle.

[52]Bernhard Riggenbach, *Das Chronikon des Conrad Pellican* (Basel, 1877). Cf. *Die Hauschronik Konrad Pellikans von Rufach. Ein Lebensbild aus der Reformationzeit,* trans. Theodor Vulpinus (Strasbourg, 1892), 21.

[53]See *Index des Livres Interdits,* vol. 1, "Index de L'Université de Paris," ed. J. M. de Bujanda, Francis M. Higman, and James K. Farge (Geneva: Sherbrooke, 1985), nos. 108-12; 233-34.

[54]See Gerald Hobbs, "Monitio amica: Pellican à Capiton sur le danger des lectures rabbiniques," in *Horizons Européens de la Réforme en Alsace* (Festschrift for Jean Rott) (Strasbourg: Librairie Istra, 1980), 81-93. The letter published by Hobbs is written in Zürich and dated June 28, 1528.

[55]". . . charissime Capito, amicam monitionem, ne hebreorum interpretibus nimium tribueres, quos certe nosti novicios esse, fereque assimiles nostris magistris Parisiensibus . . . ," in ibid., 91.

but not for grace – they remained what they were, a miserable scrap of humanity: "miserum illud genus hominum."[56]

Wolfgang Capito formed as much an unrepresentative exception in the Reformed camp as Andreas Osiander did in the Lutheran camp. Not until late in the sixteenth century – when the early Calvinists started to glimpse from the lot of the Huguenots that to be homeless and exiled was apparently not proof of the wrath of God – do we discern a first glimmer of change in Christian thinking about the Jews. The failure of the city Reformation not only uprooted the "true believers" (*electi*); it also started to undercut the poisonous legend of the "eternal Jew." The fact of the recovery of the *Veritas Hebraica* as such, however, did not provide for a similar critical edge against anti-Jewish sentiments and censures. To the contrary, it could be fitted in smoothly with the newly grown conviction that the Jews were not merely blind, but stubborn. After all, for centuries they had full access to the plain Christian truth, namely, to the *Veritas Hebraica*.

Whatever it achieved for the understanding of biblical Judaism, the Hebrew truth could not reshape the deep-seated Christian disaffection with postbiblical Jews. Unfortunately, the recovery of Hebrew, with its potential for reaching the roots of anti-Semitism, occurred just at the time of the crucial premodern mentality shift that started to reinterpret social evil as human responsibility and accountability instead of as catastrophe and "the will of God." Among all the targets for social critique – popes and lords, emperors and monks – the Jews were the only group to fit smoothly both the old vision *and* the new: while they continued to be the *instruments* of the wrath of God, they were increasingly typecast as voluntary *agents* of evil. In this way, the Jews drew the fire of conservative *and* progressive social critics alike. Hence, the campaign for the *Veritas Hebraica* was, both philologically and ideologically, not merely a setback but a failure.

In conclusion, the following awesome rhyme in an early sixteenth-century song could as well have been coined two centuries before and sung both by turbulent crowds and pious congregations:

> No city therefore can fare well
> Until it's sent its Jews to hell.[57]

---

[56]"Promissiones Dei angustiores sunt, quam ut miserum illud hominum genus conciliandum Deo hoc terreno regno muneretur . . . preter grammaticam, in qua, ut vides, eciam ipsi certant, parum Iudeis tribuendum credamus . . . ." Ibid., 91-92.

[57]Rhymed translation by Gerald Strauss in *Manifestations of Discontent,* 128.

Radical Religion and the Age of Reason

Andrew C. Fix

This essay illuminates the intellectual links between radical religious groups of the sixteenth century and the secular worldview of the early Enlightenment by focusing on a Dutch Protestant sect known as the Collegiants. The Collegiants separated from the Arminians immediately following the Synod of Dordrecht in 1620. Collegiant ideology thus incorporated the Arminian non-doctrinal and latitudinarian stress on a practical, moral Christianity in opposition to the strict confessional approach of the Dutch Reformed church. Having no creeds and maintaining open membership, the Collegiants soon attracted to their ranks Mennonites, Socinian refugees, and spiritualist followers of Franck and Schwenkfeld. As the years passed, the ideas of the Mennonites, Socians, Spiritualists and Arminians mixed in Collegiant thought to produce a uniquely secularized and rational religious doctrine that before the end of the seventeenth century led the Collegiants to philosophical rationalism and the thought of Spinoza. Fix compares the case of the Collegiants with that of Puritans and Quakers in England.

THE RELATIONSHIP BETWEEN THE PROTESTANT REFORMATION of the sixteenth century and the emergence of a largely secular and rationalistic worldview among the educated classes of Europe during the late seventeenth and early eighteenth centuries has been much debated by historians and theologians alike. Ever since historians Wilhelm Dilthey and Ernst Troeltsch clashed early in this century over what Dilthey saw as the secularizing effects of Lutheran ideas on the developing worldview of modern Europe, scholars have debated the impact of Reformation religious ideas and the struggles surrounding them on the rational and secular worldview that developed in Europe during the Scientific Revolution of the seventeenth century and the Enlightenment of the eighteenth century. Sociologist Max Weber argued from a socioeconomic point of view that the methodological religious discipline of Calvinism promoted in people an ability to deal rationally with reality and thus influenced the rise of modern capitalist institutions.[1] Historians of science and philosophy have discussed the influence of the Reformation and its religious ideas on the development of modern experimental science and philosophical rationalism in the years between 1650 and 1750. The underlying and more fundamental question of the relationship between the traditional European religious worldview and the birth of early modern science and philosophy has also been discussed. Did the traditional religious worldview contribute in any positive way to the growth of modern science and philosophy, or was the worldview of faith and authority only an obstacle to be overcome by the new philosophy and science? Did the Protestant Reformation act as an impetus for new philosophical ideas or simply retard their development? And did the radical sects of the Reformation influence the growth of the modern worldview in a negative or positive way? This paper will attempt to suggest some answers to these questions by investigating the intellectual evolution of certain aspects of the religious thought of the sixteenth-century Radical Reformation among a group of Protestant free thinkers in seventeenth-century Holland. In the thought of the Dutch Collegiants, the complex nature of the relationship between the Reformation in its radical variant and the birth of philosophical rationalism during the late seventeenth century can be studied with interesting results.

I

The question of the relationship between religion and the rise of the modern worldview of science and reason has attracted the attention of scholars ever since the Enlightenment itself. Under the influence of Enlightenment ideas, especially the philosophy of Positivism, many of the first scholars to consider this question assumed that the traditional European religious worldview had no positive influence on the growth of modern science and philosophy. Philosophers like Voltaire and Diderot emphasized the fundamental conflict and incompatibility of these two systems of thought and believed that the victory of science could only come with the defeat of the superstition and obscurantism of traditional religion. For the philosophe, an empire of reason

---

[1] Dilthey's views from his seminal "Auffassung und Analyse des Menschen im 15. und 16. Jahrhundert" (1891-92) are summarized in Heinrich Bornkamm, *Luther im Spiegel der deutschen Geistesgeschichte* (Heidelberg: Quelle and Meyer, 1955), 232-37; and in Lewis W. Spitz, *The Reformation: Material or Spiritual* (Boston: Heath, 1962), 8-16. Troeltsch's ideas can be found in his *Protestantism and Progress: A Historical Study of the Relation of Protestantism to the Modern World*, trans. W. Montgomery (Boston: Beacon, 1958; English translation, 1912). Weber's views are best expressed in his *Protestant Ethic and the Spirit of Capitalism,* trans. Talcott Parsons (New York: Scribner, 1958). An overview of the entire Protestantism and modernization issue can be found in Steven Ozment, *The Age of Reform 1250-1550* (New Haven: Yale University Press, 1980), 160-265.

could only be built on the ruins of religion.[2] Condorcet and Comte saw modern science as the mature stage of human thought replacing the infantile religious worldview of earlier generations, and nineteenth-century Positivism prolonged this viewpoint for over a century. W. E. H. Lecky's *History of the Rise and Influence of the Spirit of Rationalism in Europe,* John W. Draper's *History of the Conflict Between Religion and Science,* and Andrew White's *History of the Warfare of Science with Theology in Christendom,* all continued to see the advent of modern science as a liberating revolution freeing mankind from the grip of religious superstition. Throughout most of the nineteenth century, the belief that the progress of science would lead naturally and inevitably to the improvement of human society perpetuated the viewpoint that the defeat of religion by science was part of the great plan of human intellectual evolution. A milder form of this argument was continued into the twentieth century by such scholars as E. A. Burtt, R. F. Jones, Basil Willey, and Paul Hazard.[3]

The cataclysm of the First World War played a key role in changing the attitudes of many intellectuals regarding the nature of modern science and its relationship to social progress. With this change came new ideas about the relationship between the traditional religious worldview and the birth of modern science and philosophy. Earlier views of the inevitable victory of modern science over religious superstition preparing the way for the maturation of the human mind and the perfection of human society came to be questioned by thinkers who now rejected the thesis that traditional religion had nothing positive to contribute to the development of the modern worldview. Instead of seeing religion and science as two incompatible worldviews in constant conflict, some scholars came to believe that religious ideas had a positive influence on the birth of modern science and philosophy. Works such as Alfred North Whitehead's *Science and the Modern World* (1925), R. G. Collingwood's *The Idea of Nature* (1945), and Charles E. Raven's *Natural Religion and Christian Theology* (1953) argued that Christianity had a significant constructive influence on the development of many of the central

---

[2]See Voltaire, *Philosophical Dictionary,* trans. Peter Gay, 2 vols. (New York: Basic Books, 1963); Diderot, *Selected Works of Diderot,* ed. and trans. Lester Crocker (New York: Macmillan, 1965).

[3]See, in addition to Lecky, Draper and White, E. A. Burtt, *The Metaphysical Foundations of Modern Science* (New York: Harcourt Brace & Co., 1927); R. F. Jones, *Ancients and Moderns* (St. Louis: Washington University Press, 1961); and Basil Willey, *The Seventeenth-Century Background* (London: Chatto and Windus, 1934).

concepts of early modern science, despite the conflicts that existed between science and religion in the seventeenth century.[4]

During the 1930s two important contributions to this new conception of the positive relationship between reason and science were made. In 1934 and 1935, Michael Foster published two important articles in the journal *Mind,* in which he argued that Christian voluntaristic theology exercised an important influence on the development of empirical science in early modern Europe. In 1938 Robert K. Merton published a famous book-length article in *Osiris,* in which he maintained that the psychological implications of the English Puritan value system were conducive to the growth of modern empirical science in Britain. Building on the work of earlier scholars such as Irene Parker and George Rosen, Merton argued that the ideas and values of Puritanism had a significant positive influence on the growth of the early scientific worldview, and he backed up this contention by pointing out how many of the pioneer scientists and early members of the Royal Society had been Puritans.[5] Merton's work was much debated in the years after its initial publication. Many critics charged that Merton's arguments were too general to establish any real link between Puritanism and science, but Merton also had found many supporters who defended his methods and findings.[6]

[4]See Alfred North Whitehead, *Science and the Modern World* (New York: Macmillan, 1925); R. G. Collingwood, *The Idea of Nature* (Oxford: Oxford University Press, 1945); and Charles E. Raven, *John Ray, Naturalist: His Life and Works* (Cambridge: Cambridge University Press, 1950) and *Natural Religion and Christian Theology* (Cambridge: Cambridge University Press, 1953).

[5]See Michael Foster, "The Christian Doctrine of Creation and the Rise of Modern Natural Science," *Mind* 43 (1934): 446-68; and "Christian Theology and the Modern Science of Nature," *Mind* 44 (1935): 439-66. See also Irene Parker, *Dissenting Academies in England* (Cambridge: Cambridge University Press, 1914); George Rosen, "Left-Wing Puritanism and Science," *Bulletin of the History of Medicine* 15 (1944): 375-80; and Robert K. Merton "Science, Technology and Society in Seventeenth-Century England," *Osiris* 4 (1934): 360-36.

[6]See Eugene Klaaren, *The Religious Origins of Modern Science* (Grand Rapids: Eerdmans, 1972), 9; Charles Webster, *The Great Instauration: Science, Medicine and Reform 1626-1660* (New York: Holmes and Meier, 1976), 487; Charles Webster, ed., *The Intellectual Revolution of the Seventeenth Century* (London: Routledge, 1974); D. Stimson, "Puritanism and the New Philosophy in Seventeenth-Century England," *Bulletin of the Institute for the History of Medicine* 3 (1935): 321-34; J. R. Jacob and M. C. Jacob, "Scientists and Society: The Saints Preserved," *Journal of European Studies* 1 (1971): 87-92; Douglas Hemsley, "Religious Influences on the Rise of Modern Science," *Annals of Science* 24 (1968): 199-226; Barbara Shapiro, "Debate, Science, Politics and Religion," *Past and Present* 66 (1975): 133-38; T. K. Rabb, "Puritanism and the Rise of Experimental Science in England," *Journal of World History* 7 (1962); R. L. Greaves, "Puritanism and Science: The Anatomy of a Controversy," *Journal of the History of Ideas* 30 (1969): 346-60; J. R. Jacob and M. C. Jacob, "The Anglican Origins of Modern Science," *Isis* 71 (1980): 251-67; John Morgan, "Puritanism and Science: A Reinterpretation," *Historical Journal* 22 (1979): 535-60; P. H. Kocher, *Science and Religion in Elizabethan England* (New York: Octagon, 1969); Barbara Shapiro, *John Wilkins, 1614-1672: An Intellectual Biography* (Berkeley: University of California Press, 1969) and *Probability and Certainty in Seventeenth-Century England* (Princeton: Princeton University Press, 1983).

The first investigation of the relationship between early modern science and religion to discuss the conflicts between the two thought systems as well as the reconciliation of those conflicts achieved by seventeenth-century thinkers was Richard S. Westfall's important study *Science and Religion in Seventeenth-Century England* (1958). Westfall argued that Christian ideas played an important role in shaping the attitudes that scientists brought to the study of nature in the seventeenth century. For this reason, religion significantly influenced the conclusions of science just as science changed the way that people thought about religion.[7] In the years after the publication of Westfall's book, a number of works appeared that stressed the important role of religious ideas in the formation of many key concepts of modern science. Reijer Hooykaas's *Religion and the Rise of Modern Science* (1972) and Eugene Klaaren's *The Religious Origins of Modern Science* (1977), along with the work of Francis Oakley, J. E. McGuire, Margaret J. Osler, and Edward B. Davis, have done much to deepen our appreciation for the critical role played by religious ideas in the intellectual origins of modern science.[8]

As Robert Merton showed, the thought of the radical religious sects descended from the Protestant Reformation has provided an especially fertile field for investigating the links between early modern science and religion. Christopher Hill's book *The World Turned Upside Down: Radical Ideas During the English Revolution* again demonstrated this fact clearly. Hill argued that interest in the new mechanical philosophy was particularly prevalent among religious and political radicals during the English revolution. According to Hill, there was a close connection between empirical science and radical theology, and many Puritans favored the teaching of science because it was of practical use to the people.[9] In a broader sense, Hill maintained that radical Protestantism defeated magic and superstition and thus contributed to the process of intellectual secularization as sermons rejecting Catholic transubstantiation helped to produce a materialistic and skeptical attitude toward

[7]Richard S. Westfall, *Science and Religion in Seventeenth-Century England* (New Haven: Yale University Press, 1958), 40-69.

[8]Reijer Hooykaas, *Religion and the Rise of Modern Science* (Grand Rapids: Eerdmans, 1972); Eugene Klaaren, *The Religious Origins of Modern Science* (Grand Rapids: Eerdmans, 1977); J. E. McGuire, "Boyle's Conception of Nature," *Journal of the History of Ideas* 33 (1972): 523-42; Francis Oakley, "Christian Theology and the Newtonian Science: The Rise of the Concept of Laws of Nature" in Daniel O'Connor and F. Oakley, eds., *Creation: The Impact of An Idea* (New York: Scribner, 1969); Margaret J. Osler, "Descartes and Charleton on Nature and God," *Journal of the History of Ideas* 40 (1979): 445-56; and "Providence and Divine Will: The Theological Background to Gassendi's Views on Scientific Knowledge," *Journal of the History of Ideas* 44 (1983): 549-60; Edward B. Davis, "Creation, Contingency and Early Modern Science: The Impact of Voluntaristic Theology on Seventeenth-Century Natural Philosophy" (Ph.D. diss., Indiana University, 1984), esp. 1-14.

[9]Christopher Hill, *The World Turned Upside Down: Radical Ideas During the English Revolution* (New York: Viking, 1972), 289-92.

miracles in general.[10] In *Some Intellectual Consequences of the English Revolution,*
Hill asserted that after 1650 the mechanical philosophy largely replaced the
supernatural worldview, in part because of Puritanism's rational critique of
the mass, holy water, exorcism, and other Catholic rituals. "When the
mechanical philosophy put an abstract mechanism in control of the world,"
Hill said, "man found himself in a universe in which God and the devil no
longer took an active, day-to-day interest in humanity."[11] The toleration and
openness of the revolutionary years in England significantly contributed to
the growing rationalism that led to a decline of belief in magic. At the same
time, Hill added, the radical millenarianism of the revolution raised hopes
for a utopia on earth and linked up with Baconian scientific optimism to
create a theory of progress.[12]

The influence of radical religious ideals on the developing rationalistic
worldview was brilliantly discussed by Charles Webster in 1975 in his study,
The Great Instauration: Science, Medicine and Reform 1626-1660. Webster supported
Merton's earlier claims by arguing for the impact of Puritan millenarian ideas
on the origins of modern science. According to Webster, Puritan revolutionaries
employed science to add precision to the millennial outline drawn up by
theologians. The Puritans believed that the discoveries of science would end
the intellectual decline of humanity that started with Adam's fall and thus
help to usher in the millennium by returning to man his original dominion
over nature. Following Daniel 12:4, the Puritans believed that a great revival
of learning would be an integral part of the coming millennial paradise. They
believed that this revival of learning had already started with the rejection
of pagan Aristotelianism by the new experimental philosophy, and they saw
Bacon's *Instauratio Magna* as the blueprint for this intellectual renaissance.
Bacon held that the investigation of nature would both glorify God and
restore man's dominion over nature. He further maintained that God had
sanctioned scientific investigation through the prophecy of Daniel foretelling
the millennial increase of knowledge. The *Instauratio Magna* thus looked
forward to a great revival of learning, and Puritan science was dominated by
this millennial fervor. The Puritans pursued science for its value in confirming
the power of Providence as well as for its social utility. According to Webster,
the growth of English science was closely tied to the growth of the Puritan
party.[13]

Building upon ideas such as these, Margaret Jacob argued in *The Radical
Enlightenment* a decade ago that Puritanism aided the rise of modern science

---

[10]Ibid., 89.

[11]Christopher Hill, *Some Intellectual Consequences of the English Revolution* (Madison.: University
of Wisconsin Press, 1980), 64-66.

[12]Ibid., 59-64.

[13] Webster, *The Great Instauration,* xvi-30, 503.

because the Puritans linked their desire to promote the new science with the cause of the Puritan revolution. Puritan radicals embraced the cause of science in the service of social reform, but following the failure of Puritan reform schemes during the 1640s, a split occurred within the reform party. A group of moderates reacted against more radical reformers by adopting a latitudinarian religious position and a mechanical conception of the universe. This mechanical perspective stressed divine providence as a source of order and harmony imposed through laws at work in nature and society. The moderates championed Newtonian science because the ordered, providentially guided, and mathematically measured universe of Newton provided a model for a stable and prosperous social order based on monarchy and supported by a rational natural religion.[14]

Opposing the moderates, according to Jacob, was a party that carried on the tradition of radical Puritanism by believing the millennial paradise to be imminent. These radicals envisioned a democratic and egalitarian society without a clergy, in which the spirit of God would infuse the common people and make them inheritors of a grand new social order. Along with their social and political ideas, the radicals adopted a version of the new science that stressed materialism and pantheism. While the moderate Newtonians contributed their version of nature and society to the mainstream of Enlightenment thought represented by Voltaire, the radicals handed down their views to the radical wing of the Enlightenment led by such men as D'Holbach.[15]

II

The research of Hill, Merton, Webster, and Jacob has greatly contributed to our understanding of the ways in which radical religious ideas contributed to the formation of early modern science and the Enlightenment worldview during the late seventeenth century. In so doing, this work has shown that religious groups outside of the established Lutheran and Reformed churches of the Reformation and post-Reformation era can provide interesting insights into the nature of the relationship between religion and rationalism in early modern Europe. Ernst Troeltsch recognized this fact years ago when he pointed to the radical Anabaptists and spiritualists of the Reformation as in many ways more "modern" than the mainline Lutherans and Calvinists.[16] Hill, Merton, Webster, and Jacob have concentrated almost exclusively on English Puritanism, however, and for this reason little is known about the connections between continental religious radicalism and the coming of the

[14]Margaret Jacob, *The Radical Enlightenment* (London: Allen and Unwin, 1981), 66-105, 202.

[15]Ibid.

[16]Ernst Troeltsch, *Protestantism and Progress*, 95-96 as cited in Ozment, *Age of Reform*, 263. Some parts of the following section appeared in *The Sixteenth Century Journal* 18 (Spring 1987): 63-80.

Age of Reason. The case of the Dutch Collegiants, a radical Protestant sect that flourished in The Netherlands in the years between 1620 and 1690, can add a valuable continental European perspective on the questions investigated in England by previous scholarship.

The Collegiants were seventeenth-century heirs of the religious radicalism of the sixteenth-century Protestant Reformation on the continent. The Collegiants fused ideas from these movements with certain elements of Dutch Arminian thought to produce a unique body of religious thought that gradually evolved, over the course of the seventeenth century, into an embryonic secular and rationalistic philosophy anticipating certain aspects of Enlightenment thought. In this transformation of Collegiant thought from a radical religious ideology into a secular philosophical rationalism, many of the same processes were at work that Hill, Webster, and Jacob found among the English Puritans. Millenarianism, anticlericalism, toleration, utopianism, and universalist reform expectations were all present among the Collegiants just as among English Puritans, but among the Collegiants these ideas functioned in very different ways than among the Puritans, transforming the small Dutch group from a seventeenth-century heir of the Radical Reformation into an early outpost of philosophical rationalism. Because this striking intellectual transformation took place in Holland, the center of a vibrant intellectual life and one of the primary continental homes of the Scientific Revolution, the case of the Collegiants provides an exciting new perspective on the relationship between radical religion and the age of reason on the continent.

The Collegiant movement arose in Holland late in the second decade of the seventeenth century as a result of a dispute that took place within the Dutch Reformed Church. The dispute centered around Jacob Arminius (1560-1609), a liberal Calvinist professor of theology at Leiden University. Arminius criticized the growing trend within the Reformed church toward a rigid confessionalism and doctrinal intolerance, arguing instead for an Erasmian attitude of doctrinal latitudinarianism and an emphasis on the moral and spiritual goals of Christianity. It was Arminius's rejection of the Calvinist doctrine of predestination, which he viewed as harsh and unjust, that brought down upon him and his followers the full wrath of conservative Calvinists led by his Leiden colleague in theology, Franciscus Gomarus (1563-1641).

The religious dispute between Arminius and Gomarus quickly became intertwined with a larger political struggle between Stadtholder Maurice of Nassau and Johan Van Oldenbarnevelt, the Grand Pensionary of Holland. Oldenbarnevelt and the urban oligarchs of Holland formed a peace party opposing renewed hostilities with Spain when the twelve-year truce expired in 1621. Nassau, Oldenbarnevelt's chief rival for power within the government of the United Provinces, led a noble faction favoring a resumption of the war as well as greater centralization of the Dutch government than the oligarchs and the States of Holland were willing to permit. The followers of Arminius, called Remonstrants after the petition of grievances that they delivered to the States of Holland in 1610, found a champion in Oldenbarnevelt, whose patrician adherents disliked the stricter Calvinism of Gomarus. The conservatives looked to Nassau for protection of the official doctrines of the Reformed church against the threat of Remonstrant innovation. As the end of the truce with Spain neared, the political quarrel within the Dutch republic reached a crisis point in 1618, when Nassau managed to seize control of the government and have Oldenbarnevelt arrested. The stadtholder next moved to settle the religious dispute. A national synod of the Reformed church was held in Dordrecht during the winter of 1618-1619, and it was at this meeting that the final showdown between the Remonstrants and their opponents took place. With Nassau in control of the government, the outcome of the synod was never in doubt. The Remonstrants were expelled from the church, their ministers deposed, and many Remonstrant leaders, including the philosopher Hugo Grotius, were jailed.

Among the Remonstrant congregations left leaderless by the deposition of Arminian pastors in 1619 was the congregation in the village of Warmond, near Leiden. Rather than accept a conservative minister or disband for lack of leadership, the congregation decided to follow the advice of one of its elders, Gijsbert van der Kodde, and continued to meet without a preacher. The congregation came together to pray, sing hymns, and read scripture, relying for scriptural interpretation and religious education on the spontaneous, inspired testimony of any of their number who felt moved by the Holy Spirit to speak for the enlightenment of the group. This practice the Collegiants called "free prophecy," and it became the distinguishing feature of a new religious movement devoted to moral and spiritual religion and highly critical of the doctrinaire Reformed church. The college, as these meetings came to be called, continued to meet in secret (for fear of Calvinist persecution) in Warmond throughout 1620 before moving to the neighboring village of Rijnsburg in 1621. The Collegiant movement was born.[17]

In the years between 1620 and 1650 the Collegiant movement spread all through the United Provinces, but the most important colleges were established in Holland in the cities of Amsterdam, Rotterdam, Haarlem, and Leiden. At first the colleges were made up of a core of former Remonstrants seeking toleration and expression of their undogmatic piety. The Rotterdam college counted among its founders the Remonstrant preachers Peter Cupus and Samuel Landsbergen, and it was led in later years by the Remonstrant poet and classical scholar Frans Joachim Oudaan (1628-1692). The Amsterdam college was founded by former Remonstrant pastor Daniel de Breen (1574-1664) and the spiritualistic theologian Adam Boreel (1602-1665). Because of these Remonstrant origins, the Collegiant movement incorporated the chief Arminian

[17]J. C. van Slee, *De Rijnsburger Collegianten* (Haarlem, 1895), 16-37.

criticisms of the Reformed church: the rejection of predestination, confessionalism, and doctrinal rigidity coupled with a call for a theologically tolerant but morally and spiritually upright religion. Because of opposition to the offical Reformed church, the Collegiant movement acted as a magnet, drawing to itself the scattered groups of radical Protestants who had come to settle in Holland since the sixteenth century.[18]

The Netherlands was home and refuge for all three branches of what George Huntston Williams called the Radical Reformation of the sixteenth century: the Anabaptists, the Radical Spiritualists and the Evangelical Rationalists.[19] Anabaptism, born in Zwingli's Zurich in 1523, but soon widely spread over Switzerland, north and south Germany, and the Low Countries, sought to restore the spiritual purity of primitive Christianity to the church of the sixteenth century through strict adherence to the Bible, great moral rigor, and rejection of infant baptism. Many Anabaptists, such as Melchior Hoffman, leader of the movement in north Germany and the Low Countries, also propounded a radical millenarianism similar to that which reached its most tragic expression in the ill-fated kingdom of Münster in 1534-1535. The Radical Spiritualists, fewer in number than the Anabaptists, were led by Sebastian Franck and Kaspar Schwenkfeld. They rejected the importance of all external religious institutions, sacraments, and ceremonies as well as the relevance of theological doctrine in favor of a religion based entirely on the direct, sanctifying, and illuminating inspiration of the Holy Spirit in the individual soul of each believer. This individual inspiration they called the "Inner Light" or "Inner Word," and it brought the believer perfect religious knowledge as a means of preparing his soul to receive God's grace. Evangelical Rationalism manifested itself in part in the movement known as Socinianism, founded by Laelius and Faustus Socinus, natives of Siena who were influenced by Italian humanism and its rationalistic biblical scholarship. The Socinians flourished in Poland during the second half of the sixteenth century, rejecting the traditional Christian doctrines of the Trinity, the divinity of Christ, and Christ's satisfaction. Their criticism of Christian dogma was based on a combination of biblical literalism and a commonsense rationalism inherited from the humanists.[20]

All three of these radical religious groups experienced heavy persecution in their native countries from Catholics and Protestants alike throughout the sixteenth and early seventeenth centuries, and all three found a safe haven

[18]Ibid., 95-114.

[19]George Huntston Williams, *The Radical Reformation* (Philadelphia: Westminster, 1962), xxiii-xxxi.

[20]On the Socinians see W. J. Kühler, *Het Socinianisme in Nederlend* (Leiden: A. W. Sijthoff, 1912); on the Anabaptists see Williams; on Sebastian Franck see Siegfried Wollgast, *Der deutsche Pantheismus im 16. Jahrhundert* (Berlin, 1972); on Kaspar Schwenkfeld see R. Emmet McLaughlin, *Caspar Schwenkfeld, Reluctant Radical* (New Haven: Yale University Press, 1986).

for the private practice of their religions in tolerant Holland. The Anabaptists, from the very year of their founding, were persecuted by Catholics and Protestants alike as dangerous subverters of civil and religious order. As persecution increased after the Münster disaster, the remnants of the Anabaptist movement in northern Germany and the Low Countries sought to discourage further harassment by adopting strict pacifism under the leadership of the Dutchman Menno Simons. Many Anabaptists sought refuge in the great cities of the province of Holland, where the commercially minded civil authorities were reluctant to sanction any religious persecution without the most serious provocation. After a brief period of tension immediately following the Münster episode, which had been accompanied by smaller but equally unsuccessful Anabaptist uprisings in Amsterdam and other Dutch cities, the Mennonites were left to practice their religion in peaceful privacy by the urban oligarchs of Holland, who were soon embroiled in the revolt against Spain.[21]

Radical Spiritualism too found fertile ground for its development in Holland. Franck and Schwenkfeld spread their ideas in southern Germany during the second quarter of the sixteenth century, but the influence of their ideas was stronger and more lasting among the Dutch during the late sixteenth and early seventeenth centuries. Hounded from city to city by German authorities, these lonely prophets of inner religion established small cells of disciples in various locations in southern Germany, but they left behind no large body of followers in Germany when they died, Franck in 1543, and Schwenkfeld in 1561. Their writings found greater circulation in The Netherlands, where the works of Franck were translated into Dutch and printed several times in Holland after 1560. Franck's ideas were very popular among Dutch Protestants, especially the Mennonites.[22] The chief exponent of Franck's ideas in The Netherlands was the influential humanist and ecumenical thinker Dirck Volckertsz. Coornhert (1522-1590). Coornhert's ideas were important to many of the principal religious thinkers of The Netherlands during the late sixteenth and early seventeenth centuries, including Arminius and Boreel.[23]

Socinianism, which blossomed in Poland during the years 1580-1658, became primarily a Dutch movement during the later seventeenth century. In the years following Faustus Socinus's arrival in Krakow in 1580, the Polish monarchy was disorganized and weak and the Polish Catholic church was occupied with the challenge of Calvinism. After 1600, however, the influence

---

[21]On Menno Simons see N. van der Zijpp, *Geschiedenis der Doopsgezinden in Nederland* (Arnhem, 1952) and H. W. Meihuizen, *Menno Simons: Ijveraar voor het herstel van de Nieuwtestamentisch gemeente 1496-1561* (Haarlem: H. D. Tjeenk Willink en Zoon, 1961).

[22]Bruno Beker, "Nederlandsche Vertalingen van Sebastian Francks Geschriften," *Nederlandsche Archief voor Kerkgeschiedenis* 21 (1928): 149-60.

[23]On Coornhert see F. D. J. Moorrees, *D. V. Coornhert, de libertijn* (Schoonhoven: S. W. N. van Nooten, 1887) and H. Bonger, *Leven en werken van D. V. Coornhert* (Amsterdam: G. A. van Oorschot, 1987).

of the Counter-Reformation reinvigorated both church and monarchy in Poland, and the crown, with Jesuit prompting, undertook a brutal attack on the Socinians. The followers of Socinus were expelled from Poland in 1658 under pain of death, and while some sought refuge in East Prussia or the Rhineland, most Socinians ended up settling in Holland, especially in Amsterdam.[24] Dutch authorities were as repelled by Socinian ideas as other moderate Protestants, however, and they refused to allow the Socinians the freedom to worship publicly. But the ruling oligarchs were also motivated by a pragmatic policy of religious toleration and by a desire to avoid unnecessary disturbances of the public peace. The authorities thus turned down the repeated demands of the Reformed church to expel the Socinians and tacitly allowed them to practice their religion in private, ignoring all but the most indiscreet Socinian activities.

As the Collegiant movement grew and spread across Holland in the years after 1620, the colleges' opposition to the Reformed church and broad toleration for diverse religious opinions helped attract into the movement many Anabaptists, Spiritualists, and Socinians. The Anabaptist Mennonites were the first group of radicals to join the colleges in large numbers, and soon the Mennonites made up a substantial portion of Collegiant membership. The Rotterdam college gained many members from the local congregation of Waterland Mennonites.[25] In Haarlem, the college became heavily Mennonite and was greatly influenced by the ideas of the Mennonite preacher Pieter Langedult (1640-1687). In Amsterdam after 1650 the leadership of the college passed into the hands of the eloquent and forceful Mennonite preacher Galenus Abrahamsz. (1622-1706), who used his position in the important Amsterdam college to gain tremendous influence over the larger Collegiant movement in Holland.[26] With the Mennonites came Anabaptist ideas, including millenarianism and the belief that the established Protestant churches had compromised true Christian principles for worldly gain.

Radical Spiritualism also became an important force in Collegiantism after 1620. Amsterdam leader Adam Boreel acquired Franck's ideas through his reading of Coornhert. In his main published work, *Ad legem* (1643), Boreel followed Franck in his rejection of the sacraments and ceremonies of all external, established churches. Boreel proclaimed all visible churches hopelessly corrupt and held the only true, spiritual church to be the invisible church of true believers scattered throughout the world. Boreel passed on his spiritualism to his Amsterdam colleague Galenus Abrahamsz., whose criticism of the visible churches was widely accepted in the colleges. Galenus

[24]See Kühler and E. M. Wilbur, *A History of Unitarianism: Socinianism and its Antecedents* (Cambridge, Mass.: Harvard University Press, 1946).

[25]Van Slee, *De Rijnsburger,* 1637.

[26]Ibid., 142-44, 162-65, 178-80, 184-86.

in turn passed spiritualistic ideas on to his many Collegiant disciples, including Pieter Balling and Jarig Jelles, about whom more will be said in due course.[27]

Socinianism became part of the Collegiant movement after the arrival of the Polish exiles in Holland in 1658-1660. Denied the open practice of their religion, many of the exiles began to frequent college meetings, where they were allowed free expression of their beliefs through the mechanism of free prophecy. An atmosphere of extreme freedom of thought ruled the colleges after 1620. Unconcerned with doctrine, the Collegiants believed theological toleration to be an aspect of the pristine spirituality of the primitive church that they hoped to revive. Even Socinian antitrinitarianism provoked little hostility in the colleges. The Socinian Johannes Becius (1626-1680) became one of the leading figures of the Rotterdam college, along with the former Remonstrant preacher-turned-Socinian Frans Kuyper (1629-1692). It was not Socinian antitrinitarianism that most influenced Collegiant thinking, however, but rather the Socinians' rationalistic approach to scriptural interpretation, which they inherited from Italian humanism. For the Socinians, any religious doctrine that could not be rationally explained was false, but they insisted that everything in the Bible could be so explained.[28]

III

With this collection of Arminian, Mennonite, Spiritualist, and Socinian ideas, the Collegiant movement formed part of a broader movement of Protestant religious dissent that Leszek Kolakowski has called the Second Reformation of the seventeenth century. According to Kolakowski this movement developed both within the established Lutheran and Reformed churches and outside of these churches among individuals and independent groups. Its proponents criticized the established churches for a lack of spiritual zeal, for having compromised with the secular world, and for having abandoned the heart of true Christianity.[29] The proponents of the Second Reformation thus made many of the same criticisms of the Lutheran and Calvinist churches as had the earlier Radical Reformation. Like the earlier radicals, they considered the work of Luther and Calvin a disappointing failure, and for this reason the men of the Second Reformation believed the Protestant churches of 1620 to be as badly in need of reform as the Catholic church of 1520 had been. These new reformers saw growing confessionalism, an overemphasis on

[27]Walter Schneider, *Adam Boreel: Sein Leben und seine Schriften* (Giessen: Giessen University Press, 1911), 32-40; Herman Vekeman, *Toelichting over Galenus korte Verhandling* (Cologne: Cologne University Institute for Netherlands Literature, 1983), 29-34.

[28]Van Slee, *De Rijnsburger,* 378; Kühler, *Het Socinianisme,* 134-47; *Biographisch Woordenboek van Protestantsche Godgelerden in Nederland* (The Hague: Nijhoff, 1943), 1:365-68; *Biograpfisch Lexicon voor de Geschiedenis van het Nederlandse Protestantisme* (Kampen: Kok, 1983), 1:99.

[29]Leszek Kolakowski, *Chrétiens sans église: la conscience religieuse et le lien confessionnel au XVIIe Siècle* (Paris: Gallimard, 1969), 9-10.

external ceremonies, and doctrinal quarreling as signs that the established Protestant churches were spiritually bankrupt.

The Second Reformation of the seventeenth century flourished especially in Holland, that refuge for Protestant radicals. It comprised a group of pietists within the Dutch Reformed church who were influenced by English Puritanism and led by such men as Willem Tellinck and Jacobus Koelman; it comprised millenarian prophets like Johannes Rothe, Quirinius Kuhlman, and Antoinette Bourignon, called "the light of the world" by her followers; it included also mystic followers of Jacob Böhme such as Johannes Gichtel and Alhardt De Raedt. But the Collegiants represented the only really organized branch of the Second Reformation in Holland, and the colleges also acted as conduits by way of which the ideas of the sixteenth-century Radical Reformation became a part of the new movement. In developing their critique of the established churches, the Collegiants drew ideas from both the Radical Reformation and the Second Reformation, and in the process they developed a dramatically innovative line of religious thought. In rejecting the religion of the institutional churches the Collegiants in fact rejected the essence of the religious worldview that had dominated European thought for centuries, and in its place they put a secular, rationalistic epistemology that anticipated the worldview of the Enlightenment.

The Collegiant criticism of the Protestant Reformation and the churches that it produced was best expressed by the Amsterdam Mennonite/Collegiant Galenus Abrahamsz. in his book *Bedenkingen over den Toestant der Sichtbare Kerk Christi op Aerden Kortelijck in XIX Artikelen Voor-ghestelt*. In this tract, Galenus adopted and expanded upon a critique of the church made by earlier Radical Spiritualists like Franck, a critique which had become influential among the Collegiants through the works of Coornhert and Boreel. Galenus produced a criticism of the established churches that soon became generally accepted in the colleges.

According to Galenus, the true church of Christ had vanished from the earth with the passing of the original, spiritually pure church of the Apostles. God had given the members of the apostolic church abundant gifts of the Holy Spirit: special abilities resulting from the direct inspiration of the Holy Spirit, such as perfect religious knowledge and the ability to perform miracles. With these special gifts the early Christians built up the church and spread God's Word. When the emperor Constantine allied the Christian church to the Roman state in the fourth century, however, the church became overly concerned with worldly affairs at the expense of its spiritual mission. As punishment, God withdrew the gifts of the Holy Spirit from the church, and throughout the Middle Ages it fell ever deeper into corruption and decay. The medieval church was a corrupt, unspiritual institution badly in need of restoration to its original spiritual state, Galenus wrote. But in order for men to effect such a reform of the church they would require direct inspiration from God in the form of a renewed dispensation of the gifts of the Holy Spirit to instruct them. According to Galenus, the Reformation of Luther, Zwingli, and Calvin had not had such divine inspiration and was thus not a true reform of the church. The reformers had been pious men, but they lacked the proper instruction from God on how to rebuild the church. As a result, each man reformed differently, according to his own ideas, his own interpretation of the Bible, and his own fallible understanding of religious truth. The result was a chaotic confusion of competing "reformed" churches, each claiming to be the one true church in exclusive possession of divine truth. For Galenus, this division was evidence of the failure and spiritual bankruptcy of the Protestant Reformation.

In view of the failure of the Reformation, Galenus considered all of the visible, institutional churches of his day – Protestant and Catholic alike – as corrupt, decayed, devoid of the gifts of the Holy Spirit, and thus cut off from divine inspiration. They were merely fallible human institutions, ignorant of the true inner light of religious truth and hopelessly entangled in worldly politics. Without spiritual vigor, deprived of God's inspiration and revelation even for interpreting scripture, man's organized religion was, in Galenus's eyes, cut off from God: it was a church unholy.[30]

Galenus's critique of the established churches was inherited by the Collegiants from the Spiritualists and Anabaptists of the Radical Reformation: similar ideas can be found in the writings of Franck, Schwenkfeld, and Anabaptist authors of the sixteenth century such as Christian Entfelder. The Collegiants combined this critique of the visible churches with another complex of ideas inherited from the Anabaptist/Mennonite tradition – millenarianism – to produce a picture of the entire world cut off from divine inspiration and in religious decay. The doctrine of the millennium was an age-old Christian idea revived during the Reformation and predicting Christ's return to earth before the Last Judgment to set up a holy kingdom in which true believers would rule the earth for a thousand years and administer punishment to the enemies of God. Christ's return would put an end to centuries of persecution of God's people by the forces of evil and set the stage for an earthly paradise of the saints. The Anabaptists expected to inherit this kingdom, and thus the followers of Hoffman looked forward with great anticipation to Christ's imminent return in Münster.

Collegiant millenarianism, however, had a somewhat different tone. Collegiant chiliastic works were not dominated by the ecstatic or idealistic descriptions of the coming paradise that were so typical of much millenarian writing. Instead, they stressed the dark period of sin, suffering, and persecution of the holy people preceding the millennium. While these gloomy descriptions

[30]Galenus Abrahamsz., *Bedenckingen over den Toestand der Sictbare Kercke Christi op Aerden, Kortelijck in XIX Artikelen VoorGhestelt* (Amsterdam, 1657), 1-10; Galenus Abrahamsz., *Wederlegging van't Geschrift Genaemt: Antwoorde by forme van Aenmerckingen* (Amsterdam, 1659), 6-27.

were perhaps intended to convince the reader of the truth of the millennial prophecies by drawing a comparison between scriptural predictions of premillennial decay and the troubled condition of Europe in the seventeenth century, another effect of these pessimistic descriptions was to draw attention to the corruption and decay of the world in which both reader and writer lived. Daniel De Breen, in his work *Van't Geestelijke Triumpherende Rijk Onses Heeren Jesu Christi,* expected the eventual arrival of a holy paradise on earth. His work put greater stress, however, on the corruption of the world before the millennium: a world ruled by sinners, inhabited by people with a careless disobedience toward God, infested by false prophets, and wracked by war and natural disasters.[31]

This picture of a premillennial world in spiritual decay was enhanced in the chiliastic writings of Galenus's Mennonite/Collegiant follower Petrus Serrarius (1600-1669). Serrarius combined the millenarian picture of a world in decay prior to the Second Coming with Galenus's picture of the corruption of all established churches. In his work, *De Vertreding van de Heilige Stadts,* Serrarius wrote that Christ himself would both purify the world from sin and restore his true church in the millennium, but until that time both the world and its churches would remain corrupt and devoid of the gifts of the Holy Spirit. Because of this, any efforts made by men to reform either the church or the world would be ineffectual. Serrarius thus extended Galenus's picture of the spiritual bankruptcy of the established churches to create a vision of an entire world devoid of divine inspiration before the coming of the millennium.[32] This view spread fast among the Collegiants, influenced by both chiliasm and Galenus's spiritualistic critique of the churches. The Collegiants came to see the world in which they lived as cut off from God's inspiration and influence – as a world unholy.

The traditional providential Christian worldview, propagated and defended by the church from earliest times, was built on the assumption that God's influence and inspiration were everywhere active in the world of men. God was considered to be a casual agent in human affairs, operating in the world to control events and to inspire men with religious truth. Against this background, the Collegiant view of a secularized world devoid of God's influence was new indeed. Such a dramatic step was made possible, perhaps, by the chiliastic belief that such a situation was not permanent but would be reversed with the arrival of the millennium. When the millennium repeatedly failed to arrive on the dates assigned for its appearance, however, this view of a secularized world cut off from God began to take on an air of permanence for many Collegiants. They began to make plans for an indefinite continuation

[31]Daniel De Breen, *Van 't Geestelijke Triumpherende Rijk Onses Heeren Jesu Christi* (Amsterdam, 1653), 80-85, 97-141, 371-78.

[32]Pieter Serrarius, *De Vertreding des Heyligen Stadts, Ofte een klaer bewijs van 't verval der eerste apostolische gemeente* (Amsterdam, 1659), 7-8, 10-15, 18-20.

of pious religious life in a world unholy. Faced with the problem of how individual believers were to maintain a sincere religious life in a premillennial world in which all institutional churches were corrupt and the world itself separated from God's direction, Collegiant writers like Frans Joachim Oudaan (1628-1692), Daniel Zwicker (1621-1678), and Jan Bredenburg (d. 1691) suggested that, in lieu of divine revelation, man could only make use of his own natural reason to discover religious truth and lead a moral life. In his book *Overwegging eeniger grondstellingen door J.V.G. in zelfs redenering over de algemeene kerk ter neder gestelt,* Oudaan wrote that since men could no longer rely on divine inspiration in religion, "We have only our own understanding, however great or small, or our reason, however weak or powerful, and the dictates of our conscience, that can be our guide in these matters." Oudaan and Bredenburg also suggested that all truly pious believers should leave their corrupt institutional churches and carry on this new rational religious life in the colleges, where free thought and toleration reigned.[33] Even without claiming for reason any infallibility in divine matters, many Collegiants came to see reason as the best substitute for revelation in a world unholy. To their secularized conception of the corrupt premillennial world the Collegiants thus added a rational conception of religious life. As the Collegiants' respect for the power of reason gradually increased, this rational religion evolved into philosophical rationalism.

The Collegiants' movement toward a rational religion was greatly aided by the influence of Socinianism in the colleges. In the writings of Socinian/Collegiants like Frans Kuyper, the extent of the impact of Socinian rationalism on Collegiant thinking was evident. Kuyper took from the Socinians the idea that man's religious knowledge proceeded from two main sources: the Bible and human reason. The Bible, divinely inspired, provided man with the content of religious knowledge, but man could only interpret and understand this content by using his own reason. For Kuyper and the Socinians, a vital link existed between divine truth and human reason: all divine truth could be rationally explained, and a lack of rational explanation indicated falsity. But the Socinians did not make human reason the criterion for religious truth. For them, and for Collegiants like Kuyper who adopted their ideas, the Bible was the only criterion for religious truth because everything in scripture was both divinely true and capable of being rationally explained. This position led the Socinians and their supporters into some tortuously rationalized explanations of biblical miracles, but it also firmly established the original Collegiant idea of a rational religion. Reason was held to be not the source of religious truth but rather a vital tool for interpreting such truth

---

[33]Joachim Oudaan, *Overwegging eeniger grondstellingen door J.V.G. in des Zelfs redenering over de algemeene Kerk ter neder gestelt* (Amsterdam: 1689), 15; Jan Bredenburg, *Heylzame Raad tot Christelijke Vrede of te aanwijzing van het rechte middle tot Christelijke Vereeniging* (Rotterdam, n.d.), 6-12.

in lieu of a new dispensation of the gifts of the Holy Spirit.[34] While religious knowledge was seen as rational, reason was subservient to the biblical source of divine truth.

The spread of this rational view of religious knowledge among the once largely spiritualistic Collegiants can be traced in the Collegiant practice of free prophecy. From Collegiant writings concerning free prophecy it is clear that Collegiants prior to 1650 believed that those members who spontaneously interpreted scripture in college meetings did so through direct divine inspiration.[35] During the 1650s, however, as Socinian influence entered the colleges and the writings of Galenus and Serrarius circulated, the idea that the gifts of the Holy Spirit were no longer given to people in the corrupt premillennial world transformed the Collegiant idea of free prophecy. In later Collegiant writings such as Pieter Langedult's *De Apostolice Outheyt van de Vrijheijt van Spreecken* and Pieter Smout's *Het Helder Licht van Vrijheijt,* it is clear that the Collegiants came to view free prophecy as simply an expression of individual human reason in scriptural interpretation. It is also clear that they viewed such rational interpretation as man's only option.[36]

IV

The religion of Oudaan, Kuyper, and Smout was neither the final nor the most innovative stage in the development of Collegiant rationalism during the seventeenth century. During the last quarter of the century, Collegiant thought evolved beyond the stage of rational religion to a truly rationalistic philosophy similar in its basic assumptions to the thought of Descartes and Spinoza. In this philosophy, reason was no longer a mere tool for interpreting scripture. Reason itself became an infallible source of truths of the highest order. Some Collegiants even came to see divine revelation as unnecessary for people in possession of natural human reason.

This final step in the development of Collegiant rationalism occurred as a result of the impact of the evolving rational and secular Collegiant worldview upon the strain of Radical Reformation Spiritualism present in the colleges. In the thought of Collegiants like Pieter Balling, Jarig Jelles, and Jan Bredenburg, Inner Light spiritualism fused with a rationalistic view of religious knowledge to produce an epistemology in which reason broke free of its subservience to the revelation of scripture and presented itself as an intuitively certain source of religious truth, replacing the divine inspiration that people no

---

[34]Frans Kuyper, *Den Philosopherenden Boer* (n.p., 1646); *Tweede Deel of Vervolg van de Philosopherenden Boer* (Rotterdam, 1677) and *De Diepten des Satans* (Rotterdam, 1677).

[35]See Paschier de Fijne, *Kort, Waerachtigh en Getrouw Verhael von het eerste begin en opkomen van de nieuwe seckte der propheten often Rijnsburgers* (Amsterdam, 1671), 20-24.

[36]Pieter Langedult, *De Apostolice Outheyt van de Vrijheijt van Spreecken* (Haarlem, 1672), 13-16; Pieter Smout, *Het Helder Licht van Vrijheijt* (Rotterdam, 1679), 20, 89-97, 107-111, 158.

longer received. Thus, a crucial step toward philosophical rationalism was taken.

The early Collegiant movement had absorbed Sebastian Franck's spiritualist doctrine of the Inner Light along with his spiritualistic critique of the visible churches by way of the works of Coornhert and Boreel. Inner Light spiritualism contained a radically subjective idea of religious knowledge that held that the one vital element in religion was the indwelling of the Holy Spirit within the soul of the individual believer. This indwelling spirit provided the individual with religious knowledge by way of direct divine illumination. The Inner Light led the believer to salvation without the need of any intervention by church, clergy, sacraments, or ceremonies. This spiritualistic epistemology was well suited to the Collegiant rejection of a doctrinaire, overly confessional, and increasingly externalized Calvinism because it stressed the individual and internal nature of religion. It gave pious individuals a way to continue their religious life despite the decadence of institutional religion. Collegiant free prophecy was founded on this spiritualistic epistemology.

After 1650, the impact of the ideas of Galenus and Serrarius concerning the cessation of the gifts of the Holy Spirit changed this epistemology. In Collegiant writings concerning the religion of the Inner Light, an intuitive rationalism can be seen emerging. For Collegiants after 1650 as for those before, religious knowledge was both individual and inward. After 1650, however, the Inner Light providing the knowledge gradually came to be seen not as direct divine inspiration but as the natural light of reason.

The writings of Mennonite/Collegiants Pieter Balling and Jarig Jelles, both disciples of Galenus as well as friends of the philosopher Benedict Spinoza, illustrate this transition clearly. In Balling's work of 1662, *Het Licht op den Kandelaar,* the conception of the Inner Light was in a stage of transition from spiritual to rational. Balling referred to the Inner Light in some places as rational, in other places as spiritual, and in still other places ambiguously. In one passage he identified the Light with divine inspiration by speaking of it in the words of John 1:9: "We direct thee then to look within thyself, that is, that thou ought . . . to mind . . . the light of truth, the true light that enlighteneth every man that comes into the world . . . ."[37] In another place, however, Balling referred to the Light in unmistakably Cartesian terms: "The light . . . is a clear and distinct knowledge of truth in the understanding of every man, by which he is so convinced of the essence and quality of things that he cannot possibly doubt thereof."[38]

In Jarig Jelles' *Belijdenisse* of 1684 the ambiguity of transition began to give way to a consistently rational interpretation of the Inner Light. Jelles wrote that people receive God's grace and their salvation by following God's

[37] Pieter Balling, *Het Licht op den Kandelaar* (Amsterdam, 1662), 3
[38] Ibid., 4.

commands, and they follow God's commands by following "the light of reason, the spirit, and the truth."[39] When man is led by the light of reason, he gets a "pure intellectual knowledge of God," a knowledge enabling the individual to lead a pious life and be saved.[40] For Jelles, the Inner Light was the natural light of reason.

Collegiant rationalism reached its zenith in the works of the Rotterdamer Jan Bredenburg. For Bredenburg, the chief source of human knowledge was natural reason. Divine revelation was not entirely rejected by Bredenburg, but it was relegated by him to a minor and nearly inconsequential role as a mere supplementary source of truth or as a source of moral commands that could not be understood but only obeyed. For Bredenburg, all knowledge worthy of the name came from the light of reason.

In his *Verhandling van de Oorsprong van de Kennisse Gods* Bredenburg wrote that the light of reason gives man "a certain and infallible knowledge of the existence of God" and that divine revelation serves only to "reinforce" this natural knowledge. After providing a series of rational proofs for the existence of God, Bredenburg concluded by maintaining that divine revelation, unaided by the light of reason, could never be adequately perceived or understood by natural man.[41] In all of his writings, Bredenburg turned primarily to the natural light of reason for the knowledge necessary to lead a good and pious life. In his *Wiskunstige Demonstratie dat alle Verstandelijke Werking noodzaakelijk is* (1684) he wrote, "Reason, which takes its origin from the eternal being, offers men eternal truth and is the light . . . and the guiding star of all human practice."[42]

With Bredenburg's thought the Collegiants produced a rationalistic philosophy of knowledge similar in its assumptions to the epistemologies of Descartes and Spinoza. From a millenarian and spiritualistic worldview that owed much to the ideas of the Radical Reformation, the Collegiants developed a criticism of the institutional churches of the seventeenth century that led them to reject the entire course of the Protestant Reformation and the traditional, providential Christian worldview itself. Anabaptist millenarianism, Socinian evangelical rationalism, Inner Light spiritualism, and the spiritualistic critique of the visible churches were all combined with Galenus's vision of a failed Reformation and a cessation of the gifts of the Holy Spirit, and the result was a picture of a secularized world in which divine inspiration no longer played a role. In place of divine inspiration, the Collegiants relied on the light of reason as their primary guide in both religion and life. When

[39]Jarig Jelles, *Belijdenisse des Algemeenen Christelyken Geloofs* (Amsterdam, 1689), 34.

[40]Ibid., 36.

[41]Jan Bredenburg, *Verhandling van de Oorsprong van de Kennisse Gods* (Amsterdam, 1684), 2-8.

[42]Jan Bredenburg, *Wiskunstige Demonstratie dat alle Verstandelijke Werking noodzaakelijk is* (Amsterdam, 1684), 3.

this reliance on reason fused with the intuitive idea of the Inner Light popular in the colleges, the Collegiant conception of reason evolved into that of an infallible source of eternal truth, the Collegiants were on the brink of philosophical rationalism.

The case of the Dutch Collegiants provides an excellent example of the links between radical religion and the birth of the Age of Reason in continental Europe. The Collegiants combined many of the important ideas of the sixteenth-century Radical Reformation and the Second Reformation of the seventeenth century in such a way that they came to develop a rational and secular worldview. The case of the Collegiants also shows that important links connected the traditional, providential Christian worldview to the emerging worldview of the Enlightenment. Many of the fundamental ideas of Enlightenment rationalism developed out of a world still deeply penetrated with religious assumptions. Without the contributions of millenarianism, spiritualism, and evangelical rationalism, the evolution of the Enlightenment worldview might have taken quite a different course, at least among the Collegiants.

CLOTH HALL, BRUGES
From an old print. The tower is over 350 feet high.

Society

Haug Marschalck
Lay Supporter of the Reform

Miriam Usher Chrisman

Haug Marschalck was a mercenary soldier, paymaster of the imperial troops quartered in Augsburg. He had an active military career, fighting against Duke Ulrich of Württemberg in 1519, the peasants in 1525, the French in Italy in 1525 and 1526, and the Turks in 1529. He was, thus, deeply involved in the life of his time. In Augsburg he was called out to defend the city hall when the artisans rioted in 1524. Yet, despite taking a hard line against the peasants and artisans, he firmly believed that fundamental social changes were necessary that would produce greater equality between rich and poor. Such changes could only occur if everyone lived in accord with the scripture. He saw the people of his day caught up in the effort to serve their own interests, and this could have tragic consequences. Marschalck wrote pamphlets between 1522 and 1530 that demonstrate his strong support of the Reformation. Together his seven pamphlets provide insight into the issues that took priority in the mind of a layman and outline proposals for changes. His pamphlets are valuable because they provide a rich view of urban life and the activities and beliefs of merchants, artisans, and the poor.

IN 1962 BERND MOELLER described the fragility of urban communities in sixteenth-century Germany.[1] Peter Blickle, more recently, has written of the relationship between urban social protest and the Reformation.[2] Seen from within, the sixteenth-century city had lost the traditional norms of the common good, peace, and civility that had characterized it in the fourteenth and fifteenth centuries.[3] By 1520 many urban communities found themselves balanced precariously on the edge of social alienation and class conflict.

Lay pamphlets open up these new social realities and reveal the antagonisms that marked the relations among different groups in the city. In Augsburg, patricians, *Gross Hansen* ("big Johns" – merchants and magistrates), artisans, and the poor eyed each other with suspicion, mistrust, and, at times, malevolence.

---

[1] Bernd Moeller, *Imperial Cities and the Reformation*, ed. and trans. H. C. Erik Midelfort and Mark U. Edwards (Philadelphia: Fortress Press, 1972), 96. The original German edition was printed in 1962.

[2] Peter Blickle, "Social Protest and Reformation Theology," in *Religion, Politics and Social Protest, Three Studies on Early Modern Germany,* ed. Kaspar von Greyerz (London: George Allen and Unwin, 1984), 6-7.

[3] Hans-Christoph Rublack, "Political and Social Norms in Urban Communities in the Holy Roman Empire," in Greyerz, ed., *Religion, Politics and Social Protest,* 30-36.

Their reactions to one another and the heightening of tensions between them because of the Reformation form the substructure of the religious pamphlets written by the mercenary soldier, Haug Marschalck.

Marschalck was from Memmingen, the son of a merchant family. In Augsburg he was listed as *raisigen,* a term applied to professional soldiers from patrician or upper burgher families. Attached to the imperial troops stationed in Augsburg, he was both paymaster and reporting officer (*Berichterstatter*), as well as one of the leaders of the city's military force. He had some duties as tax collector.[4] Despite these responsibilities he ranked socially below the magisterial class, the merchants, and the high civil servants, occupying a place among the intermediate rank of city officials like tax collectors. He was literally a man in the middle, loyal to his superiors but keeping a critical eye on their behavior, aware of and sensitive to the needs of his troops, who often went unpaid. The only surviving correspondence between him and the city council is with regard to back pay for his soldiers.[5] Most of his life was spent on active military duty. In the first decade of the Reformation, he and his troops were involved in major imperial campaigns, against the Duke of Württemberg in 1519, the peasants in 1525, the French in Italy in 1525-1526, and the Turks in 1529.[6] He was at the center of the political and social conflicts of his time. In those same years he wrote seven pamphlets in support of the reform. They serve as a journal of the urban reformation, kept by a thoughtful observer. His first reactions to the reform are recorded. He defines the new faith as he understood it. His own religious and social concerns are evident.

Marschalck was an urban man living away from his own city and occupying the unpopular position of a mercenary. Firmly loyal to the emperor, he believed His Majesty would soon support the evangelical reform and thus bring peace to Germany. He was not well educated. In a dedicatory letter to the Knight Jörg von Fronsberg, he explained that he had been instructed by the Word of God as it was taught by some of the highly learned preachers in Augsburg. He had listened to them and had afterward asked them questions. They had willingly pointed out the relevant scripture to him. He had then

[4]Paul Russell, *Lay Theology in the Reformation: Popular Pamphleteers in Southwest Germany, 1521-1525* (New York and Cambridge, Eng.: Cambridge University Press, 1986), 127; Frank Hieronymus, *Basler Buchillustration 1500 bis 1545,* Ausstellung Universitäts-Bibliothek Basel, March 31 to June 30, 1984 (Basel: Universitätsbibliothek, 1984), no. 335, 35-61; *Augsburg Stadtlexicon,* ed. Wilhelm Liebhart (Augsburg: Perlach Verlag, 1985), 242.

[5]Franklin L. Ford, *Strasbourg in Transition* (Cambridge, Mass.: Harvard University Press, 1958), 16; Fr. Roth, "Wer war Haug Marschalck, genannt Zoller von Augsburg?" Beiträge zur Bayerischen Kirchengeschichte 6 (1900): 230.

[6]Russell, *Lay Theology,* 127-28.

gone back to his quarters and looked up the biblical passages for himself.[7] Not only did he look them up, but his texts show that he organized what he read by subject matter. His scriptural references were never extraneous or irrelevant, as they were in the works of some lay writers. They fitted his argument whether he was writing about the right to rebel, the dangers of material wealth, or prayer. At times his biblicism led him to lyric flights, but he was also fond of a good pun. The same pun, particularly one on Luther's name, showed up from one pamphlet to the next. He experimented with style: rhyming couplets; expository or exhortatory prose texts; a complex drama pitting the army of the devil against the army of Christ, with verses from the Old and New Testaments used as cannon shots.

His earliest pamphlets were biographies of Christ. In them Marschalck explained the new faith. A third treatise defended Luther, revealing the deep split his teaching had created among the Roman clergy. Another pamphlet described the response of the citizens of Augsburg to the reform and the divisions appearing among them. A 1525 pamphlet admonished the peasants to cease their revolt. A fifth, written in 1530, entreated the emperor to embrace the new faith at the Diet of Augsburg, which was meeting that year.[8] Marschalck observed the impact of the Reformation on all levels of society. Fiercely loyal himself to the ideal of civic peace and harmony, he clung to the hope that the Word of God would end class conflict, greed, and selfishness, and would prepare the way for a new social order.

---

[7]Haug Marschalck, *Das heilig ewig wort Gottes/ was das in ym krafft, sterck, tugend, fryd, freud, erleuchtung und leben in eym rechten Christen zu erwecken vermag* (Zwickau: n.p., 1524), fiche 1111/œ2836, fol. Ai(v). Microfiche numbers refer to the collection of H. J. Köhler et al., eds., *Flugschriften des frühen 16. Jahrhunderts,* Microfiche Serie, 1978-1988 (Zug, 1978-1988).

[8]The lack of biblical quotations, the failure to base the argument on scripture, leads me to question Karl Schottenloher's attribution of the work of the pseudonymus Johann Schnewyl to Marschalck. Three pamphlets appeared in 1526 under the name of Johann Schnewyl von Strassburg: *Wie gern wolt wiss wie ich hiess/ zu lesen mich het nit verdriess* (n.p., n.d.); *Der Blinden furer bin ich genennt// Dem der sich selbs blind erkennet* (n.p., l526); *Wider die unmilte verdammnung . . . Jacob Straussen . . . antwort* (n.p., 1526). Schottenloher argues that the writer of the pamphlets was not from Strasbourg but from Augsburg because they were printed in Augsburg and because there are references to Augsburg figures such as Urbanus Rhegius in the text. All three pamphlets support the Zwinglian interpretation of the Eucharist against the Lutheran doctrine of the real presence. Although the writer paraphrases the Bible, he cites it directly only rarely. In the pamphlets written after 1524, Marschalck was almost incapable of writing a paragraph without a direct scriptural reference; the reference was always cited, often in the text. In one case, *Wer gern wolt wissen,* fol. C2v, the anonymous writer quotes from the scripture in Latin. This does not occur in Marschalck's work; indeed, since he was selfeducated, he probably did not read Latin. Adolf Laube identified Schnewyl as a Strasbourg cleric (private communication). Cf. Karl Schottenloher, *Philipp Ulhart, ein Augsburger Winkeldrucker und Helfershelfer der "Schwärmer" und "Wiedertäufer," 1523-1529,* vol. 4, Historische Forschung und Quellen, ed. Anton Mayer and Paul Ruf (Munich: F. Daterer, 192l; reprinted, Nieuwkoop: B. de Graaf, 1967).

Marschalck defined his understanding of the new faith in two pamphlets, *The Word of God* and *The Eternal Word of God.*[9] The foundation of the faith was the Word of God, personified in Christ. Throughout the two pamphlets *Word* and *Christ* were used as synonyms. The focus of the pamphlets was God's revelation of the Word in the life of Christ. Marschalck began *The Word of God* with the first verse of John: "In the beginning was the Word and the Word was with God." Because of the Reformation, Marschalck went on, the Word of God had brought peace and triumphed over the conflicts created by the hellish rule of the devil.[10] This had been accomplished by none other than the Duke of Saxony, *Fridreych,* "rich in peace," rightly named because through him the long-lost treasure, the most worthy jewel, *Verbum Domini,* had once again been found.[11] He would firmly establish the pure Word of God until it became "a green tree with fully developed roots."[12] This was the hope that guided Marschalck's life.

The kingdom of God, continued Marschalck, was proclaimed at the first imperial diet (Reichstag) through the birth of Christ. "The most powerful, unconquerable emperor, the most powerful, mildest, and best lord, the Word of God," came to that Reichstag in the form of a small, human baby.[13] This same Christ had been proclaimed by the holy prophets. "In the small city of Bethlehem, they prepared for him a poor cradle in an open stall, where dumb animals sought both their feed and him whom we all wish to seek."[14] There the noble Word of God was laid for shelter.

> What princes . . . were the first to come to this highest Reichstag to seek you out, and who recognized your powerful majesty? What power did they have on earth? . . . It was shepherds, to be sure – poor shepherds . . . . Why should the great rich shepherds of the world gather for this? Whom did you have around you as courtiers? . . . What kinds of personages? . . . Two noble, loving, holy persons . . . . Maria, a poor daughter in terms of material things but rich

---

[9]*Eyn Edles/ schönes/ lieplichs Tractalein/ von den raynen/ hymlischen/ ewige wort (Verbum Domini) zu lob Got dem Schöpffer Hymmels und Erden un zu eren den Christlichen diener des Göttlichen worts* (n.p., probably 1522), fiche 1097/no. 2783. Otto Clemen dates this as 1522 "Haug Marschalck genannt Zoller von Augsburg," *Beiträge zur Bayerischen Kirchengeschichte* 4 (1898): 223. There were at least three other editions of this in 1524, though without dates, and one in 1530 (fiche 714/no. 1826; fiche 983/no. 2486; fiche 1312/no. 3411). *Das heilig ewig wort Gottis/ was das in ym krafft/ sterck, tugent/ fryd/ freud/ erleuchtung, und leben/ in eym rechten Christen zu erwecken vermag* (Zwickau: n.p., 1524), fiche 1111/no. 2836.

[10]*Tractatlein von dem raynen . . . ewigen wort Verbum Domini,* fol. Aii.

[11]Ibid., fol. Aii(v).   [12]Ibid., fol. Aiii.   [13]Ibid., fol. Aiv.

[14]Ibid., fol. Aiv(v). un zugericht in ainer klainen stat Bethlehem/ in ainer armen herberg/ in ainem zerrissen hawss/ in ainem offen stall in ayner klaynen armen krippen dar in die unvernünfftige thieer ire wayd suchend/ und gesucht habend/ and wir all noch zusuchen begerend . . . .

in honor, purity, virtue, and holiness. Joseph, a poor carpenter . . . .
This was the beginning of the Reichstag of all bliss.[15]

Later Christ proclaimed another Reichstag in another time, the last
judgment for those who had fought against his Word. He had come from
on high to warn men of this grim, terrible day of tears and had made his
courtiers and messengers proclaim this to men. These courtiers were poor
fishermen, a wool beater, a rug maker, pious handworkers, coarse and unlearned
people. They were neither rabbis, doctors learned in scripture, nor experienced
in human knowledge. Yet Christ had turned to them because he wanted to
be the preceptor, to teach God's Word directly to them.[16]
    Perhaps because of his social status and his place in the imperial troops,
Marschalck was convinced that earthly distinction was meaningless. Whether
it was his experience in war or his awareness of the misery of his poorly
paid men, he saw the humble as the most worthy members of society. Men
and women would have to turn away from earthly honor and abase themselves
so that Christ could work within them and transform them.[17] This was his
vision of the new teaching, his hope for what might come. But the promise
was not being fulfilled because of the divisions among the clergy. The Word
of God should have brought unity and peace. Instead, preaching had caused
schism. In a pamphlet in praise of Luther, Marschalck described the discord
among the clergy, the Romanists, and the reformers.
    Marschalck's purpose in this tract was to defend the reformer against
those who wished to discredit and destroy him. The opposition, he wrote,
had attacked him by name-calling, twisting his name to misrepresent him
and his teaching. He was not, said his opponents, the *lauterer* (the purifier),
but the *trüber* (the darkener). They called him *Lotter* (the rascal) or *Laur* (the
spy). They, the Roman clergy, charged that Luther had torn apart the bond
of Christian love and broken up the established order.[18] Unlearned priests
shrieked from their chancels that Luther's preaching against indulgences and

[15]Ibid., fols. Aiv-B, "welche Fürsten/ und mit was herligkayt seind am ersten zu dir
khomen/ die diesen hohen Reychstag bey dir un mit dir haymgesucht habend/ was grosser
tyttel . . . was gewalts haben sy auff erden gehabt . . . . es warend Hierten furwar arm Hiertten.
Du Grossmächtiger Kaiser/ du lieblicher Christus/ hast du dyse zu dir auff deinen Reichstag
berufft . . . . Was sollen dan yetz die grossen reychen Hierten der welt dar bei abnemen/ was
hettestu aber bei dir fur ain Hofgesindet/ . . . . Was warend sy fur personen. Es warend zwu
edel/ lieplich/ hailig personen . . . Maria ain arme tochter an zeytlichen guttern/ aber mer
dan uberflüssig reych an eren/ an raynigkait/ thughend/ unnd haligkait. Und dar zu mer/ ain
armer Zimmerman Joseph. . . . Diss was der haylig angefangen Reychstag aller seligkayt."

[16]Ibid., fol. Bv.

[17]Ibid., fol. Biv.

[18]*Von dem weyt erschollen Namen Luther/ wz er bedeut und wie er wirt missbraucht* (Strasbourg:
A. Farckal, 1523), fol. Aiiv. There are three copies of this pamphlet in the Köhler collection,
all without place or printer, but with the 1523 date: fiche 1533/œ3989; fiche 1346/œ3541;
fiche 10/œ41.

other money offerings had broken the harmony of the church. In fact, Marschalck charged, it was the cardinals, bishops, professors, begging monks, and papal preachers who had sat before the door of prison where the Gospel was immured, keeping the scripture in the dark.[19] But "the three Marys" had come to the tomb, Martin Luther, Andreas Carlstadt, and Philip Melanchthon. When they arrived "they saw an angel, the Christian prince Duke Frederick of Saxony, who said 'Whom do you seek here?' 'Jesus of Nazareth.' That is, they wanted the Holy Scripture, God's Word."[20] They also wanted to see the pope so that they might discuss things with him and let him know that their teachings were proclaimed in the scriptures. If he was unwilling to do this, then they wanted him to call a Christian council. Thus, concluded Marschalck, the reformers were the true *lauterer,* who proclaimed God's Word loudly, and they were also *trüber,* darkeners, because they darkened the pope's false laws. The reformers were not vagabonds but protectors, for they protected themselves with the foundations of Holy Scripture and evangelical teaching, unlike their opponents who used Aristotelian, Platonic, and other heathen proofs.[21]

Marschalck placed the struggle of the reformers in a biblical setting, the scene at the tomb, where the reformers emerged as the true protectors of the Word. He had scant hope for the conversion of the Roman clergy. "They will not be attentive to reason, for if they wish to do injury in the dark, they do not appear in daylight. They do not present themselves before the law. They go to no disputations. They do not sign their names to their books. . . . They handle everything with bans, bulls, force, and quarrels."[22] They, not Luther, were the rogues and spies. They wore red hats, became rich priests, wicked canons, and drunken provosts, whereas Luther had truly served Christ. What teacher had written as much, disputed as much, preached as much as Luther? Without the grace of the Holy Spirit, what he had done would have been impossible.[23] The first step in the Reformation had been to wrench the Word out of oblivion. Schism was the inevitable result. Luther had proclaimed the Word, but the Romanists had closed their ears. Marschalck had no solution to offer but declared that those who attacked Luther had gone too far with their scolding and blasphemy.[24]

The new teaching had not only brought dissension within the church. The divisions created among the laity were even more grievous to Marschalck. Even those who accepted the teaching did not live according to its spirit. In his pamphlet *Der Spiegel der Blinden,* probably published in 1523 but perhaps

[19]Ibid.   [20]Ibid., fol. Aiiv.   [21]Ibid.
[22]Ibid.   [23]Ibid., fol. Aiii.   [24]Ibid., fol. Aiv.

as early as 1522,[25] Marschalck described the progress of the Reformation in
Augsburg and the factions that had formed. He was outspoken in his criticism
of those who professed the new faith but had not changed their way of life.

> The three [sic] Gospels require a great understanding and good, sharp
> insight . . . [so that they may be seen] in one light and as one whole
> and brilliance. There are now many divisions, many sects, many
> heads, and all have many foolish points of view. One looks in that
> direction, the second in another, the third looks up, the fourth down.
> For Christendom and also the world, this is a bad disunity.[26]

Nevertheless, he rejoiced that the Word of God had been proclaimed
to the people of Germany. God's Word should not be changed by as much
as a letter, nor should people listen to strange or foreign teachings.[27] Christ
gave the old, right doctrines to his fishermen and disciples. The books written
at Wittenberg and at other places were based on these and taught Christ's
words to the common people. Some complained that these books attacked
Luther's opponents too harshly and were coarse and unjust. If one compared
them to those written by Luther's enemies, however, the latter were just as
coarse and were not founded on scripture.[28] In further defense of the
Wittenbergers, Marschalck pointed out that they had written their treatises
in Latin at first so that the doctrines would not be spread among the common
laymen but would be discussed only among the clergy. But the Romanists
had not wanted to learn. Then the Wittenbergers felt that they could no
longer suppress the true, clear Word or the honor of God. Although it was
unfortunate that those who did not accept God's Word must be persecuted,
the Word had to be defended and the false preachers seized, particularly the
scribes, the pharisees, and the monks.[29] Marschalck was well informed on
the state of affairs within the church. He had followed the debates between

---

[25]There were four editions of this pamphlet, three bearing different titles, one published
under the name of Haug Zoller, by which Marschalck was known, the other anonymously.
(Haug Zoller), *Durch Betrachtung und Bekarung Der bössen gebreych in schweren sünden Ist gemacht
Dyser Spiegel der Blinden* (Augsburg: Melchior Rammiger, 1522). This, according to Laube, is
presumably the earliest edition; the later editions were abridged. See *Flugschriften der frühen
Reformationsbewegung*, 2 vols., ed. Adolf Laube (Berlin: AkademieVerlag, 1983), 1:150. I used
the Laube text since it is the most complete. Other editions: (Haug Marschalck), *Ein Spiegel der
Blinden, wann Christus, derr Herr hat geredt* (Strasbourg: W. Köpfel, c. 1523), fiche 1048/no.
2651. (Haug Marschalck), *Ein Spiegel der Blinden, wann Christus der Herr hat geredt* (Basel: Adam
Petri, May 1523), fiche 1109/no. 2831. (Haug Marschalck), *Ein Spiegel der Blinden zu Erkenntnis
evangelischer Wahrheit* (n.p., 1523), fiche 1107/no. 2823.

[26](Haug Zoller), *Durch Betrachtung . . . Spiegel der Blinden*, in *Flugschriften*, ed. Laube, 128.
"Die 3 evangelii bedürfent ains grossen verstands und ainer scharpffen guten gesicht (und
dieselbig nit weydt umb sych, sonnder allain nur also) inn/ ain lyechtt unnd inn ain wessen
unnd inn ain glanntz. Nun seynnd yetz vil zertaylunngen, vil seckten, vil kopff, die haben all
vil blöder gesycht. Aines sycht da hinnaus, das ander dort hinauss, das dryt übersych, das vierdt
undersich, und ist ain boss ungleich gesycht inn der cristenhait und sunst in der welt."

[27]Ibid., 129.   [28]Ibid., 130.   [29]Ibid., 131-32.

the reformers and their opponents and was critical of the latters' unwillingness to engage in open disputations. They were weak and wished to hide the truth.

Despite the Roman priests, changes had taken place in the city of Augsburg. "What," he asked, "do you think the old priests read and learned?"[30] One out of a hundred could not read the Gospels without the help of a commentary, but some now had begun to learn to read them.[31] Moreover, whereas before thirty, forty, or one hundred people had routinely placed offerings on the canons' altars, now it was only six or eight, mostly old women. Families no longer paid for anniversary masses for their parents, nor did they have a sung mass for a deceased child. People no longer followed the custom of the churching of women. Instead they joked, "They are just as good to sleep with, blessed or unblessed."[32] He had also heard that people no longer wanted to go to confession. They wanted to speak to the priest "with a few words," receive absolution, and not pay any penitential offering.[33] Changes in daily religious habits and observances had occurred, and old customs had been abandoned but not without opposition.

Yet, there were some who wanted nothing to do with good, holy books. They did not want to hear about them or read them. "They speak out of an uneducated lack of intelligence," remonstrated Marschalck.[34] They insisted on holding to the old belief and the old customs. "Many say, 'I will follow my parents. What they did, I will do.'"[35] There were others who spoke subtly, for they did not want to make any judgment. They would not declare whether something was true or false, good or bad. They said they would wait to see what happened. Whatever side was proved right, they would join.

The citizens were divided. The conservatives held to their familiar ways, others flocked to hear the sermons, and those in between were unwilling to commit themselves. These religious differences in combination with preexisting economic and political conflicts undermined the traditional ideal of unity.[36] Marschalck believed that the root of the problem was the pursuit of wealth: "The world is being strangled by the lust for earthly goods, by evil habits, and impure desires."[37] He scolded the upper classes, the patricians and merchants. They were only interested in money and mistreated their fellow humans, overburdening them with usury. "A doctor gives a little drink which runs

---

[30]Ibid., 135.   [31]Ibid.

[32]Ibid., 147. "machent also ain spot red daraus, sprechent, sy schmeckent inen eben so wol ungesegnet als gesegnet bey in zu schlaffen."

[33]Ibid.   [34]Ibid., 135, 137.   [35]Ibid., 138.

[36]H-C. Rublack, "Political and Social Norms," 27.

[37]*Spiegel der Blinden*, 133. "Die Welt ist hart verstrickt in zeitlichem wolust mit übel gewynnung der zeitlichen güter, mit bössem gebracht, mit unrainer hofnung, und ist alles mit bessem geytz überlauffen."

through the patient's bowels, but these violent men give a syrup that runs through his house, his courtyard, his acres and fields."[38] Wealthy men and women spoiled their children, letting them dress in silk and gold garments that would be excessive even for adults. Thus, they raised their children to sin and pride. Marschalck had little hope for this rich clique. They fostered envy, hate, and greed within the city because of their arrogance, immodesty, and impiety.[39] They were some of the blindest of the blind.

More distressing were those who proclaimed themselves Christian but had not changed their way of life. They had heard the Word of God proclaimed and embraced it enthusiastically. But they did not accept it in their hearts. Here Marschalck's views reflected not only his own intense religiosity but also a mistrust of both merchants and artisans. People went to sermons or disputations, he wrote, and then went home and ran their business or practiced their craft just as they had before. The merchant went to his fairs and markets, exchanged money, bought and sold goods, all to accumulate great profits. It was not, said Marschalck, that business was shameful, but to work too hard for an overabundance, perhaps destroying your Christian brother in the process, was against the Gospel. All artisans, he believed, cheated and were willing to turn out poor, unskilled work, using a trick set of tools for the purpose.[40]

The worst and most dangerous dishonesty was practiced by the food merchants, for their customers could become very sick from contaminated food or drink. He warned against taverns where the wine was adulterated. This prevented the proper warming and strengthening of the blood and limbs of those who drank it. "Where do you think the evil rheumatism and paralysis of limbs comes from, which fifty years ago was unheard of?"[41] The doctors, Marschalck said, knew very well about the adulterated wine and warned people against it. Spices were also mixed with fillers and weakened, which could cause illness. Improper ingredients were mixed into the bread, and meat was allowed to lie around so long it became putrid.

> Oh, dear Christian brothers, we must do differently with this high, holy work. It cannot continue like this. It doesn't help just to read books and listen to preaching and praise ourselves . . . . We must put our hands into the right dough. Now what is the right dough?

[38]Ibid. "Ain artzt gibt ainem ain trinckle, daz im durch das gederm laufft, aber ain solcher grimmer mensch gibt ain syrop, der in durch hauss und hof, acker und wysen lauft."

[39]Ibid., 134.

[40]Ibid., 136.

[41]Ibid.

To love God with our whole hearts . . . our whole strength and our neighbors as ourselves. Matt. 22:37-39.[42]

If men truly followed the commandment about neighborliness, they would have to live as evangelicals. No one would hate another or cheat, whether in money-changing, buying, or selling. "The rich would help the poor and the poor would help the rich," and true brotherly love would grow.[43] If each person pursued his business or craft properly, that would be a form of prayer – "prayer without ceasing, a truly loving and friendly prayer."[44]

Marschalck was not the only resident of Augsburg who was disturbed by the dissension, the alienation of one group from another. Georg Preu, an Augsburg painter, wrote a chronicle covering the years from 1480 to 1537.[45] His history mirrored the bitterness of the common man toward the rich and powerful. His purpose was to expose the corruption of the Augsburg government. Its laws strengthened the city financially, but this was achieved, according to Preu, by the arrogant oppression of the poor. His picture of the merchant class matched that of Marschalck. The big merchants were shameless usurers who raised prices, thus making life hard for the lower orders. Those who served on the city council (*Rat*) were the sharpest in their dealings. The bakers and the butchers "stood on the same steps" as the merchants and enriched themselves without scruple at the expense of the hungry.[46] The *Rat*, the most powerful group in the city, had strongly opposed the introduction of the new teaching. "They had the devil in their hearts and the Word of God in their mouths and tried to carry water to both sides."[47] Marschalck's description of those who hurried to the Gospel preaching, praised it, and then continued to gouge their customers and debtors, was not merely a personal judgment. Preu, however, criticized Marschalck because the Gospel preaching had borne no fruit.

With the city divided so deeply on economic lines, it is hardly surprising that there were outbreaks of violence. The introduction of the Reformation in the city occurred rather late. Johann Oecolampadius had preached there in 1518 but left the following year because of his increasing Lutheran sympathies.

[42]Ibid. O lieben crislychen bruder wir müssen annderst mit dyser hohen seligen arbait umb gon, es gadt nit also zü. Es hilft nicht bücher lesen und predigen hören allain und das selb feyntlich loben und darinn disputieren und unser zeitliche handlung dannocht so gferlich übel brauchen, wir müssentt mit den henden den rechten tayg auch starck angreyffen! Nun was ist aber der recht teyg? Hat Got lyeb auss gantzen hertzen, auss gantzer seel, auss gantzem gmüt, von all dein kreften, und den nechsten als dich selbs (Matt. 22:37-39).

[43]Ibid.   [44]Ibid., 142.

[45]Georg Preu, *Die Chronik,* Die Chroniken der schwäbischen Städte, vol. 6, ed. Friedrich Roth; in turn Die Chroniken der deutschen Städte von 14. bis 16. Jahrhundert, vol. 29, series ed. Georg von Below (Leipzig: S. Hirzel, 1901).

[46]Ibid., 12.

[47]Ibid.

He was replaced by Urbanus Rhegius, then still closely associated with Johann Eck.[48] It was not until 1523 that Caspar Adler began to preach and teach from the Gospels. He was quickly silenced by the bishop of Augsburg, who imprisoned him in Dillingen, took away his books, the Bible, a Gospel, and the Epistles, and forbade him to return to Augsburg.[49] Johann Schilling, the reader in the Franciscan cloister, was the major reforming figure in these years. He preached in the Franciscan church and had a following among the artisans.[50] They were restive and provoked by the *Rat*'s refusal to support the reform. In May 1524, several journeymen, including a painter, two weavers, an arithmetic teacher, and a purse maker, undertook to prevent the consecration of holy water and salt at the Franciscan church. They asked the brother to leave the water unblessed, or at least to read the service in German so they could understand it. When he refused, one of the artisans pulled the missal out of his hands and threw it in the font. A third fished the missal out of the water and attempted to tear it with his teeth but failed because the pages were parchment. He cut it up with his knife and threw the pieces to the congregation.[51] Several of the men were taken into custody and when questioned said that Schilling had told them that holy water did nothing for the forgiveness of sins. The painter was imprisoned and the tailor exiled, but the weavers were merely warned.[52]

The *Rat* equivocated. They provided guards for the clergy, which roused the suspicions of the common people. Some, wrote Preu, wished to be evangelical, follow Christ's commandments, and eat meat on fast days. The *Rat* drew up letters permitting the preaching of God's Word. These were placed under people's doors and in the taverns. Yet men were kept in arms at night, and there was great anxiety.[53] The *Rat* had granted only a grudging acceptance of the new faith.

Later in 1524, however, the *Rat* was admonished by the emperor, princes, and lords of the empire. They demanded that those cities that held to the Gospel and the Word of God should abstain from such teaching or be placed under the imperial ban. Several mandates were received, but the people did not want them accepted. A new division was created between those who were *kaiserisch* (pro-emperor) and those who were evangelical. The *Rat* was caught between the emperor and Augsburg's citizens. The councillors were afraid of Johann Schilling, the Franciscan reader, and held him responsible for stirring up the artisans. Carefully, they negotiated with the vicar-general of the order to remove him. On August 4, 1524, Schilling left the city.[54] On August 6, according to Preu, more than six hundred commoners went to the *Rat* to petition for Schilling's return "to preach the Word of God

---

[48]Russell, *Lay Theology*, 118.   [49]Preu, *Chronik*, 24.   [50]Russell, *Lay Theology*, 120.
[51]Preu, *Chronik*, 25.   [52]Russell, *Lay Theology*, 120.
[53]Preu, *Chronik*, 25.   [54]Russell, *Lay Theology*, 121.

from the Gospels." The *Rats* response was that it could arrange with the provincial to send another Franciscan, who would be as good as the former one and more learned in scripture. The people replied by shouting, "We want the monk."[55] The *Rat* went into session and held off their answer until 12:15 p.m. Then they agreed to let Schilling preach. In the intervening time, however, the *Rat* had prepared a list of eighty-six artisans who they believed were insubordinate and stirring up unrest. On the afternoon that Schilling returned, the eighty-six were formally charged. Six hundred soldiers were called out to protect the city hall. One of their captains was Haug Marschalck.[56] The divisions that he had so clearly described had ended in confrontation. This time the *Rat* acted decisively. On September 15, two of the eighty-six were beheaded. Many of the others, fearful for their lives, left the city.[57]

The defense of the city hall did not create a conflict for Marschalck. He was, to use Preu's term, *kaiserlich,* pro-emperor. Yet he was also pro-evangelical; that had been the purpose of his pamphlets. According to those beliefs, he should have supported the artisans and the preaching of the Gospel. Two years earlier, however, Marschalck had criticized those enthusiasts who called themselves evangelical but were dishonest in their dealings with their fellow citizens. This condemnation now made it possible for him to justify the use of force against them. He saw the rioting artisans as prisoners of their own self-interests. Some evangelicals followed God's Word. Others did not. Marschalck transcended the conflicts and divisions created by the Reformation. Everyday, material life, he believed, was meaningless. The Word of God empowered him to rise above this tangible world and to enter the kingdom of God, just as Christ had. He made this clear in a pamphlet written perhaps in 1523. The dedicatory preface of the Zwickau edition is dated Augsburg, 1524.[58] The pamphlet was a continuation of the life of Christ that he had begun in *Verbum Domini.*

In this second installment, Marschalck moved to the earthly life of Jesus, undertaken "to snatch his poor sheep from the devil's mouth."[59] Athough he had become flesh for the salvation of mankind, Christ received nothing as a mortal man. He was scorned and despised by other men. He found no peace in human life, nor did he seek pleasure. He belonged to no city nor had he any home to support him in his need. He was a stranger in a strange land. While on earth he dwelled in poverty among the poor.[60] By his life he demonstrated that we were not born to any other men on earth but that we were created by God and could only be saved by God.[61]

[55]Preu, *Cronik,* 29.   [56]Russell, *Lay Theology,* 121.   [57]Ibid.

[58]*Das heilig ewig wort Gottis/ was das in ym krafft. . .in eym rechten Christen zu erwecken vermag* (Zwickau: n.p., 1524), fiche 1111/no. 2836, fol. Aiv; the Augsburg edition: (Augsburg: M. Ramminger, 1523), fiche 272/no. 777; another edition: (n.p., n.d.), fiche 1095/no. 2783.

[59]*Das heilig ewig wort Gottis,* fol. Aiiii.   [60]Ibid., fol. Aiii.   [61]Ibid., fol. B(v).

Social and religious discord, as Marschalck saw them, were manifestations of worldly life and the power of the devil, both of which had been overcome by the death of Jesus Christ. Jesus had died for all men, descended into hell, fought with the devil, and then ascended into heaven. "And he won and opened eternal life for all of us. Afterward his Holy Spirit was sent again from heaven to earth to his disciples . . . to instruct all of us and to confirm and take to heart the will of the heavenly father. That is the summary of our faith."[62] Those who remained true to the faith would not be deterred by events like the conflict between the city council and the artisans; they would recognize it as a fleeting moment, an indication of men's unworthiness and lack of understanding.

This same attitude, coupled with a strong admonition to obedience, marked Marschalck's pamphlet written against those who called themselves evangelical and yet rose in the Peasants' Revolt. Marschalck and his troops had been called out in the Peasants' War. In his pamphlet, *A Sharp Cannon against Those Who Call Themselves Evangelical and Yet Are against the Gospels,* Marschalck used scripture to describe the battle between the truth of God and the wiles of the devil. As he put it,

I have undertaken to write a short treatment, based on Holy Scripture, against the false Christians who represent themselves as Evangelicals but who are not such in the least. They want to use God's Word to cover up their avarice, rebellion, and rioting. For that reason, I have named the book after the cannon of the most praiseworthy city of Nuremberg, for that cannon is of the sort that can knock down any wall. Just so it will be shown in this pamphlet that no attack by the devil and his mob can succeed against the powerful and mighty bombardment of Holy Scripture.[63]

The pamphlet was presented as a drama. There were two castles, God's and the devil's, the former fortified and based on the love of God, even to the rejection of oneself; the other fortified with self-love, even to the rejection

<hr>

[62]Ibid., fol. Biii.

[63]*Die Scharf Metz under die, die sich evangelisch nennen und doch dem Evangelio entgegen sind* (originally Augsburg: n.p., 1525), ed. Wilhelm Lucke, in *Flugschriften aus den ersten Jahren der Reformation,* 4 vols., series ed., Otto Clemen (Leipzig: Rudolf Haupt, 1907-1911; reprinted Nieuwkoop: B. de Graaf, 1967), vol. 1, no. 3, 98130. Lucke lists three editions of the pamphlet, one a reprint by the same Augsburg(?) press, the third by a Strasbourg press (99-103), Marschalck's quotation, 105: "Gott dem almechtigen zu lob . . . hab ich fürgenommen ain kurtzen begriff auss der hayligen geschrifft zusamen tragen wider die falschen Christen, So sich unbillich Evangelisch berümen und doch nichts minders seind, Die under dem scheyn des gots worts iren geytz, embörung und auffrur begeren zeschirmen. hab darumb das buchlein wollen nemen nach dem hauptstuck der Büchsen der hochgebryssnen Statt Nürnberg, Dann die Büchs der art ist, das kain maur davor besteen mag. Also soll durch die gewältigen, kröfftigen schüss der hayligen schrifft, in dem büchlein angezaygt, kain anschlag des teuffels und seynes hauffen mügen besteen."

of God. Each castle had its own battle cry – the one, unity and peace; the other, riot and violence. Each city had its own cannon, its own leaders and captains.[64] The captain of the castle of God, none other than Jesus Christ, charged that the devil protected himself behind an imaginary Christian freedom, basing his laws on this spurious freedom to impress the *gemeine man*. Then the common men sallied forth and shot their evil arrows against their magistrates, thinking they would attain freedom. The devil's horde could be destroyed by three things: the strong shot of the Old Testament; the forceful shot of the New Testament; a barrage from both Testaments showing how God had punished division and rebellion.[65]

Marschalck described the battle, shot for shot, first from the Old Testament, then from the New. Moses, he wrote, fired first, in the first book, Genesis 13:6-9, when Abraham and Lot no longer wanted to live near one another. Abraham said to Lot, "I pray you, let us have no strife between us . . . for we are brothers." "So you see," interjected Marschalck, "Abraham, the pious patriarch, did not want to have divisions between his shepherds and his brother's shepherds. What then should we Christians do to avoid such quarreling and rebellion? I say we should give up everything we have before we give cause for such a rebellion."[66] The New Testament shots stressed peace. "The second shot comes from Mark 9:50 . . . you should have peace with one another, for as in one body all parts are in harmony with one another . . . so it should be in the spiritual body, that no one part offends another."[67]

Having fired his twenty shots, Marschalck noted that they were a manifestation of the power and force of our king, Jesus Christ, who mediated to prevent violence. Thus, the rebels should join in unity and form bonds of peace, for misfortune had always fallen on the heads of those who led rebellions, for example Lucifer, Korah, Dathan and Abiram, Ephraim and Jeptha.[68] The futility and unrighteousness of revolt were strongly asserted and entirely supported from scripture, the Word of God.

Marschalck added another dimension to the pamphlet. He built a picture of how the revolt had occurred, how men had been drawn into the peasant armies. Whether this was an accurate view or not, it provides remarkable insight into the military captain's perception of how the rebel forces had

---

[64]Ibid., 105-6.   [65]Ibid., 107.

[66]Ibid., 108: ". . . des ward Abraham gewar und sprach zü Loth: Ich bitt dich, lass uns kain zwitracht mit ainander haben, nun seyen wir doch brüder. Sihe an, Abraham, der frumm erzvatter, hatt nit mügen leyden unaynigkait zwischen seynem und seynes vettern hyrten, . . . was sollen dann yetzen wir Christen thun, zangk und embörung zu verhüten? Ich sprich, wir sollen ee verlassen alles das wir hetten, ee und wir ainer embörung ursach geben."

[67]Ibid., 114. "Der ander schuss ist Marci am 9, Ca.(v. 50) . . . air sollend fryd haben under ainander, Dann wie an ainem leyb alle glyder mitt ainander frölich seind, . . . also soll es auch in dem gaistlichen Corper zugeen, das kains das ander belaydige."

[68]Ibid., 121-22.

gathered. The common man fell because of his own selfishness, ignoring the common good.[69] God, however, promised the best fruit to a peaceful heart, "so when someone comes to you and whispers revolt in your ear, treat him as though he wanted to burn your house and entire neighborhood down."[70] The world was full of dangerous plotters, faithless and recreant men with crooked mouths and a wink in their eye. They congregated with their feet, they spoke with their fingers, they plotted strikes in their hearts. These were the kind of "evangelical" men who led revolts.[71] Then there was the secret talebearer who created unrest and anger. He was like a torch used to set wood on fire. He too must be driven from the house.[72]

The picture of men meeting in dark corners, whispering in the streets and taverns, "congregating with their feet," is yet another indication of the atmosphere that permeated the city – the anxiety, the mistrust, the fear of one group toward another, the ultimate fear of conspiracy. Marschalck ended the pamphlet on a note of victory. The devil acknowledged that if the Word of God came forth, he would be truly overcome, shot down. That Word was his death. Then all the evangelicals sang praises and thanks to Christ who had saved them.[73] From now on their help would be in the Word of the Lord who made heaven and earth. Marschalck returned to the question of the true evangelical. Only he who had taken the Gospel to heart could so be named. He would enjoy peace for the length of his days. But he who did not find such peace could not be called evangelical. Christ had conquered by his teaching and his virtuous life. He expected men to remain steadfast in peace and virtue, not to turn to violence or rebellion.[74]

By 1530 Marschalck was no longer as confident that the emperor was open to the Word of God. He addressed those gathering for the Diet of Augsburg, asking God to open them to his godly teaching so that the Christian princes and lords would turn to the right way.[75] Those who spoke against Christ, against the Holy Spirit, would now be known and recognized and would be forgiven neither on earth nor in heaven. Again he gave examples of leaders who had been destroyed by bad advice: the princes at Tyre; the king described in Isaiah 5 who had brought ruin and destruction to his people; thirty-one kings expelled from their lands as a punishment by God. "Oh woe, [if] you ruin your children . . . woe if you make edicts which forsake and scorn my Word, Isaiah 10. Oh, Charles, you noble emperor, unsheath your imperial sword, protect holy Christendom in the

---

[69]Ibid., 107.   [70]Ibid., 109.   [71]Ibid., 111.   [72]Ibid., 115.
[73]Ibid., 126.   [74]Ibid., 127.

[75]*Eyn Ermanung/ Reymens weys/ an unsern aller gnedigisten hern Carolum/ Römischer Keyser/ Ferdinandum seyner Maist. bruder/ König tzu Hungern/ und Behem/ All geystlich und weltlich Chürfürsten und Fürsten/ des heyligen Römischer Reychs/ Den löblichen pundt tzu Schwaben/ alle Geystlich und weltlich Oberkeyt* (n.p., 1530), fiche 1080/2738,, fol. Aii.

world . . . so that you will achieve eternal salvation . . . ."[76] Charles,
Marschalck noted, had many learned men to help him create a good government
so that the poor folk, who had long been blinded, would know the right
way in terms of faith.[77] All the estates of the empire would join together in
the effort against the storm of unbelief, bringing their sheep to good pasture
and the joys of salvation. "Help, Lord my God," he concluded, "for there is
need."[78] Clearly Marschalck believed the emperor and his counsellors should
be warned of the dangers of ignoring God's commandments, even as he had
warned the peasants. It was a last attempt on his part to rally the strength
of the emperor to the new faith.

Marschalck's pamphlets provide new insight into the early years of the
Reformation. The citizen body was disunited well before the advent of the
new teaching. In Augsburg the reformed faith was not clearly defined.
Marschalck did not believe it was a matter of changes in outward practice
or ceremony, or of merely listening to sermons. It was a matter of inner
spirituality. Those who heard the Word of God and modeled their lives on
the words of Christ were evangelical. The rest were enthusiasts who were
no better than the Romanists. As early as 1523 and 1524, well before the
Peasants' Revolt and the rise of Anabaptists, the reformed laity in Augsburg
were already broken into factions. The communal urban norms had not
survived the fifteenth century. "The common good" remained in the vocabulary
of the magistrates as an appeal for order, but the Reformation made it all
but meaningless. The reformed leadership was weak in Augsburg because
the bishop or the magistrates removed the stronger preachers. Johann Schilling
had no means of controlling the diverse interpretations made of his preaching
and teaching. The results were the small, particularist groups described by
Marschalck, each with its own definition of the faith, each with its own
priorities.

The Reformation had led to the edge of chaos. The artisans had risen
up in the city to force the hand of the magistrates. The peasants had risen
in the countryside. By 1530 Marschalck no longer believed that the emperor
would turn to the new faith and unite the empire. Because of the intensity
of his inner belief, his faith in the power of the Word, Marschalck's solution
was to sacralize the secular. If neither the city nor the emperor could maintain
unity and peace, the hope for unity could be lifted to the spiritual sphere.
The Holy Spirit gave Marschalck the assurance of the survival of unity in a
world ever more deeply divided.

---

[76]Ibid., fol. Aiii-Aiii(v): "O wehe yhr verdorben kinder O whei! so yhr ein radtschlag
macht. meyne wort verlast und veracht. Carle du edler Keyser werd. aus dein Keyserliche swerdt.
Beschirm die heilige Christenheit. der welt weyt und breyth. du die ewigen seligkeit. mugst
mit Fursten un Herren.

[77]Ibid., fol. Aiii(v).   [78]Ibid., fol. Aiv.

First Impressions in the Strasbourg Press

Mark U. Edwards, Jr.

Martin Luther attempted mightily throughout his life to dictate how he and his own writings should be understood. But even though he could normally control what was printed under his name, he could not control how he was interpreted by his readers. Even Luther's allies often disagreed with each other, and with the reformer himself, in their understanding of what he had said and what he stood for. So, too, did his opponents. Each treatise was received differently by different people, interpreted differently by different audiences. It was the press, then, that both connected Luther with his audience and led inevitably to a divorce between his "original intent" and appropriated meaning.

This essay examines the competing images of Luther that emerged in the vernacular press of Strasbourg during the early 1520s. Strasbourg, an imperial free city with a population of about twenty thousand, was the third greatest printing center in German-speaking lands. During the Reformation it was a major center for the printing and reprinting of Luther's works. It also saw substantial numbers of publications by supporters and opponents of Luther. In the output of this one city, Edwards traces the emergence of Luther's public image in all its complexity and even its contradictions.

OVER THE LAST TWO DECADES there has been a salutary shift in the interests of intellectual historians. From a concern with the ideas of the great theologians and intellectuals of the Reformation period, a number of us have moved to a consideration of the reception of these ideas among larger segments of the population. This profound shift is due largely to the rise to dominance in academic history of social history and the appropriation by intellectual and church historians of some of its findings, methods, and questions. Where we intellectual historians once spent most of our time studying the denizens of learned culture, we now also ask ourselves what impact, if any, learned culture had on the religious beliefs of the rest of the population. That we should entertain doubt about the influence of learned culture illustrates how far we have come. It is a salutary doubt, and it has already deepened our understanding of the sixteenth century.

However much we may disagree about details and relative priorities, intellectual historians can probably agree on the central messages of the learned conveyed in their vernacular publications. But social historians such as Gerald Strauss have challenged us with three crucial questions: who received these messages? what in the messages appealed to those who received them? and how did these messages affect the beliefs and behavior of their recipients? I propose to deal with each of these questions in turn.

First, who received these messages? At issue is literacy.[1] It has been estimated that overall literacy in Germany in the early sixteenth century was about 5 percent. Although literacy rates were higher in the cities, perhaps in the area of 30 percent, cities themselves enclosed no more than 10 percent of the empire's population. In other words, those learned in Latin were a minority among the literate; the literate were a minority within the cities; and the cities enclosed a minority of the population in the empire. The Reformation, then, was a "minority phenomenon," and the audience for the views of the learned may have been small indeed.

These simple statistics have gone a long way to debunking the romantic or confessional myth that Reformation theology galvanized a whole nation. Much to the good, they have also induced some historians to seek other

---

[1]For an exchange on the issue of literacy, audience, and "effectiveness" of pamphlet literature, see the articles by Bernd Moeller, Robert Scribner, and Steven Ozment in *Stadtbürgertum und Adel in der Reformation: Studien zur Sozialgeschichte der Reformation in England und Deutschland,* ed. Wolfgang J. Mommsen (Stuttgart: Klett-Cotta, 1979). See also the essays by Ozment, Moeller, and Scribner in *Flugschriften als Massenmedium der Reformationszeit,* ed. Hans-Joachim Köhler (Stuttgart: Klett-Cotta, 1981). Ozment originally laid out his position in *The Reformation in the Cities: The Appeal of Protestantism to Sixteenth-Century Germany and Switzerland* (New Haven: Yale University Press, 1975). Scribner continues the discussion in "Oral Culture and the Diffusion of Reformation Ideas," *History of European Ideas* 5 (1984): 237-56. The best work on publication statistics has been done by Hans-Joachim Köhler in "The Flugschriften and Their Importance in Religious Debate: A Quantitative Approach," in *"Astrologi hallucinati": Stars and the End of the World in Luther's Time,* ed. Paola Zambelli (Berlin: Walter de Gruyter, 1986) and in "Erste Schritte zu einem Meinungsprofil der frühen Reformationszeit," in *Martin Luther: Probleme seiner Zeit,* ed. V. Press and D. Stieverman (Stuttgart: Klett-Cotta, 1986), 244-81. See also Scribner's *For the Sake of Simple Folk: Popular Propaganda for the German Reformation* (Cambridge: Cambridge University Press, 1981); Richard Gawthrop and Gerald Strauss, "Protestantism and Literacy in Germany," *Past and Present* 104 (1984): 31-55; Gerald Strauss, *Luther's House of Learning: Indoctrination of the Young in the German Reformation* (Baltimore: Johns Hopkins University Press, 1978); Gerald Strauss, "Lutheranism and Literacy: A Reassessment," in *Religion and Society in Early Modern Europe, 1500-1800,* ed. Kaspar von Greyerz (London: Allen and Unwin, 1984), 109-23. On the issue of literacy in general, see especially Rolf Engelsing, *Analphabetentum und Lektüre: Zur Sozialgeschichte des Lesens in Deutschland zwischen feudaler und industrieller Gesellschaft* (Stuttgart: J. B. Metzler, 1973).

In this article I have used several widely recognized conventions. Sixteenth-century German is cited according to the conventions established by the *Martin Luther Studienausgabe* (Berlin: Evangelische Verlagsanstalt, 1979-), which places in following parentheses sixteenth-century diacritical marks that appeared above letters in the original. I have also reproduced the spelling and capitalization of the original. Following the abbreviations established by Kurt Aland, ed., *Hilfsbuch zum Lutherstudium,* 3d rev. ed. (Witten: Luther-Verlag, 1970), I use WA as abbreviation for the Weimarer Ausgabe of Luther's works (*D. Martin Luthers Werke, Kritische Gesamtausgabe* [Weimar: Hermann Böhlau, 1883-]), W2 for the second edition of Walch (Johann Georg Walch, ed., *Dr. Martin Luthers sämmtliche Schriften* [St. Louis: Concordia Publishing House, 1880-1910]), and AM for Luther's Works, American edition (Jaroslav Pelikan and Helmut T. Lehmann, eds., *Luther's Works* [St. Louis: Concordia Publishing House, and Philadelphia: Fortress Press, 1955-]).

forms by which the ideas of the learned might have been transmitted – such as sermons and other means of oral transmission on the one hand, and pictures, rituals, and other forms of nonverbal communication on the other. But I think that these statistics may conceal a more complicated situation in which the printed views of the learned reached a larger audience than the literacy statistics suggest.

While we must recognize that the theological concerns of the learned reached the general population through intermediaries, and that the message could be transformed in the process of transmission and reception (note for example the transformation of Luther's slogan "Christian freedom" in the Peasants' War),[2] we should not make the mistake of thinking that a printed message could only reach those who were able to read. It may be a conceit or at least a naiveté of our modern, literate culture to fail to recognize how easily the illiterate could gain access to the printed page. One reader could share the fruits of his or her reading with hundreds and even thousands of other people. Miriam Chrisman has shown in the case of Strasbourg that during the crucial period 1520 to 1526 the learned wrote large numbers of vernacular treatises aimed at a more popular audience.[3] These and other pamphlets of the early Reformation are replete with suggestions that the reader share his reading with the illiterate.[4] And when the reader was a preacher, the "multiplier effect" could be large indeed. The Strasbourg preacher Matthaeus Zell, in his *Christeliche verantwortung* of 1523, in which he expounded at length on Luther's teachings, stated that he was now putting in writing what he had already taught orally and at length to more than three thousand people.[5] A treatise such as Luther's *On the Freedom of a Christian* (1520) might see twelve reprintings within a year or two of its publication, representing, say, thirteen thousand copies. But one preacher such as Matthaeus Zell, who read this treatise and incorporated its message into his sermons, could multiply its influence a thousandfold or more.

And even with this I may have conceded too much to the skeptics. If we assume conservatively that each printing of a work by Luther numbered

---

[2]See my article "Luther *Schmähung*? Catholics on Luther's Responsibility for the Peasant's War," *Catholic Historical Review* 76 (1990): 461-80.

[3]Miriam U. Chrisman, *Lay Culture, Learned Culture: Books and Social Change in Strasbourg, 1480-1599* (New Haven: Yale University Press, 1982).

[4]For two examples from the early Strasbourg press, note the extended title of *Mancherley büchlin vnnd tractetlin* (Strasbourg: Schurer Erben, 1520), which is reproduced in full in n. 19 below, that speaks of those who read these books or have them read to them; and see Vadian's *Karsthans,* published in Strasbourg in 1521, in which the characters of Murner and Luther both urge Karsthans to have their books read to him, and the character of Karsthans himself speaks of having his son read the books to him (Otto Clemen, ed., *Flugschriften aus den ersten Jahren der Reformation* [Nieuwkoop: B. de Graaf, 1984] 4:88-90, 94-96).

[5]Mathaeus Zell, *Christeliche verantwortung . . . über Artickel im vom Bischofflichen fiscal daselbs entgegen gesetzt vnnd im rechten ubergeben* (Strasbourg, 1523).

one thousand copies, we are talking about an output for Luther alone of 3.1 million copies during the period 1516 to 1546. This total does not include the numerous whole and partial editions of Luther's Bible translation. And he is only one Protestant author. If, for the sake of argument, we assume that for every five treatises that Luther published, other Protestants published an additional four treatises – which is roughly the ratio found in the city of Strasbourg – then we have another 2.5 million copies. Although Catholics were badly outpublished by the Protestants in the vernacular – Luther published about five vernacular treatises to one of theirs – Catholic authors still contributed at least another six hundred thousand copies. This all adds up to a bit over six million copies, one exemplar for every two people in the empire, literate and illiterate, or twenty copies for each literate person.[6]

I suggest that publication statistics such as these show that we may need to rethink the whole issue of literacy in the sixteenth century, as well as the issue of popular interest in theology. There is another relevant statistic. On the basis of the Tübingen pamphlet (*Flugschriften*) project, Hans-Joachim Köhler has estimated that there were approximately ten thousand pamphlet editions printed within the Holy Roman Empire from 1501 to 1530. Of this total almost three quarters, or over six thousand editions, were printed between the years 1520 and 1526. At a conservative one thousand copies per edition, that makes 6.6 million copies, or more than ten copies per literate individual.[7] And on the matter of content, Köhler has estimated on the basis of samples that issues of "theology and church" appear in 98 percent of these pamphlets. The specific theological issue of *sola scriptura* is discussed by more than 70 percent of pamphlets published between 1520 and 1526. By way of contrast, the subject area "economy" was treated by only 43 percent of the pamphlets. More people were reading than some historians suspect, and they were reading about theology.

Let us now turn to the second question. What was it in the message that appealed to its recipients? Was there, as Bernd Moeller argues, a resonance between late medieval communal ideals and evangelical theology of a particularly urban sort that accounts for its appeal? Or did the evangelical message offer, as Steven Ozment contends, a new understanding of religion that liberated lay people from a clerical form of Christianity that, in the light of the new understanding, seemed burdensome, exploitative, and perhaps even fraudulent? These two positions urge us to *extend* our understanding of the Reformation's appeal from narrowly religious concerns to broader concerns involving political, social, and economic interests understood in religious terms. There is a third

---

[6]See my "Catholic Controversial Literature, 1518-1555: Some Statistics," *Archiv für Reformationsgeschichte* 79 (1988): 189-205; and my "Statistics on Sixteenth-Century Printing," in *The Process of Change in Early Modern Europe,* ed. Phillip Bebb and Sherrin Marshall (Athens, Ohio: Ohio University Press, 1988), 149-63.

[7]Köhler, "*Flugschriften* and Their Importance," 154-55.

position, found especially in the work of Peter Blickle and, to a degree, in Gerald Strauss's latest work, that argues that the essential appeal of the Reformation message was not religious but rather political or social.[8] In this view, the religious message is either irrelevant or a rationalization of a more fundamental political or social concern, called "communalism" by Blickle or "mundane life" by Strauss. If Moeller and Ozment are arguing for an *extension* of our understanding of the Reformation's appeal to include social and political concerns expressed in religious terms, then Blickle and Strauss may be said to be arguing for a *shift* in our understanding of its appeal, from religious *per se* to social and political concerns rationalized by religious terminology. In this debate, I must come firmly down on the side of those arguing for an extension rather than a shift.

To explain my preference for extending rather than shifting our understanding of the Reformation's appeal, I should like for the remainder of this essay to examine the message presented in Luther's own vernacular treatises during the initial years of the Reformation. Specifically, I wish to confine my consideration to those treatises that appeared in one particular city, Strasbourg, before Luther announced in print his rejection of Rome and began his passionate polemical battle against the papacy. Let me explain this focus.

Printing of short, relatively inexpensive vernacular works was very much intended for local consumption. In an age well before copyright existed, with shipping overland expensive and printing relatively cheap, a work generally spread through reprinting. If there was interest in Strasbourg for a work first published in Wittenberg, or at least if a Strasbourg printer *thought* there was interest in Strasbourg for a work published in Wittenberg, it was more common for the printer in Strasbourg to reprint the work than it was for the printer in Wittenberg to ship a large number of copies to Strasbourg. If the printer was correct in his expectation of local interest, then his (or her) printing of a work is a valid, although indirect, measure of public demand. If the printer reprinted the work several times, we may safely assume that he (or she) did so to meet the demands of local customers.

In sum, the reprinting of a particular work in a particular place can be used by historians as an indirect measure of local or regional demand, and

---

[8]This is clearest in Peter Blickle's *Gemeindereformation: Die Menschen des 16. Jahrhunderts auf dem Weg zum Heil* (Munich: Oldenbourg, 1985), and Gerald Strauss's *Law, Resistance, and the State: The Opposition to Roman Law in Reformation Germany* (Princeton: Princeton University Press, 1986). See especially Strauss's comment on Ozment, 210, n. 56.

not merely demand in general.[9] By concentrating on the production of one city, we are able in a rough way to identify those treatises that played the greatest role in forming the first impression that Strasbourgers had of Martin Luther and his message. To be sure, some treatises reaching Strasbourg from outside printing centers influenced the impressions Strasbourgers had of Luther and his message, even though they were not reprinted in Strasbourg. By omitting these treatises, we undoubtedly add some imprecision to our reconstruction of first impressions. Having conceded this point, I would point out that any treatise that aroused widespread interest within Strasbourg would likely have been reprinted there. By limiting ourselves to Strasbourg publications, we are unlikely to overlook many treatises that strongly formed first impressions in Strasbourg.[10]

Why, then, the choice of Strasbourg? Strasbourg, an imperial free city with a population of about twenty thousand, was the third greatest printing center in the German-speaking lands, exceeded only by Cologne and Nuremberg. During the Reformation it was a major center for the printing and reprinting of Luther's works, outproduced only by Wittenberg, Augsburg, and Nuremberg.[11] Wittenberg, for obvious reasons, is not the right place for examining the first impression Luther made on his *reading* public since Luther was available to them in the flesh. Among the remaining major centers, I chose Strasbourg over Augsburg and Nuremberg because of the fine bibliographies by Miriam Chrisman and Josef Benzing that make the study of the Strasbourg press easier than for any other major city of the Holy Roman Empire.[12]

In considering the message conveyed by Luther's early vernacular treatises, I have chosen to examine treatises by Luther that appeared in Strasbourg

---

[9]To be sure, a moment's reflection will suggest problems with this approach. Books are not consumed in one reading, so that publication dates may only reflect initial demand and thus suggest only the *beginning* of a work's influence. A work may circulate through many hands and exercise influence for years after its publication. Sermon collections, prayer books, devotional works, and whole and partial Bibles are obvious examples of such durable publication. A further difficulty: some types of printed material may circulate more widely than others. For example, there may be more centralized production and wider distribution of particularly expensive items such as Bibles. Yet by concentrating our attention on popular, relatively inexpensive treatises, we probably minimize this difficulty.

[10]In fact, almost all of Luther's early vernacular works were published in Strasbourg, so the only "outside" publications that might have significantly modified readers' first impressions of Luther would have been in Latin.

[11]See the graph in my *Luther's Last Battles: Politics and Polemics, 1531-46* (Ithaca: Cornell University Press, 1983), 23.

[12]Chrisman, *Bibliography of Strasbourg Imprints, 1480-1599* (New Haven: Yale University Press, 1982), and Josef Benzing, *Bibliographie Strasbourgeoise* (Baden-Baden: V. Koerner, 1981). I have generally found Chrisman's *Bibliography* to be more accurate and conservative in its attributions.

In an important article, Hans-Christoph Rublack has examined the content of Luther's early "bestsellers" published in Augsburg (Hans-Christoph Rublack, "Martin Luther and the Urban

before August 1520. This cutoff date is easy to explain. On July 16, 1520, Luther's *On the Papacy of Rome, Against the Highly Famous Romanist in Leipzig* left the printing press in Wittenberg. A month later, shortly after August 18, 1520, *To the Christian Nobility of the German Nation* also left the Wittenberg presses.[13] In these two vernacular treatises Luther announced to the world his rejection of the papacy. Both treatises were subsequently reprinted in Strasbourg and elicited passionate rebuttals by the Franciscan friar and author, Thomas Murner.[14] The vernacular polemical battle was engaged. From this point forward, Luther was more than a reformer of piety; he was a rebel. This change cannot but have had an influence on how the laity subsequently read and understood his works. By examining the works available up to this watershed, we limit ourselves to the works that likely formed the first impression that interested readers had of Luther and his message.

Overview of the Publications Themselves

Before the flood of polemics and controversial works appeared in the Strasbourg press in late 1520, Strasbourg readers would have found almost exclusively pastoral and devotional works by Luther available from the local press.[15] In 1519 one sermon on marriage appeared. Two other sermons, one on Christ's passion, perhaps in two editions, and the other on prayer and

---

Social Experience," in *The Transmission of Ideas in the Lutheran Reformation,* ed. Helga Robinson-Hammerstein (Dublin: Irish Academic Press, 1989), 65-82. We each characterize the content of Luther's treatises rather differently, demonstrating, if the point needs further demonstration, that the meaning of texts cannot be separated from the perspective of the reader. Briefly put, Rublack overstresses Luther's alleged "dualism" and makes him sound like an Erasmian reformer, which he was not.

It is worth stressing that this focus on vernacular works published in Strasbourg (or in Rublack's case, Augsburg) is arguably less artificial than the standard biographical approach that pays little or no attention to evidence that some treatises had much wider readership and impact than others. It may be well and good in a biography to analyze indiscriminately Latin and German works without concern for the different (although overlapping) audiences each addressed. But we need to remember that vernacular publications reached a much wider audience. Furthermore, if we are interested in issues of reception, we risk seriously misunderstanding the historical record if we give the same weight to works printed only once as we give to works that are reprinted numerous times and published over a wide geographical area. Some works were simply more significant than others in forming first impressions among a significant segment of the population.

[13]I have used Georg Buchwald, *Luther Calendarium* (Leipzig: M. Heinsius's Nachfolger, 1929), for the dates of publications.

[14]See the list of Murner's rebuttals below.

[15]Although some of the sermons and treatises that I shall discuss in the following pages may have appeared at the same time as the controversial writings of late 1520, most probably preceded the major polemics of the last quarter of the year. In any case, there is sufficient repetition of themes in these works to sketch an outline of Luther's earliest message and the impression it likely conveyed.

processions in Holy Week, appeared either in late 1519 or 1520.[16] In the
same year there appeared an edition of Luther's *The Seven Penitential Psalms*,
originally published in Wittenberg in 1517, and the *Theologia Deutsch* (*German
Theology*), a devotional treatise for which Luther had supplied a preface. Only
one work, his *Explanation of Several Articles Attributed to Him by His Opponents*,
deals in any detail with the controversy in which Luther was entangled, and
that in a very restrained fashion.[17]

In 1520 there appeared eleven sermons (or nine, if two are dated to
1519),[18] and one sermon collection that included a few other treatises, some
with mild polemical content.[19] This collection, first published in Basel in
May 1520, and reprinted in Strasbourg in October 1520, duplicated several
of the sermons that were also published individually.[20] There also appeared
some four devotional treatises (and perhaps several that I have classified under

[16]One (or three) sermon(s): a) *Ein Sermon von dem Elichen standt . . .* , b) *Ein Sermon uon
der Betrachtung des heyligen leidens Christi* (Benzing, but not Chrisman, who shows two editions
in 1520), and c) *Ein Sermon von dem gebeet vnd procession yn der Creutzwochen . . .* (Chrisman
one edition in 1520; Benzing one in 1519, attributed to a different publisher).

[17]One sermon collection: *Die syben Bu(o)sz psalme(-);* one polemic: *vnderrichtung, vff etlich
Artickel, die jm vo(-) seinen mißgünnern vffgelegt vnd zugemessen werden;* and one devotional treatise:
Theologia teütsch.

[18]a) *Ein Sermon uon der Betrachtung des heyligen leidens Christi* (two Chrisman, none Benzing,
who has one in 1519); b) *Ein Sermon von dem gebeet vnd procession yn der Creutzwochen . . .*
(Chrisman one edition in 1520; Benzing one in 1519); c) *Ein Sermon von de(-) Hochwurdige
sacrame(-)t des heiligen waren lychnams Christi, vnd von den Brüderschaffen;* d) *Ein Sermon von dem
Heiligen hochwirdigen Sacrame(-)t der Tauffe;* e) *Ein Sermon uon dem wu(o)cher;* f) (*E*)*yn Sermon
von de(-) nüwen Testament: das ist vo(-) der heilige(-) Mesz;* g) *Ein Sermon von dem Sacrament der
Büß* (two editions); h) (*E*)*In sermo(-) von dem Bann Doctor Martini Luthers;* and i) *Ein nützlich
predig . . . wie sich ein Christenmensch . . . bereiten sol zu sterben.*

[19]*Martini Luthers der waren götlichen schrifft (Doctors, Augustiner zu(o) Wittenbergk, mancherley
büchlin vnnd tractetlin. In wölche(-) ein yegklicher auch einfaltiger Lay, vil heylsamer Christlicher lere
vnd vnderweysung findet, so not seindt zu(o) wissenn, einem yegklichen Christen menschen, der nach
Christlicher ordnung (als wir alle söllen) leben will. Deren biechlin namen findest du am andern blatt,
mit zale der blättern, in wölchem yegklichs eygentlich anfahet, vnd ein epistel zu(o) denen die söllich
büchlin lesen, oder hören lesen von D. Martini Luther außgangen. Item Apologia: das ist ein schirmred
vnd antwort gegen etlicher einrede, so geschehen wider D. Martinu Luthern vnd seine Ewangelische lere,
mit fast schönen wollgegrünten bewerungen, das sein leere, als warhafftig, Christlich, vnnd göttlich
anzu(o)nemen sey* (Strasbourg: Schurer Erben, 1520).

[20]The collection contains the following (with the appropriate number, modernized short
title, and original publication date from Kurt Aland, *Hilfsbuch zum Lutherstudium*):
Aland, 742: *Auslegung deutsche des Vaterunsers für die einfältigen Laien . . . Nicht für die Gelehrten,*
1519. WA, 2:(74)80-130; AM 42:(l5)19-8l.
Aland, 557: *Ein kurze Form, das Paternoster zu verstehen vnd zu beten (für die jungen Kinder im
Christenglauben)* 1519. WA, 6:(9)11-19; W2 10:166-75.
Aland, 115: *Ein Sermon vom Sakrament der Buße,* 1519. WA, 2:(709)713-23; AM 35:(3)9-22.
Aland, 408: *Ein Sermon von der Betrachtung des heiligen Leidens Christi,* 1519. WA, 2:(131)136-42;
AM 42:(3)7-14.
Aland, 209: *Sermon de digna praeparatione cordis pro suscipiendo sacramento eucharistiae,* 1518. In
German translation. WA, 1:(325)329-34; W2 12:1342-52.

polemics but could equally count as devotional treatises): another edition of the *German Theology*, two different treatises on confession, and a brief exposition of the Lord's Prayer.[21] Finally, there were between nine and twelve treatises dealing with the controversy between Luther and the old faith,[22] some of which could also be classified as devotional works with mild polemical content (for example, *The Freedom of a Christian*, which appeared in one or two editions,[23] and *Doctor Martin Luther's Appeal or Petition to a Free Christian Council*, which appeared in two editions).[24] *On the Papacy at Rome, Against the Celebrated Romanist in Leipzig* appeared after June 26, 1520.[25] *To the Christian Nobility of the German Nation* appeared after August 18, 1520 in

---

Aland, 556: *Duo sermones de passione Christi*, 1518. In German translation. WA, 1 (335)336-45; W2 10:1176-93.

Aland, 5: *Ein Sermon von Ablaß und Gnade*, 1517 (1518). WA, 1:(239)243-46; W2 18:270-75.

Aland, 738: *Luthers Unterricht auf etliche Artikel, die ihm von seinen Abgönnern aufgelegt und zugemessen werden*, 1519. WA, 2:(66)69-93; W2 15:699-705.

Aland, 177: *Ein Sermon von dem ehelichen Stand (verändert und korrigiert)*, 1519. WA, 2:(162)166-71; AM 44:(3)7-14.

Aland, 698: *Ein Sermon von der Bereitung zum Sterben*, 1519. WA, 2:(680)685-97, 759; AM 42:(95)99-115.

Aland, 779: *[Großer] Sermon von dem Wucher*, 1520. WA, 6:(33)36-60, 630; AM 45:(231)345-410.

Aland, 60: *Ein Sermon von dem Bann*, 1520. WA, 6:(61)63-75, 630; AM 39:(3)7-22.

Aland, 392: *Ein Sermon von dem Gebet und Prozession in der Kreuzwoche*, 1519. WA, 2: (172)175-79; AM 42:(83)87-93.

Aland, 714: *Ein Sermon von dem heiligen hochwürdigen Sakrament der Taufe*, 1519. WA, 2:(724)727-37; AM 35:(23)29-43.

Aland, 655: *Ein Sermon von dem hochwürdigen Sakrament des heiligen wahren Leichnams Christi vnd von den Brüderschaften*, 1519. WA, 2:(738)742-58; AM 35:(45)49-73.

Aland, 656: *Verklärung D. M. Luthers etlicher Artikeln seinem Sermon von dem heiligen Sakrament*, 1520. WA, 6:(76)78-83; W2 19:452-59.

Aland, 476: *Ein Sermon gepredigt zu Leipzig auf dem Schloß am Tage Petri und Pauli Matth. 16, 13-19*, 1519. WA, 2:(241)244-49; AM 51:(53)54-60.

Aland, 615: *Auslegung des 109. (110.) Psalms*, 1518. WA, 1:(687)690-710; W2 5:888-921.

Aland, 761: *Von den guten Werken*, 1520. WA, 6:(196)202-76; AM 44:(15)21-114.

Spengler's *Schutzrede* is the only piece in the collection not by Luther. Published anonymously, the full title of the piece was originally *Schutzred vnnd christeliche antwurt ains erbern liebhabers gotlicher warhayt, der heyligen schrifft. auff etlicher vermaint widersprechen. mit anzaygug warumb Doctor Martini Luthers leer nit als vnchristenlich verworffen. sonder mer fur christenlich gehalten werde(-) sol. yetz widerumb corrigirt vn(-) mit ainem newen Dyalogo gebesert.*

[21]a) *Theologia teütsch* (one [Benzing two] edition, published after August 1, 1520); b) *Ein heilsams Büchlein von Doctor Martinus Luther August. von der Beycht gemacht*... (German translation in 1520); c) *(E)In kurtze vnderwisung Wie man beichte(-) sol*. . . . ; and d) *(E)In kurtze Form das Pater noster zu(o) verston, vnd zu(o) betten.*

[22]Chrisman lists twelve, Benzing nine.

[23]*Von der Freyhayt Aines Christenmenschen* (Chrisman shows two editions in 1520, Benzing one in 1520; after November 16, 1520).

[24]*Doctoris Martini Luther Appelation od(er) berüfung an eyn Christlich frey conciliu(-)* (two editions, after November 17, 1520).

[25]*Von de(-) Bapstum zu(o) Rom Wider den Hochberümpten Romaniste(-) zu Leiptzck* (after June 26, 1520, reprinted in *Drey Biechlin* in 1521 or 1522).

two to four editions.[26] *On the Babylonian Captivity of the Church* appeared in
two or three editions, sometime after October 6, 1520.[27] Only one of these
polemics, *Doctor Martin Luther's Answer to the Notice Issued Under the Seal of
the Official at Stolpen,*[28] may have appeared before midyear.[29] The rest appeared
well after midyear (since the *terminus a quo* given is the original publication
date in Wittenberg), and five or six in the last quarter of the year. So the
vernacular writings published in the Strasbourg press through the first half
of 1520 are overwhelmingly devotional and pastoral. This alone is likely to
have profoundly shaped Strasbourgers' first impression of Martin Luther and
his ideas.

To whom were these treatises addressed? Clearly, the laity. What was
their message? That one should humbly rely on God's promise of forgiveness
rather than on one's own allegedly meritorious works. Why did this message
appeal to its lay readers and hearers? Because the message explicitly dignified
the spiritual status of the laity at the expense of clerical claims and prerogatives.
Let me take up each point in turn.

The Treatises Addressed Lay Concerns

Even a simple consideration of the treatises' topics indicates clearly that
these vernacular treatises were addressed to the laity – baptism, marriage, the
Eucharist, confession, and extreme unction. One treatise instructs the laity
on how to pray the Lord's Prayer, and another instructs them on how
properly to confess. A lay ethical concern, usury, is addressed, and lay activities
such as processions and brotherhoods are examined from Luther's new religious
perspective. Even the more general treatises – one on the seven penitential
psalms, two printings of the *German Theology,* and the two mild polemics –
deal, as we shall see, with lay concerns regarding sacramental and popular
piety.[30]

The tone of these pastoral works also indicates that their intended audience
was the laity. In these writings Luther is, for the most part, not arguing with
or even addressing other theologians. He is laying out his understanding of
Christianity for his readers rather than defending it from attack by critics.
His explanation of technical issues is expressed in simple terms, undergirt
with citations of scripture and without benefit of the learned distinctions
that graced scholastic sermons and treatises of his age. He largely avoided

---

[26]*Teütscher Adel. (A)N den Christe(-)lichen Adel teütscher Nation . . .* (Benzing two, Chrisman
four editions, after August 18, 1520).

[27]*Von der Babylonischen gefengknuß der Kirchen* (Benzing three, Chrisman two editions, after
October 6, 1520).

[28]*Doctor Martinus Luthers antwort Auf die zedel, so vnd(er) des Officials zu(o) Stolpe(-) sigel ist
außgangen* (after February 11, 1520, date of first Wittenberg publication).

[29]It probably came in the second half, following the treatise to which it objected.

[30]See the listing of treatises above.

the vocabulary of theological scholarship, and in the few cases where the technical distinction was important, he patiently defined the term for the laity's benefit. In such cases he was "popularizing" the scholastic understanding of various issues as a basis for criticism or outright rejection. Throughout, his writings conveyed a tone of moral earnestness.

The Central Theological Message of the Treatises

Two interconnected themes run through most of the early works published in Strasbourg: first, that we must acknowledge our own sinfulness and surrender all reliance on our own works; and second, that we should trust God and God's promise in Christ as our only source of salvation. A few examples taken from Luther's earliest Strasbourg treatises should illustrate this well-known theme. Luther's exposition of the seven penitential psalms, which appeared in Strasbourg in 1519, returns repeatedly to our own sinfulness and wretchedness and our total dependence on God for help, strength, and salvation. Punishment comes from God to remind us of our true nature, to make us rightly humble, and to prepare us for God's gracious gift of unmerited forgiveness. A good life, Luther explained, consists not in outward works and appearance but in a sighing and troubled spirit.[31] Yet while this stress on wretchedness, humility, sinfulness, and submission to deserved punishment understandably dominates this work on penitential psalms, Luther still brings in his second theme, as can be seen in a striking commentary on the seventh penitential psalm.

> Not in my righteousness, for that is sin and unrighteousness. As he [the Psalmist] says, graciously make me true and righteous for I see some who wish to be true and righteous through their own truth and righteousness. Protect me from that! They wish to be something when they in fact are nothing, empty, liars, fools, sinners. It should be noticed here that the little words "your truth" and "your righteousness" do not refer to that by which God is true and righteous, as many think, but refer to the grace by which God makes us true and righteous through Christ, as the Apostle Paul, in Romans 1, 2, and 3, calls the righteousness of God and the truth of God, which is given to us through faith in Christ. In addition, God's truth refers not only to the Word but more to the work and fulfillment of his Word, which is due to this same grace and mercy. Just as a token or a painted gulden is not a true gulden but only represents one, and is indeed an empty thing and a deception if it is given or considered to be a true gulden, a proper gulden is the truth and without deception. In such fashion all haughty and holy lives, works, and righteousness are in relation to the righteousness and work of the grace of God a mere appearance and a deadly, harmful falseness if they are considered

[31]WA, 1:165.

true goods where there is no truth. Rather it is God's [truth] that gives the true, substantial righteousness which is the faith of Christ. For this reason the little word "truth" may also be translated from Hebrew *in fide tue,* that is, "in your faith."[32]

To a modern reader familiar with Luther's 1545 autobiographical account of his breakthrough to a new understanding of God's righteousness, this is a paragraph pregnant with significance.

Here are a few more examples. In his sermon or prayer and procession during Holy Week, Luther stressed from the outset that one must trust in God's promise. For a prayer to be truly good and heard, one must have a promise from God. "From this it follows," Luther advised his readers, "that no one obtains anything on account of the worthiness of his or her prayer but only on account of the depths of divine goodness, which anticipates all requests and desires through His gracious promise . . . ."[33] It was crucial not to doubt God's promise.[34] Above all, our prayer to God should not rely on any sense of our worthiness. In fact, it is our own sense of unworthiness that, paradoxically, makes us worthy to be heard, "because we believe that we are unworthy and we confidently venture everything on God's trustworthiness."[35] In his sermon on contemplating Christ's passion, Luther located the promise in baptismal faith. Faith, Luther explained, firmly believes that baptism has established a covenant between us and God. For our part in the covenant, we must fight against sin. For God's part, God has promised to be merciful to us and not count our sins against us.[36] In his treatise *How One Should Confess,* published in Strasbourg in 1520, Luther began with the advice that a Christian should ground his confession "on the greatest and fullest trust in the most merciful promise and pledge of God and should firmly believe that almighty God will mercifully forgive him his sins."[37] These examples could be multiplied many times over.

Appeal of the Message:
Dignifying the Spiritual Status of the Laity

What was it about these treatises that may have appealed to their lay readers and hearers? On this question, I must side with Steven Ozment in his argment with Bernd Moeller. There is very little in these treatises that, at least on the face of it, would naturally resonate with late medieval communal

[32]Ibid., 1:212-13.   [33]Ibid., 2:175.   [34]Ibid., 2:175-76. Points two and three.
[35]Ibid., 2:176.
[36]*Martin Luther Studienausgabe* 1:264. Hereafter cited as *Studienausgabe.*
[37]WA, 2:59.

ideas.[38] On the other hand, there is a great deal that, if put into effect, would "liberate" lay people from a clerical form of piety. Or to put it another way, the major themes of humility and promise provided an explicit rationale for dignifying the spiritual status of the laity at the expense of clerical privilege and authority. Luther repeatedly and explicitly drew the consequences for his readers and listeners.

Luther particularly stressed the value of ordinary lay activities, often at the expense of clerically prescribed "good works." For example, in his 1519 sermon on marriage, Luther insisted that married people could do no better work, either for themselves or for Christendom, than raise their children well.

> There is nothing in pilgrimages to Rome, to Jerusalem, or to Saint James [Compostella], nothing in building churches, endowing masses, or whatever works might be named compared to this one work, [namely] that those who are married bring up their children [well]. That is their straightest road to heaven. Indeed, heaven could not be nearer or better achieved than with this work.[39]

This was, moreover, the laity's proper and appointed work. In another early sermon, on meditating on Christ's passion, Luther continued this practice of unfavorably contrasting clerically sponsored works with what he saw as true piety. A person who rightly contemplates Christ's sufferings for a day, an hour, or even a quarter hour does better than to fast a year, pray a psalm daily, or even hear a hundred masses.[40]

Luther also insisted on the essential spiritual equality of laity and clergy. For example, in his sermon on baptism he denied that the vows of chastity, of the priesthood, or of any of the clergy were more significant or higher than baptism.

> For in baptism we all vow the same thing: to slay sin and to become holy through the work and grace of God, to whom we give and sacrifice ourselves, as clay to the potter, and in this no one is better than another. But to live according to this baptism, so that sin can be slain, there can be no one way or estate. . . . Thus it is true that there is no higher, better, or greater vow than the vow of baptism.[41]

---

[38]This point is also made by Rublack, "Luther and the Urban Social Experience," 67-70. I would, however, place Rublack in the camp of those who see the Reformation's appeal more in political and social terms than in religious.

[39]WA, 2:169-70.   [40]Ibid., 2:139.

[41]*Studienausgabe* 1:267-68. Luther did concede that there were higher estates, such as that of a priest or bishop. But he insisted that such estates should be distinguished by greater suffering and more speedy preparation for death.

Luther also undercut the sacramental authority exercised by the clergy. Consider for example, Luther's sermon on the sacrament of penance.[42] In this treatise he contrasted the forgiveness of punishment with the forgiveness of guilt. The former, under the control of the church and addressed in part by indulgences, was relatively insignificant in comparison to the latter, which is solely God's gift and reconciles the human with God.[43] Some think they may obtain forgiveness of guilt and the quieting of their hearts through indulgences and pilgrimages, Luther wrote, but,

> All that is for nought and an error. It makes things much worse because God must himself forgive sin and give the heart peace. Some trouble themselves with many good works, even too much fasting and drudgery, so that some have thereby broken their bodies and ruined their minds, believing that by virtue of their works they could do away with their sins and quiet their hearts.

But both approaches – those who seek indulgences and go on pilgrimages and those who discipline their bodies with fasting and labor – make the mistake of wanting to do good works before their sins are forgiven, while in fact the contrary is necessary because "sins must be forgiven before good works can occur."[44] The efficacy of the sacrament depends not on the sacrament itself or any human office or authority, but on faith in the promise of God.[45] On this basis Luther concluded that the forgiveness of guilt depends on no human office or earthly power, not even the office and power of pope, bishop, or priest, but solely on the Word of Christ and one's own faith in that Word.

> For he [Christ] did not want our comfort, our salvation, [or] our trust to be based on a human word or deed but rather solely on himself and his word and deed. The priest, bishop, [and] pope are only servants who hold out to you Christ's Word, on which you should rely with a solid faith as if on a solid rock. In such fashion the Word will sustain you and your sins will thereby necessarily be forgiven. For this reason, too, the Word is not to be honored on account of the priest, bishop, [or] pope but rather the priest, bishop, [or] pope [is to be honored] on account of the Word, as those who bring you the Word and tidings of your God that you are freed from sins.[46]

Luther argued further that in the sacrament of penance and the forgiveness of guilt, a pope or bishop does no more than the lowliest priest, and that when there is no priest, an individual Christian, even a woman or child, can do as much.[47] Although Luther qualified this comment with the advice that

---

[42]Ibid., 1:244-57.   [43]Ibid., 1:247.   [44]Ibid., 1:248.
[45]Ibid., 1:249.   [46]Ibid. [47]Ibid., 1:249-50.

despite this his readers should not despise the established spiritual orders, this comment cannot but have had the effect of undercutting clerical authority exercised in the sacrament. Subsequent comments reinforce this impression.[48] That clerics reserve absolution for some sins does not make the clerical sacrament any greater or better.[49] The keys are not a power but a service.[50] A priest has sufficient grounds for granting absolution when he sees that the penitent desires it. The priest needs to know no more than that. "I say this," Luther explained,

> so that people will love and cherish the most gracious virtue of the keys and not despise [them] on account of misuses by those who with banning, threatening, and harassing do little more than make a virtual tyranny out of such a lovely and comforting authority, as if Christ had established the keys only for their wishes and lordship [and] had no idea of how one should use them.[51]

Luther explicitly questioned the need for the priest to inquire into the extent of the penitent's contrition,[52] insisted that because there was no dependable rule for distinguishing between venial and mortal sins, penitents should not attempt to confess all sins but only clearly mortal sins that were oppressing their conscience at the time,[53] and stated that the best satisfaction was not assigned prayers but simply to sin no more.[54] Both the treatise and the sermon obviously simplified confession for the laity and undercut some of the conventional claims of the clergy regarding their own authority exercised in the sacrament of penance. In his treatise *How One Should Confess,* he made similar points.[55]

Luther's sermon on the ban also undercut many clerical claims and thereby elevated the status and power of the laity over their own spiritual destiny.[56] He distinguished between inward, spiritual fellowship on the one

[48]Ibid., 1:250.   [49]Ibid.   [50]Ibid., 1:253.

[51]Ibid., 1:253-54.   [52]Ibid., 1:251-52, 254.   [53]Ibid., 1:256.   [54]Ibid.

[55]In his treatise *How One Should Confess,* Luther offered advice that must have been comforting to lay Christians who dreaded the late medieval practice of confession. The Christian reader was told that before he confessed his sins to a priest, he should first confess his misdeeds and sins to God as if speaking with his closest friend (WA, 2:59). Then, in confession itself, the Christian should not worry about confessing all of his deadly sins because it was impossible to remember them all, and, in any case, all our good works, when judged by God in earnest rather than in mercy, are deadly and damnable sins. Luther also urged the Christian to dispense with the extensive and complicated set of distinctions in late medieval confessional practice between sins and the circumstances in which they were committed (WA, 2:60). He further insisted that the Christian should make a large distinction between sins against the commandments of God and sins against the commandments and laws of human beings. "For no one can be saved without the commandments of God," Luther explained, "but one can well be saved without the commandments of human beings" (ibid.). We should, Luther advised, accustom our consciences firmly to trust in God's mercy (WA, 2:64). This advice, if followed, would greatly simplify the process of confession for the laity and would likely relieve some of the anxiety associated with the sacrament even as it reduced the authority of the priest.

[56]WA, 6:63-75.

hand, and external communion on the other. No human being, not even a
bishop or pope, could give or take away spiritual fellowship. Rather it was
God through the Holy Spirit who poured this spiritual fellowship into the
heart of the human being who believed in the Sacrament.[57] Bishops and
popes could, however, cut one off from what Luther termed the "external,
bodily, and visible fellowship" of participation in the Sacrament.[58] For lay
people, however, the crucial significance of this distinction no doubt rested
in Luther's assertion that one could be under the ban and still belong to the
spiritual fellowship or communion, and vice versa. "It may often happen,"
Luther remarked,

> that a banned individual will be deprived of the Holy Sacrament and
> also of burial [in consecrated ground] and yet still be inwardly certain
> and holy in the fellowship of Christ and all the saints, as the Sacrament
> indicates. On the other hand, there are many who freely enjoy the
> Sacrament without external ban and yet inwardly are completely
> estranged and banned from the fellowship of Christ even though
> they might be buried with gold clothes under the high altar with
> all show, bells, and singing.[59]

At some length through the rest of the treatise, and with occasional heat,
Luther criticized clergy who misused the ban.[60]

Several other treatises of a largely devotional or moral character also
dealt, at least in passing, with a few issues of clerical authority. Luther's
Sermon on the Sacrament of the Body of Christ, for example, advocated that a
general council should mandate that all Christians should receive both the

[57]Ibid. 6:64.

[58]Ibid., 6:64. Luther identifies this as the "small ban" and contrasts it with the "large ban"
(ibid.). To those spiritual authorities that attempt to go beyond the "large ban" to coerce the
banned individual with the sword, Luther remarked that the secular sword belonged to temporal
rulers and not to the spiritual estate, who possessed only a spiritual sword, namely, the Word
and commandments of God (WA, 6:64). This is obviously a point of considerable interest to
laity who had fallen afoul of a clerical ban enforced by the secular authorities.

Luther also censured clerics who used the ban to collect money and to redress injuries done
to them (WA, 6:65).

[59]Ibid., 6:65.

[60]Some of them were, as a result, more deserving of the ban than those on whom they
imposed the ban (WA, 6:66-67). Some were "tyrants who seek no more than their power, fear,
and profit" in the ban. In so doing they do horrible damage to themselves "because they pervert
the ban and its work, make a poison out of a medicine, and seek only to terrify fearful human
beings and think nothing about their improvement." They will be held to account for this
(WA, 6:68). Much of the latter half of the sermon is devoted to a detailed criticism of spiritual
authorities who misused the ban or otherwise failed properly to exercise their spiritual authority.
Luther concludes, however, that wicked spiritual rulers, of which the age had many, were God's
punishment for the people's sins and, therefore, should not be resisted (WA, 6:66-75 passim).
Given the impassioned description of clerical abuses, this ultimate counsel of submission may
have lacked persuasiveness.

bread and the wine in the Sacrament, as the priests currently did.[61] In his morally earnest *Small Sermon on Usury,* Luther attacked the clerical use of *Zinskauf,* a form of annuity purchased "in the service of God." "To serve God," Luther explained with some evident exasperation, "means to keep his commands and not steal, take, take interest, and the like, but rather to live and lend to the needy. Would you tear down such true service of God in order that you might build churches, endow altars, and have [Masses] read and sung, none of which God has commanded you [to do] . . . ?"[62]

In sum, these early Strasbourg treatises urged readers to rely neither on their own efforts nor on the mediating power of clerics or clerically sponsored works, but to trust solely in God and God's promise. They questioned clerical claims to jurisdiction and power, and specifically clerical mediation between the laity and God. The clergy were to preach the Word of God, and only to that extent could they be considered intermediaries. In short, the overarching message in these writings was that the religious destiny of lay Christians was in God's hands rather than in their own. It certainly was not in clerical hands. The laity were freed from the standards of clerical piety, freed from such a thoroughgoing reliance on clerical mediation in their relations with God, and freed, above all, from concern about their own worthiness and spiritual efforts.

The Question of Reception

This was what was presented and why it might have appealed to the laity. Was it, however, the message received? A full answer to this question lies beyond the scope of this essay.[63] One measure of reception is the degree to which this message was picked up and repeated by other publicists. Unfortunately, in this regard it is difficult to measure the influence of these early treatises apart from the effect of the great vernacular polemics of late 1520, since most of the treatises published in Strasbourg in 1520 or early 1521 that characterized either Luther or his teachings came after – and even in response to – the great polemics of the last quarter of the year. Still, a brief survey is not out of place.

[61]WA, 2:742-43. Incidentally, a reply to this treatise prompted Luther to write one of the only two polemics that were published in Strasbourg during this early period, *Doctor Martin Luther's Answer to the Notice That Was Published under the Seal of the Official at Stolpen.* In this brief treatise, Luther sarcastically defended his suggestion that a general council of the church decree that laity as well as clergy should commune in both kinds (WA, 6:137-41). He verbally attacked those who used the ban and other "underhanded" means to silence critics, including burning them. He compared his treatment with the treatment meted out to Reuchlin (WA, 6:140-41).

[62]Ibid., 6:7.

[63]I am currently working on this question and hope to bring out a book-length consideration shortly. In the meantime, see my *"Lutherschmähung?"* for how Catholic controversial writers understood Luther's doctrine of Christian Freedom.

Ulrich von Hutten published a number of treatises in Strasbourg in the early years of the Reformation.[64] Three of them appeared in late 1520.[65] In these treatises, Hutten ferociously attacked the Roman papacy, the clergy, and various abuses within the church, and in two of the three he made brief mention of Luther. In the *Complaint and Warning against the Excessive Unchristian Power of the Pope at Rome and the Unspiritual Clergy,* Hutten mentioned Luther only once explicitly, in a marginal note that likened the treatment afforded both himself and Luther with that meted out to Jan Hus.[66] The treatise itself is an anticlerical, antipapal poem or song that accuses the clergy of everything from gluttony to sexual misconduct, attacks ecclesiastical practices such as indulgences and dispensations, and advocates a nationalistic attack on the papacy. In his short treatise, *Indication of How the Roman Bishop or Pope Has Acted Against the German Emperor,* Hutten excerpted various accounts of papal betrayal of the German emperor and warned the emperor to take heed of how his predecessors had been treated and not to expect anything better from the current pope. Luther is mentioned only once, on the last page, when Hutten claimed that his and Luther's writings must be acknowledged to benefit and honor the emperor and the whole German nation.[67]

As these brief summaries indicate, Hutten's writings do not help us much with understanding how Luther's writings may have been understood by his Strasbourg readers. At the very least, we can reasonably infer that Hutten himself understood Luther to be an ally in his fight against Rome and against clerical abuses. But since Luther is mentioned only twice in these treatises – once in a marginal note in *Complaint and Warning* and again in the concluding remarks of *Indication* – it is difficult to demonstrate that other readers would have made the same identification.

On the other end of the spectrum from Hutten, the Franciscan satirist Thomas Murner of Strasbourg published five polemical works against Luther

---

[64]For Hutten's treatises, I have used E. Böcking, ed., *Ulrichs von Hutten Schriften,* 4 vols. (Aalen: Otto Zeller Verlagsbuchhandlung, 1963).

[65]Hutten, *Clag vnd Vormanu(-)g gege(-) den überma(e)ssigen vnchristlichen gewalt des Bapstes zu(o) Rom, vnd der vngeistlichen geistlichen. Durch herrn Vlrichen vo(-) Hutten, Poeten, vnd Orator der gantze(-) Christenheit, vnd zu(o)uoran dem Vatterland Teütscher Nation zo(o) nutz vnd gu(o)t, Von wegen gemeiner beschwernüß, vnd auch seiner eigenen notdurfft, Jn reimens weise beschriben. Iacta est alea. Jch habs gewagt* (Strasbourg: Knobloch, Schott, Schott, 1520 [late], 1520 [Oct.-Nov.], 1520 [Nov.-Dec.]); *Ein Clagschrift des Hochberu(o)mten vnd Eernueste(-) herrn Vlrichs vo(-) Hutten gekro(e)neten Poeten vn(-) Orator an alle stend Deütscher nation, Wie vnformlicher weise vn(-) ga(-)tz geschwind, vnersu(o)cht oder erfordert einiges rechte(-)s. Er mit eignem tyran(-)ische(-) gewalt, vo(-) dem Romaniste(-), an leib, eer vnd gu(o)t beschwert vn(-) beno(e)tiget werde. . . . Ein grosses dingk ist die warheit, vnd starck über alle. iij. Esdre iiij.* (Strasbourg: Flach, 1520); *Herr Vlrichs von Hutten anzo(e)ig Wie allwegen sich die Ro(e)mischen Bischo(e)ff, od(er) Ba(e)pst gegen den teütschen Kayßeren gehalten haben, vff dz kürtzst vß Chronicken vnd Historien gezogen, K. maiesta(e)t fürzu(o)bringen. Jch habs gewogt* (Strasbourg: Schott, Schott, 1520, 1521).

[66]Böcking, *Hutten,* 3:508.

[67]Ibid., 5:383-84.

in the waning months of 1520 and early 1521.[68] But since all of these treatises by Murner responded to polemical works published by Luther *after* midyear, they cannot really be used to determine how Luther may have been understood in Strasbourg through mid-1520. Still, it is worth mentioning that Murner did single out for extensive criticism many of the reforms that we have characterized as dignifying the spiritual status of the laity at the expense of the clergy.[69]

Slightly more useful for our purposes is Laux Gemigger's *The Praise of Luther and to the Honor of all Christendom.*[70] Published in two editions towards the end of 1520 or early in 1521, this verse treatise praises Luther as "a light of Christendom" chosen by God "to tell us your divine Word."[71] Unfortunately for our purposes, it is never very specific about what Luther has accomplished except to speak the "divine truth,"[72] reveal papal and clerical rascality, teach "good morals," and question indulgences.[73] At one point, however, Gemigger suggests that Luther has taught "Christ's teaching," namely, "how we have

[68]The first treatise, *A Christian and Fraternal Admonition,* left the presses of the Strasbourg printer Johannes Grüninger on November 11, 1520. It is a reply in large part to Luther's *Sermon on the New Testament, That Is, the Holy Mass,* his *To the Christian Nobility of the German Nation,* and *Concerning the Papacy in Rome against the Highly Famous Romanist at Leipzig.* A second edition, with some changes, appeared on January 21, 1521. The next treatise followed just fourteen days later. *Concerning Doctor Martin Luther's Teaching and Preaching,* published on November 24, 1520, dealt less with Luther personally and more with his influence. It also responded to Lazarus Spengler's *Defense and Christian Reply of an Honorable Lover of the Divine Truth of Holy Scripture* . . . . As we shall see, Spengler's treatise had been published in Strasbourg in October 1520, in a reprinted collection of Luther's writings. Murner's third treatise, *Concerning the Papacy, That Is, the Highest Authority of Christian Faith,* issued from Grüninger's press on December 13, 1520. It is a reply to Luther's *Resolutiones Lutherianae de potestate Papae* of 1519, his *To the German Nobility,* and his *Concerning the Papacy in Rome Against the Highly Famous Romanist at Leipzig.* This dry treatise became a special target of the famous polemic *Karsthans.* Murner's fourth and final treatise of 1520, *To the Most Mighty and Enlightened Nobility of the German Nation,* appeared around Christmas. The last treatise of this series appeared on February 17, 1521, when Murner issued *How Doctor M. Luther, Moved by the Wrong Reasons, Has Burned the Canon Law,* attacking Luther's justification for this act of defiance. See Wolfgang Pfeiffer-Belli, ed., *Thomas Murner: Kleine Schriften,* vols. 6 and 7 of *Thomas Murners Deutsche Schriften,* ed. Franz Schultz (Berlin, 1927-28).

[69]For example, in his earliest treatise he criticizes Luther's "priesthood of all believers" (e.g., Pfeiffer-Belli, *Murner,* 6:43, 6:58-59, 6:64-65), his suggested reform of the mass (e.g., ibid., 6:51-54, 5:64-65), and his understanding of a "spiritual" church (e.g., ibid., 6:75), and he specifically accuses Luther of turning too much over to the common people (ibid., 6:84).

[70]Laux Gemigger, *Zü lob dem Luther vnd eeren der gantzen Christenhait* (Strasbourg, 1520). The title verse reads: "Wo(e)lt yemant wissen wie der hieß / Der disen spruch außgon liess / Das hat gethon Laux Gemigger student / Auß vrsach, dz man des Luthers bu(e)cher hat verprent." (Adolf Laube, Annerose Schneider, and Sigrid Looß, *Flugschriften der frühen Reformationsbewegung (1518-1524)* [Berlin: Akademie-Verlag, 1983] 1:548-57).

[71]Chrisman identifies two 1520 editions. By way of contrast, Laube et al., while also identifying two Strasbourg and one Augsburg edition, date the first edition, the Augsburg edition, as 1521, but with some uncertainty. Internal evidence suggests that the treatise was written at the earliest about the end of November 1520, and at the latest by March 1521.

[72]Laube et al., *Flugschriften,* 1:548.   [73]Ibid., 1:550-51.

turned from good to evil," and has laid out the "teaching of the evangelists
. . . without additions." Luther has also explained "God's Word and increased
faith in Christ." Luther has driven out the "evil spirit," the origin of vices,
that teaches human laws rather than God's Word, establishes different clerical
"sects," and attributes unwarranted power to indulgences in order to trick
people out of their money. "For this reason Luther was sent by God to teach
us God's Word and good morals and to drive out the Antichrist here on
earth, also to see to it that God's Word not be fully spoiled and that the
Roman tyranny be recognized, that they should have no kingdom here on
earth."[74]

Readers might have inferred from Gemigger's attacks that Luther had
criticized noble families for making monks and nuns of their children and
had raised questions about the accumulation of property in noble hands
through this action, had attacked the ban, and had challenged clerical greed.[75]
"It is the penny's shine," Gemigger remarked at one point, "that accounts
for the treatment of the pious Luther, who is unjustly and improperly treated
because he reveals to us the Roman rascality as well as their great heresy."[76]
They even seek Luther's life. "He who now dares to tell the truth must turn
himself over to death," Gemigger claimed, explaining, "If speaking kindly
makes good friends, then saying the truth makes great enemies. It is because
Luther has proclaimed to us the divine truth that people are so hostile towards
him."[77] On several occasions Gemigger labeled the papacy the Antichrist and
suggested that the clergy needed to be reformed with "cold steel."[78] Gemigger
also identified Hutten and von Sickingen as supporters both of Luther and
of the truth.[79]

The strongest evidence in the early Strasbourg press that at least one lay
person received Luther's message much as I have summarized it comes from
an originally anonymous work by the Nuremberg city secretary, Lazarus
Spengler. In October 1520, the successors to the Schürer printing house in
Strasbourg issued a collection of Luther's works in German.[80] This collection

---

[74]Ibid., 1:552-53.   [75]Ibid., 1:548-49.   [76]Ibid., 1:549-50.   [77]Ibid., 1:554.

[78]For example, "Darumb lieben diener Christi ausserwelt, / das Gottes wort nit werd gantz
verfelt / so lond [= laßt] uns auff sein in ainer gmain, / lond uns die Ro(e)mer machen mit
dem kalten eysen rain!" Ibid., 1:554.

[79]Ibid., 1:557.

[80]*Martini Luthers der waren götlichen schrifft Doctors, Augustiner zu(o) Wittenbergk, mancherley
büchlin vnnd tractetlin* (Strasbourg: Schürer Erben, 1520). This collection was first published by
Andreas Cratander in Basel in May 1520. See Laube et al., *Flugschriften,* 1:512.

included a defense of Luther written by Spengler and first published anonymously in late 1519 in Augsburg.[81]

At the outset Spengler explained that since he had been criticized for his support of Luther and accused of being a disciple of Luther, he wished to explain why he regarded Luther's teachings as in no way improper. Spengler counted Luther among those concerning whom Christendom in general, and the holy Roman church in particular, should properly rejoice as being "a special, consoling, well-grounded advocate of the holy faith and propagator of holy, evangelical, Christian teaching."[82]

Spengler offered six basic reasons for this conclusion. First, Luther's teaching and sermons are Christian and wholesome as well as consistent with Christian order and reason because they are based on the holy Gospel, the prophets, and St. Paul.[83] Second, Spengler would let each reasonable, pious person determine whether Luther's teaching was consistent with Christian order and reason. For himself, Spengler remarked, "No teaching or preaching has seemed more straightforwardly reasonable, and I also cannot conceive of anything that would more closely match my understanding of Christian order than Luther's and his followers' teaching and instruction."[84] Spengler claimed not to be alone in this opinion. "Up to this point," he remarked, "I have also often heard from many excellent highly learned people of the spiritual and worldly estates that they were thankful to God that they lived to see the day when they could hear Doctor Luther and his teaching."[85] Third, Luther's doctrine, teaching, and instruction promoted Christ and salvation rather than Luther's own advantage. The indulgence preachers did just the opposite.[86] Fourth, any reasonable and truthful person who had heard Luther or his followers must acknowledge that his troubled conscience had been relieved of many scruples and doubtful errors.[87] Fifth, since Luther was a monk, preacher, and doctor and was required by his office not to keep silent about Christian teachings, but rather to venture even his life on their advocacy, it was proper, appropriate, and necessary for Luther to speak out against indulgences and other errors and scandals in Christendom once he became aware of them.[88] Sixth and finally, Luther had to the best of his ability and in accordance with his conscience based his teaching on the Gospel. He was willing, however, to be better instructed on the basis of the truth by German or French universities, by papal judgment, or by the church.[89]

---

[81]Ibid., 12:512. The title of the second edition runs: *Schutzred vnnd christe(-)liche antwurt ains erbern liebhabers gotlicher warhayt. der heyligen schrifft. auff etlicher vermaint widersprechen. mit anzaygu(-)g warumb Doctor Martini Luthers leer nit als vnchristenlich verworffen. sonder mer fur christenlich gehalten werde(-) sol. yetz widerumb corrigirt vn(-) mit ainem newen Dyalogo gebessert.* It was published in Nuremberg by Jobst Gutknecht in 1520. The Strasbourg collection reproduced the first edition. I have not been able to determine the exact title used in the Strasbourg edition.

[82]Laube et al., *Flugschriften,*   1:501. [83]Ibid., 1:502.   [84]Ibid., 1:504-5.   [85]Ibid., 1:505.
[86]Ibid., 1:507.   [87]Ibid.   [88]Ibid., 1:509-10.   [89]Ibid., 1:510.

It is under points two and four that Spengler asked a number of rhetorical questions that should be of some interest to us. Under point two he inquired with some heat whether it was not the case that "fairy-tale preachers" had disquieted the consciences of "many simple and unlearned people," directing them "to rely more on their works than on the grace and love of God." Have not these preachers urged people to depend more on ceremonies such as rosaries, the praying of psalms, pilgrimages, fasting, the lighting of candles, holy water, and other external works than on faith, more on law than on grace, more on the flesh than on the spirit? "Haven't these same teachers," Spengler asked, "caused us countless scruples in our hearts simply with the wide-ranging, clumsy institution of confession . . . ?"[90]

This led into a sharp criticism of indulgences. Have not these teachers, Spengler went on, elevated the indulgence and its utility above grace, the treasure of faith, and the blood of Christ? Have they not turned indulgences and all the sacraments into a business? In addition, Spengler was ashamed to report, these teachers have sold souls in heaven for money and misled "poor ignorant people" into believing that, thanks to the power of indulgences, they were freed from their sins and thereby delivered unto salvation.[91]

Have not these same preachers put forward so many ecclesiastical laws that they have thereby completely tossed out the commands of Christ? Spengler continued with his rhetorical questions. Is not a person who eats meat on Friday considered more reprehensible than an adulterer or blasphemer of God? And Spengler added to this indictment the misuse of the ecclesiastical ban.[92] "In my opinion," he concluded,

> Luther has cleaned up these scruples and errors by means of well-grounded Christian references to Holy Scripture so that every reasonable person can easily understand. For this reason, we should more properly commend, thank, and praise him for [what he has done] than to denounce him as a heretic and enemy of the church. And yet, except for some shadow boxing, nothing solid, nothing based in Holy Scripture, has been offered against [Luther's arguments].

But Luther's opponents tried to use force rather than reasoned arguments to combat him.[93]

Under point four Spengler asked whether "our preachers" had not sought to ensnare consciences by multiplying sins and by offering a false reassurance through indulgences.

> In this manner the human being is made more anxious than comforted, more led into doubt than refreshed, more led into excessive fear than into love and trust of God, despite the fact that according to the holy Gospel the yoke and way of salvation is completely sweet and

---

[90]Ibid., 1:505.   [91]Ibid., 1:505-6.   [92]Ibid., 1:506.   [93]Ibid., 1:506-7.

wholesome and is to be achieved more through an orderly well-founded trust in God than in these deceptive sermons.[94]

In short, this treatise presents Luther as an opponent of those who advocate external works over an inward trust and reliance on God's grace revealed in Christ. Luther comes off, above all, as a critic of indulgences. His criticism was based, Spengler claimed, solely on scripture. Luther's concern was to reassure consciences troubled by those who advocated external works, a burdensome form of confession, and indulgences for both the living and the dead. Luther's opponents responded to him with force, Spengler claimed, rather than with reasoned arguments grounded in scripture.

Conclusion

In this age when the hermeneutics of suspicion are almost axiomatic, it may seem hopelessly naive to argue that it was the correspondence between the content of Luther's message and the concerns and interests of the laity that best accounts for its appeal. I am persuaded of this, however, by several straightforward considerations. First, the publication statistics for Luther's works show large and geographically widespread demand for his writings, and especially for those that were more pastoral than polemical in nature. Second, in my own ongoing survey of popular literature by Catholic and evangelical writers, the issues that I have found most advocated or attacked are just those issues Ozment has identified, especially issues of Christian freedom and the spiritual dignity of lay status.[95] The works by Hutten, Gemigger, Murner, and Spengler illustrate this reception at a very early period in the reform movement. Third, and perhaps most to the point, if one assumes that behavior is a good indirect measure of which ideas people found appealing, then one needs to look at what really changed in the sixteenth century. And what you find when you compare life before and after the initial decades of the Reformation is that what actually changed corresponded closely (although not, of course, exactly) to those changes that Luther and other reformers had advocated on the basis of their new, learned understanding of Christian theology.[96]

We need to be much more careful than we have been in the past to determine what actually was read, how many people read it or heard it read, what message was contained in these treatises, and – often not the same thing – what ideas different readers actually appropriated from their reading or

---

[94]Ibid., 1:507-8.

[95]See, for example, my article *"Lutherschmähung?"*

[96]See, for example, Chrisman, *Strasbourg and the Reform: A Study in the Process of Change* (New Haven: Yale University Press, 1967); Marc Lienhard and Jakob Willer, *Straßburg und die Reformation* (Basel: Morstad Verlag, 1982); and René Bornert, *La Réforme Protestante du Culte à Strasbourg au XVI(e) Siècle (1523-1598)* (Leiden: Brill, 1981).

listening. It is perhaps the fourth point – the messages actually acquired by different readers or listeners – that is the most important. For the early period of the Reformation movement, the evidence for these "first impressions" is slight. The remarks by other early Strasbourg publicists (although each was complicated by a publication after mid-1520) suggest that Luther's message of reliance on God's promise rather than on human effort, a reliance that dignified the spiritual status of the laity often at the expense of clerical privilege and authority, got through at least to other publicists. Subsequent research will reveal how much farther this message may have gone. But that we are even asking such questions is due in no short measure to the stimulating work of such historians as Gerald Strauss.

Alternatives to the Lutheran Reformation and the Rise of Lutheran Identity

Heinz Schilling

In reexamining the early triumph of Lutheranism despite the presence of dissenting Protestant voices in the urban Reformation of northern and western Germany, Heinz Schilling finds that citizens of virtually every socioeconomic position adhered ultimately to the opinion that religious uniformity went hand in hand with political stability, which is to say with the common good. Whatever their initial doctrinal convictions, religious innovators became Lutheran in the end, and the few who did not were finally isolated and consigned to the fringes of civic polity. After reviewing a number of examples, Schilling concludes that "non-Lutheran Reformation movements failed because they were a challenge to two fundamental convictions held in old European society: the idea of close interrelations between church and society, and the idea of basic harmony as a precondition of any well-ordered and peaceful state and society." The Lutheran understanding of the Eucharist coincided with "the sacral interpretation of the urban community" while Zwinglian sacramentarianism did not.

ONCE THE REFORMATION TOOK HOLD in northern and western Germany, the results were remarkably homogeneous: apart from a few special cases, the renewal of urban and territorial churches was conducted according to Lutheran principles. It was Lutheranism which over generations determined the religious, cultural, and, to a considerable extent, the political identity of the people living in these regions of Germany.[1] In view of the homogeneity of this result, we could easily fail to realize that even in this part of the empire the earliest phases of the Reformation were by no means determined by Wittenberg alone. Of course, Martin Luther stands at the beginning of almost all the Reformation movements in Germany; but in addition to those that looked to him there were from the outset ideas and persons that only partly agreed or did not at all agree with Luther and his Wittenberg followers.

The Problem

The history of the earliest Protestant movements, which were even more concentrated in towns in the Hanseatic region than in southern Germany, has had to be reconstructed largely from later sources, which were written

---

[1]Cf. for instance Joachim Whaley, *Religious Toleration and Social Change in Hamburg 1529-1819* (Cambridge: Cambridge University Press, 1985), 169-72, 186-96, 208.

mainly from a Lutheran point of view.[2] In consequence, this history has usually been told in anachronistic terms, namely as the history of an irreconcilable clash of Protestant positions. But this is the perspective of 1525 and the period after the Peasants' War and the Münster uprising, when intra-Protestant contrasts had become obvious to everyone. In order to tell the story adequately, we have to be aware of this biased perspective of the rising Lutheran orthodoxy. We have to suspect that the Lutheran monopoly on interpreting the earliest evangelical movement has meant a misrepresentation of non-Lutheran currents – concerning their share as well as their arguments.[3]

In the following, I will analyze the statements that are scattered in the literature and in the sources regarding the character and the strength of the abortive alternatives to the Lutheran Reformation; these were also alternative political and social paths into modern times. As we are well informed on the early Anabaptists,[4] this article will be centered on the currents called Sacra-

[2]For Luther's point of view, see D. *Martin Luthers Werke* (Weimar: Böhlau, 1883-1986) (hereafter WA), *Briefwechsel* (hereafter BR), concerning Danzig (1525), WA, BR, 6:319-20, cf. 305-7, 389-90; Münster (1532), WA BR 6:398-401. Cf. also Martin Brecht, "Luthertum als politische und soziale Kraft in den Städten," in *Kirche und Gesellschaftlicher Wandel in Deutschen und niederländischen Städten der werdenden Neuzeit*, ed. Franz Petri (Cologne and Vienna: Böhlau, 1980), 1-21, esp. 11, n. 49; 15-16, nn. 86-88; and 17-19. Günter Mühlpfordt, "Luther und die 'Linken' – Eine Untersuchung seiner Schwärmerterminologie," in *Martin Luther. Leben, Werk, Wirkung*, ed. Günter Vogler (Berlin: Akademie Verlag, 1986), 325-45; also Mark U. Edwards, Jr., *Luther and the False Brethren* (Stanford: Stanford University Press, 1976).

[3]Most important for a new interpretation of the "non-Lutherans" are Bernhard Lohse, "Dogma und Bekenntnis in der Reformation: Von Luther zum Konkordienbuch," in *Handbuch der Dogmen- und Theologiegeschichte*, ed. Carl Andresen (Göttingen: Vandenhoeck und Ruprecht, 1980), 2:1-164, here 28; idem, "Die Stellung der 'Schwärmer' und Täufer in der Reformationsgeschichte," *Archiv für Reformationsgeschichte* 60 (1969): 5-26, here 24; Rainer Wohlfeil, *Einführung in die Geschichte der deutschen Reformation* (Munich: Beck, 1982), 159 (with citation of further literature); Wilfried Ehbrecht, "Reformation, Sedition und Kommunikation," in *Soest, Stadt, Territorium, Reich*, ed. Gerhard Köhn (Soest: Mocker and Jahn, 1981), 243-325, here 244, 246, 280. Useless for these purposes is the old-fashioned *Reformatorenlexikon*, ed. Robert Stupperich (Gütersloh: Gütersloher Verlagshaus, 1984), as for instance the article on the Brunswick spiritualist, Gottschalk Kruse. Important on the early Reformation is Hans-Jürgen Goertz, *Pfaffenhaß und groß Geschrei* (Munich: C. H. Beck, 1987).

[4]Klaus Deppermann, *Melchior Hoffman. Soziale Unruhen und apokalyptische Visionen im Zeitalter der Reformation* (Göttingen: Vandenhoeck and Ruprecht, 1979); Hans-Jürgen Goertz, *Die Täufer. Geschichte und Deutung* (Munich: Beck, 1980); James M. Stayer, *Anabaptists and the Sword* (Lawrence, Kans.: Coronado Press, 1976); Stayer, "Die Schweizer Brüder. Versuch einer historischen Definition," *Mennonitische Geschichtsblätter* 34, NF 29 (1977): 7-34; Heinold Fast, ed., *Der linke Flügel der Reformation* (Bremen: Schunemann, 1962); Gerhard Brendler, *Das Täuferreich zu Münster, 1534/35* (Berlin: Deutscher Verlag der Wissenschaften, 1966); Günter Vogler, "Martin Luther und das Täuferreich zu Münster," in *Martin Luther*, ed. Vogler, 235-54. Additional bibliographies may be found in every issue of the *Literaturbericht* of the *Archiv für Reformationsgeschichte* beginning in 1972; the appropriate category is part 2.6, "Täufertum und heterodoxe Richtungen."

mentarian, Zwinglian, and Spiritualist.[5] A clear distinction between these and the mystic spiritualists and early Anabaptists is not possible. By inquiring into the alternatives to the Lutheran Reformation, we will also consider the extent of and the limitations upon the renewal of European society in its transition from the late Middle Ages to the early modern period, especially within the modernizing dynamism of the sixteenth century.[6]

The History of Non-Lutheran Reformers

We know about non-Lutheran currents within the early Reformation in several towns of northern and western Germany, namely for the Baltic Sea region from Livonia in the far northeast to Lübeck and Schleswig-Holstein in the west as well as for the North Sea coast, Lower Saxony, Westphalia, the Rhineland down to the imperial town of Frankfurt, and the Landgraviate of Hesse.[7] Frankfurt and Hesse were already part of the transitional region between northwestern and southern Germany, primarily influenced by the upper German and Swiss version of Reformation theology.

[5]Cf. Johannes Schildhauer, *Soziale, politische und religiöse Auseinandersetzungen in den Hansestädten Stralsund, Rostock und Wismar im ersten Drittel des 16. Jahrhunderts* (Weimar: Böhlau, 1959), 159-94, in which the author gives a social interpretation of the movement; Bernd Moeller, *Reichsstadt und Reformation* (Gütersloh: Gütersloher Verlagshaus, 1962), 65, n. 40, together with the commentary in Moeller, *Reichsstadt und Reformation*, 2nd ed. (Berlin: Evangelische Verlagsanstalt, 1987), 90-94; Gottfried W. Locher, *Die zwinglische Reformation im Rahmen der europäischen Kirchengeschichte* (Göttingen and Zürich: Vandenhoeck and Ruprecht, 1979), 633-36; most important: Ernst Koch, "'Zwinglianer' zwischen Ostsee und Harz in den Anfangsjahren der Reformation (1525-1532)," *Zwingliana* 16 (1983-85): 517-45, showing that Locher is wrong in telling us that most of the "non-Lutherans" were pupils of Zwingli. Cf. also Adolf Laube, "Radikalität als Forschungsproblem der frühen Reformationsgeschichte," *Zeitschrift für Geschichtsforschung* 35 (1987): 218-30; Mühlpfordt, "Der frühe Luther als Autorität der Radikalen," in *Die frühbürgerliche Revolution in Deutschland*, ed. Max Steinmetz (Berlin: Akademie-Verlag, 1985), 167-83; Looß, "Zur Haltung radikal bürgerlicher Kräfte vor und während des Bauernkrieges," *Zeitschrift für Geschichtswissenschaft* 36 (1988): 325-30; idem, "Radical Views of the Early Andreas Karlstadt (1520-1525)," in *Radical Tendencies in the Reformation*, ed. Hans J. Hillerbrand (Kirksville, Mo.: Sixteenth Century Journal Publishers, 1988), 43-53; Adolf Laube et al., *Die Epoche des Übergangs vom Feudalismus zum Kapitalismus von den siebziger Jahren des 15. Jahrhunderts bis 1789*, Deutsche Geschichte in zwölf Bänden 3 (Cologne: Pahl-Rugenstein, 1983), 125-26, 141-47, 151-59, 172-87, 198-203, 209-11; Horst Weigelt, *Spiritualistische Tradition. Die Geschichte des Schwenckfeldertums in Schlesien* (Berlin: de Gruyter, 1973).

[6]See my interpretation of this most important century in Schilling, *Aufbruch und Krise*, Siedler Deutsche Geschichte (Berlin: Siedler, 1988).

[7]For the general history of that region during the sixteenth century, cf. Schilling, "Die politische Elite nordwestdeutscher Städte in den religiösen Auseinandersetzungen des 16. Jahrhunderts," in *Stadtbürgertum und Adel in der Reformation*, ed. Wolfgang J. Mommsen (Stuttgart: Klett-Cotta, 1979), 235-308, forthcoming in English translation together with several of my other articles on Reformation history, in the series, Studies in Medieval and Reformation Thought (Leiden: Brill); Schilling, "The Reformation in the Hanseatic Cities," *Sixteenth Century Journal* 14 (1983): 443-56; Schilling, *Konfessionskonflikt und Staatsbildung* (Gütersloh: Gütersloher Verlagshaus, 1981), esp. 138-41, 376-79.

We are informed best about the events in the towns of Wolmar, Dorpat, and Reval in Livonia;[8] the "Wendish" Hanseatic towns – that is, above all in Wismar, but less spectacularly also in Stralsund and Rostock;[9] and in Braunschweig, one of the most important inland Hanseatic towns.[10] Traces of non-Lutheran Reformation movements can also be detected in the Pomeranian towns, mainly in Stettin and Stolp, but also in the imperial free city of Lübeck;[11] in Kiel, Schleswig, Flensburg, and Itzehoe in Schleswig-Holstein;[12] in the inland towns Celle, Goslar, Magdeburg,[13] Münster, Minden, and Soest;[14] and finally also in the West, in Wesel, Cologne, Aachen, and in

[8]Deppermann, *Melchior Hoffman*, 36-78.

[9]On these towns in general, see Schildhauer, *Auseinandersetzungen in den Hansestädten*. On Wismar, see *Hanserezesse*, ed. Klaus Friedland and Gottfried Wentz, sec. 4, vol. 2 (Cologne and Vienna: Böhlau, 1970), Rezess no. 86, art. 277-335, pp. 118-25; art. 410, p. 136; art. 475-76, p. 145; art. 597, p. 165; M. Dieterich Schröder, *Kirchen-Historie des Evangelischen Mecklenburgs vom Jahr 1518 bis 1742*, part 1 (Rostock, 1788), 81-82, 101-3, 126-27, 134-42, 151-55, 318-25, 327-30, 334, 361-67; G. C. F. Lisch, "Ueber die evangelische Kirchen-Visitation vom J(ahre) 1525," *Jahrbücher des Vereins für mecklenburgische Geschichte und Altertumskunde* 8 (1843): 37-51, 50-51; J. ten Doornkaat Koolman, "Die Täufer in Mecklenburg," *Mennonitische Geschichtsblätter* 18 (1961): 20-56, 20-39; Koch, "Zwinglianer," 517-22. On Rostock: Koolmann, "Täufer," 40-46; Axel Vorberg, *Die Einführung der Reformation in Rostock* (Halle, 1897), 36-37, 40-41, 44, 48-49, 53-54. On Stralsund: Thomas Kantzow, *Chronik von Pommern in hochdeutscher Mundart*, 2 vols., ed. Georg Gaebel (Stettin, 1897-98), 1:389-90, 394; 2:233; Wilfried Ehbrecht, "Köln - Osnabrück - Stralsund. Rat und Bürgerschaft hansischer Städte zwischen religiöser Erneuerung und Bauernkrieg," in *Kirche und gesellschaftlicher Wandel* (n. 2 above), 23-63.

[10]The most important primary source is: "Was vor ein zustannth zu Braunschweich im Kirchenn Regemennth gewessenn. Anno 1523," Stadtarchiv Braunschweig H III 7, No. 1, 23-37. Of the printed literature, see Werner Spiess, *Geschichte der Stadt Braunschweig im Nachmittelalter* (Brunswick: Waisenhaus, 1966), 1:62-65; Wolfgang A. Jünke, "Des Prädikanten Johann Kopmann Bekenntnis, ein bisher unbekanntes Dokument der stadtbraunschweigischen Reformationsgeschichte," *Braunschweigisches Jahrbuch* 58 (1977): 31-42; criticizing this interpretation is Koch, "Zwinglianer," 529-38; cf. also Olaf Mörke, *Rat und Bürger in der Reformation* (Hildesheim: Lax, 1983), 135, 145-46; Ulrich Bubenheimer, "Thomas Müntzer in Braunschweig," part 1, *Braunschweigisches Jahrbuch* 65 (1984): 37-78; idem, "Thomas Müntzer und der Anfang der Reformation in Braunschweig," *Nederlands Archif voor Kerkgeschiedenis* 65 (1985): 1-30, esp. 22-29.

[11]Georg Gaebel, ed., *Des Thomas Kantzow Chronik von Pommern* (Stettin, 1897), 399-401; Wilhelm Böhmer, ed., *Thomas Kantzow's Chronik von Pommern* (Stettin, 1835), 160-61, 165-69 (about Dr. Amandus in Stolp and Stettin); Wilhelm Jannasch, *Reformationsgeschichte Lübecks* (Lübeck: Schmidt-Röhmhild, 1958), 146.

[12]Deppermann, *Melchior Hoffman*, 84-118. Perhaps in Hamburg, too: Rainer Postel, *Die Reformation in Hamburg, 1517-1528* (Gütersloh: Gütersloher Verlagshaus, 1986), 146-59, 183, 186-91, 243-44.

[13]Koch, "Zwinglianer," 539, n. 149; 522-38.

[14]Wilfried Ehbrecht, "Form und Bedeutung innerstädtischer Kämpfe am Übergang vom Mittelalter zur Neuzeit: Minden 1405-1535," in *Städtische Führungsgruppen und Gemeinde in der werdenden Neuzeit*, ed. Ehbrecht (Cologne and Vienna: Böhlau, 1980), 115-52, esp. 149; Alois Schröer, *Die Reformation in Westfalen*, vol. 2 (Münster: Aschendorf, 1983), 280-85. Different opinions on the theology of Nicolaus Krages may be found in Martin Brecht, "Reformation und Kirchenordnung in Minden 1530," *Jahrbuch für westfälische Kirchengeschichte* 73 (1980): 34-37; Ehbrecht, "Reformation, Sedition und Kommunikation," 251-53, 261-64.

the towns of the Maas valley, above all in Maastricht.[15] In the imperial city of Frankfurt,[16] situated at the southwest corner of the region analyzed, the early Reformation was influenced more by the Upper German and Zwinglian than by the Lutheran movement; consequently, the question of Lutheran dominance and heterodox undercurrent must here be turned upside down. This picture is doubtless incomplete because there are cases like Göttingen and the Hanseatic town of Lemgo in Westfalia where we only know that preachers (Hüventhal and Peter Grossmann) presented radical opinions, but we do not know anything about their exact theological position.[17]

Besides the dominating towns, there are some territories with more or less clear traces of non-Lutheran approaches to the Reformation – the imperial earldom of East Frisia, the duchies of Jülich and Cleves on the Lower Rhine, and the Landgraviate of Hesse. In the north and in the west, in East Frisia and Jülich, Netherlandish impulses were decisive. Here political borders did not yet mean cultural or social separation, for there was a long tradition of contact with the Low Countries. In the early history of Protestantism, they played a role only insofar as they offered innovators a chance to avoid prosecution by emigrating to a neighboring territory. As from an early date the Habsburg government in the Netherlands pursued a consistent anti-Protestant policy, emigration usually took place from West to East, as, for instance, in the case of the well-known "Wassenberg preachers," who were to play an important role in Münster's shift to radical Anabaptism. In the twenties these preachers, in the western border districts of Jülich, were advocates of spiritualistic and sacramentarian views that had developed in the Maas valley and were built on the pre-Reformation theology of reform in the Netherlands (*Devotio Moderna*), and that were probably also connected with humanism.[18]

Farther to the north, East Frisia was for a long time open to almost all currents of the young Protestant movement – "real" Lutheranism, different

[15]Gerhard Goeters, "Die Rolle des Täufertums in der Reformationsgeschichte des Niederrheins," *Rheinische Vierteljahresblätter* 24 (1959): 217-36, here 221-28; Franz Petri, "Maß und Bedeutung der reformatorischen Strömungen in den niederländischen Maaslanden im 16. Jahrhundert," in *Reformation und Humanismus. Robert Stupperich zum 65. Geburtstag,* ed. Martin Greschat and Gerhard Goeters (Witten: Luther-Verlag, 1969), 212-24.

[16]Sigrid Jahns, *Frankfurt, Reformation und Schmalkaldischer Bund* (Frankfurt: Kramer, 1976), 33-34, 55-56, 148-53.

[17]Franz Lubecus, *Bericht über die Einführung der Reformation in Göttingen im Jahre 1529,* ed. Hans Volz (Göttingen: Vandenhoeck and Ruprecht, 1967), 16-24; 27-32; 44, nn. 97-98; 54-55, n. 220. See also Bernd Moeller, "Die Reformation," in *Göttingen. Geschichte einer Universitätsstadt,* ed. Dietrich Denecke and Helga-Maria Kühn, vol. 1 (Göttingen: Vandenhoeck and Ruprecht, 1987), 492-514, here 497-502; Albrecht Saathoff, *Aus Göttingens Kirchengeschichte* (Göttingen: Vandenhoeck and Reprecht, 1929), 94-95; Schilling, *Konfessionskonflikt,* 77-78, 100.

[18]Dionysius Vinne, Hendrik van Tongeren *alias* Slachtscaep, Hendrik Roll, Johannes Campanus, Johannes Klopreiss (Schröer, *Reformation in Westfalen,* 2:356-61, 396-99, referring to the older literature). Decisive for the new interpretation are Goeters, "Die Rolle des Täufertums," and Petri, "Maß und Bedeutung." Cf. also Franz Petri and Georg Droege, eds., *Rheinische Geschichte,* vol. 2 (Düsseldorf: Schwann, 1976), 36-37.

forms of Spiritualism and Sacramentalism, and Anabaptism.[19] Here it is so
difficult to distinguish between main currents and undercurrents that the
terms *norm* and *alternative* are not adequate to Frisian historical reality. Attempts
to enforce Lutheranism or the Zwinglian, Upper German version of the
Reformation as the only accepted basis for a homogeneous territorial church
failed time and again. Only during the last quarter of the sixteenth century,
that is, in the course of confessionalization, did the picture become clear:
Calvinism was established in the western parts of the country, including the
important harbor town of Emden, and Lutheranism in the eastern and southern
parts, including the capital Aurich. Nonetheless, the Anabaptists also held
their ground, although they were now clearly a dissenting minority.

While the East Frisians received some stimulus from Wittenberg,[20] they
got most of their reforming impulses from the neighboring Netherlands and
its late medieval theology of ecclesiastical and religious reform – the *Devotio
Moderna,* the Brothers of the Common Life, and humanism. Consequently,
in East Frisia a native Reformation theology developed, independent of
Luther as well as of Zwingli. This was especially evident in the Frisian
understanding of the Eucharist, in a spiritualist interpretation of salvation,
and in an independent ecclesiology.[21]

In Hesse it was not cultural and regional connections but the peculiarities
of the princely church that facilitated non-Lutheran currents within the
quickly developing Protestant territorial church. This had not been the case
at first. For when in 1524 Landgrave Philip the Magnanimous supported the
innovators openly, the head of the young Protestant territorial church was
Adam Krafft, a confirmed Lutheran. Thus, the landgraviate was shielded
from Zwinglian and humanistic impulses coming from Frankfurt, that emporium
of Reformation printing and pamphlets, which was strongly influenced by
southern German theology.[22] Franz Lambert of Avignon, the Homburg synod,

---

[19]Anneliese Sprengler-Ruppenthal, introduction to *Die evangelischen Kirchenordnungen des
XVI. Jahrhunderts,* ed. Emil Sehling, vol. 7, pt. 1 (Tübingen: Mohr/Siebeck, 1963), 312-16;
Menno Smid, *Ostfriesische Kirchengeschichte* (Pewsum: Verlag der Ostfriesischen Deichacht, 1974);
Deppermann, *Melchior Hoffman,* 139-42, 271-77.

[20]WA, *BR,* 3:115; also 2:632.

[21]For the interesting East Frisian case, which cannot be analyzed in detail here, cf. Smid,
Ostfriesische Kirchengeschichte, 115, 125-29, 132-36, 139; Sprengler-Ruppenthal (as in n. 19),
314-15, n. 17; the essays in Schilling, *Civic Calvinism in Northwest Germany and the Netherlands*
(Kirksville, Mo.: Sixteenth Century Journal Publishers, 1991); Eduard Meiners, *Oostvrieschlandts
Kerkelyke Geschiedenisse . . . ,* 2 vols. (Groningen, 1738-39), 1:53-64. Cf. also U. Gäbler, "Zur
Verbreitung des Zwinglianismus in den Niederlanden," in *Zwingli und Europa,* ed. P. Blickle,
A. Lindt, and A. Schindler (Zürich: Vandenhoeck and Ruprecht, 1985), 217-36.

[22]Walter Sohm, *Territorium umd Reformation in der hessischen Geschichte 1526-1555* (Marburg:
Elwert, 1915), 77-79; Heinrich Heppe, *Kirchengeschichte beider Hessen* (Marburg, 1878), 212-13;
without usefulness for new questions on the Hessian Reformation is Walter Heinemeyer, "Das
Zeitalter der Reformation," in *Das Werden Hessens,* ed. Walter Heinemeyer (Marburg: Elwert,
1986), 225-65; Jahns, *Frankfurt,* 56, 159-63.

and the "Reformation of the Churches of Hesse" (*Reformatio ecclesiarum Hessiae*), which were oriented towards Zwingli, remained an interlude without lasting influence on the territorial church of Hesse. On the other hand, in spite of Adam Krafft the Reformation in Hesse was never clearly Lutheran either. This became obvious when in the Marburg Colloquy on the Eucharist in 1529, the theological differences between Wittenberg and Zürich manifested themselves publicly. Numerous Hessian ministers who had seemed Lutheran now decided in favor of Zwingli's interpretation of the Eucharist.[23]

Later there were always theologians in the territorial church of Hesse who freely advocated a Zwinglian interpretation of the Eucharist; but these theologians usually did not see any difficulties in accepting the other doctrines of German Lutheranism, which became the core of the Hessian church confession.[24] This resistant Zwinglian current within a more or less Lutheran territorial church was possible because the landgrave and some of his closest counsellors approved of contacts with Zürich and again and again gave their support to Zwinglians who were persecuted in Lutheran Germany. In fact, this continued even after the Religious Peace of Augsburg in 1555 sanctioned the monopoly of Lutheranism in the empire.[25] In view of this protection by the princes, it is not possible to regard the non-Lutheran currents as alternative movements in Hesse or in East Frisia.

The sketch given here could be extended considerably for both the towns and the territories if one analyzed systematically the earliest manifestations

[23]For instance, Hartmann Ibach in Marburg (Eduard Wintzer, "Hartmann Ibach von Marburg, einer der ersten Reformationsprediger Hessens," *Zeitschrift des Vereins für hessische Geschichte und Landeskunde*, N. F. 34 [1910]: 115-83, 174-77); Dionysius Melander the Elder (Oskar Hütteroth, *Die althessischen Pfarrer der Reformationszeit*, 2 parts [Marburg, Kassell: N. G. Elwert, 1953-58], 221-22; K. Martin Sauer "Dionysius d. Ä., ca. 1486-1561, Leben und Briefe," *Jahrbuch der hessischen kirchengeschichtlichen Vereinigung* 29 [1978]: 1-36). Cf. also Johannes Hefenträger (Hütteroth, *Althessische Pfarrer*, 127-38). The theology of the early Protestant church in Hesse is interpreted in accord with the confessional loyalties of the authors: August F. C. Vilmar, *Geschichte des Confessionsstandes der evangelischen Kirche in Hessen* (Marburg, 1860) (Lutheran); Heinrich Heppe, *Die confessionelle Entwicklung der hessischen Kirche oder das gute Recht der reformierten Kirche in Kurhessen* (Frankfurt a. M., 1853) (Reformed); Wilhelm Maurer, *Bekenntnisstand und Bekenntnisentwicklung in Hessen* (Gütersloh: Gütersloher Verlagshaus, 1955) (Lutheran); Hannelore Jahr (Reformed), "Einleitung," in *Die evangelischen Kirchenordnungen*, ed. Sehling, vol. 8, pt. 1: "Hessen," ed. Hannelore Jahr (Tübingen: Mohr/Siebeck, 1965); Jahr, "Reformation und Tradition in der hessischen Kirchenordnung von 1566," theol. diss., University of Göttingen, 1955.

[24]Cf. the articles on Dionysius Melander the Elder and on Johannes Lening in Hütteroth, *Althessische Pfarrer*, 221-22, 202-9; Sohm, *Territorium und Reformation*, 77ff.; Gerhard Rau, "Hyperius, Andreas (16.5.1511-1.2.1564)," *Theologische Realenzyklopädie*, ed. Gerhard Krause and Gerhard Müller, vol. 15 (Berlin and New York: de Gruyter), 778-81.

[25]Heppe, *Kirchengeschichte*, 1:224-27, 242-46, 255-61; Kurt Jakob Rüetschi, "Baptist Johannes Wisamer von 1492 bis 1564/65). Ein Zwinglianer in Norddeutschland," *Zwingliana* 15 (1979-82): 124-35, here 133-34; Hütteroth, *Althessische Pfarrer*, 222. In the late 1530s, Bucer gained considerable influence on Philip's church policy – but without long-lasting consequences for the character of the Hessian territorial church. Cf. John C. Stalnaker, "Anabaptism, Martin Bucer, and the Shaping of the Hessian Protestant Church," *Journal of Modern History* 48 (1976): 601-43.

of Protestantism, paying close attention to the archival evidence from medium-sized and small towns. Methodologically, there is much to be said in favor of calling the early Reformation "syncretic" rather than "Lutheran" whenever direct connections to Wittenberg cannot be proved. In any case, reading Luther's works obviously does not provide a basis for concluding that Wittenberg was the only or at least the dominant influence. Especially in the western part of the empire, pre-Reformation and Upper German approaches to reform were usually combined with Lutheranism; rivalry or even opposition did not develop openly before 1525.

Ecclesiastical, Social, and Political Impact

There is no doubt that in the north and west of the empire the overwhelming majority of religious innovators became Lutheran in the end, and in fact most did so early and without problems. Only this discovery of a Lutheran identity by the majority made those who held a different opinion into a dissenting minority. The pluralism of the early Reformation polarized into an accepted Lutheran orthodoxy on the one hand and a persecuted heterodoxy on the other. Non-Lutheran dissent appeared only in exceptional cases and even then merely for a few years as a possible means toward Protestant renewal. This development, which started in 1525 and reached its peak early in the 1550s, made the non-Lutheran currents a multifarious, often contradictory alternative, one that no longer had any chance of realization. After the turning point of 1525, Lutherans and the dissenting non-Lutherans were opposed to each other. This alternative movement remained vital right into the 1530s; and it could thus often claim an influence on the Reformation process, or in a few cases even take a position of leadership. In the north and west of the empire, Lutheranism remained in close contact with popular movements in towns and countryside well after 1525, and so in northwestern Germany there existed two different types of communal reformation (*Gemeindereformation*) – the dominant Lutheran – and the dissenting non-Lutheran.

It is this simultaneity of two conceptions of communal reformation, opposed as they were in their basic theological positions, that makes the situation in northern and western Germany so interesting. My attempt to describe the position of the alternative, non-Lutheran concepts within the general context of Reformation history and to classify their possible impact on an alternative way of ecclesiastical, social, and political development will proceed in three steps. First, I will describe the theological, social, and political opinions and aims of the non-Lutheran movement; second, I will try to sketch its social profile; and third, I will analyze the reaction in the towns and the territories. On the basis of this information, in the last section I will reflect in general on the significance of the rise and defeat of alternative conceptions of reformation for the structure of early modern society and on the type of change this society was ready to accept.

It is difficult and often even impossible to give a precise and detailed description of the teachings of the early non-Lutheran reformers. If we take seriously the idea of a pluriformity in early Protestant theology,[26] we have to look at each theologian and lay preacher individually and separately. This has been done recently in a couple of cases by Ernst Koch. His results are astonishing.[27] Despite the complaints of Lutheran theologians about Zwinglian "Sacramentarians," Koch has proved that there were very few real Zwinglians in the North and West of Germany, apart from such regions as Hesse, Frankfurt, and East Frisia, which were traditionally in close contact with Swiss theology. Besides Anabaptist ideas, which appeared relatively late, the non-Lutheran Reformation currents in the regions under consideration were influenced strongly by Schwenckfeldian, quietistic, spiritualistic, and mystical ideas, and to a lesser extent by the activist and revolutionary version whose representatives Lutherans characterized as "fanatics."

In the early stage mystical spiritualism came obviously to the fore: "The Holy Spirit goes around teaching in his body like a fly" ("der heilige Geist lehre ihn im Leib herum wie eine Bremse"). This is how Gottschalk Kruse characterizd the early spiritualist Hans Horneborch from Braunschweig in 1521.[28] Notwithstanding all the differences in the ecclesiastical and theological currents within the alternative Reformation, spiritualism seems to have had the most important impact on the character and ideas of the non-Lutheran camp during the early years, mainly with regard to its concepts of the new order in church and society.

At least six points characterized the non-Lutheran strains within the early reform movement:

1. A doctrine of the sacraments that was radical in comparison with Luther's and that – first for the Eucharist, then also for baptism – emphasized subjective willingness more strongly than the objective and sacral effect of the sacramental act, and that, in consequence, could yield a more rational understanding of the sacrament.[29]

2. A purified ritual – without any traditional sacral garments, without the sign of the cross, without the laying on of hands, without benediction, and without confession.

3. The rejection of sacred pictures, which were regarded as an "exterior thing" that would inhibit the spirit striving after God.

[26]Siegfried Bräuer, "Müntzerforschung von 1965 bis 1975," *Luther-Jahrbuch* 45 (1978): 102-239, here 128.

[27]Koch, "Zwinglianer."

[28]Quoted by Bubenheimer in "Müntzer und der Anfang," 26, 28-29.

[29]Besides Zwingli and Karlstadt, sometimes Oecolampadius's influence is made responsible, as in the case of the Stralsund preacher Christian Ketelhut (Daniel Cramer, *Das Grosse Pomrische Kirchen Chronicon* [Stettin, 1628], 85). Cf. also Koch, "Zwinglianer," 538-41; Smid, *Ostfriesische Kirchengeschichte*, 125.

4. An understanding of the Bible and the Word of God that either demanded literal authenticity or was open to subjectivity and spiritualistic vagueness.

5. A corresponding conception of church and congregation, the legal and institutional framework of which more or less radically called into question church property and the regular salaries of the ministry as well as any form of hierarchy and supervision within the church; sometimes even the legitimacy of the pastorate was denied.[30]

6. In addition to these points, the revolutionary and eschatological versions of the non-Lutheran Reformation called for a violent enforcement of the reforms. Only a minority of alternative reformers held this radical opinion. Nevertheless, Lutherans cleverly declared it a general feature of the alternative movement, a "carnal" distortion of Protestant freedom.[31] In connection with this appeal to violence, these alternative reformers usually demanded the total submission of politics and society to religion – that is, they presented a monistic model of the relations between state and church, contradicting spiritualistic principles in their own camp as well as the Lutheran doctrine of Two Kingdoms. These radicals within the alternative camp wanted "to change not only the doctrine but especially also politics and the secular order" ("nicht alleine der lehre, besonder auch der politien und weltichen regiments enderen"), as a contemporary wrote critically. And soon it was said that in addition to the renewal of the church those radical reformers were eager "to rule also in the town hall" ("das rathaus mit zu regieren").[32]

The situation in East Frisia, where the spiritualistic version was exceptionally strong, shows clearly in which direction this alternative Reformation tended: When these spiritualistic reformers were forced to formulate their confession of faith in 1528, this turned out to be a manifesto in which, for the first time in history, "a church declared its own uselessness."[33] And in some places church practice really ended up in a dissolution of the organized church, as Earl Ennos II wrote in a letter to Philip of Hesse two years later: Preaching and praying would be called into question and would even be regarded as obstacles to the believer's relationship with God. The sacraments would only be accepted, if at all, as an external sign. The Eucharist was no longer to be

---

[30]Cramer, *Pomrische Kirchen Chronicon,* 75-81, 85-87, 93-96.

[31]For instance, Urbanus Rhegius in his two letters to Pomerania: *Vrbani Regii . . . Deutsche Bücher vnnd Schrifften,* ed. Ernestus Regius, pt. 3 (Nuremberg, 1562), ii-vi, vii-xi, quoted in Cramer, *Pomrische Kirchen Chronicon,* 84. Cf. also Laube, "Radikalität als Forschungsproblem," 224.

[32]*Das Chronicon Domesticum et gentile des Heinrich Piel,* ed. M. Krieg (Münster: Aschendorf, 1981), 111, 121, with regard to Nikolaus Krage at Minden.

[33]Deppermann, *Melchior Hoffman,* 135.

celebrated in church but as a daily meal in private houses with beer, water, or wine.[34]

In spite of all the differences in detail, the tendency of the alternative Reformation was clear: It declared the Reformation pastor to be just as superfluous as the Catholic priest. It questioned not only the hierarchically organized papal church but also every form of institutional church. This destroyed the interlinking of religion and society, the bonds between the ecclesiastical and the secular-political order, which had developed during the Middle Ages and which were re-established by the triumphant denominational churches of the old European period. The radically monistic version of the alternative Reformation wanted the sovereignty of religion and thus the abolition of any independent secular power. The peaceable spiritualistic version, on the other hand, wanted the other pole to collapse. According to its adherents, congregation did not manifest itself in a homogeneous and publicly organized church, either as a town or as a territorial church, but only in circles that avoided legal and institutional constraints. In its most extreme form, spiritualism abandoned the congregation completely in favor of the subjectivity of the individual Christian.

According to all available information, the social composition of the group of primary supporters – that is, of the preachers and active missionaries – was hardly different from that of the Lutheran movement. It consisted mainly of clergymen and intellectuals, above all teachers at municipal schools. Indeed, in the beginning the alternative Reformation was also a "revolution" within the clergy. It may be that Augustinians were underrepresented because of their close connections to Luther and that humanists were overrepresented because of their more rational interpretation of the Eucharist. A special social element, which did not exist in Lutheranism, is found among the "itinerant preachers" (*Wanderprediger*), who, like Melchior Hoffman, were craftsmen. Here we find some persons whose poor education and personal difficulties gave them real trouble. Johann Wulff, called Campensis, for example, failed again and again in private as well as in professional life.[35]

Regarding the group of secondary supporters, that is the passive adherents, there seem to have been sharp differences from the Lutheran movement. Compared with the Lutherans, the adherents to the alternative concept of Reformation seem to have been both higher and lower in the social hierarchy – which is only at first glance a contradiction.

Many members of the upper social strata were early supporters and protectors of the non-Lutheran reformers. Among them were noble bailiffs

---

[34]The letter is published by C. A. Cornelius, *Der Antheil Ostfrieslands an der Reformation bis zum Jahre 1535* (Aachen, 1852), appendix 1, 57-59.

[35]Horst Weigelt, "Johannes Campanus," *Theologische Realenzyklopädie*, 8: 601-4; Ehbrecht, "Reformation, Sedition and Kommunikation."

(*Amtsmänner*) and their wives, as in the case of the "Wassenberg preachers"; self-confident landed gentlemen in East Frisia, as, for example, the nobleman and *Herrlichkeitsbesitzer* Ulrich von Dornum; and many merchants and members of commercial guilds (*commerzerende Gewerbe*) like the butchers and the brewers, who tended to be social climbers. In some Hanseatic towns, such as Brunswick and possibly in Wismar, we find members of the political elite.[36] Sometimes there are lawyers, members of whose professions are usually considered to have favored Lutheranism – for instance, Dr. Westerberg in Cologne and Frankfurt and the well-known syndic and professor, Dr. Johannes Oldendorp from Rostock. Apart from their elevated social status, most of the members of these groups were highly educated.[37]

The lower strata of society were overrepresented in all those cases where the alternative Reformation could win a broad cross-section of adherents, that is, in the comparatively few cases where it was not limited to clerical and intellectual circles but became a real social movement. This was the case in the Wendish Hanseatic towns of Stralsund, Rostock, and Wismar, analyzed by Schildhauer, as well as in Brunswick, where the supporters of the non-Lutheran preachers are supposed to have lived in the "Sack," a part of the town where the lower and middle craftsmen usually resided; and in Minden, where the social identity of the followers of the preacher Nikolaus Krage declined as his positions became more radical, until only the lowly fishermen of the suburbs were left.[38]

Especially in the towns the appearance of alternative reformers provoked vehement defensive reactions. They were directed by the town councils and the Lutheran ministers and supported by the well-established channels of the Hanseatic League as well as by the new and rapidly expanding communication

---

[36]Karl-Heinz Kirchoff, *Die Täufer in Münster 1534/35* (Münster: Aschendorf, 1973), 35-37, 68-71, 86-96, and passim; Petri and Droege, *Rheinische Geschichte,* 2:37; Smid, *Kirchengeschichte,* 115-17, 125-29; Bubenheimer, "Thomas Müntzer und der Anfang," 24-25, 27; Koch, "Zwinglianer," 522.

[37]Schildhauer, *Auseinandersetzungen in den Hansestädten,* 170; Georg Waitz, *Lübeck unter Jürgen Wullenwever,* 3 vols. (Berlin, 1855-56), 1:195; 3:9, 512. The position of Oldendorp is controversial. For a Lutheran interpretation, see Erik Wolf, "Johann Oldendorp," in *Große Rechtsdenker,* ed. Erik Wolf (Tübingen: Mohr, 1951), 134-75, esp. 141-44.

[38]Schildhauer, *Auseinandersetzungen in den Hansestädten,* 181-86; Wolfram A. Junke, "Bugenhagens Einwirken auf die Festigung der Reformation in Braunschweig (1528-1532)," in *Die Reformation in der Stadt Braunschweig. Festschrift 1528-1978* (Brunswick: Limbach, 1978), 71-82, here 76-77. Ehbrecht, "Form und Bedeutung," 148-59. *Das Chronicon . . . des Heinrich Piel,* 121-22.

network of Lutheran theologians.[39] Magistrates and ministers were above all anxious about "the peaceful state of the Christians in our towns" and about "concord, peace, and love," which they regarded as preconditions for any well-ordered society. In the eyes of these officials, the doctrine of the radical reformers could only disturb Christianity and civic freedom inasmuch as

> everybody, and above all the uneducated, even women, dare to preach the Gospel and the Word of God . . . and using Christian freedom as a pretext, they live according to their own will and fancy, disregarding the ordinances and regulations; while pretending to follow Christian teaching . . . they hold secret and improper meetings. (Eyn ider, ock allermeyst de ungelerten, ock frouwen dat evangelium and dat wort Godes . . . , to prediken understan und im schine eyner christliken fryheit na synem egen willen und gevallen sunder ordeninge edder regelle levet, hemliken unde untemeliken versamelingen . . . im schine christliker lere geschen.)

The Word of God and the Gospel would be interpreted differently "from what they really meant in order to please the common people . . . and this would lead to carnal freedom, which would be followed by revolts against the magistrates and bring about the ruin of the towns."[40]

These statements quoted from the minutes of the Hanseatic diets in 1525 still related to the "Martinian sect" (*Martinische secte*) or the doctrine invented by Martin Luther. But this changed quickly and radically when it became obvious that a uniform Lutheran preaching of the pure Word of the Bible would not necessarily cause conflict and discord in the towns but could, on the contrary, "bring about harmony, concord, peace, and love in accordance with God's will."[41] The more the Lutheran Reformation produced a new basic consensus on belief and ritual in the towns and, in addition, established a legally and institutionally independent town church, the more the "deviationists" in the Protestant camp – besides the rapidly dwindling number of Catholics – became the apparent obstacles to unity. Not only the radicals were involved but also the quietists, who were not radical and revolutionary at all. It was a maxim of urban political thinking that towns that tolerated any dissent from the new Protestant unity of belief could never have a peaceful *res publica,*

---

[39]Cf., for instance, the letter of Bugenhagen to Superintendent Mag. Martin Görlitz at Brunswick on September 27, 1530, in Otto Vogt, ed., *Dr. Johannes Bugenhagens Briefwechsel* (Stettin, 1888, and Gotha, 1910; reprinted Hildesheim: Olms, 1966), no. 38, 98-99; or the letters of the Wittenbergers in the case of Campanus: Melanchthon to Bugenhagen, November 1531, in Vogt, *Bugenhagens Briefwechsel,* no. 43, 107; Luther to Bugenhagen and Görlitz on November 24, 1531, in WA, *BR,* 6, no. 1886, 321-22, and no. 1887, 232-33. See also Brecht, "Luthertum als politische und soziale Kraft," 15-19. Cf. also the material quoted in n. 43 below.

[40]Hanserezess Januar 1525, in *Hanserezesse,* sec. 3, vol. 9, no. 2, art. 97, pp. 18-19; Bericht vom Hansetag Juli 1525, ibid., no. 132, arts. 120-21, p. 264.

[41]Ibid., no. 132, art. 120, p. 264.

nor could such a church stand in a peaceful relationship with Christ because these dissenters would be either "enemy or devil" (fiant edder duvel) for the community and the church, as the lawyer Dr. Adam Pack put it in a private letter to the magistrates of Soest.[42]

Unity of belief and doctrine was not only regarded as a basic precondition for the civic peace of the individual town but should also apply to neighboring and confederated towns. In order to inform each other about dissenting preachers, the magistracies developed an intensive correspondence, which, if it was thought necessary, contained the strict exhortation not to deviate from the common course.[43] Moreover, the towns helped one another with reliable Lutheran ministers as well as by providing each other with church regulations to be used as models for reorganization.[44] On April 15, 1535, a meeting of preachers from Lübeck, Bremen, Hamburg, Rostock, Stralsund, and Lüneburg took place in Hamburg. It had the task of unifying the doctrine, ceremonies, and institutions of the different Protestant town churches as far as possible in order to make them more resistant to sectarians, papists, Anabaptists, and Zwinglians.[45] In July 1535, the Hanseatic diet passed a resolution that "a Hanseatic town afflicted with the heretical doctrine of the Anabaptists (wedderdoper) or Sacramentarians should be suspended from all rights and privileges of the League until it should refrain from its error." It was even possible to impose sanctions if "one or several private persons" were afflicted with the error and the town council did not take any appropriate measures against this.[46]

"Town-peace" and "unity of religion" were not only categories of official reaction to the alternative conceptions; they also characterized the thought and behavior of the citizens. These slogans were not just part of an ideology of the ruling classes and urban authorities – although they could be that as

[42]On the sources, see Ehbrecht, "Reformation, Sedition und Kommunikation," 289-90. Similar arguments were made by the magistrates of Erfurt on March 3, 1525 (Walter Peter Fuchs, ed., Akten zur Geschichte des Bauernkriegs in Mitteldeutschland, vol. 2 [Jena: Frommann, 1941; reprinted Aalen: Scientia, 1964], 67-68).

[43]Cf. the letters appended to Ehbrecht, "Reformation, Sedition und Kommunikation," including some from Lübeck, Bremen, Goslar, Magdeburg, Brunswick, and Einbeck (no. 1, 282-83); also from Cologne (no. 2, 283-84); Luther (no. 7, 188-89); Dr. Adam Pack (no. 8, 289-89); Bremen (no. 10, 291); Brunswick (no. 11, 291-92); Bugenhagen (no. 13, 191-96, and no. 16, 299-300); Goslar (no. 17, 200-l, and no. 19, 302); Hildesheim (nos. 3 and 4, 284-86).

[44]Besides the well-known activities of Bugenhagen, we can also recall Nicholas von Amsdorf in Magdeburg, Einbeck, and Goslar; Justus Jones in Zerbst and Halle; Urbanus Rhegius in Lüneburg, Hanover, Minden, Lemgo, and Soest; and Heinrich Winkel in Brunswick, Hanover, Göttingen, and Hildesheim.

[45]Cramer, Pomrische Kirchen Chronicon, 93-98; Schröder, Kirchen-Historie, 301-14; Schildhauer, Auseinandersetzungen in den Hansestädten, 164; Hanserezesse (cf. n. 9 above), sec. 4, vol. 2, Rezess no. 86, arts. 42-70, pp. 68-73; Hanserezesse, sec. 4, vol. 1, no. 439, art. 8, p. 415.

[46]Ibid., sec. 4, vol. 2, Rezess no. 86, art. 126, p. 83.

well.[47] These norms were the core of the old European civic mentality, which was common to the magistrates and the community of the *Vollbürger* (citizens) regardless of differences of interest in social, political, or ecclesiastical questions. Because the alternative reformers challenged this basic consensus by their teaching, or just by their appearance, they were rejected by the citizens. This was no longer a question of the actual distribution of power, which was rigorously contested between magistrates and burghers throughout the empire.[48] In these political conflicts citizens gladly accepted the support of Lutheran preachers. When communities rejected any alternative Reformation that went beyond Luther, they showed that burghers wanted to preserve the basic structure of the communal order despite vehement conflicts about the actual distribution of power. Fundamental ideological consensus and religious unity were basic norms of urban and civic life, beyond any question for the great majority of citizens. This can be proved in detail by the examples of the two radical reformers Johann van Campen in Soest and Nikolaus Krage in Minden, who both lost their guild support when their teachings began to threaten the religious unity of the burgher community.[49]

Reflections on the Significance and Meaning of the Failure of Non-Lutheran Evangelical Movements

Finally, I will summarize my findings on non-Lutheran evangelical movements within the early Reformation in northern and western Germany, and I will try to suggest the significance of the failure of the non-Lutheran concepts of change and the brilliant rise of Lutheran identity. What does the hiatus between the triumphant Lutheran identity on the one hand, and on the other the defeated alternate conceptions of religious and social renewal, formulated theoretically but with no actual chance of implementation, tell us about the character and the extent of social change within European societies at the beginning of the early modern period? I shall present my conclusions in nine theses:

1. Non-Lutheran Reformation movements failed because they were a challenge to two fundamental convictions held in old European society: the idea of close interrelations between church and society, and the idea of basic harmony as a precondition of any well-ordered and peaceful state and society.

[47]Thomas A. Brady, Jr., *Ruling Class, Regime and Reformation at Strasbourg, 1520-1555* (Leiden: Brill, 1978); Schilling, *Konfessionskonflikt*, 16-17, n. 3; 376, n. 17a.

[48]Mörke, *Rat und Bürger;* Postel, *Reformation in Hamburg;* Moeller, *Reichsstadt*, reprint; Schilling, "Politische Elite"; idem, "Reformation in the Hanseatic Cities"; idem, *Konfessionskonflikt.*

[49]For Campen, cf. Ratsprotokoll 7.1.1533, in Ehbrecht, "Reformation, Sedition und Kommuni-kation," 302-3; also ibid., 251-54. For Krage in Minden, *Chronicon Heinrich Piel*, 1211-22, analyzed by Ehbrecht in "Form und Bedeutung," 147-51; Ehbrecht, "Reformation, Sedition und Kommunikation," 253-56, 261-64. For a general treatment, consult Wilhelm Ebel, *Der Bürgereid als Geltungsprinzip des deutschen mittelalterlichen Stadtrechts* (Weimar: Böhlau, 1958).

In contrast to modern societies after the great revolutions at the end of the eighteenth century, in the *societas civilis* (civil society) of the early modern period, religion and church were not just sectional systems of society but also a central axis of the political and social system.[50] Consequently, this type of society had high structural barriers against any separation of church and state, of ecclesiastical and civic community, and against religious and ideological pluralism within one and the same community. The famous *cuius-regio-eius-religio* principle of the Religious Peace of Augsburg (1555) was the logical consequence of this fundamental outlook. The idea of religious unity was accompanied and supported by a secular model of social unity and harmony that mediated social differences and inequalities and subordinated them to a social norm of peace. This was especially marked in towns, but it was also true in territorial states, the German territories as well as the western and northern European national states. Both models of unity were deeply rooted in the civic mentality of the middle classes; they were thus not just an ideology of the ruling classes, although they could be used as instruments for stabilizing their power.

2. Both fundamental principles of early modern society were severely challenged by the religious and social changes produced by the early Reformation movement before it was tamed by clearly defined norms and doctrines. Without the imposition of a religious norm, whether Lutheran or reformed Zwinglian, the complex, multiform early Reformation theologies would have triggered a splintering that would have destroyed the links between religion and society and between church and state, on the ideological as well as on the legal and institutional level. The early evangelical renewal had already pushed this process of splintering and differentiation forward, so that notions of a fundamental change in the theoretical foundation of the social and political order appeared and were seriously discussed. As religious unity broke down, some people were eager to deny the necessity of this unity in principle.[51] They argued that a community could flourish even if its members did not share the same belief and did not belong to the same church. In their

---

[50]The following argumentation is based on my general interpretation of early modern society and its religious foundations. See Schilling, *Konfessionskonflikt,* 15-40, 191, 358-60, 365-91 (abstract in R. Po-chia Hsia, ed., *The German People and the Reformation* [Ithaca: Cornell University Press, 1988], 268-83); Schilling, "Religion und Gesellschaft in der calvinistischen Republik der Vereinigten Niederlande," in *Kirche und gesellschaftlicher Wandel,* 197-250; Schilling, "Die Konfessionalisierung im Reich," *Historische Zeitschrift* 246 (1988): 145. Cf. Olaf Mörke, "Integration und Desintegration," in *La ville, la bourgeoisie et la genèse de l'état moderne (XIIIe-XVIIIe siècles)* (Paris: Edition du Colloque International du Centre National de la Recherche Scientifique, 1988), 297-321.

[51]Cf., for example, "Das Gutachten eines unbekannten Nürnberger von 1530," in Johannes Brenz, *Werke,* part 2, *Frühschriften,* ed. Martin Brecht, Gerhard Schäfer, and Frieda Wolf (Tübingen: Mohr, 1974), 517-26, here 525, 39-41; Andreas Osiander the Elder, *Gesamtausgabe,* ed. Gerhard Müller and Gottfried Seebaß, vol. 3 (Gütersloh: Gütersloher Verlagshaus, 1979), no. 132, 631-73. Cf. also Gottfried Seebaß, "Stadt und Kirche in Nürnberg im Zeitalter der Reformation," in *Stadt und Kirche im 16. Jahrhundert,* ed. Bernd Moeller (Gütersloh: Gütersloher Verlagshaus, 1978), 66-86, here 81-82.

eyes religious and ecclesiastical pluralism did not necessarily destroy civic order and harmony but, on the contrary, could bring important advantages – for example, in the economic sector. Where such non-Lutheran alternative Reformations became a social movement in the literal sense of the word, as in some towns, they necessarily entered into alliance with fringe groups and the lower classes of society. By doing so they challenged the demand for social peace and harmony too, the second fundamental maxim of the old European concept of social order. Here again we can observe a correspondence between the actual course of events during the early Reformation period and theoretical concepts. For already during the late Middle Ages, elements of a concept of society had appeared that did not consider unity and harmony to be basic but that regarded social differences or even conflict as the basic facts of social life.[52]

3. Neither of these new concepts of society gained any broader support. On the contrary, mainly in the towns a socially broad resistance to the attacks on the two keystones of the old European model of society developed. There was a fundamental consensus between magistrates and ordinary citizens in favor of preserving religious unity as well as civic peace; these ideas aimed at securing the economic, social, and legal privileges of the citizens (*Vollbürger*) against the "non-citizen" fringe groups and lower classes, who did not possess burgher rights. When the alternative Reformation movement called the uniform sacral basis of the burgher community into question and, moreover, entered into an alliance with the "common people" – that is, the non-burgher inhabitants of the town[53] – this meant rebellion (*uproer*) and a severe challenge to the interests of the political elite as well as of the merchants and craftsmen.[54]

Aside from this, severe political risks occurred because religious disunity within an individual town or within the league of towns gave princes and the emperor an opportunity to curtail traditional urban liberties.[55]

4. The events of the Reformation in the towns of northern and western Germany contradict the idea of an antagonism between a communal Reformation or Zwinglian or other origin on the one hand and the Lutheran Reformation

[52]Cf. Thomas A. Brady, Jr., "The Themes of Social Structure, Social Conflict, and Civic Harmony in Jakob Wimpheling's Germania," *Sixteenth Century Journal* 3 (1972): 65-76.

[53]The meaning of *gemeiner Mann* within urban populations is discussed by Schilling in "Aufstandsbewegungen in der stadtbürgerlichen Gesellschaft des Alten Reiches," in *Der deutsche Bauernkrieg,* ed. Hans-Ulrich Wehler (Göttingen: Vandenhoeck and Ruprecht, 1975), 193-238, here 237-38.

[54]There is ample evidence of this fear of social unrest; cf., for example, *Hanserezesse,* sec. 3, vol. 9, no. 2, arts. 97, 103, pp. 18-19; no. 131, art. 181, p. 229; no. 132, art. 121, p. 264; no. 137, art. 10, pp. 284-85. Cramer, *Pomrische Kirchen Chronicon,* 94.

[55]*Hanserezesse,* sec. 4, vol. 2, no. 86, art. 125, p. 82. "Reichsabschied Speyer 1529," art. 5, *Neue und vollständigere Sammlung der Reichs-Abschiede . . . ,* 4 parts, ed. J. J. Schmauss and H. Chr. v. Senckenberg (Frankfurt, 1747; reprinted Osnabrück: Zeller, 1967), 2:294. See also Ehbrecht, "Köln - Osnabrück - Stralsund," 26, 30.

with its allegedly authoritarian and anti-communal character on the other. On the contrary, the Lutheran Reformation remained a popular movement well into the 1530s. It was a communal Reformation (*Gemeindereformation*) precisely because it was the guarantor of religious unity against ideological dissent and ecclesiastical pluralism.[56] It guaranteed the fundamental consensus that the old European town community obviously regarded as necessary. Wilfried Ehbrecht, one of the experts on the history of the Hanseatic League, judges that

> conflicts were solved in the traditional way – in individual towns as well as in the Hanseatic League. Groups that were no longer approved of by the community had to leave town. This held true for failed leaders of communal protest, for dismissed city councillors, and now also for the more radical religious reformers. In spite of a changing understanding of protest, the preservation of urban peace, which depended on the consensus of the burgher community . . . remained crucial.

> (. . . die Lösing war in den einzelnen Städten wie in der Hanse gleichermassen traditionell. Gruppen, die keine Billigung mehr durch die Gemeinde fanden, mussten die Stadt verlassen. Das galt für gescheiterte Anführer, abgesetzte Ratsherren und ebenso jetzt für radikalere Reformer in religiösen Fragen. Entscheidend blieb auch bei sich wandelndem Protestverständnis jeweils die Sicherung des städtischen Friedens, der vom Konsens der Bürgergemeinde . . . abhing.)[57]

The alternative non-Lutheran Reformation was rejected by the overwhelming majority of burghers because, judged by the axiom of religious unity and social peace, it was explosive and destructive. It was destructive because of its radical teaching in theology and sometimes also in politics, but even more so because of its mere existence within a dissenting minority.

[56]Franz Lau, "Der Bauernkrieg und das angebliche Ende der lutherischen Reformation als spontaner Volksbewegung," *Luther-Jahrbuch* 26 (1959): 109-34; Schilling, "Die politische Elite"; idem, *Konfessionskonflikt*, 82-84, 139-44, 376; idem, "Gab es im späten Mittelalter und zu Beginn der Neuzeit in Deutschland einen städtischen 'Republikanismus'? Zur politischen Kultur des alteuropäischen Stadtbürgertums," in *Republiken und Republikanismus*, ed. Helmut Koenigsberger (Munich: Oldenbourg, 1988), 101-44, esp. 144-51; Mörke, *Rat und Bürger*; idem, "Stadt und Reformation in Niedersachsen," in *Stadt im Wandel, Landesausstellung Niedersachsen 1985* (Brunswick: Landesmuseum, 1985), 75-87; Postel, *Reformation in Hamburg*; idem, "Motive städtischer Reformation in Norddeutschland," *Jahrbuch für Regionalgeschichte* 15 (1988): 92-107, esp. 98-99, 102-3; Moeller, *Reichsstadt*, reprint, 90-94.

[57]Ehbrecht, "Köln - Osnabrück - Stralsund," 63. Cf. the evidence of pamphlets: Heinz-Dieter Heimann, "Stadthistoriographie und Stadtreformation," *Jahrbuch für westfälische Kirchengeschichte* 76 (1983): 30-49, esp. 47-48; Heimann, "Kommunales Denken und konfessionelle Kontroverse," *Westfälische Forschungen* 34 (1984): 76-86, esp. 85-86.

5. Seen as urban rebellions of the old European type, the non-Lutheran currents within the urban Reformations can be understood as the radical extreme of urban communalism (*radikal genossenschaftlich*).[58] Most urban conflicts, the religious ones as well as the merely secular ones, proceeded into this most radical phase of a communal movement. This was at the same time the final phase and turning point of the uproar. For citizens demanded the restoration of civic normality, and this normality required a balance between the burghers' actual participation and their representation for the commonweal (*bonum commune*) by the town council and the political elite. During the Reformation period, this balance was found within the framework of the Lutheran Reformation version of religious, ecclesiastical, and social renewal. It was established during the 1530s but could guarantee civic republicanism well into the seventeenth century – at least in parts of our region.[59] Urban churches' later monopolization by the magistrates and the princes was doubtless supported by Lutheranism, but it was not at all a direct and necessary consequence of the events during the urban Reformation in a strict sense.

6. A comparison between the events in the towns and in the territories of East Frisia and Hesse shows that alternative forms of Reformation theology could evidently stand their ground more easily in territories than in towns. This was, on the one hand, a consequence of the greater spatial and social distances within the territories, whereas the spatial and social closeness of urban society, together with the civic notion of sacral unity, made the compulsion to conformity overwhelming in towns. (The case of East Frisia shows that in territories, even in small ones, it was possible as a last resort to divide the territory into separate parts with different confessions and different church organizations.) On the other hand, as in the case of Hesse, the resistance of dissenting alternative elements in Reformation theology was an expression of the prince's desire to tolerate a certain degree of theological difference, namely on the question of the Eucharist. Consequently, the existence of Zwinglian theology is no sign of communal tradition but is, on the contrary, a consequence of strong princely power.[60]

7. The history of the non-Lutheran alternative Reformation in northern and western Germany proves that the historical contingency and functionality of the different denominations and confessional churches with regard to their impact on society and politics, which came more and more to the fore in the age of confessionalization, also hold true for the very beginning of the

---

[58]The interpretation of the northwest German Reformation as a "communal Reformation" and the term *Gemeindereformation* are treated in more detail in Schilling, *Konfessionskonflikt*. See also Schilling, "Bürgerkämpfe in Aachen zu Beginn des 17. Jahrhunderts," *Zeitschrift für historische Forschung* 1 (1974): 175-231, esp. 198; idem, "Aufstandsbewegungen," 220-24.

[59]Discussed in detail in Schilling, "Städtischer 'Republikanismus'."

[60]Sohm, *Territorium und Reformation,* 76-79.

Reformation.[61] The fact that Zwinglianism became an alternative sacramentarian movement all over northern Germany but did not have any chance of attaining prominence, let alone victory, was not so much the consequence of its specific theology as it was a consequence of the principle, "one burgher community, one belief, and one church," described above.[62] In the ensuing process of monopolization, which logically followed this principle, north of the River Main Lutheranism clearly had an advantage over Zwinglianism, and of course over all the forms of radical or left-wing Protestantism. A decision between the alternatives "Luther" and "Zwingli" was all the more necessary because the differences concerned the Eucharist and thus the core of a community founded on religion – an ecclesiastical as well as a secular community. Here again Lutheranism had an advantage in the urban centers of the Hanseatic region. Its understanding of the Eucharist appealed more to the civic mentality of the sixteenth century, especially that of the craftsmen, because of the coincidence between the Lutheran sacral interpretation of the Lord's Supper and the citizens' sacral interpretation of the urban community. Zwingli's concept of a rational memorial meal attracted above all the intellectuals and not the middle-class guildsmen.

8. The defeat of the alternative Reformation was the first step towards the shift from the medieval to the early modern type of interlinkage between religion and society, between church and political order. The individual steps of this formation are well known: first the visitations and church regulations, then the confession and the oath of confession,[63] and finally the maxim "religion as the bond of society" (*religio vinculum societatis*) as it was advocated by the imperial and territorial lawyers of the seventeenth century.[64] This development was again especially marked in the towns.[65] When in the early 1560s Philip of Hesse interceded with the town council of Erfurt on behalf of the notorious Zwinglian Baptist Johann Wisamer, he received the terse answer that Wisamer would be allowed to stay in the town for a short time

[61]Schilling, *Konfessionskonflikt,* 380-91; Schilling, ed., *Die reformierte Konfessionalisierung in Deutschland - Das Problem der "Zweiten Reformation"* (Gütersloh: Gütersloher Verlagshaus, 1986), passim, esp. 79-81, 104-7, 184-86, 233-37, 374-75, 428-31.

[62]Moeller, *Reichsstadt,* reprint, 92-93; Berndt Hamm, "Stadt und Kirche unter dem Wort Gottes: das reformatorische Einheitsmodell des Nürnberger Ratsschreibers Lazarus Spengler (1479-1534)," in *Literatur und Laienbildung,* ed. Ludger Grenzmann and Karl Stackmann (Stuttgart: Metzler, 1984), 710-31, esp. 721-27.

[63]Klaus Schreiner, "Rechtgläubigkeit als 'Band der Gesellschaft' und 'Grundlage des Staates'. Zur eidlichen Verpflichtung von Staats- und Kirchendienern auf die Formula Concordiae und das 'Konkordienbuch'," in *Bekenntnis und Einheit der Kirche,* ed. Martin Brecht and Reinhard Schwarz (Stuttgart: Calwer, 1980), 341-79; Schreiner, *Disziplinierte Wissenschaftsfreiheit . . . an der Universität Tübingen (1477-1945)* (Tübingen: Mohr/Siebeck, 1981), 8-11, 13-15. For an early example of an oath of adherence to the theology of a Protestant town church, that of Göttingen, see Moeller, "Reformation," 513.

[64]Schreiner, "Rechtgläubigkeit," 375.

[65]An excellent case study is Hamm, "Stadt und Kirche," esp. 714-15, 719-23.

as a guest but that "for important reasons he could not be allowed to take up permanent residence here."[66] He was seen as a threat to the new post-Reformation urban peace and religious harmony. This development culminated in a confessional reinterpretation of medieval conceptions of salvation and unity; this is what the chronicler of Aachen, Petrus a Beeck, did at the peak of the Counter-Reformation when he defined "town" as "a union of citizens bound together not only by the city walls but especially by the common will expressed in a common confession of faith" ("civium unitatem, non modo quod uno aggere vel vallo circumagatur sed quod eodem velle, eodem nolle, eiusdem fidei symbolo . . . coalescere").[67]

9. The religious-sociological configuration of early modern confessionality that emerged from the Reformation period included the enormous dynamism of modernization.[68] At the same time it also guaranteed a degree of social and political stability and constancy that were indispensable as long as men were not institutionally and mentally ready for the separation of religion and society, of the ecclesiastical and secular orders – in other words, for the ideological and mental pluralism of the modern age. It was a marvelously anachronistic fact that the alternative currents within the early Reformation had been willing to push social change forward beyond the point possible at the beginning of the early modern period; in so doing they would have jumped over confessionalism as it emerged from the Reformation and fore-shadowed the establishment of real modernity by the Enlightenment and the revolutions at the end of the eighteenth century. The non-Lutheran reformers challenged the limits of modernization and differentiation that were so obviously established in early modern society, especially in the towns. The defeat of the alternative conceptions meant the pruning of surplus differentiation, which could not yet be sustained by the society. Instead of a utopian total differentiation, a more realistic and partial differentiation between the three main confessions occurred. Each of these confessional systems formed a coalition with the secular system in the traditional way – or, formulated differently, each entangled itself in the secular system. These confessions thereby furthered the building of the early modern state as well as the formation of an early modern society with its higher standards of rationality, discipline, civilization, and social and political justice. For this process, which lasted more than two hundred years, a close alliance of the confessional

---

[66]Quoted by Rüetschi, "Baptist Johannes Wisamer," 134.

[67]Petrus a Beek, *Aquisgranum* (Aachen, 1620). Cf. the translation by Peter Stephan Käntzeler, *Petrus a Beeck, Aquisgranum oder Geschichte der Stadt Aachen* (Aix-la-Chapelle, 1874), 329.

[68]Wolfgang Reinhard, "Gegenreformation als Modernisierung?" *Archiv für Reformationsgeschichte* 68 (1977): 226-52; Reinhard, "Konfession und Konfessionalisierung in Europa," in *Bekenntnis und Geschichte*, ed. Reinhard (Munich: Vögel, 1981), 165-89; Reinhard, "Zwang zur Konfessionalisierung?" *Zeitschrift für historische Forschung* 10 (1983): 257-77; Schilling, *Konfessionskonflikt und Staatsbildung;* idem, ed., *Reformierte Konfessionalisierung;* idem, "Die Konfessionalisierung im Reich."

churches with state and society was obviously necessary.[69] The structural
necessity of that coalition only vanished after the framework of society and
politics had been changed decisively – by state building, social formation,
and confessionalization as well as by the dramatic economic and demographic
dynamism of the second half of the eighteenth century. These changes were
the precondition of an ultimate realization of most of the basic ideas of the
early radical Reformation described above. Of course, the social, political,
and mental consequences were quite different because most of these ideas
had meanwhile been secularized by the Enlightenment, and because by 1800
the interrelation of mental impulses and material conditions was totally
different from that of the early sixteenth century.

[69]Cf. the articles of Wolfgang Reinhard (13-38), Mohammed Rassem (39-72), Albano
Biondi (73-90), and Ulrich Im Hof (119-40) in *Annali dell' Istituto storico italo-germanico in
Trento/Jahrbuch des italienisch-deutschen historischen Instituts in Trient* 8 (1982); Schilling, "Reformierte
Kirchenzucht als Sozialdisziplinierung?" in *Niederlande und Nordwestdeutschland,* ed. Wilfried
Ehbrecht and Schilling (Cologne and Vienna: Böhlau, 1983), 261-327; idem, "'History of
Crime' or 'History of Sin'?" in *Politics and Society in Reformation Europe,* ed. E. I. Kouri and Tom
Scott (Basingstoke, Eng.: Macmillan, 1987), 289-310; idem, "Kirchenzucht und neuzeitliche
Sozialdisziplinierung," in *Staat und Gesellschaft im Alten Reich,* ed. Georg Schmidt (Wiesbaden:
Steiner, 1989), 259-95.

Kinder, Küche, Kirche: Social Ideology in the Sermons of Johannes Mathesius

Susan Karant-Nunn*

One of the topics on which early Lutheran clergymen frequently preached was the nature of women, marriage, and the family. From the chancel pastors indoctrinated their congregations on the reformed vision of Christian domestic life. Johannes Mathesius (1504-1565), a Saxon living in the Bohemian silver-mining city of Joachimsthal, addressed this subject in several dozen extant wedding sermons and numerous other sermons. This paper summarizes Mathesius's teachings on women's part in the fall of humankind, the consequences of the fall, the purpose of marriage, the statuses of the spouses, and the inclinations and capacities of each. Karant-Nunn presents Mathesius's view that uncontrolled women were dangerous to themselves and society.

HISTORIANS UNIVERSALLY ACKNOWLEDGE the centrality of the sermon in early Lutheran, and generally in early Protestant, worship services. Martin Luther called the sermon "the purest offering" of a clergyman.[1] It was the focal point of reformed liturgy, replacing the Catholic elevation of the host. In addition, it is by now a platitude that the catechism and the sermon together became the chief vehicles for educating the masses in the new doctrines. They were not only to change people's minds, but also, as the reformers quickly discovered to their dismay, to introduce many to official Christian teaching. Not that the populace had been entirely ignorant, or non-Christian à la Jean Delumeau.[2] But the reformers in short order excluded from condoned belief much that had been widely popular, even beloved, as in the cases of the cults of some saints and certain rituals and festivities attached to personal stages of life and the church calendar. They drew attention instead to Christ and the Bible. *Sola scriptura, sola fide, sola gratia* were unfamiliar concepts to the laity. The pastors, once they became rudimentarily informed on these themes, were appointed, as it were, missionaries in their own parishes.

---

*Research for this paper was financed in part by a Travel-to-Collections Grant of the National Endowment for the Humanities, and in part by the International Research and Exchanges Board (IREX). The author presented a shortened version at the Sixteenth Century Studies Conference, Minneapolis, Minnesota, October 1989.

[1]*D. Martin Luthers Werke* (Weimar: Böhlau, 1883-1986; hereafter cited WA), *Briefwechsel* 3, 789, November 1, 1524; hereafter *BR*.

[2]Jean Delumeau, *Catholicism between Luther and Voltaire: A New View of the Counter-Reformation* (London: Burns and Oates, 1977).

By reason of being missionaries and because they relied upon scripture, they had to preach, and thus they acquired and honed a skill that few of them had possessed before. Visitorial tests of their acceptance of the new creed focused on whether they had married, and, often, whether they could preach acceptably on an assigned topic.

Of course, some Catholic priests had preached, and the position of preacher – as distinct from the priest who administered the sacraments – was a late medieval and thoroughly Catholic development. Some preachers, like Johann Geiler von Kaisersberg, were masterfully adept.[3] With the coming of the Reformation, however, even the village pastor had to expound from the pulpit, a task that most no doubt found quite challenging.

Out of this reformed stress upon the preached word grew a rhetorical genre far richer, more variegated and diverse than its antecedents. The sermon became a literary form as well, its content spread by means of the printing press well beyond the sanctuary to an increasingly literate lay audience. The reformed sermon elaborated upon a fifteenth-century homiletic tradition that had harmonized both humanist/intellectual and pious/emotional strains. If its rhetorical devices remained yet a long while classical, its subjects burst out of their earlier confines.

Although none of the petals on this homiletic flower were in their subject matter unprecedented in the late medieval world, wedding sermons and funeral sermons were uncommon.[4] Under Catholicism some sermons about women and about matrimony were given, even if they were not delivered precisely on the occasion of weddings.[5] But only with the advent of Protestantism did the wedding sermon develop into a significant subgenre, becoming, before the end of the sixteenth century, a widespread and even typical means of conveying a novel configuration of already available thoughts on the nature of women and the dignity of the wedded estate. Inasmuch as Lutheran nuptials ordinarily took place before the entire congregation, the opinions of the officiating cleric were made known to the community at large. The public gathering made an ideal forum for expounding moral and social themes, and a few masterful preachers fully exploited their metier. Because enthusiastic Lutheran clergymen considered the reform of society to be urgently desirable, however, they did not, as we shall see, confine pertinent

[3]Jane Dempsey Douglass, *Justification in Late Medieval Preaching: A Study in John Geiler of Kaysersberg* (Leiden: Brill, 1966, and recently reissued).

[4]Eileen T. Dugan, "The Funeral Sermon as a Key to Familial Values in Early Modern Nördlingen," *Sixteenth Century Journal* 20 (1989): 631-44.

[5]Carl Braun, *Die katholische Predigt während der Jahre 1450 bis 1650 über Ehe und Familie, Erziehung, Unterricht und Berufswahl* (Würzburg: Göbel und Scherer, 1904) contains a bibliography, the brevity of which (four pages, at end) may bear out the scarcity of Catholic sermons on these subjects.

comment to wedding sermons. Their success at persuasion is a separate question.

Johannes Mathesius is a fine example of a dedicated Lutheran clergyman and a prolific preacher of the mid-sixteenth century whose extant sermons span his twenty-three-year ministerial career in Joachimsthal, a silver-mining town just across the Bohemian border with Saxony. We possess several hundred of his sermons dealing with the full range of topics, including ninety-two wedding sermons. These provide ample material for an examination of early Lutheran teachings on women, marriage, and the family. Nonetheless, the need for scholars to study other men's sermons from this period and to compare their messages is obvious and pressing.[6]

Mathesius was a Saxon, born in Rochlitz on the Mulde in 1504. As the crow flew, Rochlitz lay only twenty-five miles west of the great medieval silver-mining center of Freiberg, and not a great deal farther to the north of the brand new boom towns of Annaberg and Schneeberg. The crazed hunt for silver and quick riches surrounded the youngster. His father, a city councillor, wanted him to become a miner and took him out of school at the age of ten to keep records for the nearby Vogelgesang mine. But the boy wanted to return to school, and he studied not only locally but in turn in neighboring Mittweida and at the Nuremberg *Gymnasium*. He received a thorough classical education, and references to Greek and Roman as well as to biblical books fill his sermons. He then proceeded to the University of Ingolstadt.

The Reformation broke out around him when he was a teenager. Being a subject of Duke George the Bearded, who tried to shield his subjects from the new "heresy," Mathesius may have learned of its doctrines only by rumor until 1526, when he read Martin Luther's book on good works.[7] Attracted by what he read, Mathesius went to Wittenberg in the spring of 1529 and heard Luther preach on baptism. Between 1529 and 1531 he studied with Philip Melanchthon, and he then taught in the Altenburg grammar school until 1532, when he was called as a school teacher to Joachimstal, the city with which his name was to be permanently connected.[8]

---

[6]See Miriam Usher Chrisman, *Bibliography of Strasbourg Imprints, 1480-1599* (New Haven: Yale University Press, 1982), 195, for books or pamphlets on marriage that were printed in Strasbourg; also 181-82 for treatises on women and marriage. Mathesius's sermons were not printed there, but they were in Nuremberg, and Strasbourgers could have owned them. See Thomas Miller, "'Mirror for Marriage': Lutheran Views of Marriage and the Family, 1520-1600," Ph.D. dissertation, University of Virginia, 1981, which treats above all the views of Cyriakus Spangenberg.

[7]Karl Friedrich Ledderhose, *Das Leben des M. Johann Mathesius* (Heidelberg: Karl Winter, 1849), 6.

[8]There is some confusion about exactly what Mathesius's position was in 1532. In his introduction to Nikolaus Herman and Johannes Mathesius, *Geistliche Lieder* (Halle: Julius Fricke, 1855), Ledderhose says that he was rector. But in *Das Leben des M. Johann Mathesius* Ledderhose says both that he was rector in 1532 (13) and that he was promoted to rector in 1535 (19).

Joachimsthal had been founded only in 1516, the result of throngs rushing in to prospect for silver. In this wild setting every stripe and conviction of preacher could find a following – Johannes Sylvius Egranus, a reform-minded humanist Catholic; Johann Bindtmann, a Dominican who preached submission and left his habit on; and even exponents of radical positions attracted followers – with the result that sects and disputations had to be prohibited.[9] We know that Andreas Bodenstein von Carlstadt had good friends there.[10] Finally, in 1534 the pastor, Magister Erhard Elling, abolished private masses and took a wife.[11] The next year Mathesius became rector of the grammar school and introduced Luther's catechism into the curriculum.

In 1540 Mathesius left Joachimsthal to return to Wittenberg. On Whitsun, June 5, 1541, he sat at Luther's commodious table and heard the reformer recount the story of his life:

This year on the day of Pentecost, the doctor told us at table his entire story – how in the year 1521 he went to Worms and stood before the emperor, confessed his teaching, and acknowledged his books. In my entire life I have never heard anything more lovely and delightful. He who has heard this business (*Handel*) with his own ears and whom it has touched can give living testimony of it. Most people speak from hearsay.[12]

Twenty-one years later, Mathesius used his recollections as the basis for a series of sermons on Luther's life which, published together in 1565, constitute the first biography of Martin Luther.[13]

Mathesius took the master's degree in Wittenberg, was ordained, and returned to Joachimsthal as deacon. He was promoted to the pastorate in 1545 when the post fell vacant. In 1543 he married Sibylla Richter, the daughter of a mine official, who bore seven children and died of puerperal fever in 1555. He mourned her until the end of his life a decade later.

---

[9]Ledderhose, *Das Leben,* 18.

[10]Carlstadt addresses "Meynem in sunderheyt geliebten bruder jn Christo Bartel Bachen Statschreiber jm Joachims tal" in the opening of his treatise, "Ob man gemach faren, vnd des ergernüssen der schwachen verschonen soll, in sachen so gottis willen angehn," of 1524. Reprinted in Erich Hertzsch, ed., *Karlstadts Schriften aus den Jahren 1523-24* (Halle: Max Niemeyer, 1956), 1:73-74. Carlstadt opines to Bach that compromises against God's will must not be made: "Each one is duty-bound, as dear as God and his neighbor are to him, to take away from the foolish their harmful and annoying things, regardless that they rage, howl, and curse as a result" (89). We may believe that some such "raging, howling, and cursing" was going on in Joachimsthal in response to efforts at reform. Georg Loesche thinks that Carlstadt visited Joachimsthal. See *Johannes Mathesius, Ein Lebens- und Sitten-Bild aus der Reformationszeit,* 2 vols. (Gotha: Friedrich Andreas Perthes, 1895), 1:75.

[11]Ledderhose, *Das Leben,* 18-19.

[12]Ibid., 33.

[13]M. Johann Mathesius, *D. Martin Luthers Leben in siebzehn Predigten,* ed. Georg Buchwald (Leipzig: Philip Reclam jun., n.d.).

Mathesius was a most assiduous preacher, and he considered himself to be utterly loyal to Luther's teachings. His parish lay in Catholic territory, and only the indispensability of its silver to the treasury of the very Catholic Holy Roman Emperor saved this clergyman from exile and possibly even from a grisly execution as a heretic.[14]

Two groups of Mathesius's wedding sermons were published in various editions during the late sixteenth century. The first series of fifteen appeared in 1563 under the title, *Vom Ehestand vnd Hauswesen, Fünfftzehen Hochzeytpredigten* to which a sixteenth was added in 1572.[15] The second collection, containing seventy-six sermons, is called *Ehespiegel Mathesij, das ist: Christliche vnd Tröstliche Erklerung etlicher vornehmer Sprüche altes vnd Newes Testaments vom heiligen Ehestande.*[16] All of these sermons were actually preached, most of them before the congregation, although occasionally people of high rank had wedding ceremonies away from the parish church and the public eye. Even so, it is significant that Mathesius expounded his concerted views on women and marital relations to nobles and magistrates, some of whom had the authority to impose their will on society at large.

Apart from wedding sermons, this prolific homiletician addressed the subject of matrimony in sermons that have come down to us in such other anthologies as *Syrach Mathesij,* drafts of sermons on the apocryphal wisdom book, *Ecclesiasticus;*[17] *Diluuium Mathesij,* fifty-four sermons delivered in 1557 and 1558 on Noah and the flood;[18] *Postilla Symbolica,* which contains a

[14]For Mathesius's involvement in politics and Emperor Ferdinand's temporary anger, see Karl Amelung, *M. Johannes Mathesius, ein lutherischer Pfarrherr des 16. Jahrhunderts: Sein Leben und Wirken* (Gütersloh: C. Bertelsmann, 1894), esp. 110-16. See related documents reprinted in Loesche, ed., *Johannes Mathesius, Ausgewählte Werke,* vol. 2 (Vienna: F. Tempsky, 1897), "Rechtfertigungsschrift an König Ferdinand," 372-77, and WA BR no. 107, 305-6.

[15]I used the 1564 edition (Nuremberg: Johann vom Berg and Vlrich Newber) as well as that reprinted in Loesche, ed., *Johannes Mathesius, Ausgewählte Werke,* vol. 2.

[16]I used the edition of 1592 (Leipzig: Johan Beyer).

[17]*Syrach Mathesij, Das ist, Christliche, Lehrhaffte, Trostreiche vnd lustige Erklerung vnd Auslegung des schönen Haussbuchs, so der weyse Mann Syrach zusammen gebracht vnd geschrieben* (hereafter *Syrach*). The edition used was Leipzig: Johan Beyer, 1589. There may have been an earlier edition since the foreword (n.p.) to Elector Christian is dated 1586; and an additional statement observes that Elector August, who died in 1586, had personally ordered these sermons to be printed. The reformers of Saxony made Ecclesiasticus (alias Syrach) required reading in many girls' schools. Ecclesiasticus, esp. chaps. 25, 26, and 42, contains a number of disparaging comments on women. See my "The Reality of Early Lutheran Education: The Electoral District of Saxony, 1528-1674, a Case Study," *Lutherjahrbuch* 57 (1990): 128-46.

[18]*Diluuium Mathesij, Das ist, Auslegung vnd Erklerung der. . . Sündfluth, die sich zur zeit Noë . . . zugetragen* (Leipzig: Johan Beyer, 1587). Hereafter *Diluvium Mathesii.*

sermon on the wedding at Cana;[19] and *Ausslegung vnd gründliche Erklerung der Ersten vnd Andern Episteln des heiligen Apostels Pauli an die Corinthier.*[20] The marital estate was unquestionably one of the themes that Mathesius considered essential to hold forth on to his spiritual charges. His opinions found their way into print and into the hands of readers well beyond the walls of the city church. I doubt that we can measure his impact, but he was certainly a prominent articulator of an emerging Lutheran model of matrimony and the proper roles and behavior of the sexes.

As we would expect of a devoted disciple of Luther, Johannes Mathesius held celibacy in doubtful regard and praised marriage highly. Oriented toward Saxony and preaching to exclusively German congregations, Mathesius should be seen as a second-generation Lutheran pastor, one for whom uprooting monasticism and clerical celibacy were not paramount concerns. Thus, the anticlerical harangues of the reformers are mainly absent from his sermons.[21] Instead, Mathesius stressed the good that is in marriage. He tells his listeners that the Son of God himself was present at the archetypal wedding and "personally led the bride and gave her to Adam in the presence of the dear little angels, who all, along with Adam, were happy and serenaded the bride."[22] He was convinced that marriage conferred human wholeness upon those who entered it: "A man without a wife is only half a person and has only half a body and is a needy and miserable man who lacks help and assistance. Indeed, the devil has him on a leash, and he is often horribly captivated, to the damage of his body, goods, honor, and also his poor soul."[23] This passage combines extolment with the common references to the dangers of not marrying. Mathesius shows a sense of the emotional dissatisfaction that must be endured by those who remain single. In his accounts of the creation of Eve, he often includes a bit of romantic embroidery: God formed Eve, he says, not just from Adam's rib, but also from a particle of his heart, and even "a piece, no more than the half, of his soul."[24] Adam's heart yearns for the missing portion, without which it cannot be content.[25] Just as God

---

[19]*Postilla Symbolica der Spruchpostill. Das ist: Auslegung vnd Erklerung der fürnembsten Sprüche des Newen Testaments . . . Gehalten in S. Joachimsthal des 1563. Jahrs* (Leipzig: Johan Beyer, 1588). Hereafter *Postilla Symbolica.*

[20](Leipzig: Johan Beyer, 1590), hereafter *Apostel Paulus an die Corinthier.* This contains 263 sermons that Mathesius preached between April 10, 1551 and August 20, 1557.

[21]See, however, *Ehespiegel,* serm. 60:191: "In their sermons the monks, to be sure, praised the nuns – the St. Claras, St. Ursulas, St. Brigittas, St. Afras, and the Eleven Thousand Virgins." The Roman Catholic Church taught that Christ came to their wedding but that he wanted to separate their wedding from the wedded estate. Daniel prophesied that "the Antichrist would be hostile to the love of women and forbid marriage. But we preach against that at weddings out of what God says in his Word about the holy estate of matrimony. . . ." See also *Diluvium Mathesii,* serm. 31:161b.

[22]*Ehestand und Hauswesen,* serm. 1:n.p., but it would be Biv.

[23]Ibid., serms. 13 and 20 (letters): ii.   [24]Ibid., serm. 12:Qqiii.   [25]Ibid., serm. 2:Eii.

gave Eve to Adam, so every man should take a wife and every woman a husband. God created marriage by his ordinance, as an office and aid for the increase and continuation of the human species.[26] Nevertheless, Mathesius does mention the possibility of abstaining from marriage for those few who have the gift of total chastity, which is to say the rare ability to refrain from all sexual activity.[27] Like Luther, he does not think many people will be capable of this. He does not state whether this dispensation is available only to men, as Luther taught,[28] or whether it might apply to women as well.

Marriage is, then, established by God; it is not an institution of second rank, as Catholic clergy thought. It gives man a companion and assistance in the manifold tasks associated with dominion over all other living things. It grants to both husband and wife the joy of spiritual intimacy; spouses' hearts are joined from the beginning by the very process of Eve's creation.

Mathesius also addresses the question of Eve's condition before the fall. In preaching on the first book of Genesis, Mathesius presents women's roles from the beginning of time. Eve was her husband's companion (*Gesellin*)[29] and helper (*Gehülffin*).[30] The assistance she rendered was always in and around the house. In fact, woman herself is a house (*haus, gebewde*), a dwelling place for her husband, or, alternatively, a strong pillar (*seule*) against which he can lean.[31] Luther, too, used the image of the house to describe woman.[32] Eve was these things even before the fall, presumably psychologically, as the repository of her husband's loving emotions. Whether she was also so physically, because of receiving a part of Adam's body into herself and sheltering and nourishing the developing infant until birth, is clear neither in Luther nor in Mathesius. Neither author takes an unequivocal stand on whether Adam and Eve actually engaged in sex before the fall and whether they did or could have had children. It is not clear from the Genesis story whether enough time elapsed in Eden before the fall for a fetus to mature.

Mathesius avers that before her disobedience, Eve was equal to Adam.[33] In the feminine domain, the household, God intended Eve and her daughters to be fully empresses. By equality Mathesius means that within their respective arenas, the domestic and the public – whatever public may have meant in the prelapsarian milieu – Eve and Adam exercised comparable authority.

---

[26]*Apostel Paulus an die Corinthier*, serm. 1:178a

[27]Ibid.

[28]WA 17 (2), Sermon "am tag Johannis des heiligen Apostels und Euangelistens Evangelion Johannis xxi," 347.

[29]*Ehestand und Hauswesen*, serm. 12:Rrii. Mathesius agrees that Christ's marriage to his church has its human counterpart in the nuptial bond between man and woman (Rriii).

[30]*Ehestand und Hauswesen*, serm. 1:Aiii. *Ehespiegel*, serm. 1:3; serm. 5:12.

[31]*Ehespiegel*, serm. 1:3; serm. 4:9-10, 11; *Ehestand und Hauswesen*, serm. 1:Aiii.

[32]WA 42:98-99.

[33]*Ehespiegel*, serm. 3:7-8.

Curiously, Mathesius sees Eve, the mother and epitome of womankind, the "grandmother of all bad women," as seriously deficient in character even before the fall. The serpent approached her and not Adam because of her innate susceptibility. She was not content being queen of the whole earth and empress of the hearth; she wanted to be a goddess, and this ambition brought the human race down from its lofty position.[34] She listened to the serpent and seduced man; and thus her responsibility for the debacle in Eden was primary.[35] Adam's fault lay merely in listening to his wife. Eve sinned first and Adam last.[36]

Because of her sin, Eve's original flaws now become egregious. Now her spirit

> was drowned in all kinds of gloom and darkness, and because of the serpent's poison, her heart was completely ruined (*verderbet*) and was spoiled with all sorts of stubbornness, anger, arrogance, spite, and cunning. Before the fall she bore the image of the son of God, but now after the fall she wears the devil's mask.
>
> And although through trust in the Mediator, she together with her husband has been raised up again and through faith in Christ has become a dwelling place of the Holy Spirit, yet horribly great darkness of spirit and obstinacy of heart remain hanging [in her], and the law of the flesh has been an animosity toward God; and out of this old flesh, just as out of an evil spring, a great many sins have gushed forth, just as the Lord Christ says in Matthew 15.[37]

Furthermore, through inheritance all women are heirs of Eve's ruined nature. The preacher does not mention either Adam here or Eve's sons. Women, he says, cannot curb and tame themselves, and God has consequently placed them under the governance of men.[38] Women, he notes elsewhere, are more inclined to all sorts of bad thoughts than men.[39]

> He [God] sees well that without [control by men] they are, all by themselves, insolent and wanton, proud and mischievous, like a frolicsome horse; for Satan has poured a good deal of his wantonness and impudence into women, as both history and daily experience bear witness. . . . So that the feminine gender does not do itself

---

[34]Johannes Mathesius, *Sarepta* [alias *Bergpostille*], *Darinn von allerley Bergwerck vnnd Metallen . . . guter bericht gegeben*, vol. 2 (Nuremberg: Dietrich Gerlatz, 1571; hereafter *Sarepta*), 7. This was originally published in 1562.

[35]See Herman and Mathesius, *Geistliche Lieder*, no. 38, "Ein Brautlied," verse 5: "Voller List aber war die Schlang / Eva das Wort Gottes abdrang / Dass sie übertrat sein Gebot / Und führt uns in Höll, Sünd und Tod."

[36]*Ehespiegel*, serm. 17:43.

[37]*Syrach*, serm. 8 on Ecclus. 25:172.

[38]Ibid.   [39]Ibid., Sermon 2 on Ecclus. 26, 175.

harm like a horse without a bridle, God put a hard bit in the mouths of Eve and all her daughters, in order to subdue and dull (*betöbern*) their appetites (*Begierde*) and lasciviousness . . . .[40]

Because she sinned, woman has become a maidservant who must submit to the bit and the bridle. And as a sign of her captivity (*Gefengnis*) she wears around her head so many ribbons and cords (*Bendel vnd Schnüre*), which are symbols of her imprisonment. There she has to serve as the maid and the vinegar jug, and the husband will command her [to do something] sooner than he will the [real] maid.[41]

Thus, women are not only to be houses in the figurative sense, but they must literally stay at home and care for the household, like the proverbial snail in its shell.[42] Whereas before the Fall the household was their empire and they were empresses over it, now they are condemned to be domestic (*heuslich*), an adjective Mathesius uses over and over to describe the good woman. Mathesius goes even further by saying that women are confined to the home (*gefangen*), first by their parents, then by their husbands. They are no longer empresses in any respect; their husbands are emperors (*keyser*) in the mundane microcosm.[43] Women, by comparison, are now lowly human beings, the "most extremely miserable creatures of all creatures on the entire face of the earth."[44] "Those who are not moved [to humility] by their labor and distress [in childbearing] but despise the Son of God will have to experience and endure much more misfortune and punishment. Yes, [the entire contents of] Pandora's box will fall upon them."[45]

With the arrival of lust, women also serve men as a remedy for the sin of concupiscence. Mathesius affirms that to marry is better than to burn.[46] From reading Luther we are well acquainted with the concept of *remedium ad peccatum,* and the reformer in turn drew the idea from St. Paul and the early church fathers.[47] Luther compared the marriage bed to a hospital in

---

[40]*Ehespiegel,* serm. 16:39.   [41]Ibid.

[42]*Ehespiegel,* serm. 69:190. For Luther's use of the same simile, see WA 42:151.

[43]Ibid., serm. 17:41.

[44]Ibid., serm. 14:36: "die aller elendeste Creatur unter allen Creaturen auff dem gantzen Erdboden."

[45]Ibid.

[46]*Ehestand und Hauswesen,* serm. 15:n.p., but would be Fffiv if numbered.

[47]James A. Brundage, *Law, Sex, and Christian Society in Medieval Europe* (Chicago: University of Chicago Press, 1987), 62-98, 185-87, 421-20. Consult also Robert C. Gregg, "Die Ehe: Patristische und reformatorische Fragen," *Zeitschrift für Kirchengeschichte* 96 (1985): 1-12. I strongly recommend, as erudite, informative, and fascinating, Peter Brown, *The Body and Society: Men, Women and Sexual Renunciation in Early Christianity* (New York: Columbia University Press, 1988).

which the disease of raging lust is treated.[48] Overall, Mathesius emphasizes
this aspect of marriage less than the reformer, but he does accept the notion
that marriage gives men the only socially and religiously acceptable outlet
for their almost inescapable carnality. Once he quotes Augustine directly and
uses the Latin *remedium,* but when preaching in German he usually prefers
the word *Arzney.*[49] Marital sex is the medical treatment of lust. As on every
other topic, he writes here exclusively from the masculine perspective, leaving
us to ask whether intercourse between husband and wife also serves as
medication for women's desire. Whatever the answer, like Luther before
him, Mathesius breaks sharply with the Catholic clerical assertion that women
were far more libidinous than men. Only occasionally, as with his use of the
word "lasciviousness" above, do we catch an echo of that view. That aside,
the Reformation did redistribute the onus of sexual culpability.

Women's chief specific duty is the production and rearing of children.
This is women's truest vocation, one they must not avoid.[50] Children are
the highest good of marriage.[51]

> The female vocation (*Beruff*) is bearing children. But bearing children,
> or *teknogonia,* comprehends all domestic work, diligence, and effort,
> such as becoming pregnant, carrying children and giving birth, nursing,
> nourishing, feeding, looking after them, taking on the housekeeping,
> teaching and instructing the children in what is best, saving something
> for them, economizing and setting aside, honorably endowing them
> and marrying them off, and whatever wiping up, clothing, and
> cleaning goes with it.[52]

Wifehood, motherhood, and housewifery are inseparable points toward which
every female should orient herself. A daughter should pray, "Heavenly Father,
my dear God . . . Let me [among others] become a good housekeeper . . .
so that I may be an adornment to my baptism and vocation and praise you
along the path that you have commanded for me."[53] A housewife should
pray, "Lord Jesus Christ . . . help through your goodness that in conformity

[48]"Ein Sermon von dem ehelichen Stand," WA 2:168-69.

[49]For example, see *Apostel Paulus an die Corinthier,* serm. 1:178a. *Ehespiegel,* serm. 64:207:
". . . propter officium et remedium creata est uxor."

[50]In his fourth sermon on Ecclesiasticus 25 (*Syrach,* 169), Mathesius expresses his horror
over the discovery of some dead infants, murdered, he assumes, and buried by their mothers.

[51]*Ehespiegel,* serm. 7:20-21.

[52]Ibid., serm. 67:219-20.

[53]Johannes Mathesius, *Oeconomia Oder Bericht vom Christlichen Hausswesen* (Erfurt: Georg
Bawman, 1577), n.p. but between D pages and E pages. This edition is a stunning example of
the sixteenth-century printing art. It is heart shaped, bound down the middle, and opens on
both sides. It contains the Nikolaus Herman German translation (pp. 269-73) of Mathesius's
Latin "Epithalamion oder Brautlied," first given by the pastor in 1560.

to your command I humble myself before my husband and raise my child to fear you and to live in decency . . . ."[54]

Mathesius paints a rather touching picture of the loving family when he advises the wife,

> When the husband comes home from afar, or from his official duties, business, or craft, she should open the door and go toward him and receive him in a friendly way. She should teach her little children to draw their father a little heart, give him a little kiss, and put their small hands in his. For another thing, she should set upon his lap the children who are too small to speak.
>
> One finds many who take their husband's damp hat and coat, and who warm up a shirt for him if he comes home from work damp with sweat.[55]

Mathesius continually holds up wives and mothers of the Bible and classical literature as models of the good woman: Sarah, Rebecca, Rachel, Abigail, Anna (Samuel's mother), the Sunamite (II Kings 4), Susannah, Esther, Mary of Bethany, Nausicaa, Penelope, Cornelia, and Veturia (the mother of Coriolanus).[56] The one male example that he sets before women is Zacharias – because he was silent![57] In virtually all his wedding and other pertinent sermons, Mathesius employs stock adjectives to describe the traits of personality and character that the Christian female should cultivate. She should be pious, faithful, devout, loyal, chaste, bashful, timid, quiet, helpful, gracious, loving, encouraging, hardworking, happy, peaceable, frugal, motherly, obedient, humble, domestic, modest, longsuffering, fertile, compassionate, practical, gentle, patient, submissive, and clever. Women's adornment should be inner virtue and not outer sparkle.[58] In one sermon, Mathesius opines that the four cardinal feminine virtues are faith, love, chastity, and decorum. "Girls ought to work and sew these four words into their embroidery. That is the females' catechism and decalogue."[59] It is surely a fine piece of understatement when he says that "a domestic, clever, reasonable, modest, honorable, and understanding wife is a powerful good and a great treasure on earth and in keeping house."[60]

In one of his sermons on Ecclesiasticus 25, Mathesius declares that neither Jesus Syrach nor he meant to malign all women. "We want," he said, "if God wills it, to live out our days in the praise of women."[61] Several of the

---

[54]*Oeconomia,* in part n.p., and in part Diiii.

[55]*Syrach,* serm. 7 on Ecclus. 25:171.

[56]These names are found throughout Mathesius's pertinent sermons. See also *Postilla Symbolica,* 62.

[57]*Oeconomia,* n.p., but between pages paginated A and those paginated B.

[58]*Ehespiegel,* serm. 38:122; serm. 29: passim.

[59]Ibid., serm. 67:220.   [60]*Postilla Symbolica,* 62-63.   [61]*Syrach,* serm. 4 on Ecclus. 25:168b.

sermons from which his harshest criticisms are drawn, when taken as a whole, praise the married estate and stress the love and forbearance that partners are to extend to one another. Especially the first fifteen sermons of *Vom Ehestandt vnd Hauswesen* are informed with warmth, the product of a mind that intended to foster affection and domestic harmony in the marriages beginning before him. Of some Catholic, clerical, and learned opinion he was openly critical. He lists and rejects the worst slanders of "the wise men and philosophers," who called woman "an unreasoning animal, an evil worm, an evil grass, a bitter herb, a sweet evil, a necessary misfortune, . . . an obstacle to eternal life, a hindrance and inconvenience to the saints, . . . a sow stall, a miner's arseleather [*arschleder,* worn by silver miners to protect their backsides in the low shafts], one of the seven deadly sins, worms, a sweet poison, a sewer, a trash can [*Schmeisshaus*] . . . ."[62] Nonetheless, as a man of his time he continued to regard females with prejudice, as a potential, and often an actual, threat to the stability of society. He was a well-educated man who knew not only Luther but the Bible and the classics. He had imbibed with his studies the misogyny that was rampant in late medieval clerical circles, and he had digested it. If women's heavenly redemption lay in divine hands, their only acceptable earthly salvation lay in human, masculine ones. Women must fulfill the assignment that God has given them; quite literally, they must accept their calling (*vocatio, Beruf*). A salient difference between men and women is that among men, a variety of vocations are in evidence, whereas for womankind there is a single, unified calling, that of Christian housewife and mother. On this point Mathesius was, as he believed himself always to be, in complete agreement with Luther, his hero and his model. No matter what women's actual livelihoods and vicissitudes might be, their identity and their satisfaction were to be derived from their ties to husband, children, and home.

Does the pastor envision no public function for women? Certainly not in preaching or teaching. He observes that Mary Magdalene was a preacher (*Predigerin*) of the Gospel, but that was an aberration.[63] He fully concurs with St. Paul that women must be silent in the churches, and he thanks God that no women in Joachimsthal were attempting to preach.[64] Mathesius mentions only two activities that women ought to carry on in the community. One is treating one another's "female" illnesses, including pregnancy and tending sick children; here he accords to skilled and experienced women – but not to all women – the right to practice healing. He praises the medications of pious matrons at court and in the cities, and he says that Mary Magdalene

---

[62]*Ehespiegel,* serm. 5:12.

[63]*Ehestand und Hauswesen,* serm. 11:Ooii.   [64]*Ehespiegel,* serm. 67:219.

was known for her herbs and curative concoctions.⁶⁵ All citizens, however, must shun witchcraft and other sorts of betrayal.⁶⁶

A second approved undertaking for women is serving the needy (*Handreichung*) and assisting the church in those practical ways that circumstances might dictate. Mathesius speaks here of "pious matrons," suggesting that the older, or at least the mature, woman, whose children no longer need her constant oversight, may have time to give Christian aid to her church and less fortunate neighbors. Women may serve the church if this does not conflict with their responsibilities at home.⁶⁷

All in all, Mathesius's estimation of womankind is less positive than his estimation of marriage. To be sure, women are co-heirs of God's grace, and just like men they are instruments (*werckzeuge*) of God's will: "Even though they are well a foolish [*blöd*] and weak tool of God . . . nevertheless God has accomplished much healing and relief [*wolfart*] through the feminine sex, and Christianity has been served by women's help and profession of faith."⁶⁸ Yet despite his praise and promotion of marriage, and despite the love for his wife that he professed throughout the years that remained to him after her death, Mathesius expresses again and again his opinion that women are severely flawed and dangerous if not supervised. For this reason, I am convinced that we must begin to distinguish between the advocacy of marriage and the praise of women qua women.

If this preacher's wedding and other relevant sermons were directed, as they were, to a mixed audience, what message were men to take with them? First, they were to comprehend women's inescapable weakness and incapacity. To some degree this had been a consistent strain in Western thought since at least the fifth century, though in lay circles probably not an entirely convincing one. Not the theme itself but its insistent, incessant public repetition is here the novelty. Women's inferiority was articulated not by some celibate priest or friar but by a married pastor, not to clergy alone in an effort to help them subdue the flesh, but to the entire populace. Furthermore, the pastor now had the tacit support of the local magistracy and the higher echelons of authority. The Protestant church in the urban setting came to be unified in a way that its Catholic predecessor had never been. Women and men were to take the pastor's teachings to heart. For his part, Mathesius fully intended to indoctrinate his human flock.

Second, men were to grasp the centrality of marriage to social stability. They were to realize that structurally the husband is God's representative in

⁶⁵Ibid., serm. 62:200. Mathesius may have thought of Anna, wife of Elector August of Saxony, an avid collector of herbs and medicinal recipes.
⁶⁶Ibid., 197-98.
⁶⁷See, for instance, *Ehespiegel,* serm. 45:159.
⁶⁸*Ehestand und Hauswesen,* serm. 11:Oo-Ooii.

the household, and God's will for human society depends on his accepting this obligation as well as this honor. Mathesius envisions the family as the basic agency through which Christ's word is disseminated and order maintained.

Third, men are to receive instruction in their own proper deportment within marriage. In these sermons, the division of labor and sex roles are not merely reflected as facts of life; rather, the common reality has now become ideology. Women *must* stay in the home; they *must* bear children if they are able; they *must* submit to their husbands' judgments in all matters including the domestic; they *may not* be divorced from him if he is tyrannical and cruel,[69] unbelieving and obstinate,[70] even if he becomes a Catholic,[71] and probably even in the case of adultery, since many who wander will return to the right path.[72] If one spouse becomes an Anabaptist, then they may separate, but Mathesius does not say that they may divorce.[73] No matter how badly husband and wife act, they must stay together, unless, of course, one attempts to kill the other or a child. In that case, the magistrates must do their duty. But even then, the innocent party should not be permitted to remarry.[74] Mathesius's very conservative opinions did not determine the judgments actually handed down in such instances, and he, after all, resided in a Catholic land where diocesan consistories still at least nominally held sway. Nevertheless, divorce was a scarce commodity in all Lutheran territories; there was no really liberal policy in the sixteenth century.

Divorce being all but impossible, then, men must master their wives. To allow women to gain the upper hand is more than humiliating; it undermines social order and it offends God. Amazingly, Mathesius had read Luther's (and Bugenhagen's) 1528 letter to the humanist scribe of Zwickau, Stephan Roth, which severely admonished him for not having his wife under control.[75] The Joachimsthal pastor declares, "One should check and restrain [*stewren vnd wehren*] the malice [of women], says Luther in a letter to Stephan Roth [about] how one should deal with a bad wife."[76]

Fourth, barring the misfortune of a self-assertive wife, husbands should love their wives as themselves, should be patient and forbearing, tender and

---

[69]*Ehespiegel,* serm. 37:120: "Merckts wol: Des Mannes Tyranney vnnd Grawsamkeit, oder Vngleicheit des Glaubens vnnd der Religion, hebet oder trennet das Band des Ehestandes gar nicht auff."

[70]Ibid., 122.

[71]*Apostel Paulus an die Corinthier,* serm. 3:181b. Unless he refused to allow his wife to continue in the true faith.

[72]Ibid., 181b.   [73]Ibid., 183a.   [74]Ibid., 181a.

[75]WA BR, 4: no. 1253, April 12, 1528.

[76]*Ehespiegel,* serm. 61:195. As far as I know, Luther's letter was not in print but was probably among the papers that Roth left when he died in 1545. Roth had taught in Joachimsthal as a young man and could have retained connections there; the two may well have been acquainted. Unfortunately, most of Roth's voluminous correspondence has never been published and languishes unread in the Zwickau Ratsschulbibliothek.

considerate. They must remember that women are the weaker vessel and do not have the ability to meet men's higher standard.[77] A husband should try not to notice each thing that his wife does wrong but "peer through his fingers" instead. "Married couples live in concord the longest when one is blind and the other deaf, says the clever King Alfonso. Whoever notices and fights over everything and talks and inveighs against everything, and never occasionally looks through his fingers or lets things pass by his ears – he must always be at war."[78] Notwithstanding the husband's honor and majesty, he should not behave like a lion in the house, always sour looking, rebuking, grumbling, and hitting. If he does he will embitter his wife, who will then rarely be the apple of his eye and the comfort of his heart.[79] Mathesius tells his congregation in a Christmas sermon that the ornithic symbol of the wedded pair is the kingfisher, "who carries his aged spouse to sweet water."[80] Nevertheless, husbands will find that they have to discipline their wives from time to time. ". . . God . . . gave him [the husband] two hands – just as he gave worldly authority the sword and the schoolmaster the rod – so that the bad wife may be broken of her intention and behavior. . . ."[81]

Fifth, whereas the wife is confined to the household, the husband is obliged to provide her with a living. He must nourish, house, and clothe her and their children and servants. If a woman is to regard her husband as her lord, she must be able to count on his protection and sufficient maintenance. Women should never be the breadwinners. This would be like spanning the horse in back of the wagon. And to live from a wife's inherited money makes of the husband a minstrel in his own home.[82] Mathesius does not specifically criticize women contributing something to their families' livelihood, but theirs must be a secondary and subordinate enterprise, ever giving way to the immediate requirements of the family and ever appropriate to their housekeeping vocation.

Mathesius holds Isaac out to men as the model of the good husband and householder. Six sermons in *Vom Ehestand und Hauswesen* take as their texts portions of the Genesis story of Isaac.[83] The pastor evidently does not consider

[77]As one might expect, the phrase "weaker vessel" appears with regularity, e.g., *Ehespiegel*, serms. 14:36; 61:195. See *Ehespiegel*, serms. 41 and 42, on men's behavior toward their wives, 137-45.

[78]*Ehestand und Hauswesen*, serm. 4:N. The last phrase is literally: ". . . der muss nimmer kein schwert einstecken."

[79]Ibid., serm. 12:Qqii.

[80]Johannes Mathesius, *Auslegung vnd Erklerung des vhralten vnd aller Ersten Euangelij von des Weibes Samen* (Leipzig: Johan Beyer, 1587), Aiiii.

[81]*Syrach*, serm. 8 on Ecclus. 25:172.

[82]I suppose that "minstrel," a derogatory label at this time, is meant as someone who is expected to "perform" for his living. *Ehestand und Hauswesen*, serm. 4:Mii.

[83]Serms. 3-8, only partly paginated.

it a flaw in Isaac that his wife conspired with Jacob to deceive him and succeeded.

My purpose in sketching the salient features of Mathesius's teachings on women and matrimony is to show that one well-known, popular, second-generation Lutheran pastor propagated, in person and through the printed book, a view of private reformed society that may – after other men's sermons have been scrutinized – prove to have been characteristic of the new faith. I also wish once again to raise the issue of whether, in what ways, and to what degree reformed clerical opinion actually departed from the Catholic. I shall offer several tentative conclusions, with the understanding that when other men's homilies have been more closely studied, these conclusions may have proved to need modification.

1. Mathesius intended and believed that his views coincided with Martin Luther's. For the most part they do, but I have never detected in Luther the notion of a particularly virulent and specifically feminine strain of original sin, one that was transmitted exclusively by Eve to women alone. The sources of this idea need to be identified, but it surely does not derive from reformed thought. While present in his sermons on Ecclesiasticus, which was an important source too for the authors of *The Hammer of Witches,* this is not a prominent theme in Mathesius.

2. We should cease to regard the elevation of marriage as synonymous with the elevation of womankind. The over-close identification of the two involves a logical fallacy. Marriage could have been promoted for reasons that were in part antifeminine. Mathesius's sermons frequently juxtapose high praise of the marital condition with the depiction of the very defective nature of women. This seems a curious inconsistency, but it is possible that marriage was now more actively praised and promoted in part because women were perceived to be *worse* than before and more in need of the male discipline that the nuptial bond imposed upon them. In theory at least, unless women relinquished the last vestige of their independence, the social order was felt to be threatened.

3. So many derogatory estimations of women are to be encountered in the sermons and treatises of Mathesius (not to mention Luther[84]) that I am tempted to inquire whether Lutheran clergy may not at base have taken over and incorporated much traditional Catholic clerical misogyny, to which they added (not at all cynically) sufficiently mitigating and encouraging language to render credible their insistence that all marry. There is a curiously monastic flavor to the life Mathesius advocates for women: not poverty, to be sure, but chastity, obedience, and stability. Lutheranism liberates men from monastic vows, but women must live as semi-nuns. Catholic expressions of misogyny

---

[84]See Merry E. Wiesner, "Luther and Women: The Death of Two Marys," in *Disciplines of Faith: Religion, Patriarchy and Politics,* ed. James Obelkevich, Raphael Samuel, and Lyndal Roper (London: Routledge, 1986), 295-308.

had generally been confined to a narrow celibate group, not the laity at large. With the triumph of Lutheranism, some of these same negative sentiments were pressed hard and regularly upon a much wider audience – in fact upon everyone, clergy and laity alike. All the same, the most extreme vituperation, incompatible with the happy association of the sexes, was abandoned.

4. Mathesius's stress upon the husband as God's representative in the home, and the application to him of words like "honor," "glory," and "majesty" widen the ideological gap between men and women. In describing the place of men, Mathesius uses language often reserved for the deity, and yet he calls women "the lowest creatures on earth." Mathesius drives a verbal wedge between the sexes even while claiming to reconcile them. Did the Reformation actually seek to increase the distance between laymen and laywomen? Or did it reinforce a distance that had begun to grow independently in those urban circles affected by the revival of classical ideas? The considerable discrepancy between the grammar school curricula offered to boys and to girls in the towns hints further at a desire to separate the male and female spheres.[85] What had often in the late Middle Ages been de facto differences between the sexes now hardened into de jure separation.

5. Did Lutheran preachers like Mathesius hold forth so vehemently on the desirability of marriage in part to justify their own abandonment of celibacy to a public that was not entirely convinced that the godly cleric *should* indulge his sexual appetites?[86] It is certainly true that late medieval complaints about clerical incontinence were rife, but did popular opinion overwhelmingly accept a married pastorate, or would it have preferred simply an end to hypocrisy and the enforcement of abstinence?

6. There is a curious paradox in the transition from Catholic to Lutheran marriage. Under Catholicism, we well know, marriage was in principle a sacrament. Yet the ceremony usually took place at the church door or away from the church, with a priest in attendance to pronounce his blessing. The church actually made little fuss over the ritual and took a rather minor part in it. The couple's consent, with or without ecclesiastical participation, created the bond. By contrast, Lutheranism purported to secularize the tie, and yet it moved the rite into the church and before altar and congregation. Lutheranism insisted that a duly authorized clergyman actively preside, demanded that he preach on the sanctity of marriage to all in attendance, and subsequently kept couples under closer supervision than Catholicism ever had. The impression left by Protestant attentiveness and avid pronouncement is one of sacralizing marriage. We ought to look not just at changes in theology, but also at actual behavior as we identify the secular and the sacred.

[85]See my "The Reality of Early Lutheran Education," n. 17 above.

[86]Steven Ozment notes that the laity occasionally did have trouble adjusting to a married clergy. See *The Age of Reform 1250-1550: An Intellectual and Religious History of Late Medieval and Reformation Europe* (New Haven: Yale University Press, 1980), 394-95.

7. Evidence has begun to accumulate of women's deteriorating economic position in Europe after 1450.[87] Is it nothing more than a coincidence that women were losing ground in the most concrete sphere, the workaday world, at the same time that Mathesius and others were promoting their withdrawal into the home? I am not suggesting that any connection between the two was consciously drawn.

8. Is it only by chance that authoritarian principles were gaining in Germany at the territorial level (and indeed at the local level too – although here they were forced to give way to the princes) during the very period when Mathesius was articulating the authoritarian governance of the household? Does the microcosm in any sense reflect the macrocosm? Certainly, Mathesius saw a correspondence between the divine and the various human hierarchies.

In a thought-provoking essay, Wolfgang Reinhard searches for the roots of modernization across confessional boundaries during the Reformation and Counter-Reformation era. He finds remarkable similarities between the Reformation and the Counter-Reformation, between Lutheranism and Calvinism, and between the ways in which they used the process of confessionalization to achieve the goal of a collective mentality.[88] Among the seven methods Reinhard lists are the dissemination of new norms, propagating belief in these and preventing those who disagree from doing likewise, achieving discipline among those who adhere to the new teaching, and employing ritual to reinforce the views being introduced.[89] We could find in Mathesius's sermons a manifestation of just such efforts. Mathesius presents to a lay audience new norms for the relationship between husband and wife: husbands rule absolutely, their wives submit in all things and stay at home. The sermons may be seen as propaganda for these norms. Nor was Mathesius's power

[87]Examples of this evidence may be found in Martha C. Howell, "Women, the Family Economy, and the Structures of Market Production in Cities of Northern Europe during the Late Middle Ages," in *Women and Work in Preindustrial Europe,* ed. Barbara A. Hanawalt (Bloomington: Indiana University Press, 1986), 198-222; Susan C. Karant-Nunn, "The Women of the Saxon Silver Mines," in *Women in Reformation and Counter-Reformation Europe: Public and Private Worlds,* ed. Sherrin Marshall (Bloomington: Indiana University Press, 1989), 42-43; Erika Uitz, "Zu denauf eine Verbesserung ihrer gesellschaftlichen Stellung hinzielenden Aktivitäten der Frauen in den deutschen Städten des Spätmittelalters," *Untersuchungen zur gesellschaftlichen Stellung der Frau im Feudalismus, Magdeburger Beiträge zur Städtegeschichte* 3 (1981): 47-69; Kurt Wesoly, "Der weibliche Bevölkerungsanteil in spätmittelalterlichen und frühneuzeitlichen Städten und die Bestätigung von Frauen im zünftigen Handwerk (insbesondere am Mittel- und Oberrhein)," *Zeitschrift für die Geschichte des Oberrheins* 128 (1980): 69-117; Merry E. Wiesner, *Working Women in Renaissance Germany* (New Brunswick, N.J.: Rutgers University Press, 1986), esp. 149-85 and 187-98.

[88]Wolfgang Reinhard, "Zwang zur Konfessionalisierung? Prolegomena zu einer Theorie des konfessionellen Zeitalters," *Zeitschrift für historische Forschung* 10, no. 3 (1983): 257-77. See also his "Gegenreformation als Modernisierung," *Archive for Reformation History* 68 (1977): 226-51; and "Konfession und Konfessionalisierung in Europa," in *Bekenntnis und Geschichte,* ed. W. Reinhard (Munich: Vogel, 1981), 165-89.

[89]Reinhard, "Zwang zur Konfessionalisierung?" 263-67.

confined to the pulpit. As his correspondence reveals, he was in a position to insist on conformity.[90] The emerging Lutheran nuptial rite, although its Catholic antecedents were clearly visible, contained innovations that symbolized the new order of things: the performance of the ceremony before the altar and in the presence of the congregation; the wedding sermon as instruction of the bridal pair and the public; the concerted effort to eliminate the long-traditional sexual pranks that attended the bedding of the pair. Changes in Lutheran teaching on marriage and in Lutheran practice thus provide a good example of the methods of confessionalization.[91]

9. The image of women's place that Mathesius's sermons convey may be summed up with three German words: *Kinder, Küche, Kirche*. Preachers of the Reformation era like Mathesius shifted their emphasis to elements of social belief that were already available but not widely popular, elements that before had been invoked chiefly by Catholic clergy and intellectuals. These preachers now enthusiastically inculcated them on the laity. They minted the ideology that is represented by the slogan, "*Kinder, Küche, Kirche.*" Compared to the medieval clerical advocacy of shunning women, they did effect a reconciliation between the clergy and the female sex, and some would call this elevation. But in lay terms, they did not plainly elevate women.

Johannes Mathesius composed an elegy to his beloved wife Sibylla. Here is an excerpt from it:

> Oh, what a pious wife she was!
> Her heart all faith, modesty, truth, and love;
> Like a vineyard she was fruitful,
> To her husband she was truthful,
> And never with his views disputeful.
>
> The Psalter was her favorite book,
> To church it with her always took.

---

[90]Mathesius sought and obtained from Philip Melanchthon advice on marriage cases under the pastor's control. See Mathesius's surviving correspondence in Loesche, ed. *Johannes Mathesius, Ausgewählte Werke*, 2:223-371.

[91]The leader in developing a theory of confessionalization is Heinz Schilling. He has published extensively on the subject. Among many others, see the following: *Konfessionskonflikt und Staatsbildung: Eine Fallstudie über das Verhältnis von religiösem und sozialem Wandel in der Frühneuzeit am Beispiel der Grafschaft Lippe*, Quellen und Forschungen zur Reformationsgeschichte, 48 (Gütersloh: Gütersloher Verlagshaus, 1981); summarized in "Between the Territorial State and Urban Liberty: Lutheranism and Calvinism in the County of Lippe," in *The German People and the Reformation*, ed. R. Po-chia Hsia (Ithaca: Cornell University Press, 1988), 263-83; "Die Konfessionalisierung im Reich," *Historische Zeitschrift* 246 (1988): 1-45. Thus far, Professor Schilling's treatment has concentrated on territorial and urban politics and the interaction of groups such as classes and guilds rather than on the family, an institution that obviously crossed all social and economic boundaries. It is quite apparent that authorities did try to "confessionalize" the family. See Lyndal Roper, *The Holy Household: Women and Morals in Reformation Augsburg* (Oxford: Clarendon Press, 1989).

A gentle spirit who could understand,
She had a truthful tongue, a generous hand.
Tended child and kitchen, ran her house,
She told her husband before she went out.
A humble woman and constantly patient,
She hated show, shunned ostentation.
Reticent, obedient, upright, and mild,
With everyone in peace she dealt.
Ever conciliatory, harsh with none,
She never differed with her husband.[92]

[92]Loesche, ed., *Johannes Mathesius, Ausgewählte Werke*, vol. 1:*Leichenreden*, 66-67.

Success and Failure of the Reformation: Popular "Apologies" from the Seventeenth and Eighteenth Centuries

Hans-Christoph Rublack

German Lutheran pastors of the early modern period quoted and commented on the practical accounts lay people gave of their attitude to Lutheran religion. These "apologies" form a vital source for studying the attitudes toward religion of the simple layfolk, mostly in rural areas. Many people resented the elaborate and disciplining demands placed on their lives by the church, and many objected to the threatening images of hell and the devil to which they were exposed by Lutheranism. What they sought was an assuring pastoral care and the ritual highlighting of the "rites de passage." Until the eighteenth century religious knowledge of doctrinal matters was hardly internalized by most peasants, although some were able to read the Bible and even cited it in their arguments. As a result, anticlericalism prevailed, together with attitudes that ranged from open hostility to the church to religious indifference. These attitudes should not be mistaken for secularism, however, because laymen claimed to have immediate access to God, and they believed in the reality of the devil. They accepted the restricted form of the Lutheran service and identified Lutheran religion largely with preaching, but they continued to use religious formulas to ward off evil. What made pastoral preaching alien to the simple folk may be defined as cultural distance. Laymen objected to the learned character of the Lutheran message as well as to what they felt to be interference in their traditional lives by the clergy. The "Apologies" of the laymen may be considered as instruments of negotiation aimed at defending their practice of religion and asking the pastors to adapt their teaching to the needs of everyday life.

I

LUDWIG WITTGENSTEIN SUGGESTS that the form and content of the apologies and excuses that people consider tenable is a reflection of their thoughts and life-style. This opinion may have been shared by the Stuttgart court preacher Felix Bidembach when, in March 1601, the subject of his sermon centered on the apologies used by "the children of this world" to mitigate their sins.[1] The following quotation typifies these apologies: "Of what consequence is

---

[1]Felix Bidembach, *Kurtze Predigt / von den viererley ge = meinen vnnd vermeinten Auszreden / oder Entschuldigungen der Weltkinder / dardurch sie jhre Suend zu bemænteln / oder zuuernichten begeren / vnd dannenhero in sicherheit gerhaten . . . .* (Tübingen: Georg Gruppenbach, 1601).

it when I have done something that is not quite correct? This does not make me automatically devilish."[2] What these "children of this world" challenged was the preaching of the law, a central concern of Lutheran sermons throughout the early modern era. Resentment prevailed among the laity on this point and was noted by the preachers. This was particularly marked in instances in which the preacher endeavored to admonish his congregation. In 1581, Conrad Porta observed that the preachers' use of admonitions made the laity suspect that this was an inherent attempt at clerical domination: "People become angered at the preachers and say the parsons wish to be lords."[3] In 1766, at the end of the ancien régime, another pastor, Gottfried Merkel, warned his colleagues, "You can be taken as a little pope in your village," and further cited laymen who claimed that "one is no longer sure how one should approach the pastor since he scolds us at every turn. It is almost as if one is facing death on the occasions when one has some business to attend to in the parson's house."[4] The sentiments cited above gain perhaps their most succinct expression in the Swabian saying, "In every parson you will find a little pope."[5]

The laity rejected that preaching of the law which exhorted them to change their life-style. They asked at the end of the seventeenth century, "Why do the clergy become involved in matters that do not concern them."[6] Johannes Mathesius had already reported in 1559, "Parsons exaggerate the fires of hell to prompt the laity to make sacrifice."[7] Laymen tended to recognize and minimize this type of spiritual rhetoric with such comments as "If the parsons could not talk of the devil nor the shepherds of the wolf,

---

[2] Ibid., 8-9: "Was ists dann mehr / wann ich gleich das gethan habe / es ist wol nicht gar recht / dass aber einer gleich solte darumb des Teuffels sein / das ist nicht."

[3] Conrad Porta, *Pastorale Lvtheri.* . . . (Eisleben: Andreas Petri, 1582): 102v; preaching the law has the effect, that "die Leute zuernen / vnd vnwillig werden vber die Prediger / sagen die Pfaffen wollen Herrn sein."

[4] Gottfried Merkel, *Briefe über den Charakter und die Pflicht eines evangelischen Predigers,* vol. 1 (Berlin: Christian Friedrich Voss, 1766), 135: "Man kann in seinem Dorf fuer einen kleinen Pabst gehalten werden." "Man weisz bey nahe nicht mehr, wie man mit unserem Herrn Magister reden soll. Alle Augenblicke faehrt er uns an. Es ist, als wenn man in den Tod gehen sollte, wann man auf der Pfarre etwas zu verrichten hat."

[5] "In jedem Pfäffle stecket e Päbstle." Hermann Fischer, *Schwäbisches Wörterbuch* 1 (Tübingen: Lauppsche Verlagsbuchhandlung, 1904), 999-1000.

[6] Johann Ludwig Hartmann, *Reine Lehrer und feine Zuhoerer / aus Act. XX. So bezeuge ich nun / dasz ich rein sey von aller Blut etc.* . . . (Rothenburg o.d.T.: Noah von Millenau, 1679), 46: "Was gehet dieses die Geistliche an, was sie nicht brennet / sollen sie nicht löschen."

[7] "Einer spricht / o die Pfaffen machen die helle heisz / das man opffern solle." Johannes Mathesius, *Leychpredigten Ausz dem fünfftzehenden Capitel der I. Epistel S. Pauli zun Corinthiern. Von der aufferstehung der Todten vnd ewigem leben* . . . . (Nuremberg, 1559), lv.

they would have very little to say."[8] In instances where the pastor had not prepared a sermon based on the biblical text of the day, he would inevitably fall back on the theme of the "fires of hell." The layman chose, however, to counter this religious emphasis, claiming that the devil was not as black as the clergy wished to paint him.[9]

Thus the laity's understanding of God diverged from the image of the God of wrath conveyed to them in the sermons. Bidembach is quoting popular opinion when he writes, "God is a good man with whom one can live more harmoniously than with the parsons."[10] One could rely on his grace and even argue with him, even if one did not always live up to Christian norms. The quotation continues, "It is a poor servant indeed who cannot risk enraging his lord. Who can model himself at all times on heavenly virtues? Surely our Lord and God would not respond immediately with the fire of hell when we have trespassed. Surely such [small] failings would not be taken so seriously."[11] The concept of a gracious God who was not distanced from mankind but who knew the imperfections of human life typified the popular lay Protestant perspective. This may have been the popular version of the priesthood of all believers.

These elements of popular religion were noted by Lutheran pastors, such as Balthasar Köpke, minister at Neu-Brandenburg, who published a *Praxis catechetica* in which he records several excuses of the common country folk used to apologize for their un-Christian, irregular, and unrepenting way of life when they are admonished to do true repentance and improve their lives by the Word of God.[12] The Swabian and pietist village pastor Andreas

[8]Bidembach, *Kurtze Predigt*, 15: "Die Pfaffen machen allezeit ein ding groesser / als es an jhme selbsten ist," "vnd koenten die Pfaffen nicht vom Teuffel / vnd die Schaefer vom dem Wolff sagen / so wuesten sie sonst nicht viel zu reden." This refers to a late medieval lay tradition that the parsons would starve if they did not talk about hell. Peter Dinzelbacher, "Die Realität des Teufels im Mittelalter," in *Der Hexenhammer. Entstehung und Umfeld des Malleus maleficarum, von 1487*, ed. Peter Segl, Bayreuther Historische Kolloquien 2 (Cologne and Vienna: Böhlau, 1988), 151-75, esp. 171.

[9]Tobias Wagner, *Kohlschwartzer Teufel* (Ulm: Balthasar Kühne, 1643), 34-35, argued against those "welche dafuer halten / ob solte der Teuffel nicht so schwartz seyn / als wie die Pfaffen fuergeben."

[10]Bidembach, *Kurtze Predigt*, 14: "Gott sey gut Man / vnd besser mit jenem auszukommen / dann mit den Pfaffen."

[11]Ibid, 9: "Es ist ein schlechter Knecht (sprechen die sichern Leut), der seinen Herrn nicht erzuernen darff: Wer kann sich alle zeit an Himmel heben: Solt vnser HERR vnd Gott gleich mit dem hoellischen Fewr woellen darein schlagen / wann einem jrgend ein Fusz entgangen ist: vnd sich vbersehen hab. Es wuerdt so boese nicht werden."

[12]Balthasar Köpke, *Praxis Catechetica, Etliche Aussfleuchte der gemeinen Leute auff dem Lande / Womit sie ihre Suende und un = christliches / unordentliches / unbuszfertiges Wesen pflegen zu entschuldigen / wann sie aus Gottes Wort zur wahren Buss und Besserung diss Lebens ermahnet werden. Gezeiget / und aus Gottes Wort nach dem Catechismo Lutheri beantwortet*, 2nd ed. (Frankfurt: Johann David Zunner, 1697). Köpke (1646-1711) was pastor at Fehrbellin and Nauen in Kurbrandenburg (Christian Gottlieb Jöcher, *Allgemeines Gelehrtenlexikon . . .*, ed. Johann Christoph Adelung, supp. vol. 3 [Bremen, 1784], 670).

Hartmann wrote *Three Dialogues of a Preacher and a Penitent*[13] as well as an
*Unprejudiced, Plain and Well-meaning Concept Which a Village Pastor May Use
to Guide the Congregation Entrusted to Him.* One century later, in 1802, a similar
report was made by Christian Victor Kindervater in his tract, *On the Useful
Administration of the Office of a Preacher, Concerning Schooling and Education of
the Village Congregations. With an Appendix on Pastors Adapting to Village
Circumstances.*[14] This evidence can be corroborated by the vast Lutheran
pastoral literature, in addition to prefaces to postils, and weather and funeral
sermons. Although these texts reflect the opinions and observations of Lutheran
pastors, they also contain a wealth of popular statements that merit our
analysis and interpretation. The details thus culled from this material can be
supported not only by a qualified use of the visitation records but also by
archival evidence at the local level.[15] Such an approach brings situations and
points of conflict to light as well as displaying irregularities in the moral
and spiritual world of the pastor. This latter aspect will not be dealt with
here.[16] The zeal with which the pastors sought to impose elements of official
church teaching may have negated the improving effect they desired. The
answer to the questions, what the official Lutheran teaching achieved and
what popular religion was, can be found in quoting the frustrated statements
of Lutheran ministers.[17] Such an approach would, though, confirm the results
of Gerald Strauss's research and extend the validity of his findings by at least
one century. In addition, we can gain valuable insights into the religion of
the people in their arguments against the constraints that the teaching of the
law imposed on their lives. There are two points which thus emerge, one

[13]Andreas Hartmann, *Drey Gespraech Zwischen einem Prediger und Beicht = Kind* (Tübingen:
Elias Minner, 1710); idem, *Unvorgreiflich = Einfaeltig = und wolgemeinter Entworff / wie ein
Dorf = Pfarrer seiner anvertrauten Gemeinde erbaulich vorstehen moege* (Ulm: Georg Wilhelm Kühne,
1710). Andreas Hartmann (1677-1729) was pastor in Truchtelfingen (1709), in Döffingen
(1712), and then at the Stuttgart orphanage (1715-16) (Christian Sigel, *Das evangelische Württemberg,*
vol. 2, 11, 556 [Manuscript in Württembergische Landesbibliothek Stuttgart]; Jöcher, *Allgemeines
Gelehrtenlexikon . . . ,* 2 [1750]).

[14]Christian Victor Kindervater, *Ueber nuetzliche Verwaltung des Predigtamts, Schulunterricht,
Bildung der Gemeinden und den Lebensgenuss auf dem Lande. Nebst einem Anhange über das Verbauern
der Landprediger* (Leipzig: Georg Joachim Göschen, 1802). The title page refers to him as preacher
at Pegau.

[15]James Kittelson, "Success and Failures in the German Reformation: The Report from
Strasbourg," *Archiv für Reformationsgeschichte* 73 (1982): 153-75; idem, "Visitations and Popular
Religious Culture: Further Reports from Strasbourg," in *Pietas et Societas. New Trends in Reformation
Social History. Essays in Memory of Harold J. Grimm,* ed. Kyle C. Sessions and Phillip N. Bebb,
Sixteenth Century Essays and Studies, 4 (Kirksville, Mo.: Sixteenth Century Journal Publishers,
1985), 89-101.

[16]For a beginning see Hans-Christoph Rublack, "Der wohlgeplagte Priester. Vom
Selbstverständnis lutherischer Geistlichkeit im Zeitalter der Orthodoxie," *Zeitschrift für historische
Forschung* 16 (1989): 1-30.

[17]For the sixteenth century, cf. the long list in Ignaz Döllinger, *Die Reformation, ihre innere
Entwicklung und ihre Wirkungen im Umfange des Lutherischen Bekenntnisses,* vol. 1, 2nd ed. (Regensburg,
1851); vol. 2 (Regensburg, 1848), passim.

confirming Strauss, the other modifying his findings. The Reformation, or, more precisely, two centuries of Lutheran teaching, yielded both failure and success. We should not take the pastors' complaints at their face value, but to believe that their preaching had no effect whatsoever would be misleading.

II

It is beyond dispute that Lutheran pastors met resistance from their congregations. In part this can be attributed to the clerics' aloofness and otherworldliness. It could not be expected that a layman could come to terms with the apparent incongruity of a statement from his pastor that it was better that he be ill and weak and have God's grace than to be healthy and strong and yet lose his soul, when another Lutheran pastor claimed that health was considered a value surpassing honor, wealth, and possessions.[18] Equally abstruse appeared a pastor's response to a peasant's inquiry concerning the carpenter he should employ to build his house: "I do not know of any better than the Lord our God." The peasant's response, "I have to find a human being who can build my house," was as obvious as it was indicative.[19] Pastoral replies of this kind were considered to be removed from reality.[20] A similar reaction is found in the unwillingness of laymen to accept the preachers' position that all men were but sinners: "since the world, as one says, has not been made for the sake of fools."[21] Popular etymology taught

---

[18]Johann Ludwig Hartmann, *Gruel des Segenspre = chens / Durch allerley gewisse Formulen / Characteres / Kraeu = ter / Ceremonien / bey allerley Kranck-heiten / Jaegern / Schmiden / Hirten / Vieh / Aertz = ten / Hebammen / etc. bey verlornen Sachen / Bannen der Gespenster / Otter vnd Schlangen beschweren: Auch allerley Aberglauben vnd an = dern. / / Samt Bericht von Alraunen oder Galgen = Maennlein / auch Diebs = Daumen / vnd Spiritibus fami = liaribus* (Nuremberg: Wolfgang Moritz Endter, Johann Andreae Endters seel. Soehnen, 1680), 7: "Ach wie viel tausendmal zutraeglicher und besser waere es dir / du waerest mit Gottes Hulde und Gnade kranck oder schwach / und haettest darneben Gottes Gnade und ein gut Gewissen / denn dass du mit seiner Ungnade und ewigen Zorn / auch mit Verlust deiner armen Seelen / mit boesem nagendem Gewissen / soltest frisch und gesund sein." Ibid., 270, quoting Chrysostom: "Citius mors Christiano est subeunda, quam vita ligatur redimenda," which he translated, "Darum soll ein jeder lieber in Gottes Namen kranck seyn / dann in des Teuffels Namen gesund werden." The rhyme was by Adam Klopfer (in Bonifacius Stoeltzlin, *Bethesda, Oder Geistliche Haisz = Apothek und Seelen = Cur* . . . . [Ulm: Balthasar Kühne, 1660]):
Das allerhoechste Gut / das ieman wird gegeben /
nechst Gottes Gnad und Huld / ist ein gesundes Leben;
wer damit ist begabt in dieser Zeit und Welt /
der hat was uebertrifft Ehr / Reichtum / Gut und Gelt.

[19]A. Hartmann, *Drey Gespräch,* 19: "Ich weiss keinen bessern / als den HERRN unser GOTT," and "Ich muss doch sonsten auch einen Menschen haben / der mir mein Hausz baut."

[20]Ibid., 189: "zu wunderlich und zu hoch."

[21]Bidembach, *Kurtze Predigt,* 9: "Denn die Welt / spricht man / ist nicht vmb der Narren willen geschaffen," only fools showed no mercy, but God was gracious and merciful.

that God was goodness itself and therefore just and pious.[22] This made it possible to negotiate with him. God had to be indulgent, he had to have people in heaven as heaven was not made for geese.[23]

There is no secularized element or attitude detectable in the religion of the people. God and the devil were accepted as real and central elements of Christian religion. Those places where popular religion departed from official religion were demarked by the pastors. From another perspective, the "apologies" were part of a process of negotiation between laymen faced with the necessity of survival in this world and pastors concerned with God's holy order and the life beyond. In order to negotiate, men and women adopted the language of the official religion, even to the point of quoting Scripture to fend off claims alien to their life. An example of this is the skillful response of the peasant woman who quoted I Corinthians 4:1. When asked if she was concerned about her eternal salvation, she said, "This is mainly the concern of the officials and you pastors, as you are stewards of the mysteries of God."[24] Laypeople had to care for their living. They had no time to be concerned about their own or their neighbors' salvation, and when this attitude was challenged and called a bald excuse, a not untypical response was, "Do I have to drop my business and deal with purely spiritual things?"[25]

A more sophisticated strategy was an alternative choice of terminology to describe the sins of which one was accused. Thus we find "whoring" juxtaposed with "friendliness." Andreas Hartmann's peasant plainly stated that such friendliness counted as a proof of sincerity.[26] Under certain circumstances promiscuity would seem unavoidable. A petition of the congregation at Büchenbach near Schwabach claimed that a vicar had sinned with the pastor's daughter, "staying daily about her in the house."[27] As the devil used to

[22]Johann Ebert, *Einfeltige Wetterpredigt / Bey erbaermlicher Leich = bestattung sieben Christlicher Personen / als . . .* (Schleusingen: Sebastian Schmuch, 1607), B iiir. Similarly A. Hartmann, *Entwurff,* 37: "For eternal God derives his name from goodness in that he is a good and pious God." ("Dann der ewige Gott habe je seinen Namen von der Guete / das er sey ein guter vnd frommer Gott.")

[23]Bidenbach, *Kurtze Predigt,* 14: He [God] had to admit argument "vnd ein Auge zuthun. Er muesse doch Leut haben im Himmel / der Himmel seye ja den Gaensen nicht geschaffen."

[24]A. Hartmann, *Einfaeltige und Schrifftmaessige Anweisung Wie die Land = Leute und andere / die eine Hauss = haltung fuehren / ihre allgemeine Feld = und Hauss = Ge = schaeffte und taeglichen Wandel Zur Ehre dess Drey = Einigen Gottes und Erbauung ihrer Seelen heilsamlich anwenden und einrich = ten koennen* (Ulm: Georg Wilhelm Kühne, 1709), 243: "Das geht nur Ampt = Leut / und euch Geistliche fuernemlich an; denn ihr seyd Hausshalter ueber Gottes Geheimnniss."

[25]Ibid., 67: "Ein gemeiner Mann / wie ich bin, und der den ganzen Tag hart schaffen muss / wenn er sein Stuecklein Brod erwerben will, hat nicht der weil . . . ." "Muss ich dann mein Geschaeffte ligen und stehen lassen / und mit lauter geistlichen Dingen umgehen?"

[26]Bidembach, *Kurtze Predigt,* 9. The Swabians termed making love (*Buhlschaft*), friendliness (*Freundlichkeit*); see Fischer, *Schwäbisches Wörterbuch* 5 (1908), Sp. 1756.

[27]Nuremberg Landeskirchliches Archiv (hereafter LKA) Markgräfliche Konsistorialakten (hereafter MKA) spez. 145: "um welche Er taeglich im Hauss geweszen."

persecute all preachers and teachers of the word, they added, so he seduced the vicar. Moreover, some rulings of the consistory essentially seemed to contradict the proclaimed norms, as when in a case of double promise of marriage it was ruled that the man had to marry the one with whom he had already had intercourse.[28]

Premarital intercourse was incriminated by both church and state, and social control was advocated by the village establishment. There were, however, strategies to circumvent public control. In Ansbach in 1714, marriages by civic judges were forbidden, as people had praised this as a cheaper alternative to going to "street and church" and giving the pastor his due.[29] A couple might find a friendly pastor by paying him more or by going to a neighboring territory. In Ansbach, Hohenlohe proved a favorable location.[30]

Avarice, which violated one of the principal norms of a society without economic growth, was defended by some laymen as "good housekeeping." But this practical account had to be justified by the size of the household. "I need my own things, times are meager, so I must keep my house in order to survive."[31] This line of argument appealed to central norms of the old regime: the "house" and its survival. Clerical admonitions and impositions which challenged or interfered with socially accepted behavior and approved identity were resisted. People said, "One cannot always live up to heaven." The simple folk did not comprehend a notion of sin as something essentially internal. They played what ministers called "the ancient flute": "I am not evil, I have done nobody any harm, all my life I have been pious and honest, nobody could say I have done wrong."[32]

There is archival evidence to confirm this type of evasion and negotiating. In a circular letter, dispatched in 1714, the dean of Schwabach complained about the laity's failure to attend Sunday service and the unsatisfactory knowledge of the catechism among young people. In response, the pastor of Aurach cited the keeping of oxen as the main obstacle. "For I am boldly told [by my parishioners] that this is their chief means of subsistence, and those were the best two hours for cattle to graze," since after service it was too hot in summer. They did not hesitate to forward this message to the dean with the additional note that should an order be issued, they would contest it on

[28]Nuremberg LKA Dekanat Schwabach 38, 12/12/1714.

[29]Ludwigsburg Staatsarchiv B 70 S 79*, 6/22/1705; B 70 S 78*, 7/30/1714.

[30]Ludwigsburg Staatsarchiv B 70 S 79*, 10/23/1749.

[31]A. Hartmann, Drey Gespraech, 39: "Ich brauch das Meinige / die Zeit ist klemm / so muss ich hausen / dass ich mich mit den Meinigen hinauss bring."

[32]Ibid., 35: "Ich bin nicht böss / thu niemand kein Leyd / ich hab mich mein Lebtag fromm und redlich gehalten / komm ein Mann daher / und sag mir etwas unrechts nach."

grounds of their need to ensure their livelihood.[33] When some years later, in 1721, the consistory again ordered attendance at Sunday service, the village mayors, at the pastor's request, informed the villagers as follows: "The pastor sends greetings. You are not to drive oxen out to graze during church services . . . . You are free to do it anyway if you wish, but I will not."[34] Immediate challenge came from a villager who stated that he would bring the matter before the margrave. Other peasants responded more elegantly, indicating that they would send their children to catechism teaching, stressing that it already was an established custom to say a prayer when the bell tolled.[35] These events prompted a pastor to comment in the 1717 visitation how careful the peasants were to defend their old customs.[36]

III

The role of ritual and attention to detail therein was another trait of the religion of the people. Thus, an alteration in ceremony or custom occasioned confusion. In 1716, a pastor described the difficulties that arose in the practical application of a change in the baptismal rite, which required that water be sprinkled three times on the forehead and/or the chest. The established usage at Weissenburg had been to sprinkle three times on the chest, which now prompted the question, "how this threefold sprinkling should be done, whether twice on the forehead and once on the chest, or twice on the chest, and once on the forehead." Clarity on this issue was deemed essential prior to introduction of the new rite in order to avoid undue disturbance within the community and the inevitable question, whether baptisms previously performed according to the old practice retained their validity.[37] Religion was identified with a set of sanctifying ceremonies and "rites of passage."

Priority was given to religious support at death. Büchenbach near Schwabach, having been ruined during the Thirty Years' War, and having lost its pastor through incorporation with Schwabach, applied for a pastor again in 1660. The community maintained that people were dying without religious comfort

---

[33]Nuremberg LKA 30/I, 12/22/1714: "Denn man wendet mir ohne Scheu ein: Es liege ihre meiste Nahrung dran, es wären die besten 2. [sic] Stunden, da das Vieh fresse"; "so hätte man Ursach seine Nothdurfft darweider einzubringen."

[34]Nuremberg LKA Dekanat Schwabach 36, 10/21/1721: "Der Pfarrer lässet euch grüszen, ihr sollet die ochsen nichts mehr unter der Kirche austreiben . . . . Wollet ihrs nun thun – stehets euch frey. ich [sic] thue es nicht."

[35]Nuremberg LKA Dekanat Schwabach 86.

[36]Ibid.: "die alt gewohnheiten zu defendiren."

[37]Nuremberg LKA Dekanat Schwabach 35, 7/15/1716: "nun läst sichs aber hier fragen, wie dann die trina adspersio solle geschehen, ob sie 2mal auf die Stirn, und nur 1mal auf die brust, oder 1mal auf de brust, und 1mal auf die Stirn, weiln der gemeine Mann sich sonsten daran stossen dörffe, wo man ihn solches nicht vorher ordentlicherweise anzeige, denn sie wohl so schlimm, dass Sie einwenden und sagen, entweder ist mein kind vorher recht, oder unrecht getaufft worden."

and communion.[38] Wealthy people spent money on funerals, as a pastor in Wiesenbach found, "one more than the other."[39] But otherwise, commented a Swabian pastor, Johann Erhard Cellius, in 1625, heavenly bread was so cheap "that we [the people] are fed up with it every day, and there is even a saying, 'There is nothing cheaper than God's word and poverty'; or, put even more briefly, 'Parsons and beggars.'"[40] But burials, like weddings, were an opportunity to demonstrate one's social status. Rich people refused to be buried at the same time as poor ones.[41] In the eighteenth century the academic elite gave preference to nonpublic weddings, on grounds of economy.[42]

Hence rituals, even confession, had become "socialized." When attending confession, people presented the pastor with victuals and flax, and some pastors adapted readily to this procedure. The laity could expect to be received in accordance with the value of their offerings.[43]

In this context religious ritual and social reputation complemented and reinforced each other. Zacharias Rivander cited a particularly good example. A farmhand who had never taken part in communion and was not able to pray was rejected as a godfather and was teased so mercilessly by the stable boys that he lost his sense of reason and ultimately committed suicide.[44]

Popular religion attributed to rituals a meaning alien to their intentions. Pastor Köpke negatively put it that the common people in the country attended church, confession, and communion, and they are godparents, but they do not know "what all this means."[45] Johann Jacob Moser continued that they said morning and evening prayers as well as grace "by means of established formulas, and beyond this they do nothing but wait for the meals. . . . At most they abstain from cardinal sins."[46] When asked about praying before the meals, a peasant's wife pointed to the bowl with the inscription:

[38]Nuremberg KLA MKA spez. 145.

[39]Ludwigsburg Staatsarchiv B 70 L 84, ca. 1616: "gibt Immer einer mehr alss der ander."

[40]Johann Erhard Cellius, *Buszspiegel Ander Theil*. . . . (Tübingen, 1625), l0: "Himmelsbrot" (heavenly bread) is so cheap, "dasz wir dessen alltag Vrdruesz werden / vnd selbsten gleichsam ein Sprichwort darausz machen: Es ist doch ja nichts wolfeilers / als Gottes Wort vnd Armut: oder noch kuertzer: Pfaffen vnd Betler."

[41]Nuremberg LKA Dekanat Schwabach 38, 1711.

[42]Nuremberg LKA Dekanat Schwabach 39 I.

[43]Ludwigsburg Staatsarchiv B 70 S 76, 4/23/1695; Nuremberg LKA Dekanat Schwabach 43.

[44]Zacharias Rivander, *Fest-Chronica*, 1591, 2, 64: "das zeucht er jhme so zum Sinne / dasz er gleich gar wanwitzig wird."

[45]Köpke, *Praxis Catechetica*, 3. Similarly Johann Jacob Moser, *Theologia Pastora = lis exemplaris viva Oder: Schoene und geseegnete Amts = Fuehrung einiger noch lebenden treuen Knechte Gottes, Mit einer Vorrede: Von dem Hasz der Welt und Amts = Seegen, als ordentlichen und noethi = gen Kennzeichen rechtschaffener Prediger* (Züllichau: Waisenhaus, Gottlieb Benjamin Fromman, 1740), A 3r.

[46]Moser, *Theologia Pastoralis*, A 3r: "vermittelst gewisser Formuln und über diss wird nichts gethan / als der Nahrung abgewartet" . . . Kommts in praxi hoch / so huetet man sich fuer aeusserlichen groben Suenden."

"Eat and drink, but on God think."[47] There was no time for talking about religion, but when someone asked her, "Did you finish your meal," she would say, "Thanks be to God!"[48]

The meaning commonly ascribed to religion certainly was assistance and comfort at death, a particular brand of "civil religion." The peasants put this principle bluntly, as Moses Pflacher reported, "Dear children, you need not learn how to pray. Let those pray who have no bread."[49] There was a saying, rendered by Martin Hammer, that peasants "are pious as long as the bad weather threatens the village."[50] It was only in 1784 that ringing the bell during thunderstorms was forbidden in Ansbach. "Many imagined that the bells had the power to dispel the storm, whereas experience teaches that by long tolling of bells the thunderstorms are rather attracted," as enlightened science had put beyond any doubt.[51]

Laymen sought religious comfort in the troubles of life and death. Pastors complained that they were only called to administer to the dying and that here the expectation was that they could instantaneously work a miracle.[52] At the end of the seventeenth century, a pastor rendered this in poetic form:

> Alas! In these last days
> the state of the common man is such

[47]A. Hartmann, *Drey Gespraech,* 265: "Trinck und iss / Gott nicht vergiss."

[48]Ibid., 272: "Ich denck schon an unsern HERRN GOTT / dann wenn ich nach dem Essen von jemand gefragt werde, Hast gessen / so sag ich GOTT Lob."

[49]Moses Pflaucher, *Postill / oder Pre = digten / Vber die Sontaeg = liche / vnd der fuernembsten Fest / Euan = gelien / da auff ettliche Euangelia / zwo oder drey Predigten gericht / auch an ein jede Predigt ein Tabula gehenckt / in welche nicht nur Articulum Rhetoricum / sondern auch res ipsae begrif = fen sind . . .,* ed. Georg Antwander (Tübingen: Georg Gruppenbach, 1602), 509: "Liebe Kinder / jhr doerffet nicht lernen beten / habt ohn das gnug zu essen: lasset die beten / die kein Brot haben."

[50]Martin Hammer, *Die Sagitta pestilentia, Pestilentz Pfeil / das ist: Auszfuehrlicher Bericht von dem Goettli = chen ZornPfeil der Pestilentz / Wannenher derselbe seinen Vrsprung Natuerlich vnd Vbernatuerlich habe / dass fuer allem Gott der HERR die Welt aus gerechtem Gericht / heimsuche vnd straffe / durch was Mittel er dieselbe vnter vns Menschen wircke / wel = cher gestalt diese Straffe beides Leiblich vnd Geistlich gelindert vnd abgewendet / Auch bey allen Anfechtunge / sies eyn Leiblich oder geist = lich mit Trost begegnet werden koenne. Dobey zum Ende angedeutet wird / wie man sich / nach ausgestandener Zuechtigung / Christlich vnd froemlich verhalten / vnd Gott hertzlich wegen geleisteter Huelffe dancken solle* (Leipzig: Johann Boerner and Rehefeld, 1613), 405: "Dass sie so lange from seyn / als das Wetter vber dem Dorffe stehet."

[51]Nuremberg LKA Dekanat Schwabach 28, 3/29/1784: "veile sich die Einbildung gemachet, als hätten die Glocken Krafft und Stärke die Gewitter zu vertreiben; die Erfahrung hingegen lehret, dasz durch das lang und starcke Läuten der Glocken die Gewitter ehender herbeygezogen, als vertrieben werden." See the discussion in Barbara Goy, *Aufklärung und Volksfrömmigkeit in den Bistümern Würzburg und Bamberg,* Quellen und Forschungen zur Geschichte des Bistums und Hochstifts Würzburg 21 (Würzburg: Kommission Schöningh, 1968).

[52]Köpke, *Praxis Catechetica,* 204: "Da sol als dann Gott Wunder thun / und augenblicklich helffen." A. Hartmann, *Entwurf,* 143, confirms this attitude of the laymen. Felix Bidembach, *Manuale Ministrorum Ecclesiae . . . .* (Frankfurt, 1613), 137: "Quod non nisi rebus desperatis venit ad Christum."

That he does not believe in God's work
And he behaves as though blind and deaf.
Arrogantly he says
Is all this still true?
But when God afflicts people
Greatly and punishes them

. . . .

Then faith is conveniently at hand.
When a town, a village, and even a country
is engulfed by thunder and lightning
and even flood announces God's wrath . . . .[53]

Johann Ludwig Hartmann's experience was that the laymen ". . . gladly listen as long as pastors talk about religious comfort and God's grace."[54] But when they preached about the law, they were resented and not listened to, and the people even said, "Let the pastor scold, he can't do otherwise."[55] As Hartmann Creidius of Augsburg knew in the seventeenth century, there were

---

[53]Johann Ebert, *Einfeltige Wetterpredigt,* F jr:
Leyder / in dieser letzten Welt /
Sichs umbs gmein Volck also verhelt /
Das sie die Gottes Werck nicht glauben /
Stelln sich / als wern sie blind vnd tauben /
Duerffen vermessend sprechen hoch /
Wer weisz / ob dieses wahr sey noch?
Aber / wenn Gott die Leut heimsucht /
Ihnen starck zuschickt / straff vnd Zucht
Das die Heylgen Arme vnd Reichen /
Grosse vnd klein / pflegen zu zeichnen /
Da koempt der Glaub jhnen zur Hand/
Wenn eine Stadt / Dorff / ja gantz Land /
Durch Donner vnd Plitz wird angezuendt /
Auch Wasserflut Gottes Zorn ankuendt /. . . .

[54]J. L. Hartmann, *Reine Lehrer,* 46.

[55]"Ja man sagte: Lasz den Pfaffen schmaehlen / er macht es nicht anders." Johann Gottlieb Adami, *Der Gewissenhaffte Beicht = Vater / Wie er seyn soll Seinem hohen und theuern Ampte nach verschwiegen / Seiner geheiligten Person nach Exemplarisch / und wider die Laster seiner Beicht = Kinder Straeflich.* . . . (Leipzig, Dresden: Johann Christoph Zimmermann, Johann Christoph Mieth, Verleger, 1694), 184. See also Melchior Volz, *Christliche Predigt / Von der Frucht = barkeit vnd reichem Segen des 1603. Jar / vnd wie man Gott darfuer dancken / vnd seine Gaaben recht gebrauchen / vnd wol anlegen solle.* . . . (Tübingen: Georg Gruppenbach, 1604), 34-35: "Etliche woellen sich Gottes Wort nicht gern mehr straffen lassen. Haltens fuer ein Last / vnd lassen sich geduencken / wann sie nur des Lasts der Pfaffen ab weren / so wolten ohne sie viel basz hausen vnd auszkommen." ("Some no longer want to be punished by God's word, take it as a burden, but think that if they got rid of the burden of the parsons, they could live better in their houses and have their living.") Or the Saxon court preacher Paul Jenisch in his sermons *Von der Kinderzucht.* . . . (Leipzig, 1609), 153: "Many take preaching not as an instigation for life, but as one to death. If one teaches law, it beats like a hammer into their hearts, and that they do not like. If one preaches on grace, their hearts tell them that as long as they do not repent, they cannot partake of grace. Thus they stay in their sins until the end of this life and earn eternal death."

some "who often stated that parsons are dispensable, for they don't do anything but scold from the pulpit; if you go to church just once on Sunday and listen to the sermon, this is sufficient."[56] Martin Hammer perceived resistance rather than indifference in this: "Many turn against the preachers and say: Those parsons cannot but prophesy misfortunes, fire, pestilence, war, hail, etc. They wish such things to come upon us, and it seems as if they welcome them."[57] Hartmann's *Manual for Pastors*[58] had the layman say, "Preach mildly and softly to us, as it pleases our ears and we like to hear it." At the end of the eighteenth century, a doctor reported a scene at a deathbed: "The longer the minister talked about death and dying, the more he disquieted the heart of the sick by threats, causing shortness of breath, unwillingness in the patient to listen to him, and lack of confidence. The more the pastor endeavored to enlighten the mind of the patient with pleasant notions and quiet him by assuring him of the hope of eternal life, the more he intruded."[59] During the same period, Christian Kindervater was of the opinion that what a peasant took away from confession was "the comforting conviction that he was absolved from all the sins that he had committed up till then, perhaps even from thefts that he had in mind for the same day."[60]

Apart from indifference, pastors perceived ignorance. Many village pastors did not prepare their sermons, Erasmus Sarcerius noted, adding, "It is all the same to the peasants, they do not understand anyway."[61] Köpke summarized a popular attitude: "If we all were learned, we would not need priests";[62]

[56]"die sich offt verlauten lassen / man koenne der Pfaffen wol entrathen / sie thun doch nichts / als schelten auff den Cantzeln / wann man den Sontag einmal zur Kirchen geh / und Predigt hoeret / so hab man ubrig genug." Hartmann Creidius, *Postilla Epistolica Das ist: Schrifftmaessige Erklaerung aller Sontaeglichen Episteln / wie die selbige von Ad = ventbisz auff Pfingsten / in der Christlichen Kir = chen verlesen werden* (Frankfurt: Johann Beyer, 1653), 1:39.

[57]"dann jhr viel fallen auff die Prediger vnd ruffen / Ey die Leut koennen nichts / dann von Vnglueck propheceyen / mit Fewer / Pestilentz / Krieg / Hagel etc. drawen / sie wundschen vns solches an Halsz / vnd scheinet / als sehen sie es gerne." Hammer, *Die Sagitta pestilentia,* 318.

[58]J. L. Hartmann, *Hand = Buch fuer Seelsorger / In / Sechs hieneben specificirten Theilen vorstellend Monita, Alloquia, Suspiria, Colloquia, Dicta, Exempla, Cantica, Superpondia, etc. Bey Kranckheiten und allerhand Zufaellen. Auf vieljaehriges Begehren vor = mals publicirt.* . . . (Nuremberg: Wolfgang Moritz Endter, 1699), 7.

[59]As quoted in Jutta Dornheim and Wolfgang Alber, "Ärztliche Fallberichte des 18. Jahrhunderts als volkskundliche Quelle," *Zeitschrift für Volkskunde* 78 (1982): 28-43, esp. 36.

[60]Kindervater, *Ueber nuetzliche Verwaltung,* 8-9: ". . . alles, was er [der Bauer] etwan aus dem Beichtstuhle zu seiner Erbauung mit hinweg nimmt, ist die troestliche Ueberzegugung, dass er für seine bisherigen Sünden, vielleicht für die Diebereyen, die er denselben Tag wohl noch auszuführen Lust hat, vollkomnen Erlass empfangen habe."

[61]Erasmus Sarcerius, *Pastorale Oder Hirtenbuch /.* . . . (Eisleben: Urban Glaubisch, 1562), 145v: "denn (wie etliche sagen) es gild den Bawren alles gleich / sie verstehens nicht."

[62]Köpke, *Praxis Catechetica,* 10: "Wann nur alle Gelehrten waeren / so beduerfften wir keiner Priester nicht."

and "A peasant will always be a peasant, he will never turn into a scholar."[63] Ignorance prompted crime. The Nördlingen preacher Georg Matthäus Beck made a young woman blame her infanticide on it: "O ignorance, o ignorance! How much do you lead me into misery and trouble of heart!"[64] Somewhat more realistically, Kindervater stated that nobody who was plagued continuously by hunger was likely to read a book, taking for granted that such a person could not pay for one.[65] The pastors complained about religious illiteracy: "It is, alas, well known that, as in other places, but particularly in villages, the common folk lie buried in great ignorance and stupidity; they need to be taught the first letters of the Word of God."[66] Even in a university town like Tübingen, a professor thought the lower classes to be ignorant and crude-minded who did not know anything about God's Word. He disapproved as well of the attitude of the elite which made them look down on the Bible from their high thoughts and self-made wisdom, "as if upon something that they had known for a long time."[67]

That the Reformation had failed in this respect was clearly pointed out by Köpke: "Most of them [the laity] are as they were before; they leave the candle on the candlestick and live in their own ignorant way."[68] Many had forgotten the catechism they had been taught in their youth, and just as many had never learned it at all.[69] That this was nothing new can be deduced from Jacob Heerbrand's statement of 1583, in which the Tübingen professor noted that after God had sent his prophet Luther, preaching had continued for sixty-six years. However, God's call to repent had not been heard, which had caused Him to send comets.[70] This view was confirmed more emphatically by Jakob Andreae, who saw no improvement of life in the Protestant part of Germany, where the Word of God had been spread. "People say, 'We understand that we can gain eternal life by faith in Jesus Christ alone. . . .

[63]Ibid., 44: "Ein Bauer bleibt doch ein Bauer / und wird nimmer ein Gelehrter." A. Hartmann, *Anweisung,* 8, had the peasant say, "Ich bin ein Bauer / und kein Pfarrer" ("I am a peasant and no pastor").

[64]Georg Matthäus Beck, *Die von dem barmherzigen Gott hochbegnadigte arme Suenderin und Kindes-Mörderin.* . . . (n.p., 1716), 13: "O Unwissenheit! O Unwissenheit! wie bringst du mich in allen Jammer und Herze-Leid."

[65]Kindervater, *Ueber nuetzliche Verwaltung,* 11.

[66]"Bekannt ist leyder! dasz das gemeine Volck / wie in andern orten / also fuernehmlich auf dem Dorff / in grosser Unwissenheit und Thumheit gleich begraben liegt und bedarff / dasz man es die erste Buchstaben der Goettlichen Wortelehre" (A. Hartmann, *Entwurf,* 120-21).

[67]"als auf etwas, das sie schon lange wissen" (Johann Gottlieb Faber, *Predigt Von dem grossen Schaden, den die hartnaeckige Verachtung des goettlichen Worts nach sich zieht.* . . . [Tübingen, 1766], 9).

[68]Köpke, *Praxis Catechetica,* 2: "die meisten stellen sich gleich wie vorhin / lassen das Licht immerhin stehen auff dem Leuchter / und leben dabey in muthwilliger Unwissenheit."

[69]Ibid., 3: "Die meisten wissen nichts vom Catechismo / viel haben ihn in der Jugend gar nicht gelernet / viel haben es laengst wiederumb vergessen."

[70]Jacob Heerbrand, *Buszpredigt aus Jonas.* . . . (Tübingen, 1583), 19-20.

As we cannot pay for it with fasting, almsgiving, prayers, or any other good work, let's not be bothered with this kind of work.'" Andreae complained that excessive eating and drinking replaced fasting and that modesty was replaced by pride. Luxury of dress and disregard of the poor were held to be symbols of rejecting Catholicism. Protestantism was characterized by failure to attend Sunday service and by drunkenness, which made it no longer possible to determine "whether [one] is Lutheran or Papist."[71]

Similarly, people pleaded their innocence based on their ignorance and inadequate understanding: "To tame old dogs needs a lot of leashes,"[72] and, "Is it that sinful not to know much? As they say, ignorance does not commit sins."[73] Then they claimed that it was impossible to work and read at the same time. "While working who can think of God? That is impossible. If one wants to read and pray, one has to sit down or walk, and get a book, and we do not always have time for that."[74]

Kindervater realized in 1802 that the peasants' ignorance in religious matters was to be attributed to their traditionalist attitude. There was an "order of things" that they had been accustomed to from their youth: "Concepts they are taught have very little meaning for them."[75] ". . . Everything he [the peasant] knows, and what he believes to be either useful or dangerous in human life, he takes from experience. . . . Peasants have an inherent distrust of change and are not easily convinced by rational argument."[76] Tradition and reputation were mutually reinforcing. It was not pride that made peasants hold such lavish weddings. It was, rather, "an age-old custom. If you do not do it, people talk about it, to the detriment of your reputation."[77]

The same traditional attitude is to be found in the expectations of the laity concerning the outward appearance of the minister. In a dialogue,

---

[71]Jacob Andreae, *Christliche / notwendige vnd ernst = liche Erinnerung / Nach dem Lauff der jrdischen Planeten gestelt / Darausz ein jeder einfaeltiger Christ zusehen / was fuer Glueck oder Vnglueck / Teutschlandt diser Zeit / zugewarten. Auss der vermanung Christi / Luc. 21 in fuenff Pre = digen verfasset.* . . . (Tübingen, 1567), 140 et seq., "Wir haben / sprechen sie / gelehrnet/ das wir allein durch den Glauben an Jhesum Christum selig werden . . . wir koennen es nit mit vnserm Fasten / Allmuossen / Gebetten / oder andern Wercken bezalen / Darumb so lasz vns mit disen Wercken zufriden."

[72]"Alte Hunde baendig machen / dazu gehoeren viel Stricke" (Köpke, *Praxis Catechetica,* 28).

[73]"Ist es denn so grosse Suende nicht viel wissen? Man sagt ja / Unwissenheit suendigt nicht" (ibid., 19).

[74]"Wer kan bey der Arbeit an Gottes Wort gedencken? dasz ist unmüglich. Wann man wil lesen und beten / musz man sitzen / gehen und ein Buch zur hand nehmen / wozu wir nicht allemal Zeit haben" (ibid., 24).

[75]"Der Unterricht durch ihm beygebrachte Begriffe ist sehr unbedeutend" (Kindervater, *Ueber nuetzliche Verwaltung,* 274-75).

[76]"Der Bauer hegt gegen alles Neue ein gewisses Vorurtheil, und Gründe überzeugen ihn nicht so leicht" (ibid., 29).

[77]Köpke, *Praxis Catechetica,* 325 et seq.

published in *Calendar for the People* in 1787, a peasant praises the late pastor and contrasts him with the new minister, who adheres to enlightenment. The old one had kept to the letter of the catechism and had urged children to learn its questions, answers, and texts by heart.[78] The new type of ministers complained that their parishes opposed them if they did not do everything in the same way as their predecessors. At the beginning of the eighteenth century, one successor did not wear a biretta in the pulpit, but a wig instead,[79] nor did he have a beard.[80] His successor, in turn, was told that "a pastor without a wig is no preacher, but a good-for-nothing, and [that] they did not want a good-for-nothing." Peasants criticized the preachers on the content of their sermons and the manner in which they were delivered.[81] Such criticism was common even at the beginning of the seventeenth century. For some the pastor was too young or too strict, for others too old or too mild.[82]

IV

The belief in demonic possession was a recurrent theme of contemporary literature.[83] Demons were found not only among the wicked but often among

[78]Johann Christoph Fröbing, ed., *Calender fürs Volk,* Beyträge zu einer Bibliothek fürs Volk 5 (Hanover, 1787), 278: "der blieb hübsch beym Buchstaben des Catechismus und drang darauf, dass die Kinder Fragen, Antworten und Sprüche fein auswendig wüssten."

[79]Ibid., 281 et seq., 289: "Der Mann, der keine lange Mähen von Ziegenhaar und keinen Priesterrock trägt, der ist auch kein vollkommener Prediger." ("The man who does not wear long goat's hair and priest's gown is not a perfect preacher.")

[80]One hundred fifty years before, Philipp Schickhart had called it a strategy of ministers who wanted to gain authority and reputation to have a large beard (Philipp Schickhart, *Ordinations Predigt / Sampt gewonlichem Actu, Beyder Einsegnung zweyer Jungen Kirchendiener zu Brackenheim*. . . . (Tübingen: Cellische Druckerei, 1608), 10.

[81]Conrad Schlüsselburg, *Postilla, Das ist: Auszlegung der Epi = steln vnd Euangelien auff die fuer = nembste Fest vnd Feyertage durch das gantze Jahr*. . . . (Frankfurt: Johann Saur, Drucker; Peter Kopf, Verleger, 1604), preface.

[82]Friederich Balduin, *Postilla Oder Auszlegung der Sontaeglichen / vnd vornemb = sten Fest Evangelien vber das gantze Jahr / aus vnterschiedlichen Predigten vieler Jahren also zusammen ge = tragen / dasz des Texts rechter Verstand / vnd heilsamer Ge = brauch von Anfang bisz zum Ende des Evenge = lij oerdentlich gezeiget wird* (Wittenberg, 1624, 1625), 2:89.

[83]Wolfgang Brückner and Rainer Alsheimer, "Das Wirken des Teufels. Theologie und Sage im 16. Jahrhundert," in *Volkserzählung und Reformation. Ein Handbuch zur Tradierung und Funktion von Erzählstoffen und Erzählliteratur im Protestantismus,* ed. W. Brückner (Berlin: Schmidt-Verlag, 1974), 394-416; R. Alsheimer, "Katalog protestantischer Teufelserzählungen des 16. Jahrhunderts," in ibid., 417-519; recently Wolfgang Zimmermann, "Teufelsglaube und Hex-enverfolgung in Konstanz 1546-1548,"in *Schriften des Vereins für Geschichte des Bodensees* 106 (1988): 29-57; Johann Conrad Dannhauer, *Scheid = vnd = Absag = Brieff / Einem vngenannten Priester aus Coellen / auff sein Antworts = Schreiben / an einen seiner vertrawten guten Freunde / ueber das zu Straszburg also titulir = te vom Teuffel besessene Adeliche Jung = fraewlin gegeben*. . . . (Strasbourg: Jacob Thiel, 1654); Philo, *Magio logia Das ist: Christlicher Bericht von dem / Aberglauben unnd Zauberey. Der Welt / ohne einige passion der Religionen fuergestellt* / (Augsburg: Matthias Enderlin, Isni, Verleger, Johann Heinrich Mayer, Drucker, 1675); A. Hartmann, *Warhafftige und mit Vielen Glaubwuerdigen Zeugen bewaehrte Relation Was sich Zu Doeffingen Hochfuerstl. wuer = tembergischen Herschafft / und Boeblinger Amts / mit Zwey besessenen Weibs = Per = sonen im Monath Decembr. 1714. merck = lich zugetragen hat*. . . . (1716). The subject is unresearched as to Lutheran

the pious too.[84] Thus, the devil took possession of the pious daughter of a
blacksmith who lived honorably and in the fear of God, eagerly attended
church and received the sacraments, and "even read the common evangelical
booklets."[85] The devil spoke from within her, and though she prayed for
release he did not go out of her. This was achieved only with the aid of
hymns sung by a pastor and members of the congregation. Before disappearing,
the devil gave notice of who his future victims would be: "All those who
do not readily go to church and wish to read by themselves at home, who
do not attend the sacrament, who indulge in excess eating, drinking and in
usury – these are all mine with body and soul if they do not repent."[86] This
was a genuine clerical admonition of the laity.

Even those who attended the church services were found to be inadequate.
Martin Chemnitz cites the example of the offended preacher, describing his
congregation: "Some fall asleep, some listen without devotion, some chat
during the sermon, some walk out."[87] A Saxon minister, Johann Samuel

---

orthodox theology; cf. Georges Tavard, "Art. Dämonen, Kirchengeschichtlich," *Theologische
Realenzyklopädie* 8 (1981): 275-300. Cf. the interpretive article by H. C. Erik Midelfort, "The
Devil and the German People: Reflections on the Popularity of Demon Possession in Sixteenth-
Century Germany," in *Religion and Culture in the Renaissance and Reformation,* ed. Steven E.
Ozment, Sixteenth Century Essays and Studies, 11 (Kirksville, Mo.: Sixteenth Century Journal
Publishers, 1989), 99-119.

[84]Valerius Herberger, *Epistolische Hertz = Postille* (Leipzig, 1693), 2:99: "Wie gehets etlichen
Menschen? Etliche Leute haben Gottes Wort hertzlich lieb, gehen gerne zur Kirchen, fuehren
ein gottselig Leben: Der Teuffel ist ihnen desswegen gehaessig, plaget sie mit wunderlicher
Melancholie und schwermuetigen Gedancken, sie haben schwere Anfechtungen in ihren Hertzen,
als wenn sie die groesten Suender waeren nicht auswerwelt, sie koenten nicht selig werden etc."
(What is the experience with some people? Some love God's Word with their heart and lead
a godly life. Therefore, the devil hates them, plagues them with amazing melancholy and sad
thoughts. They have great afflictions in their hearts, as if they were the greatest sinners, were
not among the elect, could not be redeemed.") Christian Schriver reports how the devil took
possession of a pious virgin (*Das verlohrne und wieder gefundene Schaefflein / . . . ,* 5th ed.
[Magdeburg: Johann Lüderwaldt, 1688], 321).

[85]*Warhafftige vnd Erschroeckliche / / Geschicht / / / So sich begeben vnnd zugetragen hat auff
der Platten. . . .* (Eisleben: Peter, 1584), A2.

[86]Ibid.: "Alle die nicht gerne zu Kirchen gehen / woellen selbst daheim lesen / zum
Sakrament nicht gehen / in Fressen / Sauffen / vnnd wucher ligen / seind alle mein mit Leib
vnnd Seel / so ferrn die selben nicht Busz thon woellen . . . ." Possessed people were often
full of vice. Christian Scriver reports that the devil had paid a vagrant printer in accordance
with their agreement and pact "und saget / das Geld waere gut zum Sauffen / zum Spielen /
zu Huren / im Krahm aber tauge es nicht" ("and said that the money was good for drinking
and gaming but could not be used for trading." *Das verlohrne und wieder gefundene Schaefflein,*
171.)

[87]"wie da etliche schlaffen / etliche ohne Andacht zuhoeren / ettliche unter der Predigt
schwätzen / etliche zu der Thuer hinausz gehen vnter der Predigt" (Martin Chemnitz, *Postilla
Oder Auszlegung der Euangelien / welche auff die Sontage / auch die fuernembste Fest vnd Apostel Tage
in der Gemeine Gottes abgelesen vnd erklaeret werden* [Frankfurt: Johann Spiess, 1593], 412). One
century later Michael Baumann wrote, "They go to church as the dog into the kitchen, and sit

Adami, tells the story of the zealous preacher who had to interrupt his sermon to prompt the listeners, "Wake the pastor's wife up!" Philip Jakob Spener admonished his daughter, when she was about to marry a minister, not only to abstain from falling asleep during service, but to listen to God's Word as if it concerned her.[88] In the nineteenth century Carl Büchsel, after scolding a parishioner who habitually slept in church, received the reply, "At home I am plagued by flies so that I cannot rest, but in church it is nicely cool; in winter I do not attend church."[89] After twenty-three years of similar experiences, the Augsburg pastor Bernhard Albrecht compiled a prayer book that includes a prayer against sleeping and chatting during services:

> Help me, O Lord Jesus, through your might that I do not doze in this your house. For he who wants to profit from God's Word should not sleep or snore. Help me not to chat or behave willfully. For he who really pays attention will not annoy others by chatting, does not show off his apparel, and does not let his eyes wander to note how others are dressed.[90]

---

there in such devotion, that someone falls asleep while the sermon is preached or leaves before the benediction, but the rest of the day they sell at the market. If one asked in this present congregation why so many chairs were vacant and so many people not present, they would answer, 'Oh, there is a market.'" ("Solte man eben jetzo in gegenwaertiger versamlung fragen / warumb so viel Stuehle leer / vnd so viele Leute nit zugegen seyen? . . . 'Ey es ist ein Marckt.'") *Evangelische Gewissens Postill Dasz ist Der Andere Theil dess hiebevor ausz Gefertigten Gründ = Riszes desz wahren Christenthumbs ausz denen Sonn = und Feyertaglichen Evangelien* (Frankfurt: Thomas Matthias Götz, 1668), 90-91.

[88]Philipp Jakob Spener, *Lehrreich Zuschrifft an seine Frau Tochter Von denen noethigen Pflichten Einer jeden sonderlich aber einer Priester = Frau Zum gemeinen Nutzen bekannt gemacht. . . .* (Leipzig: Michael Blochberger, 1731), 24.

[89]Carl Büchsel, *Erinnerungen aus dem Leben eines Landgeistlichen,* 6th ed. (Berlin, 1861), 17: "Zu Hause setzen einem die Fliegen so viel zu, dass man nicht zur Ruhe kommt, in der Kirche dagegen ist es so schön kühl; im Winter gehe ich auch nicht in die Kirche."

[90]Bernard Albrecht, *Hausz = und Kirchen = Schatz* (Hamburg, 1660), 440: "Hilf / O HERR Jesu / durch deine Krafft / dasz ich in diesem deinem Haus nicht schlummere. Denn were Gottes Wort mit Nutz anhoeren wil, der musz nicht schlaffen und schnarchen. Hilff / dasz ich nicht plaudere / oder Fuerwitz treibe. Denn wer recht auffmerckt / der ist mit keinem Geschwaetz andern aergerlich / er bespiegelt sich nicht in seinen Kleidern / er wandert nicht mit den Augen herumb / er sihet nicht / wie andere Leut bekleidet sind." This originally appeared in 1618. On Albrecht cf. Rublack, "Augsburger Predigt im Zeitalter der Orthoxie," in *Die Augsburger Kirchenordnung von 1537 und ihr Umfeld,* ed. Reinhard Schwarz, Schriften des Vereins für Reformationsgeschichte, 196 (Gütersloh: Gütersloher Verlagshaus Gerd Mohn, 1988), 123-58, esp. 132.

Simon Musäus informs us that most of his audience fell asleep,[91] and the
excuse was that God's Word "was something old and they would rather use
the time for sleeping."[92] The famous and pious theologian Johann Gerhard,
however, was praised in a funeral sermon, for he had attended church twice
on Sundays, and "nobody ever saw him asleep."[93] Chatting, someone confessed,
is a great sin. "But as to sleeping I do not know. It so easily happens that
during singing and preaching your eyes close."[94] Lay people were simply not
used to listening for a longer time: "They cannot help falling asleep, they
are sorry." "Others say even if they sleep they very well hear what is
preached."[95]

In warning against violating the third commandment, pastors provided
a rich collection of examples of God immediately punishing those who did
not go to church: "A farmer who always went to the mill to grind corn on
Sundays, one Sunday had all his corn turned to ashes."[96] Ministers found it
easy to relate deviant behavior to damages incurred, a pattern associated with
the popular magic that they disparaged.

Laymen suspected pastors of being professionally ambitious. When the
clerics admonished them to listen to God's Word, the laity thought they did
so in part because they wanted to show that they attracted large audiences.[97]

The devil could be active even in church, for he was "God's ape." An
Augsburg cobbler submitted to diabolical insinuations from 1671 to 1677,

[91]Simon Musäus, *Postilla das ist / Auszlegung der Euangelien / durchs gantze Jar / an Sonntagen vnd gewoehnlichen Festen / in der Kirchen vblich vnd gebraeuchlich / in drey vnterschiedliche Theil getheilet /*. . . . (Frankfurt: Nicholaus Basseus, 1583), 2:244r; Bonifacius Stöltzlin, *Catechismus = Hand. Das ist: Ordenliche / einfaeltige und Schriftmaes = sige Erklaerung / Des kleinen Ca = techismi D. Martin Luthers / der Sechs Hauptstukken / der Hausz = Tafel / des Un = derrichts fuer die Communicanten / und der Kinder = Gebetten. Ini CXXXVIII. Predigten verfaszt /*. . . . (Ulm: Balthasar Kühne, 1666), 200: the majority of the listeners forget the sermon.

[92]Christian Gerber, *Unerkannte Suenden der Welt /* . . . , 5th ed. (Dresden: Christoph Heckel, 1708), 15: God's Word was "was Altes / man schlaefft lieber unter der Zeit."

[93]"wobei man den D. Gerhard niemals schlafen gesehn," quoted by August Tholuck, *Vorgeschichte des Rationalismus 1: Das akademische Leben des siebzehnten Jahrhunderts mit besonderer Beziehung auf die protestantisch-theologischen Fakultäten 1: Die akademischen Zustände* (Halle, 1853), 67.

[94]Köpke, *Praxis Catechetica*, 74: Chatting "ist grosse Suende. Aber was das Schlafen betrifft / weisz ich nicht. Es kan leicht geschehen / dasz unter dem Singen and Predigen einem die Augen zufallen."

[95]Stöltzlin, *Catechismus = Hand*, 199-200: "Sie koennen ihme nicht thun / es seye ihnen leid." "Andere sagen / wann sie gleich schlaffen / so hoeren sie doch / was man predigt."

[96]Ibid., 193. Another farmer had his stores burned "this very night," again because he had ploughed on a Sunday; another man's hand grew together with his plough and he suffered for two years. A woman who made her maids spin on Sunday burned to death with two children in her house. The wife of a nobleman who went hunting on Sunday gave birth to a child with a dog's head, "and it barked like a dog."

[97]Chemnitz, *Postilla*, 406: "wann wir armen Prediger euch Zuhoerer vermahnen zum fleissigen Gehoer desz Goettlichen Worts / wir thun das darumb / dasz wir viel Zuhoerer moegen haben."

noticing "that he [the devil] went to church with him, talked to him there, and wanted to prevent his taking the sacrament. When he prayed, the evil one prayed as well; when he sang, the devil joined in; and he was even such an excellent bass singer that the cobbler was amazed and assumed that everybody else also heard him sing."[98] Satan wished to be disturbing, however, for once during a sermon in the Hospital of the Holy Ghost, the cobbler "felt a wind press his innards, but he held it in for honor's sake." He heard the devil comment, "Only a thief suppresses his fart; oh you fool, why don't you release it?"[99]

V

For Lutherans conjuration was devilish because it trespassed against the first and second commandments. Practicing it was traditional, and the need for it increased as a consequence of the Reformation, which dissociated the holiness of God from earthly works.[100] The reform diminished the number of sacraments and shifted the focus of the service from sacrament to preaching. To take sacramentals out to defend against danger was no longer possible.[101] But the crises of life continued,[102] and the lay people invoked conjurations against the illnesses of humans and cattle, against ghosts and appearances of the devil, to ease pregnancy and delivery,[103] as well as during hail and

---

[98]Christoph Ehinger, *Daemonologia, oder Etwas Neues Vom Teufel / . . . Den sichern / vnbaendigen / Gottlosen / Cyclopischen Welt = Kindern / die bald nicht mehr glauben / dass ein Teufel sey / zur Uberzeugung / Warnung / und Busz /. . . .* (Augsburg: Gottlieb Goebel, Verleger, Jacob Koppmayr, Drucker, 1681), 23: "mit ihme zur Kirch gangen / mit ihm geredt / und von disem Hochheiligen werck abhalten wollen / hat er gebettet / so hat der Boesswicht mit gebettet / hat er gesungen / hat er auch mit gesungen / und zwar einen so vortrefflichen Bass, dasz er sich verwundern meussen / und nicht anderst gemeinet / iederman hoere ihn singen."

[99]Ibid., 43: "kam ihm heimlich ein Wind in Leib . . . den verhielt er Ehrenhalben." He heard the "hoellischen Schandvogel" say, "Der Dieb verhaelt den Furtz / ey du Narr / warum laessest du ihn nicht hinausz?"

[100]J. L. Hartmann, *Greuel des Segensprechens,* 20, points to the tradition of conjuration from papal times.

[101]Robert W. Scribner, "Ritual and Popular Religion in Catholic Germany at the Time of the Reformation," *Journal of Ecclesiastical History* 35 (1984): 47-77. Reprinted in Scribner, *Popular Culture and Popular Movements in Reformation Germany* (London: Hambledon Press, 1987), 17-48.

[102]J. L. Hartmann, *Greuel des Segensprechens,* 10-11, divides spells into three categories: 1. those designed to prevent future evils; 2. those that are to remedy present threats; and 3. those that help one to achieve fortune.

[103]Ibid., 141; 108-9. The midwives' practice was – if everything else had failed – to call in the husband in childbirth, as an ultimate resort to have him embrace his laboring wife from behind, "and to say thrice, 'In the name of God the Father, God the Son, and God the Holy Ghost'"("und dreymal sprechen heissen: Im Namen Gottes des Vatters / Gottes des Sohns / und Gottes des Heil. Geistes").

lightning storms. Such "superstitious" practices increased.[104] The world was
flooded with superstition and soothsaying.[105] Somewhat more precisely, Johann
Ludwig Hartmann stated that spells against worms and shrinking parts of
the body were common, "and some people earn a lot of money from this,
and they live almost everywhere."[106] When pastors incriminated these practi-
tioners' activities, laymen argued that they used "merely good words" and
that "they only speak of God. How can this be unrighteous?"[107] In fact, the
soothsayer invoked God and the Trinity: "What is done in the name of the
LORD or in the name of God is right."[108] "God's name is no curse," runs a
Swabian saying.[109] As "words spoken in the pulpit have power and effect,
so they are also powerful in soothsaying."[110] Pastors called upon the Trinity
in baptism,[111] as well as in prayers: "One prays and calls God by words; why
is it impossible to bless and say spells with certain words?"[112] Protestants
seemed to impute holy power to the spoken word; why, then, was the old
practice of soothsaying, which employed many of the same words, held not
to be legitimate? As God had created and blessed everything, one ought to
be able to use objects for spells as well.[113] Laymen adapted to the new terms

[104]Conrad Wolfgang Platz, "Dasz Segensprechen vnnd Beschwoeren vnrecht / vnd ein
Zauberey Seund: neben ableinung allerley Einreden," in *Consiliorum Theo-logicorum Decas I. et
II. Das ist / Zweinzig Theolo = gischer Bedencken / Bericht / oder Antwort / auff mancherley (in
Glaubens / Gewissens vnnd andern mehr Sachen) zutragende Faelle / vnd vorfallende Fragen / oder
Handlungen gerichtet / vnd mehreren Theils vor vielen Jaren gestellet . . .* , ed. Felix Bidembach, 2
vols. (Tübingen: Georg Gruppenbach, 1605), II(2): 267-301, preface. According to the preface,
it was first printed in 1562. Platz had studied in Tübingen and served as pastor at Biberach
from 1560 to 1595 (*Jöcher-Adelung-Rotermund* 6 [1819]: 378-79).

[105]Christof Vischer, *Einfelltiger / vnd in der heiligen Goett = lichen Schrifft wolgegruendter
be = richt wider den aberglaubischen alt = uettelischen Segen / damit man Men = schen vnd Vieh wider
allerley seuchen / mit greuwlichem missbrauch Gott = liches worts / zu helffen vermeinet* (Schmalkalden:
Michel Kröner, 1571), H[6v]. Sarcerius, *Pastorale*, 168r-69r.

[106]J. L. Hartmann, *Greuel des Segensprechens*, preface, iijv: "manche Leute . . . verdienen
viel Geld damit; Es sind fast aller Orten solche Leute wohnhafft."

[107]Platz, *Segensprechen*, 282: these are but "lauter gute Wort," "man sagt nur von Gott /
wie wollte dann das unrecht sein?" Similarly, J. L. Hartmann, *Greuel des Segensprechens*, 35,
247-48.

[108]Platz, *Segensprechen*, 282-83, "Was im Namen des HERRN / oder im Namen Gottes
beschicht / das ist recht."

[109]Fischer, *Schwäbisches Wörterbuch* 3 (1911), Sp. 757: "Gottes Name! ist net geflucht."

[110]Platz, *Segensprechen*, 293: "die gesprochene Wort in der Predigt auff der Cantzel / haben
jhre Krafft vnd Wuerkung. Derowegen seind sie auch im segnen kraefftig." J. L. Hartmann,
Greuel des Segensprechens, 247-48: "Wie nun Gottes Wort habe herrliche Krafft / die Seelen zu
bekehren / und der Menschen Hertzen zu erweichen / also koenne es auch in andern Zufaellen
helffen." ("Just as God's word has wonderful power to convert souls and to move men's hearts,
so it is capable of helping in other contingencies.")

[111]J. L. Hartmann, *Greuel des Segensprechens*, 252-53.

[112]Platz, *Segensprechen*, 294: "Man bittet vnd rueffet Gott an / mit Worten / wolte man
dann nicht auch doerffen segnen vnd beschwoeren / mit gewissen Worten?"

[113]Ibid., 296.

of negotiation, but they ignored any precise theological deductions. It was difficult to make the differences clear, and pastoral endeavors were as continuous as they were vain. According to Georg Christoph Zimmermann, Franconian peasants at the beginning of the eighteenth century always turned first to wise women. They resorted to the pastor when social relations were concerned. He reported that a wealthy blacksmith sought out a wise woman when money was stolen.[114] Only after she had pronounced who the thief was did he come to the parsonage and ask the pastor to do him the favor of calling in the one accused, and in his capacity as confessor persuading him to restore the money. Only if this succeeded would the victim refrain from going to court.

VI

Peasants and pastors perceived the cultural distance that separated them. Peasants well understood that pastors defined religion in terms of knowledge and that they considered ignorance irreligious. As long as they were illiterate, the peasants were not able to meet Protestant expectations. They were not capable of understanding why there should be any need for a learned religion. They took themselves as grown-ups to be incapable of learning. Youth was the time for learning; afterwards one had a weak head.[115] For adult life it was experience that mattered. Physical labor was real labor, and this admitted of no thinking about God.[116] If pastors expected spiritual growth, they were frustrated: "Throughout the years one's work for such people is without results – this is the painful feeling the preacher very often gets."[117]

A Lutheran pastor communicated religious knowledge; this was the core of his understanding of his profession. He called himself a teacher in the

---

[114]Georg Christoph Zimmermann, *Den in vielen Stuecken allzuaberglaubigen Christen / hat ein viel Jar lang / unter denselbigen vor dem Herrn lehrender Diener Gottes, bey genauer Observation sehen und kennen lernen.* . . . . (Frankfurt, Leipzig: Brevinus Noricus Fago = Villanus [Büchenbach] auf Kosten des Authoris 1721), 32 et seq. She, of course, named the smith's next-door neighbor as the thief.

[115]Köpke, *Praxis Catechetica,* 28-29.

[116]Ibid., 206. Peasants thought their labor alone was labor; the officials and the pastors earned their money easily, by walking around and playing. A. Hartmann, *Einfaeltige Anweisung,* 2-3, has them ask why, if work was a consequence of the Fall, the nobles and pastors did not work (*schaffen*): "They just command and eat well and drink, and you do nothing but preach and pray. We as peasants have to maintain you." To this the minister quotes Prov. 12:12 [?], demonstrating that preaching tires the body, labor of the mind being "the heaviest work in the world" ("allerschwehrste Arbeit unter der Sonnen").

[117]Kindervater, *Ueber nuetzliche Verwaltung,* 8: "dasz man Jahr aus Jahr ein für solche Menschen grösstentheils umsonst arbeitet, dieses schmerzliche Gefühl hat leider! der Prediger sehr oft."

sixteenth century just as his successors during the Enlightenment did.[118] Only
in the eighteenth century did the peasants begin to read religious books.[119]
Protestantism as a book religion then finally found its home in the country.[120]
But the Lutheran demand that fathers teach at home what was preached in
church was often inverted. If one could serve God just as well at home as
in church, then it was possible to stay at home. In the opinion of pastors,
this attitude developed at the devil's instigation.[121] You can read God's Word
in your little book. The pastors "say nothing new, you have heard everything
before." Simon Musaeus complained that even the crudest people, "if they
can read a German postil at home, believe they don't need to go to any
church."[122]

What was accepted was one service on Sunday and the image of the
pastor reading from a book. When children played pastor, they enacted this

[118]Pflacher, *Postil oder Predigten*, 163, 373; Kindervater, *Ueber nuetzliche Verwaltung*, 21:
"Alles, was die Menschen gottesfürchtiger, gerechter, billiger, gemeinnütziger, mit der Vorsehung
zufriedener, und den Uebergang in ein besseres Leben ihnen leicht macht, das habe ich zu
lehren. . . ."("Everything that makes human beings more God-fearing, just, fair, attentive to
the common good, content with providence, and facilitates their passage to eternal life, I have
to teach them.")

[119]Köpke, *Praxis Catechetica*, 48: "Ir duerfft euch eben so sehr ueber Unwissenheit nicht
klagen. Man find auff dem Lande auch manchen rechtschaffenen verstaendigen und klugen
Mann / welcher / ob er wol nur ein Bauer ist / dannoch so wol seine Bibel / und andere
Buecher und Postillen hat / und wol so viel verstehet als mancher Priester." ("You need not
complain so much about ignorance. In the country we find many a righteous, sensible, and
intelligent man who, though he is but a peasant, nevertheless has his Bible, other books and
postils, and equals some priests in understanding.") See also A. Hartmann, *Drey Gespraech*, 6:
Peasants read Bibles and postils on holy days. N. Breining, "Die Hausbibliothek des gemeinen
Mannes vor einhundert und mehr Jahren," *Blätter für württembergische Kirchengeschichte* NF 13
(1909): 48-63, as to Besigheim; Martin Scharfe, *Die Religion des Volkes, Kleine Kultur und
Sozialgeschichte des Pietismus* (Gütersloh: Gütersloher Verlagshaus Gerd Mohn, 1980), 33-34, for
Tübingen and Feldstetten; Hans Medick,"Buchkultur auf dem Lande: Laichingen 1748-1820.
Ein Beitrag zur Geschichte der protestantischen Volksfrömmigkeit in Altwürttemberg," in
Glaube, Welt und Kirche im evangelischen Württemberg, (Stuttgart: Calwer Verlag, 1984), 46-68;
Richard Gawthrop and Gerald Strauss, "Protestantism and Literacy in Early Modern Germany,"
Past and Present 104 (1984): 31-55.

[120]Max Weber, *Gesammelte Aufsätze zur Religionssoziologie* 1 (utb 1488) (Tübingen: Mohr,
1988), 505: "Je mehr nun die Religion Buchreligion wurde, desto literarischer und daher desto
mehr ein priesterfreies rationales Laiendenken provozierend wirkte sie." ("The more religion
became a religion of the book, the more literary and therefore the more liberated from priests
it became, and the more it provoked rational thinking in the laity.")

[121]Pflacher, *Postil oder Predigten*, 83. Johannes Gigas, *Postilla / Das ist / Auszlegung der
Euangelien / durchs gantze Jahr / an Sonntagen vnnd gewoehnlichen / Festen / sampt andern Predigten
/ in drey vnterschiedliche Theil getheilet /. . . .* (Frankfurt: Nicolaus Basseus, 1582), 1:90, relates
the argument: I believe for myself, so why should I go to church? I can pray in my chamber.
Similarly Köpke, *Praxis Catechetica*, 68: "da gedenckt man als dann gar zu hause zu bleiben /
und in der Postill etwas zu lesen / weil doch solches eben wol Gottes Wort sey." ("They believe
they can stay ever at home and read a little in their postil, for it too is God's Word.")

[122]Musäus, *Postilla*, 2:244r: "Da ist kein Filtz so grob / wann er nur eine Teutsche Postill
daheim lesen kan / so leszt er sich beduncken / er doerffe in keine Kirche gehen."

scene.[123] Some lower class people had difficulty in meeting the standard of decorum for churchgoing because they lacked a Sunday dress. The Hamburg pastor, Balthasar Schupp, invented the figure of Corinna, an honorable but hypocritical whore, who said that she could not attend service as she had no Sunday dress. She wanted "to read the postil in bed, and pray in bed and sing."[124] As the content of sermons was repetitive, some allowed themselves to stay away occasionally: "One may go to the dear church just as well some other time and make up what one has missed."[125] The service on Sundays provided an opportunity besides the inn to get together with others, especially for women. Some felt they had to make excuses for staying away,[126] but then they behaved like balking asses which "are talked to for a long time but then shake their heads and do just as they had before."[127] The image held up as desirable was that of a sheep – Protestant teachers did not want to promote emancipation.[128]

Traditionalism incorporated deep-seated prejudice against newfangled things: "No, we cannot be talked into this" (in this case abandoning carnival). "Pastors are chatterers. May what they threaten come upon them! We want to have fun, not respect what the pastors say."[129] People refuted preaching that was designed to change behavior – to improve it, as the pastors called it. In the sixteenth century, Erasmus Sarcerius noted the popular meaning

---

[123]Gregor Strigenitz, *Ieremias vocatus et confirmatus. . . .* (Leipzig: Franz Schnellbolzens Erben, Drucker, Bartholomus Vogt, Verleger, 1601), 11: "O wie offt geschichts noch heutigs tags / dasz Kinder in Hauesern / wenn sie beysammen sind / der Kirchen spielen / da tritt eines vnter jhnen auff / nimpt ein Buch / vnd predigt den andern fuer / vnd betten mit einander." ("O how often does it happen even today, that children, when they gather in houses, play church. One of them steps forward, takes a book, and preaches to the others, and they pray together.") Another piece of evidence for preaching as the core of the service can be taken from the Swabian saying about a woman with a hunchback: "She is a pastor's daughter; she has the pulpit on her back." ("Sie ist eine Pfarrerstochter, sie hat die Kanzel auf 'm Buckel") Fischer, *Schwäbisches Wörterbuch* 1 (1904), 1015.

[124]Johann Balthasar Schupp, *"Corinna, Die erbare und scheinheilige Hure / Beschrieben / und allen unkeu = schen Leuten zur Warnung. Mit einer Vorrede / und einem Anhang / gestellet,"* in *Schriften* (n.p., n.d.), 469.

[125]Köpke, *Praxis Catechetica,* 362: "In die liebe Kirch kan man doch hernach wol kommen / und dasselbe wieder nach holen / wa man etwa verseumet."

[126]Pflacher, *Postill oder Predigten,* 171: they went to church "damit sie nicht fuer Vnchristen gehalten werden"("as they did not want to be taken as un-Christian.")

[127]Ibid.: "als wann man einem stettigen Esel lang zugesprochen, so schuttelt er die Ohren darueber vnd bleibt auff seinem Esels Kopff vnnd Trapp."

[128]Gigas, *Postilla,* 230: Listeners are to adopt the "sheeps' way" (*Schafs art*): knowing their shepherd's voice and following him, they readily give milk and wool and allow themselves to be punished and embalmed.

[129]Sebastian Artomedes, *Christliche Auszlegung vnnd Erklerung der Sontags vnd Fest Evangelien vber das gantze Jahr / mit etzlichen zugetha = nen Predigten aus Moyse / aus den Psalmen vnd Propheten /* (Leipzig: Thomas Schürer, 1613), 1:256: "Nein, des sind wir nicht zu bereden, die Pfaffen sind Waescher / es kom vber jhren hals / was sie vns drewen / wir wollen lustig sein / vnd die Pfaffen nicht ansehen."

inherent in the saying, "One cannot always live up to heaven," that is, "People have whored in the past, and they will likely do so in the future." A model of defence against admonition could be found in Noah's days, when people had mocked, "He does not know what he is talking about. Nothing that he warned us about has happened; we are still living, and life is as it has always been. Why does he find fault with us? We want to eat and drink, marry and have wedding feasts, and have a good time. Why should we pay attention to him when he doesn't do anything for us?"[130] There was the argument in the negotiation: "Let him who is without sin cast the first stone. . . . The person who has never fallen down can never get up."[131] The aspect of religion that mattered was ritual. In the eighteenth centiry, Andreas Hartmann had to point out that to be a Christian meant more than mere churchgoing.[132]

The evidence presented above, all drawn from pastoral experience, demonstrates a high degree of continuity from the Reformation period through the end of the old regime. The spectrum offered here was certainly reduced. There were now more citizens reading religious books just as there were rural artisans who turned pietist. Too, the pastoral standards of evaluation changed. There were certainly some successful implementations of Protestant belief and practice as well as failures. But why did pastors consider their level of success to be so minimal? In the long run, they might have noticed that the apologies of the people had adapted to Protestant terms. However, the clergymen saw only the defensive nature of these arguments, and they viewed all apologetics as evidence of a lack of valid religiosity. From the parsons' perspective, the apologists were sinful if not outright deviant. Historians must perceive behind the apologetic arguments the reality of peasant life, centered and rooted in house and subsistence, primarily concerned with survival, the meaning of which was concentrated in concrete experience and communicated in the phraseology of age-old wisdom. One of the very common "excuses" for superstitious practices was the saying, God helps those who help themselves.[133] The lay apologists adapted official religious language

---

[130]"Man hat fur vns Hurery vnd Ehebrecherey getrieben / so wird mans auch wol nach vns treiben." Gregor Strigenitz, *Diluvium: Das ist / Auszlegung der schrecklichen / vnd doch auch zu = gleich troestlichen Historien der Suendflut /. . . .* (Leipzig: Bartholomäus Vogt, 1613), 2v: "Ey / er weisz nicht viel was er saget / hat lange also geprediget / ist dennoch nichts drauff erfolget / wir leben noch allesampt / vnd es stehet wie es lange gestanden. Was hat er mangels an vns / wir woellen essen vnd trincken / freyen vnd Hochzeit halten / vnd guter dinge seyn / vnd jhn nicht ansehen / er gibt vns nichts darzu."

[131]Erasmus Sarcerius, *Pastorale oder Hirtenbuch;* idem: *Von jährlicher Visitation* (1555), 179r: "Wer kein Suender ist / der hebe den ersten stein auff / vnd werffe. . . . Wer nie fiel / der stuende nie auff."

[132]A. Hartmann, *Drey Gespraech,* 6.

[133]Zimmermann, *Den in vielen Stucken allzuaberglaubigen Christen,* 411: "Heist es doch: Mensch hilff dir / sagt Gott / dann will ich dir auch helffen."

for purposes of defending the familiar realm of self-help and social cooperation
– the same principles that have been seen to prevail in early modern medical
practice.[134] Where possible, the people resisted the social disciplining of
Lutheran preaching.[135] Clearly this realm could not be self-sufficient or
autonomous, as life was open to want, death, and catastrophes.[136] So what
laymen then asked for was spiritual comfort, which validated their life. But
to preserve their social identity they adapted the terms of Lutheran Protestantism
to fundamental social norms. The shifting of the central accent in religion
from administering sacraments to communication by preaching forced upon
them new strategies of negotiation: They had to use arguments to resist a
highly compact and reflected interpretation of the world of official religion.
Those who easily assume a successful attempt at acculturation by clerical
elites have to face the evidence the pastors themselves presented, and they
more often attested their failure.

---

[134]Barbara Duden, *Geschichte unter der Haut. Ein Eisenacher Arzt und seine Patientinnen um
1730* (Stuttgart: Klett, 1987), 114.

[135]As to social disciplining, see Stefan Breuer, "Sozialdisziplinierung. Probleme und
Problemverlagerungen eines Konzeptes bei Max Weber, Gerhard Oestreich und Michel Foucault,"
in *Sociale Sicherheit und soziale Disziplinierung. Beiträge zu einer historischen Theorie der Sozialpolitik,*
ed. Christoph Sachsse and Florian Tennstedt (Frankfurt: Suhrkamp, 1986), 45-69.

[136]Ernst Shubert, *Arme Leute, Bettler und Gauner im Franken des 18. Jahrhunderts,* Veröffentlichungen der Gesellschaft für fränkische Geschichte, series 9, vol. 26 (Neustadt/Aisch: Degener
Verlag, 1983), 13-31 for a description of Franconia at the end of the old regime.

The Emperor and Pope, Bologna, 1530

Politics

Between State and Community: Religious and Ethnic Minorities in Early Modern Germany

R. Po-chia Hsia*

In the medieval Empire, German Jews were the personal property of the kings. Their legal status, specified in imperial charters and defined by the term "Imperial Chamber Serfs," reflected their privileged and simultaneously precarious position in a Christian society. During the fourteenth and fifteenth centuries, the imperial Jewish regalia were conceded, in most areas of the empire, to territorial princes and imperial cities. Territorial and urban Jewish statutes provided the legal framework that shaped the daily lives of the Jewish communities in the empire.

Beginning with Maximilian's reforms, the emperors in the sixteenth and seventeenth centuries tried to reassert their rights over the Jews. Through imperial mandates and the Imperial Aulic Court, the Habsburgs attempted to reintegrate the Jews into the imperial constitution. Contested by princes and cities, the attempt to regain the *Judenregalia* achieved limited success. This paper examines the tensions between the imperial court and the territories in light of different pieces of legislation regarding the Jews. It analyzes the nature of the state in the Holy Roman Empire, constructed on a multiple array of contradictory laws and political interests, and the peculiar position of the Jews in the Christian polity.

THE CONCEPT OF ETHNIC AND RELIGIOUS MINORITIES seems at first glance rather unproblematic in the context of German history. Surely, Jews and gypsies were ethnic minorities, just as various sects such as the Mennonites, Moravians, Hutterites, Socinians, and Schwenckfeldians belonged to the category of religious minorities. It seems that the definition of minority or marginal status always involves a self-defining center, the "we" that creates "the other." But can this differentiating center be identified in the old Reich? Who defined social boundaries in the central Europe of the sixteenth and seventeenth centuries?

Let us return briefly to the problem of defining ethnic and religious minorities. The very concept itself is based on contemporary social sensibilities. Minority status connotes marginality; minorities are opposed to majorities,

*This is a revised version of a lecture delivered on June 1, 1989, at the German Historical Institute, Washington, D.C. I am grateful to Hartmut Lehmann, Hanna Schissler, and Erik Midelfort for critical comments. This essay is dedicated to the memory of Bruno Kindermann.

outsiders to insiders, marginality to core. Our notions of human rights, civic rights, justice, and discrimination underlie the articulation of this concept. Marginality is often seen as defined by race and religion. While not denying the historical existence of these categories, the application of these concepts to the study of central Europe between the fifteenth and eighteenth centuries involves the risk of anachronism and historical oversimplification: Were Jews marginal because of their race or their religion? What was the status of the Sephardic Jews in Hamburg who were described as the Portuguese nation? Were gypsies persecuted because of their race or their unsettled, migratory way of life? After all, the pamphlets that warned of gypsies also cried out against beggars, robbers, soldiers, and other wandering folk. While the marginal status of the Anabaptist sects seems obvious, what can the examples of the major Christian confessions tell us? Until the Peace of Westphalia (1648), Calvinists did not have any legal status in the Holy Roman Empire and were often the object of vilification by both Catholic and Lutheran authorities. Catholics themselves often suffered political and social discrimination, as François Fuchs reminds us in his study of Catholic Strasbourgers between 1529 and 1681. Only after the French annexation of the Alsatian city could Catholics attain citizenship.[1] The persecution of religious minorities did not end in 1648; the massive expulsion of Protestants from the territory of Salzburg occurred in 1731, when confessional stability had long been achieved in the empire.[2]

There is another problem with the theme. The juxtaposition of the concept of religious and ethnic minorities alongside that of German history conjures up the specter of National Socialism. The danger of writing teleological history is a real one. To understand the recent past, some historians argue, one must go back to the origins of intolerance and persecution in German history. With this idea Joachim Hohmann begins his book on the persecution of gypsies in Germany at the beginning of the fifteenth century, when gypsies made their first appearance in written documents. Hohmann then describes the persecutions as reflected by imperial and territorial legislation – the imperial diets of 1496 and 1498 declared gypsies to be beyond the pale of law, and in the sixteenth century they were suspected of being Turkish spies. He takes this story to its tragic climax in the Hitler regime, and ends with a critique of the Federal Republic.[3] Other historians, less polemical and politically engaged than Hohmann, have nonetheless adopted the concept

---

[1]François J. Fuchs, "Les catholiques strasbourgeois de 1529 à 1681," *Archives de l'église d'Alsace* 38 (1975): 141-69.

[2]For a discussion of the historical background and the events leading up to the expulsion, see Franz Ortner, *Reformation, katholische Reform und Gegenreformation im Erzstift Salzburg* (Salzburg: A. Pustet, 1981).

[3]Joachim S. Hohmann, *Geschichte der Zigeunerverfolgung in Deutschland* (Frankfurt: Campus, 1981).

of minority without sufficient critical reflection. *Minderheiten* have become fashionable in German historiography: a recent meeting of the Southwest German Study Group for Research on Urban History was devoted to "Minorities and Marginal Groups in Urban Society,"[4] and a popular lecture course at Freiburg University resulted in a volume on the history of the Jews in early modern Germany.[5] "Core and margins," "insider and outsider," "plurality and prejudice" – these are the ideas that have informed much of the research on religious and ethnic minorities.

While not denying the reality of persecutions, to many a leitmotif of central European history, the imposition of concepts of center and marginality and the unquestioning acceptance of religious and ethnic categories can create a false sense of familiarity with the past. Central Europe under the old Reich was radically different not only from twentieth-century Germany, but also from the Germany of the nineteenth century. The identity-giving structures of the old regime, a society of estates (*Ständegesellschaft*), must be understood on their own terms. A distinctive vocabulary of social differentiation was articulated in the pamphlets and government ordinances of the early modern centuries: *Hausvolk* and *fahrendes Volk* distinguished the settled from the vagrants; *ständisch, nebenständisch,* and *außerständisch* described the degree of conformity to established social categories. The challenge, therefore, is to render an accurate translation of historical representations into contemporary social categories.

I

For the history of minorities in central Europe, the Reformation represented a crucial watershed. During the late Middle Ages, the empire had a sense of social cohesion defined by common adherence to Christianity. Marginality, hence, referred primarily to non-Christian groups or to heretical movements. The history of Jewish communities in the empire between the Black Death of 1349 and the Reformation of 1517 bears out this pattern of marginalization. Although the First Crusade in the eleventh century destroyed the Jewish communities of the Rhineland, the scale of this persecution paled in comparison with the massacres that took place during the outbreak of the plague epidemic in German cities in 1349 and 1350. As Frantisek Graus has recently documented, the scale of the anti-Semitic massacres was enormous, spreading from the Bodensee in the south to the north.[6] Particularly troubling, he argues, was

---

[4]Bernard Kirchgässner and Fritz Reuter, eds., *Städtische Randgruppen und Minderheiten. 23. Arbeitstagung des Südwestdeutschen Arbeitskreises für Stadtgeschichtsforschung* (Sigmaringen: Thorbecke, 1986).

[5]Bernd Martin and Ernst Schulin, eds., *Die Juden als Minderheit in der Geschichte* (Munich: DTV, 1981).

[6]Frantisek Graus, *Pest-Geissler-Judenmorde. Das 14. Jahrhundert als Krisenzeit* (Göttingen: Vandenhoeck & Ruprecht, 1987).

the degree of systematic planning undertaken by magistrates prior to the executions and expulsions of Jews, even before the actual advent of the plague.

To a surprising extent, the Jewish communities in the empire recovered after the midcentury massacres and began to resettle in many of the communities from which they had been expelled. The crucial development during this period was the denial of citizenship to the Jews. In sharp contrast to their legal rights during the High Middle Ages, the Jews were usually only given residence permits contingent upon the payment of protection money and the goodwill of the magistrates. A new wave of anti-Semitism broke out at the beginning of the fifteenth century when the magistrates of the imperial cities began to expel their Jews. Markus Wenninger, who has studied these late medieval expulsions, argues that the Jews had become financially dispensable for the urban populace.[7] But in addition to the economic motives of anti-Semitism, the intensification of popular piety in Christian society also played a crucial role, as reflected in the increase in ritual murder and host-desecration accusations and trials during the fifteenth century.[8] From scattered sources, we have some indication that the rise of persecution during the fifteenth century led to Jewish emigrations. Many left the empire for Italy, some en route to Palestine; others left Franconia for Venetian territory. The Jewish community in Trent, destroyed by the fury of the 1475 ritual-murder trial, consisted of immigrants from German-speaking central Europe.[9] This long-term trend of marginalizing Jews culminated in 1519, when the Regensburg community was expelled. By the second decade of the sixteenth century, only two imperial cities had any sizeable Jewish populations – Frankfurt and Worms.

The pattern of urban expulsion transformed the character of German Jewry. With dispersion the Jews settled in smaller clusters, but in a much larger number of small and midsize communities.[10] Although deprived of protection and civic status by imperial cities, Jews gained protection under many territorial rulers, ranging from powerful princes to petty knights. The dispersion of the Jewish communities helped to determine their subsequent settlement pattern in rural Franconia and in the German Southwest. Their legal status also began to improve. With the reception of Roman law at the end of the fifteenth century, some jurists were prepared to consider Jews as

[7]Markus Wenninger, *Man bedarf keiner Juden mehr. Ursachen und Hintergründe ihrer Vertreibung aus den deutschen Reichsstädten im 15. Jahrhundert* (Vienna/Cologne: Böhlau, 1981).

[8]R. Po-chia Hsia, *The Myth of Ritual Murder: Jews and Magic in Reformation Germany* (New Haven: Yale University Press, 1988).

[9]For documentation, see my forthcoming book, *Trent 1475: Stories of a Ritual Murder Trial* (New York: Yeshiva University Library).

[10]For a preliminary analysis of Jewish communities in central Europe based on the data gathered in the *Germania Judaica*, vol. 3 (1350-1517), see Michael Toch,"Siedlungsstruktur der Juden Mitteleuropas im Wandel vom Mittelalter zur Neuzeit," a paper delivered at the 37. Historikertag, October 13, 1988, Bamberg.

concives of the Holy Roman Empire.[11] Also, Charles V and his successors pursued an active policy, with varying degrees of vigor, in reclaiming the *Judenregalia* that had been effectively lost to the urban magistrates and territorial rulers.[12] Between the sixteenth and eighteenth centuries, the Imperial Chamber Court and the Aulic Court (*Reichshofrat*) in Prague (later in Vienna) regularly received and deliberated on cases brought by Jews against delinquent debtors or against unjust oppressors.[13]

II

Gypsies, however, continued to suffer persecutions into the late eighteenth century. The imperial diets of Lindau (1495) and Freiburg (1498) declared void Emperor Sigismund's 1435 Letter of Protection for the gypsies.[14] It seems that the chief reason for persecution against the gypsies was the suspicion that they were Turkish spies. The 1530 Diet of Augsburg expressly made this accusation, echoed again in the 1551 diet, also in Augsburg, which ordered all gypsies to leave the empire within three months. Gypsies were considered beyond the pale of law. In 1571 a young man in Frankfurt stabbed a gypsy to death but was released by the magistrates on the ground that "not only should such people not be tolerated and suffered in Germany, but also those who would act against such heathens or gypsies would not have committed any injustice or violence. . . ."[15] In the Thirty Years' War, while some gypsy bands hired themselves out as soldiers, masterless soldiers joined roving gypsy bands as well. After the war, in the second half of the seventeenth century, persecutions intensified; gypsies were accused of kidnapping Christian children for sale as slaves to the Turks, a variant in the theme of accusing Jews of kidnapping and murdering Christian children.[16] In the first half of the eighteenth century, when religious executions, including witch-hunts, had practically ceased, the persecution of gypsies further intensified, as reflected in the harsh tones of territorial legislation. In 1725 Frederick William of Prussia even ordered that all gypsy men and women older than eighteen years were to be hanged without trial.[17] Gypsies were often charged with magic: in 1749 a gypsy woman and her eight-year-old daughter were executed

---

[11]See Wilhelm Güde, *Die rechtliche Stellung der Juden in den Schriften deutscher Juristen des 16. und 17. Jahrhunderts* (Sigmaringen: J. Thorbecke, 1981).

[12]The best discussion of the relationship between imperial authority and the Jewish communities in sixteenth-century Germany is Selma Stern, *Josel of Rosheim. Commander of Jewry in the Holy Roman Empire of the German Nation* (Philadelphia: Jewish Publication Society of America, 1965).

[13]Sabine Frey, *Rechtsschutz der Juden gegen Ausweisungen im 16. Jahrhundert* (Frankfurt a. M.: P. Lang, 1983).

[14]Hohmann, *Zigeunerverfolgung,* 16-18.

[15]Ibid., 18.

[16]Ibid., 25.

[17]Ibid., 27.

in Landshut for magic.[18] There were, however, a few attempts to integrate the gypsies. In 1726 the Count of Wittgenstein allowed a group of gypsies to settle on his land, and in 1762 Maria Theresa and Joseph tried to settle gypsies and turn them into peasants.[19]

III

If this brief survey of the history of the persecution of Jews and gypsies in late medieval and early modern central Europe seems straightforward, the actual explanation for this development is more complex. It is obvious that both Jews and gypsies were perceived by the Christian majority as ethnic and religious minorities in Germany. But that very Christian majority, the center that defined marginality, was itself undergoing a process of disintegration and fragmentation. The sixteenth century destroyed Christian unity. No longer was a single religious identity the common assumption of membership in society. By the mid-sixteenth century, the proliferation of Christian groups had created a fragmented religious landscape. Alongside the three major Christian confessions – Catholic, Lutheran, and Calvinist – were a multitude of smaller groups: numerous Anabaptist sects; followers of spiritualist leaders such as the Schwenkfeldians; Socinians; and even Christian converts to Judaism. These groups shattered forever the picture of a unified Christendom. Central Europe, in the meantime, became a haven for religious refugees: Calvinist exiles from France, England, and the Netherlands settled during the second half of the sixteenth century in Emden, Wesel, Cologne, Frankfurt, and Strasbourg; from the turn of the century, Portuguese Jews arrived in Hamburg in successive waves.[20]

The constitutional framework to accommodate this diversity was established in the Religious Peace of Augsburg (1555) and later, after the Thirty Years' War, in the Peace of Westphalia (1648). While the constitutional guarantees confirmed limited toleration of religious dissent and safeguarded the political positions of the three major Christian confessions, they established the de facto situation in central Europe where every social group was potentially in the position of being a religious minority. Many princes took the provision of *cuius regio eius religio* to heart and tried to enforce confessional conformity upon their subjects. Resistance to state coercion was widespread and extended across all confessional barriers. Thus in Franconia, in the village of Bergrheinfeld in the vicinity of Schweinfurt, a community under the joint jurisdiction of the bishops of Würzburg and Eichstätt, the Lutheran villagers successfully

[18]Ibid., 33.

[19]Ibid., 43-44.

[20]On Calvinist exiles in German cities see Heinz Schilling, *Niederländische Exulanten im 16. Jahrhundert* (Gütersloh: Gerd Mohn, 1972); on Sephardic Jews in Germany see Jonathan Israel and Joachim Whaley, *Religious Toleration and Social Change in Hamburg 1529-1819* (Cambridge: Cambridge University Press, 1985).

resisted the Counter-Reformation for 150 years.[21] Or take the example of the six villages in the parish of Eschwege in Hesse-Kassel. In 1608 Landgrave Moritz introduced Calvinism in his land and encountered widespread resistance. Officials questioned 749 men and women in Eschwege and recorded the people's reasons for refusing communion and disobeying their prince.[22] The resistance of religious minorities also troubled the Lutheran territorial century, separatist communities came under investigation by the territorial church and government in Württemberg. In two investigations, in 1718 and 1725, authorities sent out by Stuttgart discovered that the unity of throne and altar was precisely the reason for separatist resistance. Separatists held the Lutheran clergy in contempt, describing them as thieves and murderers who received their offices by buttering up powerful patrons. In defiance of the state, the separatists rejected official church rituals as necessary for salvation.[23]

We have seen three examples of nonconformist resistance to the state. But the process of confessionalization – the interrelated processes by which the consolidation of the early modern state, the imposition of social discipline, and the formation of confessional churches transformed society – created a confessionally mixed and fluid landscape, even where state coercion was not directly present. The bishopric of Osnabrück and the city of Oppenheim in the Rhineland are two representative examples.

The Reformation had made significant advances in northwest Germany by the late sixteenth century. By that time the metropolitan city of Osnabrück was mostly Lutheran, while the rural parishes around it were confessionally mixed, with divisions often running through the same village, if not the same household. During the Thirty Years' War, Catholic and Swedish armies battled one another throughout these lands, and many parishes experienced no fewer than five reformations of religion, one with each passing army. The Peace of Westphalia provided for the alternation of a Catholic with a Lutheran prince-bishop to govern the territory. The confessional picture of the region looked like a jigsaw puzzle, with over three-quarters of the communities containing sizeable religious minorities; confessional divides ran through parishes, villages, households, and families; mixed marriages were quite common. While this confessional jigsaw proved most troubling to the clergy, it did not seem to bother the common people. Most seemed to show a great deal of flexibility, toleration, and eclecticism in confessional matters. In re-Catholicized churches, Lutherans did not withdraw from parish life; they sat in the same pews that had long been in the possession of their families, put in their share of church maintenance, and served as overseers

---

[21]See R. Po-chia Hsia, *Social Discipline in the Reformation. Central Europe 1550-1750* (London: Routledge, 1989), 139, 141-42.

[22]Ibid., 135-36.

[23]Ibid., 139.

of the church. They attended mass, went on processions, and sometimes even carried pictures of saints. What the laypeople cared about, both Lutherans and Catholics, was not the presence of other religious minorities but the moral conduct of their clergy. In 1668, for example, the parishioners of Ankum – a parish with a Catholic majority and a sizeable Lutheran minority – jointly complained to the cathedral chapter about their curate, "a man who speculated more on the depth of the beer barrel than on the mysteries of the Gospels."[24]

The case of Osnabrück seems to suggest that the concept of religious minority, itself derived from nonconformity to official religion, was irrelevant or at least unimportant to the common people. Among the three major Christian confessions, peaceful coexistence proved the norm. In the wine-growing town of Oppenheim on the Rhine, a Calvinist, a Lutheran, and a Catholic community coexisted after the Reformation. In 1698 the Calvinists made up 46.5 percent of the population, the Lutherans 32.5 percent, and the Catholics 21.1 percent. In addition, there were a few Jewish families. In spite of differences in marriage patterns, fertility rates, child-rearing habits, household size, literacy, and life expectancy, not to mention culinary ideas, work habits, medical treatment, and rituals of death and burial, the Oppenheimers of the seventeenth and eighteenth centuries went their different ways in peace. They married one another, stood as godparents, did business, and managed government. The remarkable thing was not the multiconfessionality of the urban community or the implied minority status of many of its citizens, but the stable and long-lasting social peace achieved in a complicated social and political framework.[25]

As I have argued, the confessionalization of central Europe from the sixteenth to the eighteenth centuries undermined the very concepts of center and margin, of in-group and out-group, concepts central to the identification of religious and ethnic minorities. The long-term consequence of confession-alization was an increase in social tolerance, not religious conformity, for the social groups in central Europe. For the individual, confessionalization also created a larger social space for the construction of social and personal identities. For those who took their beliefs seriously, a bewildering array of religious ideas and practices was made available by confessional competition. There are records of many individuals, not just intellectuals, crossing confessional and religious divides during the centuries of the old Reich. One example

---

[24]On Osnabrück see Theodor Penners, "Zur Konfessionsbildung im Fürstbistum Osnabrück. Die ländliche Bevölkerung im Wechsel der Reformationen des 17. Jahrhundert," *Jahrbuch der Gesellschaft für Niedersächsische Kirchengeschichte (JGNKG)* 72 (1974): 25-50; and Franz Flaskamp, "Die grosse Osnabrücker Kirchenvisitation an der oberen Ems. Ein Beitrag zur Geschichte der Gegenreformation," *JGNKG* 70 (1972): 51-105.

[25]See Peter Zschunke, *Konfession und Alltag in Oppenheim. Beiträge zur Geschichte von Bevölkerung und Gesellschaft einer gemischtkonfessionellen Kleinstadt in der frühen Neuzeit* (Wiesbaden: F. Steiner, 1984).

should suffice to illustrate this expansion of social space for the individual as a result of the Reformation.

Stephan Isaac was born in the Jewish faith in 1542 in the imperial city of Wetzlar. In 1546 Stephan's father, Johann Isaac, converted and joined the Lutheran church before accepting the position of professor of Hebrew at Marburg University. When Johann Isaac and his family moved from Marburg to Louvain in 1547, they converted to Catholicism. Young Stephan grew up as a fervent Catholic, attended university, entered the priesthood, and was elected a canon at St. Ursula's collegiate church in Cologne. Yet Stephan did not find his successful church career completely fulfilling. In the early 1580s, when Calvinism made significant gains in the Rhineland, Stephan began to question many Catholic practices. He criticized the people for praying to pictures of the Virgin Mary and the saints, and he attacked popular belief in magical healing and miracles. Disciplined by his superiors, Stephan left the Catholic church and converted to Calvinism. Although this is a colorful example, Stephan's life was by no means unique.[26] It shows the fluidity of religious and ethnic boundaries in early modern Germany, where the competing identities of Jew, Lutheran, Catholic, and Calvinist were subsumed under a personal quest for self-knowledge. In the history of German Jewish assimilation, the wave of conversions at the end of the eighteenth and the beginning of the nineteenth centuries, and the phenomenon of Jewish high society in Berlin, had their origins in the sixteenth century.[27]

IV

The enlargement of social space, the multiplication of its dimensions, and the growth of religious tolerance were also significant results of the rise of the territorial state. *Staatsräson*, or reason of state, supplanted religion as the motive force behind the restructuring of society.[28] The example of Brandenburg-Prussia, the future power behind the unification of Germany, is especially instructive.

The success of the Hohenzollerns in creating a rational, dynamic, and expansionist state can be traced back to the conversion of Johann Sigismund to Calvinism in 1613. In a Lutheran society, with the Junkers firmly entrenched in the estates and controlling the territorial Lutheran church, the adoption of a minority religion by the ruling house represented an instrument for the advancement of absolutism. From the beginning, the toleration of religious

---

[26]The autobiography of Stephan Isaac, *Wahre und einfältige historia Stephani Isaaci* (n.p., 1586), is edited and reprinted by Wilhelm Rotscheidt in *Quellen und Darstellungen aus der Geschichte des Reformationsjahrhunderts*, vol. 14 (Leipzig: M. Heinsius, 1910), 175.

[27]For the Jewish elite in Berlin see Deborah Hertz, *Jewish High Society in Old Regime Berlin* (New Haven: Yale University Press, 1988).

[28]For the rise of toleration in early modern Europe see Joseph Lecler, *Toleration and the Reformation*, 2 vols. (New York: Association Press, 1960).

and ethnic minorities by the rulers of Brandenburg-Prussia formed a central policy of their power politics. Calvinist refugees were welcomed to Prussia, the most numerous and well known being the French Huguenots expelled by Louis XIV after the revocation in 1685 of the Edict of Nantes, which had created the legal framework for the existence of the Protestant minority in France. Similarly, many of the Protestants expelled from Salzburg also emigrated to Prussia. Another group protected by the Hohenzollerns were Jews. After the expulsion of Jews from Vienna, the financiers and bankers among them were welcomed by the Berlin court. During the course of the eighteenth and nineteenth centuries, Berlin grew to become the center of German Jewish life, surpassing Frankfurt, Prague, and Vienna.[29]

The promotion of trade, finance, and economic growth, prominent among Prussia's motives for religious toleration, is also reflected in the urban history of early modern Germany. The leader in this regard was the great Hanseatic seaport of Hamburg. As Joachim Whaley has shown, in spite of the establishment of Lutheran orthodoxy in the Elbian city, the patrician, commercial ruling class in Hamburg consistently protected Calvinists, Catholics, Jews, Anabaptists, and foreign merchants, often against the agitation of Lutheran pastors and the anger of the populace.[30]

The relationship between mercantilism and toleration is even more clearly seen in the founding of new cities, which the urban historian Heinz Stoob has called "cities for exiles" (Exulantenstädte).[31] The movement for urban foundations began after the Thirty Years' War, when princes competed to attract immigrants and capital to repopulate their devastated territories. Thus Friedrich von Wied declared the village of Langendorf on the right bank of the Rhine as the site for his new residence, where all immigrants, regardless of their religious belief, could worship in private. The settlement, which came to be called Neuwied, attracted Calvinists and Anabaptist groups. By 1770, the 2,905 residents included 125 Mennonites as well as Moravian Brethren, Hutterites, and other separatists. Other mercantilist cities included Mannheim, founded in 1607 by Friedrich IV, Count Palatine; Glückstadt, founded in 1617 by Christian IV, King of Denmark, where Mennonites, Quakers, Jews, Lutherans, German Calvinists, Remonstrants, and Counter-Remonstrants all enjoyed freedom of worship; Frankenthal and Neu-Hanau, promoted respectively by the Elector Palatine and Philip Ludwig II, Count

---

[29]See Selma Stern, Der Preussische Staat und die Juden, part 1 (Tübingen: J. Mohr, 1962); and Otto Hintze, "Calvinism and Raison d'état in Early Seventeenth-Century Brandenburg," in The Historical Essays of Otto Hintze, ed. Felix Gilbert (New York: Oxford University Press, 1975), 88-154.

[30]Whaley, Religions Toleration. For the central significance of mercantilism in the toleration of Jews see Jonathan I. Israel, European Jewry in the Age of Mercantilism 1550-1750, rev. ed. (Oxford: Clarendon Press, 1989).

[31]Heinz Stoob, Forschungen zum Städtewesen in Europa, vol. 1 (Cologne/Vienna: Böhlau, 1970).

of Hanau-Münzenberg, as potential rivals to Frankfurt; and lastly Altona, founded in 1602 by Count Ernst of Holstein-Schaumburg to rival nearby Hamburg.

This new wave of urban foundations, with legal guarantees for religious and ethnic minorities, stood in sharp contrast to the policies of many of the older imperial cities, where confessional conformity persisted over mercantilist considerations. Cologne, perhaps, stands as the most telling example. In spite of the presence of sizeable Lutheran, Calvinist, and Anabaptist minorities in the mid-sixteenth century, the city gradually closed its doors to non-Catholics. In the seventeenth century Protestants were denied citizenship and subjected to heavier taxes, and Jews were denied the right of residence. Not surprisingly, many Protestants emigrated to Mühlheim, across the Rhine in Hohenzollern territory. Religious toleration in Mühlheim helped to establish the foundation for the city's economic growth during the eighteenth century. Its population grew from 763 (those over ten years old) in 1708 to 3,062 adults in 1784. Conversely, Cologne suffered an economic and demographic decline, seeing its population drop from 43,000 in 1715 to under 40,000 in 1775.[32]

V

The society of the old Reich was a complex society of estates: the definition of core/majority versus marginality/minority gradually began to shift from religious and ethnic categories to sociopolitical categories defined by the princely territorial states. Hence, order and stability could cover all social groups across ethnic and confessional barriers. Power created identity. Perhaps the most poignant example was provided by an unholy alliance created to finance Emperor Ferdinand II's pursuit of the Counter-Reformation in the early years of the Thirty Years' War. After the reconquest of Bohemia, a number of Habsburg privy councillors put together a consortium to collect and supply silver to the imperial mint in order to increase the war chest. The consortium was founded in 1622 with the right to mint coinage for Bohemia, Moravia, and Lower Austria. The political support came from men prominent in the Bohemian government, including Governor Liechtenstein and General Wallenstein, who put up nominal sums. But the real financial backing came from two men: Hans de Witte, Bohemia's richest financier, a native of Antwerp who had emigrated to Prague as a young merchant apprentice, a Calvinist nonetheless; and Jakob Bassevi, Prague Jew and merchant, prominent in the silver trade.[33]

If the apex of old regime society included men of power and wealth, regardless of race or religion, bands of outlawed bandits also included men and women of different backgrounds. Around 1700 Saxon authorities hunted

[32]Hsia, *Social Discipline,* 84-88.
[33]Golo Mann, *Wallenstein,* trans. Charles Kessler (London: A. Deutsch, 1976), 175-77.

down groups of outlaws who robbed churches and smuggled merchandise. The notorious bandit leader Niklaus List, as the police discovered, cooperated with another band of vagrant Jews. In its repression of criminality and in its defense of property and order, the state was merciless toward all bandits, Jew and Christian alike.[34]

To speak of early modern central Europe as a single entity is obviously to ignore its multiple, complex constituent parts. This larger perspective, nonetheless, allows for a comparison with the states of western Europe. By way of conclusion, the following hypothesis seems worthy of consideration as a way of rethinking the history of early modern central Europe.

Early modern central Europe was a pluralistic, complex society, more tolerant of differences than England, France, or Spain. In England, the repression of Catholics became an enshrined state policy after the reign of Elizabeth I. The persecution of "recusants" ranged from political disenfranchisement to executions of Jesuit missionaries. By the time of Cromwell, the identification of Protestantism with the national character was consolidated by the war of conquest in Ireland, an aggression that legitimated the marginalization of religious and ethnic groups. A similar historical process can be observed for Catholic France and Spain. The consolidation of royal power in seventeenth-century century France precluded the toleration of Huguenots. With the revocation of the Edict of Nantes in 1685, Louis XIV completed the work of his predecessors, notably Richelieu and Mazarin, and reversed the historical development of the previous century that weakened central, royal power in the interest of regional and religious differences. And just as Protestantism became synonymous with English national identity, the Spanish empire was unthinkable without its Catholicism. While the English made religious and ethnic minorities out of the Catholics and Irish, Spain had its *conversos* and *moriscos,* whose outward and purported inner differences were never accepted by the society they inhabited.

In the complexity of its constitutional framework and social composition, the old Reich resembled rather the United Provinces of the Netherlands. Created out of a traditional patchwork of particularist interests and privileges, Dutch society, although centered in a Calvinist state religion, offered many interstices allowing religious and ethnic minorities to flourish. In its archaic, traditionalist constitution, the Holy Roman Empire likewise created a society that tolerated religious and ethnic differences to a far greater degree than the more centralized states of western Europe.

---

[34]Uwe Danker, *Räuberbanden im Alten Reich um 1700. Ein Beitrag zur Geschichte von Herrschaft und Kriminalität in der frühen Neuzeit,* 2 vols. (Stuttgart: Suhrkamp, 1987).

Ideology Meets the Empire: Reformed Convents and the Reformation

Merry E. Wiesner

Though western Europe provides the most famous examples of female rulers in the sixteenth century, a number of territories of the Holy Roman Empire were also ruled by women. The most unusual of these were the free imperial abbeys whose overlord and special patron was the emperor. The abbess of such an institution, including renowned medieval foundations like Quedlinburg and Gandersheim, had jurisdiction not only over the abbey itself, but also over the lands and villages belonging to it, which made her a *Landesherr* (territorial ruler).

Because of their long traditions of power, independence, and prestige, free imperial convents were often the most vocal and resolute opponents of the Protestant Reformation. There were also a few abbesses who accepted the new theology and energetically introduced it into their territories. The story of these abbesses allows us to observe the interplay of religious, political, and gender ideology against a background of family and feudal relationships; it reveals the chasm that could exist between Protestant ideology and the actual course of the Reformation.

IN DECEMBER 1564, STEPHAN MOLLITOR, a Wittenberg-trained pastor, chose a rather strange text for the funeral sermon of the abbess of Gernrode: "Woe to you, O land, when your king is a child" (Ecclesiastes 10:16). He then used the text not only to criticize the fact that the new abbess was only fifteen years old but also to rail against female rulership in general.[1] Molliter was not alone in his disparagement of female rule, of course; John Knox's *First Blast of the Trumpet Against the Monstrous Regiment of Women* had appeared only six years earlier. Among those joining their voices were François Hotman, Michel de Montaigne, Thomas Becon, and George Buchanan. These attacks led others, including John Aylmer, John Case, Torquato Tasso, and John Leslie, to defend female monarchy.[2] The debate over gynecocracy hinged on questions about what we would now call the social construction of gender:

---

[1]Dr. Franke, "Elisabeth von Weide und Wildenfels: Aebtissin des freien weltlichen Stiftes Gernrode 1504-1532," *Mitteilungen des Vereins für Anhaltische Geschichte und Altertumskunde* 8 (1899): 328; Hans K. Schulze, *Das Stift Gernrode* (Cologne: Böhlau, 1965), 51.

[2]Summaries of the debate over female rule may be found in Paula Louise Scaling, "The Scepter or the Distaff: The Question of Female Sovereignty, 1515-1607," *The Historian* 41, no. 1 (1978): 59-75; Ian MacLean, *The Renaissance Notion of Woman* (Cambridge: Cambridge University Press, 1980).

How could a queen exhibit the manly qualities necessary for ruling while still remaining a woman? If her private moral virtues came into conflict with her political duties, which should take precedence? How could a married queen be a monarch over her own husband at some times, yet a wife to him at others?

Most of those involved in the debate over female rule lived in western Europe, where the issue was not simply a theoretical one in the century of Mary and Elizabeth Tudor, Mary Stuart and Catherine de Medicis. Knox had been inspired to write his attack by the dreadful (in his eyes) spectacle of two Catholic queens on one island – Mary Tudor and Mary Stuart. Stephan Molliter was also speaking from personal experience, for forty years earlier he had been called to Gernrode when the abbess of the free imperial abbey there decided to become Lutheran, and, like any good Lutheran prince, hired Protestant preachers to convert her territory.[3] Molliter had thus spent his entire pastoral career under the jurisdiction of not only women but abbesses, women whose very existence seemed to contradict Lutheran teachings. No wonder the poor man was upset.

Although "Lutheran abbess" may sound like an oxymoron, it is not. During the sixteenth century, a number of convents and abbeys transformed themselves into Protestant establishments, in some case with surprisingly little loss of power or independence for the abbess. Most of these were located in several areas of central Germany that became Protestant, particularly the duchies of Lüneburg and Brunswick/Calenburg and the bishoprics of Magdeburg and Halberstadt. These same areas of the Holy Roman Empire also saw some convents which successfully resisted all attempts by Protestant secular nobles to close them or to force them to give up their Catholicism; these convents remained as Catholic institutions within Protestant territories, in some cases until the nineteenth century. The abbesses of many of these Lutheran or Catholic convents continued to play an active political, religious, and cultural role in the empire, despite attacks on female rule and grave doubts on the part of their fellow Lutherans about the possibility of a truly Christian (that is, Lutheran) convent life. I would like to explore the story of these convents – Quedlinburg, Gandersheim, Heiningen, Gernrode, Lüne, Meyerdorf, Althaldensleben, Marienborn, Barsinghausen, Mariensee, Wennigsen, Wülfinghausen, Ebstorf, Isenhagen, Medingen, Walsrode, and Wienhausen – in an attempt to understand what factors allowed the abbesses apparently to overcome both gender and religious ideology.

Medieval historians have, of course, long recognized the tremendous power wielded by abbesses. Three of the abbeys under consideration – Gandersheim, Quedlinburg and Gernrode – were free imperial abbeys, whose abbesses were the most powerful women in the empire. Free imperial abbeys were

---

[3]Franke, "Elisabeth von Weide," 328; Schulze, *Das Stift Gernrode,* 64.

institutions whose only overlord was the emperor; the abbess had jurisdiction not only over the abbey itself, but also over the land and villages belonging to it, which made her a *Landesherr* (territorial ruler). These three abbeys were not convents in the technical sense of the term inasmuch as their residents had never taken formal vows or been strictly cloistered. They were generally termed secular endowments (*weltliche Stifte*), and the residents could leave if they chose or if family circumstances required it. They belonged to no order and were only vaguely under the jurisdiction of a bishop.[4] Each of them had been established in the ninth or tenth century and had a long tradition of learning and cultural activity; Quedlinburg and Gandersheim in particular had European-wide reputations. Their ties to the emperors were extremely close, as they had either been founded by one of the Ottonians or received imperial privileges shortly after their founding. All of the abbesses and most of the residents were from the nobility, and their families had frequently made large bequests to the abbeys. Thus, by the time of the Reformation, the abbeys had received centuries of imperial and noble patronage, with their rights and privileges confirmed by both pope and emperor.

These three abbeys were not only recipients of patronage, however, but also sources of it. Long before the Reformation, the abbesses had received the right to name most church officials in their territories. (Matilda, the sister of Otto II and the abbess of Quedlinburg in the tenth century, was even called "metropolitana" – overseer of bishops – by her biographer.)[5] Each abbess also appointed secular officials such as toll collectors, bailiffs, and legal personnel. She had the right to mint money or to grant minting privileges, and many of the coins bear portraits of the abbess herself or her family's coats of arms.[6] Except for the emperor, she was the ultimate legal authority in her territory, and apparently, because she was not cloistered, she did hear some cases herself. As a free imperial ruler, she sent a representative to the imperial diet, and she frequently brought specific cases to the emperor if she felt her rights were being infringed upon. The abbess was also a source of artistic patronage, hiring builders, sculptors, painters, and musicians; and of social patronage, supporting hospitals, orphanages, and occasionally schools. The noble residents of the abbey did not do any manual labor themselves, so the abbey hired local women and men to cook, clean, and tend the gardens.

[4]They may thus be compared with Fontevrault and the Paraclete in France, which also had close ties to the French royal house. Penny Schine Gold, *The Lady and the Virgin: Image, Attitude and Experience in Twelfth-Century France* (Chicago: Unive..ity of Chicago Press, 1985).

[5]Suzanne Wemple, "Sanctity and Power: The Dual Pursuit of Early Medieval Women," in *Becoming Visible: Women in European History,* ed. Renate Bridenthal, Claudia Koonz, and Susan Stuard, 2nd ed. (Boston: Houghton Mifflin, 1987), 148.

[6]Alan M. Stahl, "Monastic Minting in the Middle Ages," in *The Medieval Monastery,* ed. Andrew MacLeish (St. Cloud, Minn.: North Star Press, 1985), 65-67.

The other convents were not independent in the way these three abbeys were but were under the control of regional nobles. This did not mean that their abbesses were not powerful figures, however. Because the convents were landowners, they had control over the residents on that land and the same sort of patronage that free imperial abbesses had, though on a smaller scale. The other convents were also allied with noble houses, for most of their residents were noble; in some cases they were also allied with a religious order, to which, at least in theory, they could turn for support or assistance.

The political and intellectual high point for many of these convents was the eleventh century, before the Gregorian reforms ordered strict cloistering for women and the universities emerged to provide advanced education for men only. Most of them were not moribund in the later Middle Ages, however, as evidenced by their involvement in pre-Reformation reform movements designed to return convent life back to its original standards of religious observance. Particularly after the Council of Constance, many convents passed stricter rules, and nuns traveled from one reformed convent to another to help others restore discipline. In the 1440s, for example, three nuns from the reformed convent at Heiningen near Goslar stayed for three years at the convent at Neuwerk, helping the nuns there to make similar reforms.[7]

Some convents enthusiastically accepted reform, but others were less willing, particularly if the impetus for reform came from outside the convent and the nuns could see that other than spiritual factors were involved. In many areas of Germany, bishops used reforms to try to curtail the power of prominent abbesses and take over convent property; in other areas secular rulers were the instigators. For example, in 1469 the convent of Wienhausen was forcibly reformed by Duke Otto of Lüneburg, who removed all objects of value from the premises, noting that poverty was part of the strict rule of St. Benedict. The abbess, Katherine von Hoya, violently objected, and all the nuns agreed with her, telling Otto that obedience to the abbess was an even more important part of Benedictine life. Otto then carted the abbess and most of her assistants off to one of his castles and placed Wienhausen under the authority of the abbess from a nearby convent who had been more amenable to his reform moves. Under continual pressure from the duke and from high officials of the Benedictine order, the nuns at Wienhausen agreed to elect a new abbess, but only if the old one were allowed to return to the convent and live out the rest of her days in peace. The new abbess and the nuns had to agree to Otto's reforms, but they immediately began encouraging local noblewomen to give gifts of money and goods to replace the confiscated (or, more accurately, stolen) property.[8]

[7]Lina Eckenstein, *Women Under Monasticism* (New York: Russell and Russell, 1963 [1896]), 418.

[8]*Chronik und Totenbuch des Klosters Wienhausen* (Wienhausen: Kloster Wienhausen, 1986), fols. 19-41.

The reform at Wienhausen predated the Protestant Reformation by more than half a century, but in many ways it prefigured later attempts by Protestant rulers to introduce Lutheran teachings. Indeed, the later chroniclers at Wienhausen, who were nuns, date all further events at the convent from this reform, not from the Lutheran one, indicating which event was more significant in the minds of the nuns themselves. Though such reforms could be financially disastrous for convents, they did bring back high standards of spirituality.

Long traditions of power, independence, and prestige combined with a reinvigorated spiritual life to make reformed convents the most vocal and resolute opponents of the Protestant Reformation. Duke Ernst of Brunswick, who had been trained at the University of Wittenberg, began to introduce the Reformation in his territories in the 1520s. Almost all of the male monasteries agreed with very little pressure to disband and give their property to the duke, but all of the female convents in his territories refused even to listen to Protestant preachers. In Walsrode and Medingen, the nuns locked the convent doors and took refuge in the choir of the chapel; Duke Ernst first pleaded with them personally, then ordered the gates forcibly opened and a hole bashed in the choir for his Protestant preacher to speak through.[9] In Lüne, the nuns lit old felt slippers to drive out the preacher with smoke, sang during his sermons, and when ordered to be quiet did their rosaries. They were forbidden to hold public mass, and so they held it in their private quarters or the convent granary.[10] The nuns in Heiningen refused to give any food to the Protestant preachers sent to the convent, hiding whatever they had, and none gave in to ducal pressure to leave, despite promises of a 20-gulden dowry.[11]

The prioress and the convent residents at Ebstorf answered ducal threats with a letter stating that though they had no wish to oppose his wishes, they knew their only salvation lay with the Catholic Church. Though they were "poor uneducated women," they knew the church fathers approved of convent life, and they had read praises of virginity in the Bible; so how could they listen to someone who preached against convents? Both the duke and his chief reformer Urbanus Rhegius were very upset by this letter, replying that it was unseemly for a woman to address a prince on matters of theology. Rhegius went on to comment that if it was proper for a father to discipline his children, why should not the duke, as the father of his country, force

---

[9]Adolph Wrede, *Die Einführung der Reformation im Lüneburgischen durch Herzog Ernst den Bekenner* (Göttingen: Dietrich, 1887), 127, 217.

[10]Ulrich Faust, ed., *Die Frauenklöster in Niedersachsen, Schleswig-Holstein und Bremen,* Germania Benedictina, vol. 11: Norddeutschland (St. Ottilien: EOS-Verlag, 1984), 384.

[11]Gerhard Taddy, *Das Kloster Heiningen von der Grundung bus zur Aufhebung,* Veröffentlichungen des Max-Planck Instituts für Geschichte, 14 (Göttingen: Vandenhoeck and Ruprecht, 1966), 120, 122.

them to hear about the true religion?[12] He also noted that the letter could not possibly have been written by the prioress herself as its grasp of theology and church tradition was impossible for a woman.

The prioress of Ebstorf was not the only woman to show a clear understanding of theology, however. The visitations accompanying the Reformation in the bishoprics of Magdeburg and Halberstadt found many nuns able to argue very skillfully in favor of their Catholic beliefs. The abbess at Althaldensleben, for example, pointed out that if she had accepted the first Protestant teachings introduced into the convent, she would now be branded a Philipist and have to change her beliefs again. As she was uncertain what further changes the Protestants might make, she preferred to stay with the old Catholic teachings.[13]

Convents in other parts of Germany also opposed the Reformation with similar tactics, but what makes these central German convents different is the fact that the nuns were often successful.[14] Of the twenty-two female convents in Magdeburg and Halberstadt, eleven were still in existence and still Catholic in 1648, despite having been plundered repeatedly in both the sixteenth-century wars of religion and the Thirty Years' War. None of them, I might add, owed its Catholic status to the Edict of Restitution. This rate of survival is much higher than that of male monasteries, of which six out of twenty-nine survived to 1648. That any convents or monasteries survived in Protestant areas is of course somewhat unusual, and Franz Schrader attributes this to their strong spiritual life, economic independence, and banding together, combined with differences in opinion among Protestant authorities about how they should be handled.[15] Schrader makes no attempt to explain the gender difference, however, though it is rather striking and was commented upon by both Protestant and Catholic contemporaries. In the sixteenth century, Bishop Heinrich Julius, who became Lutheran, noted, for example, that the continuation of Catholicism in the convents was "the result of the resoluteness of the nuns. . . . The monks, though, are very lukewarm in the practice of

---

[12]Wrede, *Die Einführung der Reformation,* 218.

[13]Franz Schrader, *Ringen, Untergang und Überleben der katholischen Klöster in den Hochstiften Magdeburg und Halberstadt von der Reformation bis zum Westfalischen-Frieden,* Katholisches Leben und Kirchenreform im Zeitalter der Glaubensspaltung, 37 (Münster: Aschendorff, 1977), 43.

[14]For the situation in two other areas of Germany see Franz Binder, *Charitas Pirckheimer: Aebtissen von St. Clara zu Nürnberg* (Freiburg: Herder'sche Verlagshandlung, 1878); Lorna Jane Abray, *The People's Reformation: Magistrates, Clergy and Commons in Strasbourg 1500-1598* (Ithaca: Cornell University Press, 1985); and Francis Rapp, "Zur Spiritualität im Elsässischen Frauenkloster am Ende des Mittelalters," in *Frauenmystik im Mittelalter,* ed. Peter Dinzelbacher and Dieter R. Bauer (Ostfildern: Schwabenverlag, 1985). Rapp notes that some Strasbourg convents also survived into the seventeenth century, which would make Alsace an interesting case for comparative purposes.

[15]Schrader, *Ringen, Untergang, und Überleben,* 86.

their Catholic religion."[16] In 1625, a Catholic missionary reported back to the papal nuncio in Cologne that "the four women's convents [in Magdeburg] have remained truer to their beliefs and vows than the men's monasteries, who have almost all fallen away."[17]

The convents in Brunswick and Lüneburg were not successful in their struggle to remain Catholic, but by becoming Protestant they were able to survive the Reformation as religious institutions for women. Most of them fought theological change as long as they could, but they finally put independence and spiritual practices above mere theology and agreed to accept Lutheran doctrines as long as their lives were not radically changed. Indeed, it is often difficult to tell exactly what religion a convent followed at any particular point, as Catholic and Protestant women lived together and their observances and rules were a mixture of both. Lüne, for instance, was forced to accept a Protestant ordinance in 1555, which declared that the convent was now an educational center (*Ausbildungsstätte*) for women; but the women wore Benedictine habits and described themselves as belonging to the Benedictine order until 1610.[18] In 1573, Duke August passed a new convent ordinance that allowed all residents to leave whenever they wished, but later a nun in Heiningen who did not wish to leave and marry was punished and had all her goods confiscated.[19] The first Lutheran pastor was sent to Wienhausen in 1529, and the duke later took away much of the convent's land and all its prayer books. Church services were not switched from Latin to German until 1602, however, and until the 1640s residents who died provided in their wills for candles to be lit perpetually for the repose of their souls. The first woman willingly left the convent to marry only in 1651.[20]

Free imperial abbeys could hold out longer against military and political pressure than those under the control of nobles, as we can see in the case of Gandersheim, which fought the Reformation for decades. The abbey was surrounded by the territory of the dukes of Brunswick, some of whom were vigorous Lutherans who wanted abbey lands for the support of their new university. Duke Julius (ruled 1568-89) attempted to have his own candidates installed as abbesses, and during much of his reign there were actually two abbesses, one elected by the residents and one chosen by the duke. Both attempted to collect taxes and tolls, and the elected abbess continually received imperial letters of protection, which were of little practical use in asserting her rights. Finally, in 1588, the elected abbess was allowed to return and assume her rightful place after the body of a newborn child was found in

[16]Quoted in Schrader, ibid., 54.

[17]Quoted in Schrader, ibid., 74.

[18]Faust, *Die Frauenklöster*, 385.

[19]Taddy, *Das Kloster Heiningen*, 138.

[20]*Chronik Wienhausen*, fols. 70, 82, 88, 89.

the abbey's cellar and the duke's appointee admitted that she had borne the child, which had died soon thereafter.[21] Despite the confession, there have always been doubts about whether the child was actually hers or whether the abbey residents had pressured her into confession; she was, in any case, imprisoned for the rest of her life.

In political terms, the abbey won, for the duke gave up his claims to abbey land and agreed that it would remain a free imperial endowment. Later abbesses continued to receive imperial recognition and to send representatives to the diet. In religious terms, the duke won, for the abbess elected in 1589 and all those who followed her were Protestant, no longer requesting papal recognition. Anna Erika, elected in 1589, clearly placed politics and abbey traditions over religion, however; she had backed the elected abbess who preceded her in a long dispute with the duke, despite the fact that the two women differed in religion.[22]

Outside pressure was not always responsible for an abbey's accepting the Reformation. In Gernrode and Quedlinburg the abbesses themselves accepted the new theology and energetically introduced it into their territories. They took to heart Luther's early teachings on the possibility of a truly Christian convent life, which were also expressed in statements of faith such as the Wittenberg Articles of 1536: "If certain persons of outstanding character, capable of living a life under a rule, feel a desire to pass their lives in the cloister, we do not wish to forbid them, so long as their doctrine and worship remain pure."[23] They chose to ignore his more negative opinions, most fully expressed in De votis monasticis (1522).[24]

Elisabeth of Weide and Wildenfels was elected abbess of Gernrode in 1504, the first free imperial abbess to open her abbey to Lutheran teachings. She sent a representative to the Diet of Worms in 1521, in part to ask for the emperor's assistance in getting land she felt was the abbey's back from local nobles who had confiscated it, but also to get a firsthand report about what Luther was saying. Five years later she began to reform her territories, bringing in the later so ungrateful Stephan Mollitor, and appointing Lutheran pastors in the villages under her rule. One of these was soon driven from his post by Johann von Anhalt, a local nobleman who had long had designs on abbey land and who argued that the abbess had no right to appoint married

[21]Kurt Kronenberg, *Die Äbtissinnen der Reichsstifts Gandersheim* (Bad Gandersheim: Gandersheim Kreisblatt, 1981), 103-6.

[22]Ibid., 109-11.

[23]"Wittenberger Artikel, 1536," *Quellenschriften zur Geschichte des Protestantismus* 2 (Leipzig: A Deichert, 1905), 75.

[24]For a discussion of Luther's changing ideas on the possibility of chaste convent life, see Bernhard Löhse, *Mönchtum und Reformation – Luthers Auseinandersetzung mit dem Mönchsideal des Mittelalters. Forschungen zur Kirchen und Dogmengeschichte* 12 (Göttingen: Vandenhoeck and Ruprecht, 1963).

Lutheran clergy. The abbess appealed to the emperor, who valued imperial tradition more than religion in this case and ordered Anhalt to allow the pastor to resume his duties. Elisabeth also appealed to both the pope and the emperor in 1527 to force local bishops to stop taxing her subjects; despite her Lutheran appointments, both pope and emperor took her side against the bishops.[25] Gernrode continued to receive imperial privileges at least until 1577.[26]

Anna von Stolberg, abbess of Quedlinburg from 1515 to 1574, controlled nine churches, a hospital, and two male monasteries. She accepted the Protestant Reformation in the 1540s, started a consistory, made all priests swear to the Augsburg Confession, and set the salaries for both church and school officials. Despite vehement objections from the order, she turned her Franciscan monastery into a city school for both girls and boys, an interesting gender reversal of the usual pattern of male authorities transforming convents into schools or using convent property to fund scholars at universities. Though these actions gave clear proof of her religious ideas, when she asked for a coadjutor abbess to help her in her later years, she received both imperial and papal confirmation of the woman she chose. Seventeenth-century abbesses were confirmed by the emperor alone but continued to exert both secular and spiritual authority. In 1680 the abbess Anna Sophia issued a new baptismal ordinance, and in 1700 the abbess Anna Dorothea gave out an "edict against the separatists."[27]

Given Lutheran ideas about the power of secular authorities in matters of religion and the near impossibility of a truly Christian convent, these abbesses might appear naive at best. Indeed, what happened later at Gernrode would seem to bear this out. By 1532, the princes of Anhalt were putting pressure on the nuns to elect an abbess of their choice, and by 1541 they ordered the abbess to report to them on the state of religion in her churches. After 1564, all the abbesses were members of the house of Anhalt and were chosen as children, remaining in the convent only until they married.[28] The pattern was repeated in several other convents, leading some historians to dismiss all post-Reformation convents as simply residences and finishing schools for noble daughters.[29] The problem with this is that not all convents came under strict princely control. In Quedlinburg and Gandersheim, the abbesses retained their secular independence and their religious authority. The Lutheran convents in Brunswick and Lüneburg and the Catholic convents

---

[25]Franke, *Elisabeth von Weide,* 319.

[26]Schulze, *Das Stift Gernrode,* 10.

[27]Friedrich Ernst Kettner, *Kirchen und Reformations Historie des Kayserl. Freyen Weltichen Stiffts Quedlinburg* (Quedlinburg: Theodore Schwan, 1710), 123-64.

[28]Schulze, *Das Stift Gernrode,* 50-51, 66.

[29]Cf. Erhard Stiller, *Die Unabhängigkeit des Klosters Loccum von Staat und Kirche nach der Reformation* (Göttingen: Vandenhoeck and Ruprecht, 1966), 71.

in Magdeburg and Halberstadt also continued to recruit new members, maintain schools, and control land and population. What accounts for their endurance?

The easiest explanation for the abbeys' survival lies in the networks of patronage in which they were enmeshed. In the case of the free imperial abbeys, the Hapsburg emperors were not willing to move against or even reprimand institutions where female members of their own family had resided and whose connections to former emperors were stronger than their own. The free imperial abbeys represented Hapsburg ideas of what the empire should be in an era of increasingly strong secular territorial rulers, a fact not lost on the abbesses. Elisabeth von Weide, for example, played on imperial pride when she commented that bishops taxing her subjects were attempting to limit imperial power.[30] In other convents, noble residents used their family connections and ties to religious orders to put pressure on secular rulers. The abbesses in Brunswick, for example, sent both their male relatives and local clergy to the emperor to request a letter of protection; the letter was issued, though it was not of much use against Duke Ernst's drastic measures.[31]

In the case of convents controlled by local nobles, regional peculiarities provide part of the answer to the question of longevity. The duchies of Brunswick and Lüneburg were unusual in that the holdings and income from the convents never became simply part of the ducal treasury. They were administered by ducal officials, but as a separate fund, which exists to this day.[32] This has been dismissed as simply a bureaucratic distinction, but it did give convent residents officials who were specifically responsible for their interests and to whom they could go with complaints, which they did.[33] The decision to leave convent income as a separate fund was first made by Duchess Elizabeth of Brunswick, who ruled during the minority of her son. Elizabeth wrote a long advice manual to her son about how to be a good ruler, in which she specifically noted that all convent income was to be used for charitable, educational, and religious purposes; she said that no nuns should be ordered out of convents or convents left without lands or income because "to leave them just like that would be un-Christian and unloving."[34] Though her son paid no attention to the rest of her advice, he, and his successors, followed her on this point. Protestant rulers throughout much of Germany

[30]Franke, *Elisabeth von Weide,* 319.

[31]Wrede, *Die Einführung der Reformation,* 131, 224.

[32]"Klosterfonds und Klosterkammer Hannover," *Niedersachsen, Zeitschrift für Heimat und Kultur* 82 (March 1982): 21.

[33]Taddy, *Das Kloster Heiningen,* 146.

[34]"Unterrichtung und Ordnung . . . ," in *Deutscher Fürstenspiegel aus dem 16. Jahrhundert,* ed. Friedrich Karl von Strombeck (Braunschweig: Friedrich Vieweg, 1824), 57-130. (It is tempting to make a connection between her action and the fact that all the monastic establishments that survived in her territories were for women, though this would probably be pushing the evidence a bit far.)

used economic pressure to force convents and monasteries to close, confiscating their lands and holdings, and this small difference in Brunswick may have been more significant than it initially appears to be.

Political factors also entered in in both Brunswick and the bishoprics. In the sixteenth century, Brunswick was divided politically between two branches of the same ruling house. The convents were often caught in power struggles between the two branches, as well as among the emperor, pope, and both the Protestant and Catholic dukes. The initial efforts through plunder and destruction of the Protestant dukes to force the convents to convert had not worked; the second round of efforts, begun under Duke Julius in 1538, were more moderate and more concerned with securing the outward allegiance of the convents than their theological change.[35] Because territories flopped back and forth between Protestantism and Catholicism, depending on the whims of the current duke and the military situation, it worked to everyone's advantage to obscure the exact religious affiliation of a convent; that way, depending on the outcome, Catholic orders and authorities did not have to admit ever losing control, and Protestant authorities could claim an early date of conversion.[36] The situation in the bishoprics was somewhat similar, with episcopal and other church authorities disagreeing on how convents should be handled.[37]

The convents' role as a source of patronage was also instrumental in their survival. Positions as officials were often handed down within the same family for generations, a source of income that would be lost if the abbey were dissolved. The convents continued to absorb poorer women as support staff, making lower-class families more willing to accept a convent in their midst. I have not found a single example of popular protest against any of these convents after the initial wave of convent storming in the 1520s. In May 1525, Elisabeth von Weide was, in fact, able to convince a group of peasants intent on storming Gernrode to return home by reminding them of all she had done for them; though her words were very patronizing, the fact that she neither took any revenge on the leaders nor allowed her brother to do so is certainly partly responsible for the fact that the abbey was left alone after that.[38]

Patronage and political circumstances alone are not enough to explain the abbeys' continuation as Lutheran institutions. After all, male monasteries were also linked to the emperor and noble houses and provided services to local populations. To my knowledge, only one male monastery, the Augustinian house of Möllenbeck, near Rinteln on the Weser River, accepted Lutheran

[35]Taddy, *Das Kloster Heiningen,* 128.

[36]Stiller, *Die Unabhängigkeit,* 14.

[37]Schrader, *Ringen, Untergang, und Überleben,* 86.

[38]Franke, *Elisabeth von Weide,* 326-27.

theology, yet continued as a monastic establishment, and then only until 1675.[39] As mentioned above, many fewer male monasteries put up a fight against the Reformation, and those that did capitulated much faster than female houses. In the ability of the four abbeys to survive, gender played as important a role as political connections.

Why were women's religious institutions more successful in their efforts to remain in existence? The answer to this question involves both external and internal factors. To look first at external factors: after initial attempts to convert or disband them, women's religious establishments were allowed to survive because they were not viewed to be as great a threat as monasteries. The residents were, after all, women. Gender stereotypes about female weakness may have provoked opposition to female rule, but they also enabled men to take actual examples of that rule less seriously, at least at the local level. We can see this in the language of documents such as the Peace of Augsburg; in the clause termed the "Ecclesiastical Reservation," church officials who gave up Catholicism after 1552 were to lose their positions. Though the framers were certainly aware of the existence of female-headed abbeys, the language was completely male-specific.[40] Abbesses were simply not as significant in practical terms as abbots or bishops. (Sixteenth-century writers did not generally use the generic male, as evidenced by the frequency with which "male and female" or "he and she" show up in documents.)

Though noble and upper-bourgeois families hungered for abbey lands, they were also unwilling to bear all the consequences of closing the abbeys. What would they do with their daughters if they were closed? The cost of dowries was rising in early modern Germany, and even wealthy families could often not afford to marry off all their daughters; they wanted an honorable place to send those daughters for whom they could not find an appropriate marriage partner. The problem was particularly acute in the case of the free imperial abbeys, for all the residents were noble. As six noblemen wrote to Duke Heinrich of Brunswick when he first spoke of suppressing all monasteries, including Gandersheim, "What would happen to our sisters' and relatives' honor (*Ehre*) and our reputation (*Rumes*) if they are forced to marry renegade monks, cobblers, and tailors?"[41] The lack of available marriage partners among the nobility was certainly understood by the abbey residents as well; studies of convents and other *Stifte* that admitted both bourgeois and noble women have found that noble women tended to stay until death in convents that were forbidden to admit new members, while the bourgeois

[39]François Biot, *The Rise of Protestant Monasticism* (Baltimore: Helicon, 1963), 65-67.

[40]"Augsburger Reichstags abschiede," in *Geschichte in Quellen*, ed. F. Dickmann, Renaissance, Glaubenskämpfe, Absolutismus, 3 (Munich: Beck, 1966), 204-10.

[41]Johann Karl Seidemann, *Dr. Jacob Schenck, der vermeintlicher Antinomer, Freibergs Reformator* (Leipzig: C. Hinrichs'sche, 1875), Anhang 7, 193.

residents left.[42] Convent life for daughters was more integrated into noble than middle-class family patterns, and so it was harder for both the residents and their families to give up these foundations.

There were also internal factors that contributed to the continuation of the convents. Most of these convents were institutions with long-established traditions of political power and cultural importance. The residents were very aware of their position and fought any attempt, whether theologically motivated or not, to restrict their independence. They realized, too, that as women they had no position in the Lutheran church outside the abbey, and so they were more adamant than their monastic brothers about keeping the convents flourishing.[43] Former monks could become pastors in the Protestant churches, but for former nuns the only role available was that of pastor's wife, an unthinkable decrease in status for a woman of noble or patrician birth.

That the firmness of the nuns resulted from loyalty to their own traditions, and not simply loyalty to Catholicism, can be seen by their reaction to Counter-Reformation moves, particularly those proposed by the Jesuit order. When with the Edict of Restitution Heiningen was returned to Catholicism, the Jesuits wanted to take over part of the convent's income, but the nuns adamantly refused. The Jesuits tried again in 1644 by sending two representatives, but the nuns would not let them in the door.[44] The Counter-Reformation church was appalled to learn that the convents in Magdeburg and Halberstadt allowed anyone in to hear mass, which it regarded as a flagrant violation of cloister regulations. It ordered the nuns to stop, but they paid no attention.[45]

Abbesses clearly recognized their special status and reflected it in their writings as well as actions. Anna Sophia of Quedlinburg, for example, published a number of hymns and a book of meditations entitled *Der treue Seelenfreund Christus Jesus*.[46] Her book included a long introduction and afterword discussing the special duties that virgins had to praise God, and comparing the women in her convent to both the vestal virgins and biblical women such as Deborah, Hannah, Judith, and Mary. She quoted Augustine about virgins praising Christ and mentioned Anna Maria von Schurman's recent book advocating

[42]Christina Vanja, *Besitz- und Sozialgeschichte der Zisterzienserinnenklöster Caldern und Georgenberg und des Prämonstratenserinnenstiftes Hachborn in Hessen im späten Mittelalter,* Quellen und Forschungen zur hessischen Geschichte, 45 (Darmstadt: Historische Kommission für Hessen, 1984), 195.

[43]The same gender difference was found in France during the Revolution, when nuns were much more likely than monks to stay in their communities. (Olwen Hufton and Frank Tallett, "Communities of Women, the Religious Life, and Public Service in Eighteenth-Century France," in *Connecting Spheres: Women in the Western World, 1500 to the Present,* ed. Marilyn Boxer and Jean Quataert [New York: Oxford University Press, 1987], 76.)

[44]Taddy, *Das Kloster Heiningen,* 184.

[45]Schrader, *Ringen, Untergang, und Überleben,* 58.

[46]Published by Georg Sengenwald, Jena, 1658.

women's education, which had been published in Utrecht in 1641 in Latin.[47]
Her work was regarded as theologically suspect by some Lutheran theologians,
who thought that she stressed the ubiquity of Christ's presence too strongly
in her comment that women could feel this presence equally with men. The
book of meditations was later judged acceptable, however, and was reprinted
several times.[48] Anna Sophia made no general statements about the capabilities
of all women, but she did stress those of her noble coresidents; she clearly
recognized that identification with her class would take her further than
identification with her gender.

Although in practice the continuation of convents was rarely challenged
after the mid-sixteenth century, there were still theoretical doubts about the
abbesses' spiritual and temporal powers, particularly among Lutherans. Even
those Lutheran commentators who chose to praise the abbesses felt it necessary
to justify and explain their power. Friedrich Kettner, who wrote a long
history of Quendlinburg that was published in 1710, included a long discussion
about why the titles "abbess," "prioress," and "canoness" could legitimately
be maintained, using examples from the New Testament and early church
to show that these were not later popish inventions. He also gave a wonderfully
convoluted argument about why the authority of a woman should not be
the curse it is deemed to be in Isaiah 3:12 ("I will give you children to be
your oppressors and women to be your rulers . . ."). It seems that Isaiah
was not talking about the female sex here but about those of feminine
temperament (*Gemuth*), according to Kettner, who then included a long list
of ancient and contemporary female rulers.[49]

The abbesses' temporal authority was questioned in that most theoretical
milieu, the university law school. The early seventeenth century saw frequent
debates in schools such as Rostock and Ingolstadt about whether women
could succeed to feudal holdings, debates which included the case of abbesses.[50]
Their case was also taken up in discussion about the temporal power of the
clergy in general.[51]

In the long run, at least until 1807, doubts and debates did not matter.
Patronage networks combined with ambivalence about gender and religious
ideology to allow abbesses a wide range of powers. Class proved itself more

[47]Una Birch, *Anna von Schurman: Artist, Scholar, Saint* (London: Longmans, 1909), 188.
[48]Ibid., 130.
[49]Ibid.
[50]MacLean, *The Renaissance Notion*, 74-75.
[51]Ibid., 75.

important than either gender or religion, a fact which we might view as demonstrating once again the "backward" nature of the Holy Roman Empire. I choose to see matters slightly differently. Heinz Schilling has recently rightfully stressed the political and cultural triumph of the nobility in Germany after the Thirty Years' War.[52] From this perspective, we can view these abbesses as harbingers rather than as throwbacks.

[52]*Aufbruch und Krise: Deutschland 1517-1648* (Frankfurt: Siedler, 1988). Carolyn Lougee has pointed out that at least in France, seventeenth-century noble culture was in many ways dominated by women (*Le Paradis des Femmes: Women, Salons, and Social Stratification in Seventeenth-Century France* [Princeton: Princeton University Press, 1976]). This was also true in the Holy Roman Empire, where women were secular rulers as well as abbesses. Hostility toward the nobility and clergy in France was of course indirectly responsible for the end of the abbesses' power and independence, for the abbeys in the empire were secularized and their lands confiscated following Napoleon's conquests, conquests which had their roots in the French Revolution. Recent analysis of the Revolution and of the thinkers who contributed to it, especially Rousseau, has pointed out the gendered content of the critique of the nobility: Rousseau, Diderot, and others regarded the prominence of women among the nobility as a sign of that class's decadence. (See several of the essays in Samia Spencer, ed., *French Women and the Age of Enlightenment* [Bloomington: Indiana University Press, 1985]; Susan Miller Okin, *Women in Western Political Thought* [Princeton: Princeton University Press, 1979]; and Joel Schwartz, *The Sexual Politics of Jean-Jacques Rousseau* [Chicago: University of Chicago Press, 1985].) In the democratic ideology of the Revolution, gender differences far outweighed those of class, in the same way that they did in the republican ideology of Renaissance Florence (see Diane Owen Hughes, "Invisible Madonnas? The Italian Historiographical Tradition and the Women of Medieval Italy," in *Women in Medieval History and Historiography,* ed. Susan Mosher Stuard [Philadelphia: University of Pennsylvania Press, 1987]). Though we may criticize the abbesses for being elitist, membership in and identification with the aristocracy was the only road to political power available to women in the early modern period.

Imperator Caefar Diuus Maximilianus
Pius Felix Augustus

Emperor Maximilian I, by Albrecht Dürer

Some Peculiarities of German Histories in the Early Modern Era

Thomas A. Brady, Jr.

Professor Brady, an expert on the historiography as well as the history of the Holy Roman Empire, looks again at the idea of Germany's *Sonderweg*, both its positive versions among the followers of Leopold von Ranke and some negative ones after World War Two. Noting that the Holy Roman Empire, in view of its long survival, cannot have been as weak as is alleged, he examines "three dominant characteristics of the Holy Roman Empire during the early modern era: first, the traditional, non-national character of the imperial monarchy; second, the prominence of small states; and third, the active participation in public life by the church in the guise of the three confessions. . . ." Brady shows how these features already set Germany apart from the nations to its west, as, one after another, they diverged from the late medieval European pattern into "centralized governance, commercialized warfare, and seaborne empire." With frequent reference to the work of Peter Blickle, Brady points to the rural communes of the Rhine and Danube basins. Here ideas of liberty and quality persisted among peasants and villagers and provided a model that was feared by some and emulated by others, even beyond the region. Such popular communalism included control of religion. The people adhered tenaciously to their own variety of Christianity and resisted confessionalization. Thus, Brady concludes, only after 1800 did Germany really begin its *Sonderweg* – toward, not away from, the West.

> *And without the vehemence of passion history was only chronicle.*
> Gerald Strauss[1]

I

THE BEWILDERING POLITICAL MAP of central Europe before 1800 displays "the contrast between posture and power" in the old Holy Roman Empire.[2] Strewn across it are purple blotches for ecclesiastical territories and bright red pimples for the free cities; and the explorer who digs behind the big, showy pieces – Prussia, Austria, Bavaria, and Saxony – finds curious things: Imperial free abbesses and prince-provosts, heads of military-religious orders and free knights, and free peasants, notably the thirty-nine free villages and

---

[1]Gerald Strauss, *Historian in an Age of Crisis: The Life and Work of Johannes Aventinus, 1477-1534* (Cambridge: Harvard University Press, 1963), 247.

[2]Idem, "The Holy Roman Empire Revisited," *Central European History* 11 (1978): 290-301, here at 291.

hamlets on the Leutkirch Heath in Upper Swabia, whose folk until 1806 appointed their sheriffs and judges and owned no lord but the emperor. No wonder later writers wrote the empire's epitaph with a sense of wondering incomprehension.[3] Lord Bryce spoke in 1866 for the majority:

> So, too, is the Holy Empire above all description or explanation; not that it is impossible to discover the beliefs which created and sustained it, but that the power of those beliefs cannot be adequately apprehended by men whose minds have been differently trained, and whose imaginations are fired by different ideals. . . . Something more succeeding generations will know, who will judge the Middle Ages more fairly than we, still living in the midst of a reaction against all that is mediaeval, can hope to do, and to whom it will be given to see and understand new forms of political life, whose nature we cannot so much as conjecture.[4]

Long reflection on our incomprehension still whets one's sympathy for the perennial attempts to plot a straight line from some point in the Germanys' pasts to Germany's present in 1871, 1914, 1933, 1945, or even 1990. Every line so drawn pays tribute to the idea of a German special path or *Sonderweg*, a course on which the Germans diverged from the patterns of the European "West," whether the latter be understood as "Western civilization," "modern Europe," "modernity," "the modern world," "democracy," "freedom," "the free market," "civilization," or even – more candidly – England, perhaps flanked by France and the Low Countries.[5] Though the negative form of the idea of *Sonderweg* took shape during the Great War as an inversion of one of the "ideas of 1914,"[6] an older, positive form "had been developed, with widely varying meanings, since the early nineteenth century as a by-product of the development of modern German national consciousness."[7] It was largely the work of the academic historians, those self-appointed guardians of the New Germany's political culture, who "rationalized German history of the eighteenth and nineteenth

---

[3]Ibid., 290-91.

[4]James Bryce, *The Holy Roman Empire*, rev. ed. (New York: Clarke, Given and Hooper, n.d.), 388.

[5]I comment on this point in "The Rise of Merchant Empires, 1400-1700: A European Counterpoint," in *The Economics of Merchant Empires*, ed. James D. Tracy (Cambridge and New York: Cambridge University Press, 1991).

[6]See Klaus Schwabe, "Zur politischen Haltung der deutschen Professoren im Ersten Weltkrieg," *Historische Zeitschrift* 193 (1961): 60-134; idem, *Wissenschaft und Kriegsmoral. Die deutschen Hochschullehrer und die politischen Grundfragen des Ersten Weltkrieges* (Göttingen: Vandenhoeck and Ruprecht, 1969).

[7]Bernd Faulenbach, *Ideologie des deutschen Weges. Die deutsche Geschichte in der Historiographie zwischen Kaiserreich und Nationalsozialismus* (Munich: C. H. Beck, 1980), 6.

centuries as a meaningful historical process which culminated in 1871."[8]
They helped to create "the ideology of the German way," a vision of "the
special problematic of German history, which arose from the Germans'
political life in a European context and included the specific political and
cultural accomplishments of the Germans."[9]

The classic point of origin for "the German way" lay in Martin Luther
and his reformation. "Within German historical scholarship," writes Jaroslav
Pelikan, "the Reformation occupies a position analogous in some ways to
that of the Civil War in American historiography, as the crucial and (in a
quite literal sense of the term) epoch-making event by which the nature of
an entire national community and of its history has been defined."[10] This
idea reflects the character of academic history in the Second Empire as a
Protestant discipline, scarcely disturbed by the marginalized dissents of Catholics,
Social Democrats, and others.[11] Ranke's disciples, who gave the tone, echoed
"the Master's" dictum, that "[in the Reformation era] for the first time the
German spirit assumed a general form without regard to a foreign model."[12]
They treasured and guarded his identification of "the German nation, or at
least its 'productive,' future-oriented sections, with Protestantism," and they
tended "to summarize the whole of German history under the heading 'From
Luther to Bismarck.'"[13]

The positive form of this idea of *Sonderweg* was a casualty of the era from
1918 to 1945, though in the opinions of some, notably Gerhard Ritter, it

[8]Ibid., 7. This sense of the historians as political tutors to the nation is forcefully expressed
by Gerhard Ritter's *Geschichte als Bildungsmacht. Ein Beitrag zur historisch-politischen Neubesinnung*
(Stuttgart: Deutsche Verlags-Anstalt, 1947). See, for comparison, William H. McNeill, "Mythistory,
or Truth, Myth, History, and Historians," and "The Care and Repair of Public Myth," in his
Mythistory and Other Essays (Chicago: University of Chicago Press, 1986), 3-22, 23-42.

[9]Faulenbach, *Ideologie des deutschen Weges,* 6.

[10]Jaroslav Pelikan, "Leopold von Ranke as Historian of the Reformation: What Ranke
Did for the Reformation – What the Reformation Did for Ranke," in *Leopold von Ranke and
the Shaping of the Historical Discipline,* ed. Georg G. Iggers and James M. Powell (Syracuse:
Syracuse University Press, 1990), 89-98, here at 90. On the role of the Reformation in the idea
of "the German way," see Faulenbach, *Ideologie,* 125-31.

[11]For the social basis, see Wolfgang Weber, *Priester der Klio. Historisch-sozialwissenschaftliche
Studien zur Herkunft und Karriere deutscher Historiker und zur Geschichte der Geschichtswissenschaft
1810-1970,* Europäische Hochschulschriften, ser. 3, no. 216 (Frankfurt, Bern, and New York:
Peter Lang, 1984), 208-9. See my comments in "From the Sacral Community to the Common
Man: Reflections on German Reformation Studies," *Central European History* 20 (1987): 229-45,
here at 235-39.

[12]Quoted by Faulenbach, *Ideologie,* 125.

[13]Wolfgang J. Mommsen, "Ranke and the Neo-Rankean School," in *Leopold von Ranke
and the Shaping of the Historical Discipline,* 136-37. See Karl Kupisch, *Durch den Zaun der Geschichte.
Beobachtungen und Erkenntnisse* (Berlin: Lettner-Verlag, 1964), 337-41.

lived far into the postwar age.[14] Its negative form proved more durable. Geoffrey Barraclough's influential *Origins of Modern Germany* pronounced that "generations of strife" and "the religious changes" of the Reformation era "brought about . . . a further rise in the power of the princes, which ushered in the period of princely absolutism."[15] A. J. P. Taylor added with customary certainty that "the moment for making a national middle-class Germany was lost in 1521 perhaps forever, certainly for centuries."[16] And the Leipzig historian Max Steinmetz wrote that the Reformation era witnessed the failure of "the first attempt of the popular masses to create a unified national state from below."[17] These quotes testify to the power of the old idea of the *Sonderweg* as sixteenth-century Germany's path away from "the West."

Nowadays, after a long generation of several Germanys, boundaries are once again coming into flux. It is a time for reflection on inherited truths, even apparently discarded ones. Recent literature on the Reformation and early modern eras sheds much light on the old thesis of the German *Sonderweg* since the sixteenth century. It undermines in particular the residual credibility of the belief that in the Reformation era the German-speaking world embarked on a path of authoritarian political development, which led it away from the path taken by the peoples of western Europe and thus from the common European heritage.

II

Two recent developments cast bold new light on the histories of German-speaking peoples in the early modern era: a new picture of their world as a whole, and the discovery of the movement for popularly based, decentralized governance at the end of the Middle Ages. The traditional picture of the Holy Roman Empire during the early modern era offered merely a series of stepping stones from the politically supine late medieval empire to the wars of liberation against Napoleon. The stones, Heinz Schilling recently noted,

[14]See Gerhard Ritter, *Europa und die deutsche Frage. Betrachtungen über die geschichtliche Eigenart des deutschen Staatsdenkens* (Munich: Münchner Verlag, 1948), esp. 7-150; in English: *The German Problem: Basic Questions of German Political Life, Past and Present,* trans. Sigurd Burckhardt (Columbus: Ohio State University Press, 1965), 9-150. On Ritter's place in this tradition, see Faulenbach, *Ideologie,* passim; and on the role of Luther and the Reformation in Ritter's thought, see Klaus Schwabe, "Zur Einführung: Gerhard Ritter Werk und Person," in *Gerhard Ritter. Ein politischer Historiker in seinen Briefen,* ed. K. Schwabe and Rolf Reichardt, Schriften des Bundesarchivs, 33 (Boppard am Rhein: Harald Boldt, 1984), 22-31.

[15]Geoffrey Barraclough, *The Origins of Modern Germany,* 2nd rev. ed. (Oxford: Basil Blackwell, 1947), 373.

[16]Quoted by Thomas A. Brady, Jr., "The Common Man and the Lost Austria in the West: A Contribution to the German Problem," in *Politics and Society in Reformation Europe: Essays for Sir Geoffrey Elton on his 65th Birthday,* ed. E. I. Kouri and Tom Scott (London: Macmillan, 1987), 142-43.

[17]Quoted by Brady, ibid., 143.

were named "Peasants' War," "Luther and the Reformation," "Thirty Years' War," and "Frederick II and Prussia."[18] Thirty years of research in the presence of multiple German states have changed this picture entirely by thrusting into the foreground three dominant characteristics of the Holy Roman Empire during the early modern era: first, the traditional, non-national character of the imperial monarchy; second, the prominence of small states; and third, the active participation in public life by the church in the guise of the three confessions, Catholic, Lutheran, and Reformed or Calvinist.[19]

Though not free of occasional whiffs of conservative nostalgia, the effort to rehabilitate the empire as a successful political structure has gone a long way toward forcing us to a new appreciation of its durability and relative workability. If we begin with its revitalization during the reigns of the emperors Maximilian I (r. 1493-1519) and Charles V (r. 1519-1556), the empire's three-hundred-year life does not rank it among the most ephemeral of European states and state-like formations. Much evidence has accumulated, too, to show that its judicial, law-keeping, fiscal, and military structures were tolerably effective, provided one accepts their differences from comparable organs of the centralized national monarchies of western Europe. In Gerald Strauss's memorable words, "Though clearly an awkward colossus with a baroque façade and a labyrinthine structure, the Holy Roman Empire no longer strikes us as quite the sideshow monstrosity depicted in the older historiography."[20] Assiduous scholars have documented the workings of imperial institutions, such as the High Court (*Reichskammergericht*) and the regional bodies (*Kreise*), which "performed concretely and effectively what the empire as a whole stood for but could not do: the preservation of fragmented sovereignty, of the privileges of the weak as well as the strong, and of the

[18]Heinz Schilling, *Aufbruch und Krise: Deutschland 1517-1648, Das Reich und die Deutschen* (Berlin: Siedler, 1988), 9.

[19]H. Schilling, "Vom Aschenbrödel zum Märchenprinzen – Geschichtswissenschaft und historisch-politische Kultur in Deutschland," in *Wes Geistes Wissenschaften? Zur Stellung der Geisteswissenschaften in Universität und Gesellschaft, Vortragsreihe der Justus-Liebig-Universität Gießen im Wintersemester 1988/89*, ed. Schilling and Conrad Wiedemann (Gießen: Verlag der Ferber'schen Universitätsbuchhandlung, 1989), 35-49, here at 42.

[20]Strauss, "The Holy Roman Empire Revisited," 301. For orientation to the literature, see Volker Press, "The Holy Roman Empire in German History," in *Politics and Society in Reformation Europe*, 51-77; Georg Christoph von Unruh, "Die Wirksamkeit von Kaiser und Reich," in *Deutsche Verwaltungsgeschichte*, ed. K. G. A. Jeserich, H. Pohl, and Georg Christoph von Unruh, vol. 1: Vom Spätmittelalter bis zum Ende des Reiches (Stuttgart: Deutsche Verlags-Anstalt, 1983), 270-78.

complex and shifting political relationships on which the feudal order in
Germany rested."[21]

The durability of the Holy Roman Empire is closely linked to the second
characteristic, the prominence of small states. We may begin with the
conventional comparison, which holds, with justice, that the state building
process occurred in the German-speaking world on a "territorial" level rather
than a "national" one. What does this mean? Once upon a time, it meant
that, unlike the Portuguese, Spanish, French, and English, the German nation
evolved no centralized state adequate to its needs. This meaning, however,
loses all force in the face of our recognition that nations as we know them
are more or less creations of the states, rather than vice versa. "Nations,"
writes Ernest Gellner, "Can be defined only in terms of the age of nationalism,"
which is "essentially, the general imposition of a high culture on society
[and the] generalized diffusion of a school-mediated, academy-supervised
idiom, codified for the requirements of reasonably precise bureaucratic and
technological requirements."[22]

Sixteenth-century Europe did witness the emergence of a new type of
state, but it had less to do with national community than with three interlinked
characteristics: centralization, militarization, and empire.[23] The "national"
kingdoms of Europe's western tier were all conquest states, built and rebuilt
through the subjugation of some peoples by others. "The new monarchy,"
V. G. Kiernan writes, "bore an essentially warlike character that it was never
to lose. War for it was not an optional policy, but an organic need, . . .
[and] the whole state apparatus that rulers were putting together piecemeal
was largely a by-product of war."[24] Political consolidation began with conquest
and ended with "an exchange of resources, including plunder, to merchants

---

[21]Strauss, "Holy Roman Empire Revisited," 296-97. On the *Reichskammergericht*, see V.
Press, *Das Reichskammergericht in der deutschen Geschichte*, Schriftenreihe der Gesellschaft für
Reichskammergerichtsforschung, no. 3 (Wetzlar: Gesellschaft für Reichskammergerichtsforschung,
1987). On the Kreise, see James Allen Vann, *The Swabian Kreis: Institutional Growth in the Holy
Roman Empire, 1648-1715,* Studies Presented to the International Commission for the History
of Representative and Parliamentary Institutions, vol. 53 (Brussels: Éditions de la librairie
encyclopédique, 1974); Helmut Neuhaus, *Reichsständische Repräsentationsformen im 16. Jahrhundert.
Reichstag – Reichskreistag – Reichsdeputationstag,* Schriften zur Verfassungsgeschichte 33 (Berlin:
Duncker and Humbolt, 1982).

[22]Ernest Gellner, *Nations and Nationalism* (Ithaca, London: Cornell University Press, 1983),
55, 57. See Bernard Guénée, *States and Rulers in Later Medieval Europe,* trans. Juliet Vale (Oxford:
Basil Blackwell, 1985), 49-65. See also John A. Hall, *Powers and Liberties: The Causes and
Consequences of the Rise of the West* (Berkeley: University of California Press, 1985), 217-23, who
argues that nations in the modern sense are the agendas of nation building, which result from
the state's drive for development.

[23]This paragraph recapitulates my argument in "The Rise of Merchant Empires, 1400-1700,"
in which the notes provide access to the literature.

[24]V. G. Kiernan, "State and Nation in Western Europe," *Past and Present* 31 (July 1965):
20-38, here at 31.

in return for goods and credit."[25] War and trade were complementary ways of gaining control of what had belonged to others, and their marriage was consummated in the military revolution, in which innovations in management, organization, and weaponry spread like wildfire across sixteenth-century Europe.[26]

Charles Tilly has characterized this process with the pungent comment that "war making and state making – quintessential protection rackets with the advantage of legitimacy – qualify as our largest examples of organized crime."[27] Although some of the military innovations behind it sprang to life in the German-speaking world – one thinks of Swiss infantry and of the German *lansquenets* and *Reiter* – their political consequences made very slow headway in the empire. This was so partly, perhaps, because during the two centuries between the Hussite Wars (1420-1433) and the Thirty Years' War (1618-1648), the empire's German-speaking heartlands enjoyed relative respite from major wars, and partly because the major German-speaking military power, Austria, was for long engaged in wars of a quite un-European type.[28] By the eighteenth century, of course, one German-speaking power, Prussia, had managed to become large enough, ambitious enough, and predatory enough to imitate the western monarchies, but its poverty, unnourished by seaborne empire, forced Prussia to super-militarize itself into a social caricature of them.[29] Eighteenth-century Prussia thus became the first part of the German-speaking world to try to remake itself in the image of the West.

The other, smaller German states hardly tried to keep pace. T. C. W. Blanning's study of eighteenth-century Mainz reveals how the hopelessly "backward" ecclesiastical principalities, of which the empire contained dozens, illustrate "the astonishing ability of the political and social establishment in Germany to absorb, adapt and even utilize progressive and potentially disruptive

[25]Eric R. Wolf, *Europe and the People without History* (Berkeley: University of California Press, 1982), 105. As Charles Tilly so pungently puts it, "War making and state making – quintessential protection rackets with the advantage of legitimacy – qualify as our largest examples of organized crime." Charles Tilly, "War Making and State Making as Organized Crime," in *Bringing the State Back In,* ed. Peter B. Evans, Dietrich Rueschemeyer, and Theda Skocpol (Cambridge: Cambridge University Press, 1985), 169-91, here at 169.

[26]See the masterful synthesis by Geoffrey Parker, *The Military Revolution: Military Innovation and the Rise of the West,* 1500-1800 (Cambridge: Cambridge University Press, 1988); also William H. McNeill, *The Pursuit of Power: Technology, Armed Force, and Society since A.D. 1000* (Chicago: University of Chicago Press, 1982), 79-81.

[27]Tilly, "War Making and State Making," 169.

[28]I have made this point in "Imperial Destinies: A New Study of the Emperor Maximilian I," *Journal of Modern History* 63 (1991): forthcoming; and see Parker, *Military Revolution,* 35-38.

[29]This argument about imitation owes not a little to Perry Anderson, *Lineages of the Absolutist State* (London: NLB, 1974), 195-278.

forces."[30] All in all, it is at least likely that, with the exception of Prussia and perhaps the Austrian borderlands, the inhabitants of the empire, especially in its southern regions, retained far more local control of their institutions and bore less crushing burdens of taxation for military and imperial purposes than did the subjects of the western European monarchs. For this order, which in most respects preserved what had been built during the later Middle Ages, they paid a double price. First, the decentralized polity left the empire susceptible to civil war (in the seventeenth century) and invasion (in the eighteenth). Secondly, from one of medieval Christendom's heartlands the German-speaking world became a part of the less developed semiperiphery as the centralized monarchies of the West promoted development through their competitions for empire.

The third major characteristic of early modern Germany flowed from the Reformation. Across the length and breadth of the empire there arose after 1555 "more or less stable church structures with their own doctrine, constitutions, and religious and moral styles," the formation of which proceeded in close cooperation with the territorial states.[31] They are called "confessions," and their uncovering and mapping have become a major theme of the historiography of post-Reformation Germany.[32] Beginning with Ernst Walter Zeeden, historians have laid bare the development of a firm sense of collective religious identity in the two generations between the Peace of Augsburg (1555) and the onset of the Thirty Years' War (1618) and in the two generations between the war's end and the early eighteenth century.[33] These four generations, not the Reformation generation, created the confessional map of the German-speaking world and linked the structure, welfare, and work of the churches more closely to the power of the states than had ever before been the case. Confessionalization is thus to be seen as the specially German form of Christian reform in the Reformation and Counter-Reformation, and as a modernizing force, as in concert with the state the churches promoted rationaliza-

[30]T. C. W. Blanning, *Reform and Revolution in Mainz, 1743-1803,* Cambridge Studies in Early Modern History (Cambridge: Cambridge University Press, 1974), 3, quoted by Strauss, "Holy Roman Empire Revisited," 299.

[31]Robert Bireley, S.J., "Early Modern Germany," in *Catholicism in Early Modern History. A Guide to Research,* ed. John W. O'Malley, S.J., Reformation Guides to Research 2 (St. Louis: Center for Reformation Research, 1988), 11-30, here at 11-12, quoting Ernst Walter Zeeden.

[32]For orientation to the literature, see Bireley, "Early Modern Germany," 25-29.

[33]Ernst Walter Zeeden, et al., eds., *Repertorium der Kirchenvisitationsakten aus dem 16. und 17. Jahrhundert in Archiven der Bundesrepublik Deutschland,* vol. 1: *Hessen* (Stuttgart: Klett-Cotta, 1982), 16 (introduction).

tion, bureaucracy, social discipline, individualism, and a sense of supraethnic community.[34]

A traditional monarchy, small states, and widespread confessional networks – these three characteristics reveal how organically the Holy Roman Empire of the early modern era prolonged and filled out the structures of late medieval Germany, namely, the weak royal power, the emergence of territorial states, and the interpenetrating of lay and clerical institutions and forms of authority. In the light of these features, and measured against the characteristics of Europe around, say, 1350, in the eighteenth century the Germanys were the most European lands in transalpine Europe. They had adhered more or less to a common pattern from which the countries of Europe's western tiers, one after the other, had diverged into the enterprise of centralized governance, commercialized warfare, and seaborne empire.

<h1 style="text-align:center">III</h1>

Nowhere in the German-speaking world did the old ways and old patterns endure longer or with greater tenacity than in the old imperial heartlands in the Rhine and Danube basins. Nowhere did people counter more stoutly the "western" political strategy – concentration and state building – with their own strategy of dispersion and parliament and commune formation.[35] The development of communes, which allowed the ideals of liberty and equality to take root in the structures of local life, preceded by several centuries the struggle for succession to feudal governance between the partisans of concentration and those of dispersion. The German-speaking South, especially between the central highlands and the Alps, fostered and fixed decentralized forms of governance with special effectiveness and longevity.

Peter Blickle has usefully defined communalism as the movement which, between about 1250 and about 1500, transferred local governance from feudal magnates to corporations of townsmen and villagers.[36] Urban communes are a well-understood force in European history, but rural communes, though

[34]Bireley, "Early Modern Germany," 12, citing the work of Jean Delumeau. See in general Wolfgang Reinhard, "Gegenreformation als Modernisierung? Prolegomena zu einer Theorie des konfessionellen Zeitalters," *Archiv für Reformationsgeschichte* 68 (1977): 226-51; idem, "Zwang zur Konfessionalisierung?" *Zeitschrift für historische Forschung* 10 (1983): 257-77.

[35]Gerald Strauss, *Law, Resistance, and the State: The Opposition to Roman Law in Reformation Germany* (Princeton: Princeton University Press, 1986), 96.

[36]Peter Blickle, *Deutsche Untertanen. Ein Widerspruch* (Munich: C. H. Beck, 1981), 51-54; idem, "Der Kommunalismus als Gestaltungsprinzip zwischen Mittelalter und Moderne," in *Gesellschaft und Gesellschaften. Festschrift zum 65. Geburtstag von Ulrich Imhof*, eds. Nicolai Bernard and Quirinus Reichen (Bern: Wyss, 1982), 95-113; idem, "Communal Reformation and Peasant Piety: The Peasant Reformation and Its Late Medieval Origins," *Central European History* 20 (1987): 216-28, here at 221-23. For an overview of Blickle's ideas, see Brady, "From the Sacral Community," 242-44. See also Heide Wunder, *Die bäuerliche Gemeinde in Deutschland* (Göttingen: Vandenhoeck and Ruprecht, 1986).

they also appeared in many parts of Europe – including France and England[37] – came to play a lasting role in local, sometimes even in regional, governance only in certain parts of the Holy Roman Empire, namely, the German South, or roughly the upper basins of the Rhine, the Rhone, and the Danube, which also formed a zone of intense and lasting communal formation in the towns.[38] Here, by contrast with Italy, the communal ethos did not give way to signorial experiments or atrophy into a deadened oligarchical order.[39] What is far more startling, however, than the vitality of urban communes is the rise of rural ones. Though not unknown in other European lands, rural communes developed most lavishly and freely in the Alpine uplands, where the weak fabrics of royal and feudal authority allowed the countryside to awaken from the long sleep of history without motion.[40] The communes acquired political aspirations, they sometimes gained voice in territorial parliaments, and in a few favored places they formed independent rural republics. Where else did rural folk ever claim, as the people of the Valais did in 1619, "to be a free people, as in a free republic"?[41]

Although the formation of communes in the German-speaking world dates back to the thirteenth century, it took on political significance in the fourteenth century and maintained it until the sixteenth.[42] The movement's most spectacular creation, the Swiss Confederacy, arose from the union in

[37]This subject needs to be disentangled from the notorious statism and individualism of the French and English literatures respectively. I have commented on the literature's treatment of French rural communes in "The Rise of Merchant Empires, 1400-1700," at n. 86. On English rural communes, see Clifford S. L. Davies, "Die bäuerliche Gemeinde in England (1400-1800)," trans. Helmut Gabel, in Aufstände, Revolten, Prozesse. Beiträge zu Bäuerlichen Widerstandsbewegungen im frühneuzeitlichen Europa, ed. Winfried Schulze, Geschichte und Gesellschaft. Bochumer Historische Studien 27 (Stuttgart: Klett-Cotta, 1983), 41-59, here at 52-55; Margaret Spufford, Contrasting Communities: English Villages in the Sixteenth and Seventeenth Centuries (Cambridge: Cambridge University Press, 1974).

[38]On communalism in general, see Antony Black, Guilds and Civil Society in European Political Thought from the Twelfth Century to the Present (Ithaca: Cornell University Press, 1984). On the geography of German-speaking communalism, see Brady, Turning Swiss: Cities and Empire, 1450-1550, Cambridge Studies in Early Modern History (Cambridge, New York: Cambridge University Press, 1985), 5-6, 9-11, 28-30; Peter Blickle, "Kommunalismus und Republikanismus in Oberdeutschland," in Republiken und Republikanismus im Europa der frühen Neuzeit, ed. Helmut G. Koenigsberger and Elizabeth Müller-Luckner, Schriften des Historischen Kollegs. Kolloquien 11 (Munich: R. Oldenbourg, 1988), 57-75, here at 74.

[39]Schilling, "Gab es im späten Mittelalter und zu Beginn der Neuzeit in Deutschland einen städtischen 'Republikanismus'? Zur politischen Kultur des alteuropäischen Stadtbürgertums," in Republiken und Republikanismus, 101-43, here at 115-16.

[40]I allude to Emmanuel Le Roy Ladurie, "History that Stands Still," in E. Le Roy Ladurie, The Territory of the Historian, trans. Ben Reynolds and Sian Reynolds (Chicago: University of Chicago Press, 1979), 1-27.

[41]Quoted by Blickle, "Kommunalismus und Republikanismus in Oberdeutschland," 57-75, here at 57. Schilling, "Gab es . . . einen städtischen 'Republikanismus'?" 143, believes that Blickle's unification of urban and rural communes under the term"communalism" is too specially German, but that is also true of the phenomenon itself.

[42]Blickle, "Kommunalismus and Republikanismus in Oberdeutschland," 72.

1291 of what a later pamphleteer called "the poor little bunch of peasants, . . . the Swiss."[43] During the next two hundred years, the confederacy underwent a political and military expansion that made it the only rural-urban federation in European history. It exerted considerable political influence on its neighbors, and it acquired the image of a nemesis of the South German feudality. Briefly, the confederates "gained world-historical significance" for "the Swiss way of war."[44]

The Swiss Confederacy also exerted a powerful demonstration effect on the rest of South German communalism.[45] Not only did the Swiss actively support the formation of "little Switzerlands" in neighboring lands, such as the Swabian Allgäu, Vorarlberg, the Graubünden, and the Valais, but they also provided the entire zone with a model of state construction from the bottom up. When the communal movement rose to its last peak in the first quarter of the sixteenth century, this model of governance worked powerfully in all the regions in which local communal authority was already well established.[46] One such region was the Tyrol, the subject in 1525 of a most imaginative popular constitution, the basis for which is illustrated by this report of 1421 from the Stubai Valley: "When a judge is to be appointed in the Stubai, the neighbors have the right to elect three of the neighbors and present them to the prince's sheriff; he then chooses a judge from among the three, whichever seems best."[47] So powerful did this demonstration effect become by 1520, that a Netherlandish councillor warned the Emperor Charles V that without a strong royal hand, "the whole German land would become one vast commune."[48]

The confederacy also symbolized communalism's menace to aristocratic power. By 1500 the identification of "Swiss" with "peasant" and "rebel" had become a cliché of South German political discourse, the content of which is revealed by a late fifteenth-century verse which warns the nobles that:

> The common man can't be beaten
> For the Swiss take no prisoners.
> Therefore, let's get out of here,
> For they are wild with anger

---

[43]"An die Versammlung gemeiner Bauernschaft," in *Flugschriften der Bauernkriegszeit,* ed. Adolf Laube and Hans Werner Seiffert (Berlin: Akademie-Verlag, 1975), 133, line 33.

[44]Hans Delbrück, *Geschichte der Kriegskunst im Rahmen der politischen Geschichte,* vol. 4: *Neuzeit* (Berlin, 1920; reprinted, 1962), 1.

[45]For details, see my *Turning Swiss.*

[46]Blickle, *The Revolution of 1525: The German Peasants' Wa. from a New Perspective,* trans. Thomas A. Brady, Jr., and H. C. Erik Midelfort (Baltimore: Johns Hopkins University Press, 1981), 171-80.

[47]Blickle, *Gemeindereformation. Die Menschen des 16. Jahrhunderts auf dem Weg zum Heil* (Munich: R. Oldenbourg, 1985), 175.

[48]Quoted in my *Turning Swiss.*

And will murder and despoil
The nobles on the spot.[49]

This same image inspired Emperor Maximilian in 1499 to call the Swiss "wicked, crude, contemptible peasants, who despise virtue, nobility, and moderation in favor of arrogance, treachery, and hate for the German nation."[50] When he discovered how deeply such vices had penetrated his own army, the emperor flung his glove to the ground and cried, "You can't fight Swiss with Swiss!"[51]

The word "Swiss" thus came to stand for "the common man," another contemporary term, which Blickle has defined as "the peasant, the miner, the resident of a territorial town; in the imperial cities he was the townsman ineligible for public office."[52] The name distinguished all such folk from those who by birth, wealth, prestige, power, or simple self-regard were wont to say to themselves, as Owen Glendower does in I Henry IV (III.1), "I am not in the roll of common men." The phrase, "the common man," included women and children only by vague association, though the Swiss tended to relative liberality in these matters. After the Battle of Marignano, for example, widows of the fallen were permitted to speak in the Landesgemeinde, or assembly, of Schwyz; and in Uri, Unterwalden, and Zug the age of political majority was set at fourteen, instead of twenty-five or thirty, the usual age in urban communes.[53]

Lest we be tempted to place a political "Golden Age of the Common Man" in our textbooks alongside the ever-rising middle class, we should remember that the zone of real liberation from feudal lordship remained relatively small, mainly those uplands which, though poor, were also relatively open both to the outside world and to internal change.[54] What became reality in such regions remained merely an agenda among the lowland farmers, who lacked not the political will but the armed force. Machiavelli put the point

[49]Rochus Freiherr von Liliencron, ed., Die historischen Volkslieder der Deutschen, 5 vols. (Leipzig, 1865-1896; reprint, Hildesheim: Georg Olms, 1966), 1:433, no. 93, lines 184-88. I take the translation from my Turning Swiss, 36.

[50]Hermann Wiesflecker, Kaiser Maximilian I. Das Reich, Österreich und Europa an der Wende zur Neuzeit, 5 vols. (Munich: R. Oldenbourg, 1971-86), 2:337, 5:76.

[51]Ibid., 2:347.

[52]Blickle, Revolution of 1525, 124.

[53]Louis Carlen, Die Landsgemeinde in der Schweiz. Schule der Demokratie (Sigmaringen: Jan Thorbecke, 1976), 12-13. In general, however, Lyndal Roper is correct in arguing that communal institutions remained closed to women's participation. See her study, "'The Common Man,' 'the Common Good,' 'Common Women': Gender and Meaning in the German Reformation Commune," Social History 12 (1987): 1-22.

[54]Pier Paolo Viazzo, Upland Communities: Environment, Population and Social Structure in the Alps since the Sixteenth Century, Cambridge Studies in Population, Economy and Society in Past Time (Cambridge: Cambridge University Press, 1989), esp. 154-73.

with his usual terseness: "The Swiss are heavily armed and wholly free." ("Svizzeri sono armatissimi e liberissimi.")[55]

The time for political action proved rather brief, for the long late-medieval depression, which fed popular aspirations by raising the value of human labor, gave way to the sixteenth-century increase of people, prices, and state authority, which undermined the security, and hence the potential or actual political voice of working people in the South German towns, as well among the artisans and journeymen as among the working women;[56] it had the same effect on the land, as well in the nucleated villages of Franconia as in the dispersed settlements of Upper Austria.[57] All in all, during the sixteenth century the common people became more vulnerable, more divided, more subject to manipulation and pacification, and more concentrated on survival than they earlier had been.[58] This new, harder time took the political steam from South German communalism.

Some historians, it is true, hold that objective economic conflicts of interest made impossible any cooperation between popular political aspirations in town and land.[59] The record nonetheless documents instances of such cooperation, especially in the great Peasants' War, when heavy action often found burghers standing by the peasant rebels. Here, for example, is an eyewitness account by Jacob Sturm of Strasbourg from the free city of Heilbronn in April 1525:

[55]*The Prince,* chap. 12, in Niccolò Machiavelli, *The Chief Works and Others,* trans. Allan Gilbert, 3 vols. (Durham: Duke University Press, 1958), 1:48; Italian: *Il Principe e Discorsi sopra la prima deca di Tito Livio,* ed. Sergio Bertelli, 2nd ed. (Milan: Feltrinelli, 1968), 55. See Leonhard von Muralt, *Machiavellis Staatsgedanke* (Basel: Benno Schwabe and Co., 1945), 127, who cogently connects this sentence with the title of *Discorsi,* 1:55: "Where there is equality a princedom cannot be established; where there is none, a republic cannot be established." *The Chief Works and Others,* 1:306; Italian: *Il Principe et Discorsi,* 254.

[56]Jean-Pierre Kintz, *La société strasbourgeoise du milieu du XVIe siècle á la fin de la Guerre de Trente Ans 1560-1650. Essai d'histoire démographique, économique et sociale* (Paris: Editions Ophrys, 1984); Knut Schulz, *Handwerksgesellen und Lohnarbeiter. Untersuchungen zur oberrheinischen und oberdeutschen Stadtgeschichte des 14. bis 17. Jahrhunderts* (Sigmaringen: Jan Thorbecke, 1985); Merry Wiesner, *Working Women in Renaissance Germany* (New Brunswick, N.J.: Rutgers University Press, 1986).

[57]Thomas Robisheaux, *Rural Society and the Search for Order in Early Modern Germany* (Cambridge: Cambridge University Press, 1989); Hermann Rebel, *Peasant Classes: The Bureaucratization of Property and Family Relations under Early Habsburg Absolutism, 1511-1636* (Princeton: Princeton University Press, 1983).

[58]The general trend, of course, affected most of Europe. See Peter Kriedte, *Peasants, Landlords and Merchant Capitalists: Europe and the World Economy 1500-1800,* trans. V. R. Berghahn (Cambridge: Cambridge University Press, 1983), 18-60.

[59]This is the position of Tom Scott, *Freiburg and the Breisgau: Town-Country Relations in the Age of Reformation and Peasants' War* (Oxford: Clarendon Press, 1986). His skepticism is shared by Schilling, "Gab es . . . einen Republikanismus?" 143; idem, "Die deutsche Gemeinde-reformation. Ein oberdeutsch-zwinglianisches Ereignis vor der 'reformatorischen Wende' des Jahres 1525?" *Zeitschrift für historische Forschung* 14 (1987): 325-32.

The rebels moved to Heilbronn, where, after threats to cut down the vines and pressure from the common man, especially from the women, the honorable senate had to open the city to them on Easter Tuesday [April 18]. Today [April 22] their commander, Jörg Metzler of Ballenberg, came with many other captains into the city and moved into a special chamber in the city hall. They hold their deliberations there, having posted their own men at the gates, and do what they please . . . . The Heilbronners have to put up with all this.

Perhaps, but Sturm also reported how many Heilbronners joined the rebels:

A placard has been posted ordering all citizens and journeymen who want to join the army to assemble at one of the gates. The senate had to let depart anyone who will.

Heilbronn's mayor stood weeping at the gate as his people streamed out to join the rebels.[60] The behavior of these and many other burghers in 1525 recalls to mind an old Saxon legal adage: "Only a wall separates burgher from peasant."

Political cooperation between burghers and peasants reflected the many correspondences between urban and rural communal life.[61] The town had its wall, the village its fence; the town its council and mayor, the village its jurors and headmen; the town its law book, the village its regulations (*Weistümer*). Town and land also shared a political discourse based on "traditional guild and communal ideals of corporate friendship, brotherhood and love" and the unifying values of peace and the common good.[62] In the town halls and the village courts, men spoke of "law and order," "justice," "neighbors," "the common good," "the honor of God," "Christian brotherly love," and, by the eve of the Reformation, the "godly law." This vocabulary served, on the one hand, the magistrates of Nuremberg, who introduced a law book of 1478 with the statement,

As peace, concord, and due obedience of the whole community is protected, defended and promoted by an appropriate and fair administration of justice – therefore, to the praise of God and to the salutary

[60]Jacob Sturm to Strasbourg, Heilbronn, April 22, 1525, in *Politische Correspondenz der Stadt Straßburg im Zeitalter der Reformation* ed. Hans Virck, et al., 5 vols. (Strasbourg: J. H. Ed. Heitz; Heidelberg: Carl Winter, 1882-1933), 1:196, no. 344.

[61]See Blickle, "Kommunalismus und Republikanismus in Oberdeutschland," 72; idem, *Gemeindereformation,* 167-79.

[62]Black, *Guilds and Civil Society,* 69-70. See Blickle, *Gemeindereformation,* 196-204.

and blessed increase of the common weal of this honorable city, as well as of the entire community, these statutes have been codified.[63]

It also served, on the other hand, rural communes such as that of Pfalzen in the Tyrol, which in 1417 opened a statute with these words:

> To all who may see, hear, or read this open document, we, the body of neighbors who reside in the village of Pfalzen, have established, constructed, and made with enthusiasm, unanimity, and sound judgment a union (*ain ainung*), in order to promote the honor, piety, and welfare of our descendents. We therefore establish, decree, and order that . . . .[64]

By the fifteenth century, the South German and Swiss rural commune had become a tiny but structurally and morally complete counterpart to its urban sister.

The South German-Swiss communal experience is striking, not because of communal formation itself, which occurred in many parts of Europe, but because in this zone communalism entered the realm of governance and, however briefly and incompletely, devolved political voice upon ordinary people. Not on all persons, of course, nor on the most ordinary, for the big folk – patricians and merchants in the towns, inheriting heads of prosperous households in the village – almost always set the tone of communal life. Yet, by European standards communalism created political voice for remarkably broad strata of the population.

Equally striking is peasant participation in the parliamentary governance of many small South German states, mainly in an arc across the Swiss Confederacy's northern boundaries, reaching from the Tyrol and Vorarlberg in the east to Baden and the prince-bishopric of Basel in the west.[65] Through their representation in these parliaments, and often through the courts as well, the rural communes defended their collective rights, sometimes with great success.[66] In the absence of centralized territorial states, individuals, too, could pursue justice very high into the empire's judicial hierarchy. There was, for example, the case of Linsers Hans, a peasant from around Wolfisheim near Strasbourg.

[63]Quoted by Hans-Christoph Rublack, "Political and Social Norms in Urban Communities in the Holy Roman Empire," in Peter Blickle, Winfried Schulze and Hans-Christoph Rublack, *Religion, Politics and Social Protest. Three Studies on Early Modern Germany,* ed. Kaspar von Greyerz (London: George Allen and Unwin, 1984), 26, the translation of which I have slightly revised.

[64]Blickle, *Gemeindereformation,* 173.

[65]F. L. Carsten, *Princes and Parliaments in Germany from the Fifteenth to the Eighteenth Century* (Oxford: Clarendon Press, 1959), 424. The point has been developed thoroughly by Peter Blickle, *Landschaften im alten Reich. Die staatliche Funktion des gemeinen Mannes in Oberdeutschland* (Munich: R. Oldenbourg, 1973).

[66]See Winfried Schulze, *Bäuerlicher Widerstand und feudale Herrschaft in der frühen Neuzeit,* Neuzeit im Aufbau, vol. 6 (Stuttgart-Bad Cannstatt: Frommann-Holzboog, 1980).

Hans's trouble began in a Wolfisheim tavern one winter afternoon in 1524, when a dispute over a sale led to drawn knives and a stabbing. After convictions by a civil proceeding before the village court and by a criminal hearing before the seigneur, Linsers Hans appealed to the senate of Strasbourg and, failing to get his way there, to the High Court of the Holy Roman Empire (*Reichskammergericht*). What is more astonishing, when the High Court sent for the record of the trial of first instance, the village court of Wolfisheim produced the indictment, the testimonies, and the verdict – all in writing.[67]

The documentation of such institutions, movements, representation, and rights has become the stuff of historical literature on early modern Germany. They formed one sector of the much despised German particularism, that bewildering, confusing, decentralized, and unnational structure, which protected, on the one hand, the growth of Bavaria and Prussia as important states and, on the other hand, the liberties of Tyrolean valleys, the burghers of Strasbourg, Memmingen, and Isny, the upland communities in the southern Black Forest, and the five villages of the "Free Folk on the Leutkirch Heath." If this picture clashes radically with the fashionable view of European rural society as "stable, stabilized, and balanced,"[68] locked in the nearly timeless sleep of the *longue durée*, the puzzle must be unraveled elsewhere and by others.

IV

Communalism sought, as much as did centralized states, to bond to itself the power of religion, through which "individual desires come together in agreement to press their claims, and hearts become united."[69] Zürich's reformer, Ulrich Zwingli (1485-1531), acclaimed the importance of religious bonds to the urban community: "a Christian city is nothing more than a Christian commune."[70] Religious communalism, however, was by no means restricted to the cities, and we are gradually learning that parallel to religious communalism in the German-speaking cities, which culminated in the urban reform, ran religious communalism on the land, which culminated in the "rural reformation."

The reigning orthodoxy about popular religion in late medieval and early modern Europe is informed by the Anglo-French acculturation thesis,

---

[67]Strasbourg, Archives Départementales du Bas-Rhin, 3B 707: Linsers Hans vs. Arbogasts Hans. The stabbing took place on January 7, 1524. The dossier is incomplete, and the appeal's outcome is unknown. My thanks go to Leah C. Kirker for her transcription and analysis of the dossier's central document.

[68]Emmanuel Le Roy Ladurie, "Rural Civilization," in *The Territory of the Historian*, 79-110, here at 103.

[69]Ibn Khaldûn, *The Muqaddimah: An Introduction to History*, trans. Franz Rosenthal, abridged ed. N. J. Dawood (Princeton: Princeton University Press, 1957), 125.

[70]*Huldreich Zwinglis sämtliche Werke*, ed. Emil Egli et al., 14 vols. to date (Berlin, Leipzig, Zürich, 1905-), translated by Thomas A. Brady, Jr., "In Search of the Godly City: The Domestication of Religion in the German Urban Reformation," in *The German People and the Reformation*, ed. R. Po-chia Hsia (Ithaca: Cornell University Press, 1988), 20.

which holds that Christianity hardly influenced the rural people until the seventeenth century, when "seeking to eliminate the worship of saints and to put an end to the cult of the dead, . . . Catholicism finally found itself digging its own grave."[71] Undeterred by such solemnities, Peter Blickle and his team at Bern have begun to uncover a deep, broad movement of religious communalization in the pre-Reformation era.[72] Through their headmen and courts, villages requested the establishment of parishes and the provision of parish priests, and they often demanded both a voice in the nomination of pastors and the repatriation of alienated tithes to support their priests.[73] Where such rights were secure, they were defended, as in the village of Ehringen near Nördlingen, where the village statutes proclaimed "that the commune of Ehringen has the power to elect its pastor . . . , and if the commune is not satisfied with him, it may give him notice within three months."[74] In central Switzerland the communes installed and deposed their priests, some of whom had to submit to annual reviews and confirmations. Such rights were extremely rare outside the Swabian-Alemannic and Alpine lands, and they were by no means the rule within this region.

The fundamental problem of pre-Reformation religion, it seems, was the localization of control of the religious personnel, institutions, and resources so as to provide more faithful, more regular, and cheaper religious service by the clergy to the laity. By 1500, perhaps only one hundred of the three thousand or so towns in the empire had acquired the right to appoint their own parish priests, though there was mounting pressure to transfer patronage rights and tithes to the towns and villages. The Reformation gave this movement a powerful legitimating idea: the godly law, God's plan for the world as contained in the Bible. Based on the godly law, the Reformation movement's twin goals around 1520 became the preaching of the Word of God and local control of religious life. The connection between biblicism and local control is visible everywhere, even where the local communes had no political aspirations. Such was the case in the margraviate of Brandenburg-

[71]Le Roy Ladurie, "Rural Civilization," 99-101. See the trenchant critique of this thesis by Richard C. Trexler, "Reverence and Profanity in the Study of Early Modern Religion," in *Religion and Society in Early Modern Europe, 1500-1800,* ed. Kaspar von Greyerz (London: George Allen and Unwin, 1984), 245-69.

[72]Blickle summarizes the findings in "Communal Reformation and Peasant Piety: The Peasant Reformation and Its Late Medieval Origins," trans. David Luebke, *Central European History* 20 (87): 216-28. For the historiographical context, see his introduction to *Zugänge zur bäuerlichen Reformation,* ed. Peter Blickle, Bauer und Reformation 1 (Zürich: Chronos, 1987), 11-18. What follows is based on this collection, on Blickle's own *Gemeindereformation,* and on Franziska Conrad, *Reformation in der bäuerlichen Gesellschaft. Z .r Rezeption reformatorischer Theologie im Elsass,* Veröffentlichungen des Instituts für europäische Geschichte Mainz 116 (Wiesbaden: Franz Steiner, 1984).

[73]See Rosi Fuhrmann, "Die Kirche im Dorf. Kommunale Initiativen zur Organisation von Seelsorge vor der Reformation," in *Zugänge zur bäuerlichen Reformation,* 147-86.

[74]Quoted by Blickle, *Gemeindereformation,* 181.

Ansbach in Franconia, where Margrave Casimir installed a new pastor at Wendelstein in 1524. Immediately, the headman and court of the village instructed the pastor that "we hold you to be no lord but only a servant (*ein Knecht und Diener*) of the community, so that we have to command you, and not you us. And we order you to proclaim faithfully the Gospel and the Word of God purely and clearly, according to the truth and without human additions."[75] In 1525 the rebel armies of Upper Swabia formed their "Christian Association" "to the honor and praise of God Almighty, to the exaltation of the holy Gospel and God's Word, and to the furtherance of justice and the godly law"; and they proclaimed that "we want henceforth to have the power and right for the entire commune to appoint and depose its pastor."[76] Finally, the Ilanz Articles of April 1524 bound the Graubünders as follows: "So that the Word and Christ's doctrine is proclaimed more faithfully to the common man, who should not be led into error, from henceforth no one, whether pastor, chaplain, monk, Roman appointee, or of whatever status he may be, shall be appointed to any post, if he does not reside among our Leagues."[77] Behind this provision lay the desire for regular, inexpensive, and faithful service by the clergy to the laity, which, it was believed, could be secured only through local control.[78]

Religious communalization aimed to secure the benefits of a rich and varied ritual life, the popularity of the symbols and actions of which by no means disappeared with the coming of the Reformation.[79] The Christianity of ordinary, German-speaking folk, indeed, impresses through "the extraordinary tenacity of popular resistance to imposed doctrines and observances," as exemplified by its startling power to clothe a new figure, such as Luther, in old garments, the attributes of a Catholic saint.[80] After reflection on this power, Gerald Strauss suggests that following the Reformation's "early hyperactive and emotionally charged heroic phase," the common people tenaciously

---

[75]Quoted by Blickle, *Gemeindereformation*, 27-28.

[76]Ibid., 34.

[77]Ibid., 52-53.

[78]Our one satisfactory study of a pre-Reformation diocese confirms this belief. Francis Rapp, *Réformes et reformation à Strasbourg. Église et société dans le diocèse de Strasbourg (1450-1525)*, Collection de l'Institut des Hautes Études Alsaciennes 23 (Paris; Editions Ophrys, 1974).

[79]This is the main message of Robert W. Scribner's pioneering studies of religious ritual, which are now easily accessible in Robert W. Scribner, *Popular Culture and Popular Movements in Reformation Germany* (London, Ronceverte: Hambledon Press, 1987), especially "Cosmic Order and Daily Life: Sacred and Secular in Pre-Industrial German Society," 116; "Ritual and Popular Belief in Catholic Germany at the Time of the Reformation," 1748; and (previously unpublished) "Ritual and Reformation," 103-22.

[80]Gerald Strauss, *Luther's House of Learning: Indoctrination of the Young in the German Reformation* (Baltimore: Johns Hopkins University Press, 1978), 302. See R. W. Scribner, "Luther Myth: a Popular Historiography of the Reformer," and "Incombustible Luther: the Image of the Reformer in Early Modern Germany," in his *Popular Culture and Popular Movements*, 301-22, 323-54.

resisted the Reformation's attempt "to replace the permissive climate of medieval Catholicism with an authoritarian creed."[81]

This stubborn quality of popular Christianity often resisted confessionalization quite successfully. Cases are known, for example, from the mid-sixteenth century of men who served simultaneously as Catholic priests and Protestant pastors.[82] Where no strong state developed to impose and guard confessional boundaries, popular Christianity never lost this quality. This was the case in the Graubünden, a land – now in Switzerland – which possessed three languages, two confessions, one small city (Chur), and hardly any state. Once past the (extremely disruptive and savage) Wars of Religion, its people settled into a way of life in which the two confessions functioned in a common culture.[83] At least this is the conclusion suggested by stories of how it fell to the Capuchin priests to protect both Catholic and Protestant Bündner communities from demons and other evil spirits.[84] Of the most famous such priest, Eberhard Walser, Capuchin superior ("dr Supeeri") at Mastrils, it was said that "he drove many devils over the Mastrils hill and out of the Prättigau."[85] Peter Walser died in 1905.

A story from the town of Ilanz (Romansh: Glion), the ancient market town of the Surselva, also illustrates the transconfessional role of Catholic exorcists in the Graubünden. In the cellar of a former tavern at Ilanz, the spirits of two innkeepers, man and wife, often appeared to visitors and said: "So many thumbs also make a measure." This was their punishment for having cheated customers by sticking their thumbs in the pitchers while drawing wine. The present owners, who were Protestants, sent for the Catholic priest from a nearby village to drive the spirits from their cellar. The priest agreed, but only if the householders would ask their own Protestant pastor to join him in the task. As the two brothers of the cloth stood before the house, the priest asked, "Will you go in and bring them out?" The pastor went in but shortly returned to report that the spirits refused to come. Then the priest went down into the cellar and brought the spirits out, and he and the pastor led them through the town. After the priest banished them to a cave along the Rhine, they never bothered mortals again. This event happened

---

[81]Strauss, *Luther's House of Learning*, 30-33.

[82]Bireley, "Early Modern Germany," 13, citing Ernst Walter Zeeden, *Die Entstehung der Konfessionen. Grundlagen und Formen der Konfessionsbildung im Zeitalter der Glaubenskämpfe* (Munich: R. Oldenbourg, 1965), 74, 77.

[83]For orientation, see Friedrich Pieth, *Bündner Geschichte*, 2nd ed. (Chur: F. Schuler, 1982), 119-250.

[84]See Scribner, "Ritual and Popular Belief in Catholic Germany at the Time of the Reformation," 44-47, for an explanation of why this remained a Catholic task.

[85]Arnold Büchli, *Mythologische Landeskunde von Graubünden. Ein Bergvolk erzählt*, 4 vols. (Disentis: Desertina, 1989), 1: 574-75.

"a long time ago," said the informant in 1943.[86] The historian, heeding the folklorist's warning that all is not ancient which seems so,[87] does not have to believe these practices extremely old in order to appreciate their point: in the absence of a centralized state, post-Reformation religion could not be thoroughly confessionalized. Through the process of confessionalization, we may conclude, the state "became the true beneficiary of the union with the Reformation."[88]

V

The long survival of the Holy Roman Empire's late-medieval characteristics – a traditional monarchy, small states, close union of religion and governance, and communalism – mocks every notion of a new departure, turning point, or *Sonderweg* among the German-speaking peoples before 1800.[89] Thereafter did begin a new story, a *Sonderweg* not away from "the West" but toward "the West," a passage of German-speaking peoples from the Germanys to Germany. Nothing impelled them in this direction more than their experience of French imperial rule under Napoleon – so much so, that Thomas Nipperdey opens his account of nineteenth-century Germany with the words, "In the beginning was Napoleon."[90] The shocking appearance of a truly western ruler among the Germans is also suggested in a scene by the Alsatian writer René Schickele. As one of Napoleon's regiments – German speakers from Alsace – marches into Rheinweiler, a small town in Baden, the soldiers are heard to sing:

> Gott Vater hat einen Sohn, Und der heißt Napoleon.[91] (God the Father has a son, And his name's Napoleon.)

[86]Ibid., 2:399-400.

[87]Hermann Bausinger, "Traditionale Welten. Kontinuität und Wandel in der Volkskultur," *Historische Zeitschrift* 241 (1985): 265-87.

[88]Karlheinz Blaschke, "The Reformation and the Rise of the Territorial State," trans. Thomas A. Brady, Jr., in *Luther and the Modern State in Germany,* ed. James D. Tracy, Sixteenth Century Essays & Studies 7 (Kirksville, Mo.: Sixteenth Century Journal Publishers, 1986), 75.

[89]I would add this fourth characteristic to Heinz Schilling's three (see note 19), despite his strictures in "Die deutsche Gemeindereformation" (n. 59).

[90]Thomas Nipperdey, *Deutsche Geschichte 1800-1860. Bürgerwelt und starker Staat* (Munich: C. H. Beck, 1983), 11.

[91]René Schickele, *Maria Capponi* (Munich: Kurt Wolff, 1925), 70.

Curious Georgics: The German Nobility and Their Crisis of Legitimacy in the Late Sixteenth Century

H. C. Erik Midelfort

The argument is made that assaults by such prominent writers as Sebastian Franck, Nicodemus Frischlin, and Cyriakus Spangenberg upon the German aristocracy provoked a vehement and even violent response because the German nobles felt seriously wounded. Writers like the three named pointed out that despite pretensions to valor and virtue, the German nobles were perhaps more conspicuous for their drinking and impiety. One result of this assault upon the legitimacy of the German aristocracy was the rise of special chivalric schools; another was the growing concern for the purity of blood lines as a way of proving the nobles' legitimate claim upon privilege. Parallel developments can also be observed in Spain and France. The essay questions the views of Otto Brunner, whose *Adeliges Landleben* is a major work in the field, and aims at stimulating further work on the German aristocracy.

Shall a godless soldier own these well-tilled fields, a barbarian these crops? (Impius haec tam culta novalia miles habebit barbarous has segetes?)

Virgil, *Bucolica* 1.70-71

MORE THAN FORTY YEARS AGO OTTO BRUNNER (1889-1982) published a remarkable book, a study of the life and significance of a minor Austrian poet of the seventeenth century, Wolf Helmhard von Hohberg.[1] In the life of this member of the *Fruchtbringende Gesellschaft* (Society of the Fruitful), Brunner taught his readers to see a noble world on the edge of collapse, a world governed by the principle of lordship (*Herrschaft*) that was about to be taken over by the principles of rational economy and the centralized bureaucratic state. The *Grundherr* (lord of the land) was sinking to nothing more than a *Grossgrundbesitzer* (large land owner); the *Herrenschicht* (ruling order) was becoming a leisure class.[2] Fighting with the temptations of nostalgia, Brunner stated clearly and openly that there could be no return of the noble world; it was gone forever. But the spiritual crisis of the modern age lay in the sad fact that the new forces of politics and bourgeois economy had not yet succeeded in creating "stable forms of human cooperation and a corresponding

---

[1] Otto Brunner, *Adeliges Landleben und europäischer Geist. Leben und Werk Wolf Helmhards von Hohberg, 1612-1688* (Salzburg: O. Müller, 1949).

[2] Ibid., 323, 339.

217

spiritual life."[3] That was what Wolf Helmhard von Hohberg had had in large measure – a life of responsibility and culture that connected with the "noble" values of old Europe going all the way back to Aristotle. Brunner's strategy as a historian was to create the appropriate social categories for a genuinely historical sociology that would avoid imposing modern social forms upon the helpless past. Instead of speaking of state, economy, and class, Brunner extracted alternate terms with which to understand a lost world: lordship, household (*das ganze Haus*), and estate. By listening closely to Hohberg's language as he described the ideal life of nobles on the land, Brunner exercised a neo-historicist capacity that he had first unfolded in his study of medieval lordship, *Land und Herrschaft*.[4] It is not my direct purpose here to raise the methodological and philosophical problems that Brunner's strategy entails.[5] Nor do I wish to inquire here into the process by which *Adeliges Landleben und europäischer Geist* served to rehabilitate Brunner's academic career, which had run aground at the end of World War II.[6] Although these would be fruitful tasks, I think we need instead to take a closer look at the German nobility in the early modern period. So influential has Brunner's work been that certain features of noble life have threatened to disappear from our historical consciousness altogether.

Central to Brunner's understanding of Hohberg was the idea of crisis. In Hohberg's poetry and especially in his major work on agriculture and the noble way of life, *Georgica Curiosa* (1682), Brunner thought he could sense the quiet, civilized, illusion-loving retreat of a noble ethos in crisis.[7] Echoing

---

[3]Ibid., 10, 339.

[4]Otto Brunner, *Land und Herrschaft. Grundfragen der territorialen Verfassungsgeschichte Südostdeutschlands im Mittelalter,* Veröffentlichung des Instututs für Geschichtsforschung und Archivwissenschaft in Wien 1 (Baden bei Wien: R. M. Roherer, 1939); in 1959 the first postwar edition appeared under the title *Land und Herrschaft. Grundfragen der territorialen Verfassungsgeschichte Österreichs im Mittelalter* (Vienna: R. M. Rohrer). The charge of "neo-historicism" comes from Hans-Ulrich Wehler, ed., *Geschichte und Soziologie* (Cologne: Kiepenheuer und Witsch, 1972), introduction, 11.

[5] See, e.g., D. M. Nicholas, "New Paths of Social History and Old Paths of Historical Romanticism. An Essay Review on the Work and Thought of Otto Brunner," *Journal of Social History* 3 (1969/70): 277-94; Winfried Schulze, "Theoretische Probleme bei der Untersuchung vorrevolutionärer Gesellschaften," *Theorien in der Praxis des Historikers. Forschungsbeispiele und ihre Diskussion* (Sonderheft 3 of the journal *Geschichte und Gesellschaft*, ed. Jürgen Kocka (Göttingen: Vandenhoeck und Ruprecht, 1977), 55-74; John B. Freed, "Reflections on the Medieval German Nobility," *American Historical Review* 91 (1986): 553-75. Otto Gerhard Oexle, "Sozialgeschichte – Begriffsgeschichte – Wissenschaftsgeschichte. Anmerkungen zum Werk Otto Brunners," *Vierteljahrsschrift für Sozial- und Wirtschaftsgeschichte* 71 (1984):305-41; Fransisek Graus, "Verfassungsgeschichte des Mittelalters," *Historische Zeitschrift* 243 (1986): 529-89.

[6]Robert Jütte, "Zwischen Ständestaat und Austrofaschismus. Der Beitrag Otto Brunners zur Geschichtsschreibung," *Jahrbuch des Instituts für deutsche Geschichte* (Tel-Aviv) 13 (1984): 237-63.

[7]In his table of contents to *Adeliges Landleben,* Brunner crystallized his view of the threat under which the noble culture of the seventeenth century lived: "Die Krise: der moderne Staat, 124." Interestingly, Brunner does not use the word *Krise* on 124.

the famous portrait of late medieval Burgundian culture by Johan Huizinga (*The Waning of the Middle Ages*), Brunner thought he could sense desperation and denial in the aristocratic love of fantasy. Poetry, novels, drama, epic, and shepherd romance all pointed to an aristocratic world in trouble:

> For this world was threatened by such new tendencies as the modern state, the "bourgeois way of life" (*Bürgerlichkeit*), and the "natural system of the intellectual disciplines" (*Geisteswissenschaften*). Therefore the poetry of this period was much more an "art of illusion" than was true for the noble world of the Middle Ages. Such poetry reached its high point in opera, a creation of the early seventeenth century.[8]

Nobles of the seventeenth century also took refuge in the teachings of Neo-Stoicism, especially in the works of Justus Lipsius and Guillaume du Vair, who taught noblemen how to subdue their affections for the world even as they counseled statesmen to use whatever means necessary to preserve the peace and order of the state.[9] Such refuge, however, was not secure for more than a few years beyond the death of Hohberg in 1688. In 1690 Leopold I published his *Robotpatent* (Decree on Forced Labor) for Bohemia, which together with the patents of 1717 and 1738 provided "the first examples of state intervention in the inner life of the lords' lands."[10] The forces of rational economy would combine with those of the state to make the "whole house" a useless political and economic entity and to liberate politics and economics from the aristocratic ethical web within which they had been understood for over two thousand years.

So a crisis was at hand, but one that was curiously undramatic. Brunner's crisis in fact stretched forward from Hohberg through the next 160 years, down to 1848 at least. This observation may appear banal; historians have often dealt in crises of so long a duration that the crisis itself becomes almost undetectable.[11] The specific problem is that Brunner here represented a position that saw the history of the German nobility, or at least its ethos, as virtually unchanging, in all essentials, for hundreds of years, stretching back to Aristotle or even Homer. This strong sense of temporal continuity was matched by Brunner's sense of the homogeneity of noble culture. His celebrated analysis of the intellectual world of the Austrian nobility was based in large part upon thirteen catalogs of noble libraries from the first half of the seventeenth century.[12] Brunner argued that the contents of these libraries all contributed

---

[8]Ibid., 124.   [9]Ibid., 129-30.   [10]Ibid., 315.

[11]For an effort to restore the idea of crisis to some precision and usefulness, see Randolph Start, "Historians and 'Crisis'," *Past and Present* 52 (1971): 3-22; Volker Press suggests a much more dramatic and explosive crisis in the sixteenth century, but the contestants are the same as Brunner's, and the victor (the state) is the same as well: "Wilhelm von Grumbach und die deutsche Adelskrise der 1560er Jahre," *Blätter für deutsche Landesgeschichte* 113 (1977): 396-431.

[12]Brunner, *Adeliges Landleben*, 158-66.

to one homogeneous noble culture, so that the most modest collection was only an imperfect reflection of what the largest assemblage, that of Job Hartmann von Enenkel, more fully displayed: the astonishing erudition of the Austrian nobility.[13] Moreover these seventeenth-century libraries reveal a culture that, while it had become more classically learned and more able to read Greek and Latin, was essentially similar to that revealed by the few surviving catalogs of medieval noble libraries. It did not occur to Brunner to wonder whether such collections were typical in the seventeenth century, to say nothing of how typical their medieval predecessors were. And yet, investigations such as those of Rudolf Endres have shown that the Franconian nobles in 1525 were not especially bookish. Of fifty-eight Franconian noble families who compiled lists of damages after the Peasants' War in order to claim reimbursement for their losses, only six seem to have had any library at all.[14] The castle at Egloffstein had a library of five books, Wachsenroth had only "some German books," while Wichsenstein could boast of only three books. Only the library of Christoph von Seckendorf revealed an educated interest in the world of learning. These were, of course, Franconian nobles, not Austrian, but Brunner's method, if applied to these inventories, might have pumped up Seckendorf's collection as affording us the "fullest view" of a Franconian noble's library. It seems more accurate to note, with Endres, that these nobles rarely had much education or any books.[15]

Another problem is that Brunner assumed that whatever he found in Hohberg's *Georgica Curiosa* was characteristic of a specifically aristocratic frame of mind. Hohberg, for example, took little interest in making his farming more rational and efficient. His bookkeeping methods were primitive; he could not tell which of his crops were profitable or which of his operations were losing money. Brushing aside the few places in which Hohberg did pay attention to planning and profits, Brunner concluded that aristocrats like Hohberg were wedded to a traditional economy in which market forces were not supposed to be dominant.[16] But of course it was not only aristocrats who thought in traditional ways about the business of farming, as Brunner surely

[13]Of the largest fifteenth-century library he discovered, Brunner characteristically wrote, "Den umfassendsten Einblick in eine Adelsbibliothek des 15. Jahrhunderts gibt uns das Bücherverzeichnis der Elisabeth von Volkenstorf." Ibid., 150. It does not seem to have occurred to Brunner that so large a collection gives us a view of the "fullest noble library," not the "fullest view of a noble library."

[14]Rudolf Endres, *Adelige Lebensformen in Franken zur Zeit des Bauernkrieges.* Neujahrsblätter der Gesellschaft für fränkische Geschichte 35 (Würzburg: F. Schöningh, 1974), 32.

[15]Ibid., 33-34. The great noble libraries mainly date from the seventeenth century: Eva Pleticha, *Adel und Buch: Studien zur Geisteswelt des fränkischen Adels am Beispiel seiner Bibliotheken vom 15. bis zum 18. Jahrhundert* (Neustadt and der Aisch: Degener, 1983).

[16]Brunner, *Adeliges Landleben,* 293-305; cf. Wolf Helmhard von Hohberg, *Georgica Curiosa, Aucta, das ist umständlicher Bericht und klarer Unterricht von dem Adelichen Land- und Feldleben, auf alle in Teutschland übliche Land- und Haus-Wirtschaften gerichtet* (Nuremberg, 1695), part 1, book 1, chaps. 2 and 21-24.

knew. In Hohberg's day his *Georgica Curiosa* had only one serious rival as a complete, encyclopedic guide to running a farm and household: the enormous *Haus- Feld- Artzney- Koch- Kunst- und Wunderbuch* of Johann Christoph Thiemen.[17] This book, although aimed at a far less learned and aristocratic readership, reveals just as traditional a view of the market and of bookkeeping and efficiency in general. It appears that Brunner's nostalgia got the better of him at this point. "The world we have lost" was for him an "aristocratic" world with an unquestioned aristocratic ethos. Perhaps that is also the reason why Brunner had so little to say about Hohberg's Protestant Christianity and the way in which religious duties pervade the *Georgica Curiosa*.[18] Such elements were not specifically aristocratic.

I make these remarks not to give *Adeliges Landleben* a final, belated review. It was and is in many ways a wonderful book. But Brunner's brilliant picture of a slowly dying noble ethos has blinded too many historians to crosscurrents within the noble ethos, as well as to the crisis that German nobles had to overcome in the sixteenth century – a crisis of legitimacy. Of course, one such crisis has long absorbed the attention of scholars under the name of the Peasants' War, but it has long been customary to see that conflict more as a peasant uprising or rebellion (or most recently a revolution) than a crisis for the German aristocracy. Even the most astute scholars have assumed that unless the peasants could come up with a new ideological basis for social change, the nobles could successfully illegitimize any protest by pointing to the Old Law as the basis for noble power. Thus Peter Blickle, to name only one, dramatically portrays the ideological struggle between "feudalism" and "biblicism" as if feudal relations were so universally accepted that only a radically new form of legitimacy stood any chance of mobilizing a successful workers' movement.[19] This makes a certain sense from the point of view of modern ideological politics,[20] but there were other strategies with which the discontented could unsettle the nobilities of Europe. One of the simplest was to take nobles at their word when they claimed that their rights and privileges depended upon their own virtue and the virtue, valor, and heroism of their ancestors. Not all observers in 1525 thought of the nobles as transparently virtuous, and despite the abject defeat of the peasants and the "common

---

[17]The full title merits comparison with the *Georgica* of Hohberg: *Haus- Feld- Artzney- Koch- Kunst- und WunderBuch. Das ist, Ausfürliche Beschreib- und Vorstellung wie ein kluger Haus Vater und sorgfältige Haus-Mutter wes Standes und Würden sie auch immermehr seyn mögen . . . höchst-glücklich fortpflanzen mögen* (Nuremberg, 1687).

[18]See Hohberg on the Jews and Anabaptists, e.g., and on the education of children: *Georgica Curiosa*, part 1, book 1, chaps. 74-75, and book 3.

[19]Peter Blickle, *The Revolution of 1525: The German Peasants' War from a New Perspective*, trans. and ed. Thomas A. Brady, Jr. and H. C. Erik Midelfort (Baltimore: Johns Hopkins University Press, 1981), 87-93.

[20]See, e.g., Donald Kelley, *The Beginning of Ideology. Consciousness and Society in the French Reformation* (Cambridge: Cambridge University Press, 1981), 1-10, 301-36.

man," not all observers after 1525 could see virtue as the central characteristic of the German nobility. Yet without virtue the best laid legal claims might ring hollow.

That is what makes the 1531 critique of noble life by Sebastian Franck in his *Chronica, Zeytbuch, und Geschychtbibell* so truly interesting. It is customary to regard his explosive portrayal of noble selfishness and violence, of drunkenness and gluttony, of vanity and hunting and injustice as little more than the exaggerations of a moralist.[21] Brunner, in particular, performs one of his more remarkable acts of historical legerdemain in reducing Franck to a mere echo of the Franciscan tradition of poverty and spirituality, a tradition supposedly seized upon by the bureaucrats of the absolutist state in order to devalue the noble world.[22] Such an approach to Franck might be plausible if Franck had presented only an outraged moral revulsion at the noble decadence he saw about him. Actually he offered more, but we must learn to listen to his language. I want to call attention to the famous preface to the second part of Franck's *Chronica*, where he discussed the eagle. For twenty-one pages Franck analyzed the nature and characteristics of the eagle and all the other animals commonly used by princes and lords in their coats of arms: bears, wolves, hawks, panthers, foxes, lions.[23] Why, Franck asked leadingly, did the princes and lords of the world consistently choose such worthless and horrid creatures as their symbols? The answer lay close at hand and depended on the sixteenth-century version of ethology, the science that tries, among other things, to understand human nature by looking at its common basis in the nature and behavior of other animals. In the sixteenth century the detection of such common traits was facilitated by the assumption that, like men, most

---

[21]Endres, *Adelige Lebensformen*, 8.

[22]"Quellen, wie die Chronik der Grafen von Zimmern, die sich deutlich als Schwanksammlung erweist und daher z. B. vom Studium an italienischen und französischen Universitäten nur die dabei erlebten 'lächerlichen und schimpflichen Geschichten' erzählt, oder die Erinnerungen des Hans von Schweinichen, bedürfen einer kritischen Würdigung. Die üblichen Formeln stammen offenbar aus den von H. Gumbel . . . widergegebenen Sätzen Sebastian Francks: 'Sie treiben keine ander handtierung dan jagen, beyssen, sauffen, prassen, spillen; leben von rent und zins und gülten in überfluss gar köstlich. Hier wird die spiritualistische, aus der 'Armutbewegung' kommende Wurzel der Abwertung der Adelswelt deutlich, die sich von den Predigten der Bettelmönche des 13. Jahrhunderts bis zu Abraham a Sancta Clara verfolgen lässt. Darüber and über das Aufgreifen dieser Formeln durch die Bürokraten des absolutistischen Staates und ihre Weitergabe an die Publizistik des 19. Jahrhunderts, vgl. S. 286 f., 311 u. 327. Der ganze Prozess ist ein bemerkenswerter Beitrag zum Problem des Zusammenhangs von Säkularisierung und Spiritualismus, der soviel zum Abbau der Adelswelt beigetragen hat." *Adeliges Landleben*, 354, note to 166.

[23]I have used the first two editions: Sebastian Franck, *Chronica, Zeytbuch und Geschychtbibel von anbegyn biß ihn diß gegenwertig MDXXXI Jar* (Strasbourg, 1531) and its extension (Ulm, 1536; reprinted Darmstadt, 1969). The "Vorred vom Adler" is at fols. 119r-125r in the 1531 edition; in 1536 it was expanded on fols. 142-62; note that the pagination jumps from 144 to 155, and 160 is misprinted as 140.

animals lived in societies or polities and exhibited virtues, vices, thoughts and feelings, social institutions, and social failings.

As Keith Thomas has reminded us recently, sixteenth-century men and women had no hesitations about classifying plants and animals according to human needs.[24] Man was the measure of all things, and fortunately nature responded to the measurement with a rich storehouse of lessons for man. The result was that a commentary on the "lordly" animals could shift imperceptibly to a commentary on the lords, a shift made all the more easily in German owing to the etymological closeness of the words *Adel* and *Adler*. All of this may be an overly elaborate way of saying that Franck's views on the eagle were of immediate importance. In Franck's opinion, eagles were notoriously rapacious, dishonorable, and un-Christian birds. The eyes, beak, and talons bespoke violence and belligerence; its habitat was lonely, lofty, and uncivil. While other animals had natural allies (such as the symbiotic relationship between the trochilus and the crocodile), eagles had none; they did, however, attract a worthless crowd of hangers-on, eager to feast off the bloody bits left behind by the tyrannical eagle.[25] Unlike other animals, the eagle killed its own babies, selecting but one for survival and eliminating the rest, behavior that reminded Franck of ancient tyrants and Roman emperors. Feared by all and loved by none, the eagle had to live in high places, the tops of trees or mountains, "aware that everyone does reasonably hate him whom everyone must fear."[26] Other animals bowed to the eagle and paid him obeisance out of fear alone, "just as with evil princes." So notorious was the eagle that the story of the love of an eagle for a maiden "isn't believed even by those who'll believe anything."[27]

We would not be mistaken in hearing in Franck's fable a serious contribution to German political theory as well as an Erasmian response to Machiavelli.[28] Eagles, however, were not merely bloodthirsty. Some of their hatred for other birds was ideological, such as their enmity against cranes, which came "perhaps because they (the cranes) prefer democracy, the equal lordship of

[24]Keith Thomas, *Man and the Natural World. A History of the Modern Sensibility* (New York: Pantheon, 1983), 51-71; Rodney Needham, *Primordial Characters* (Charlottesville, Va.: University of Virginia Press, 1978); John Berger, "Animals as Metaphor," *New Society* 39 (March 10, 1977): 504-505. Georges Gusdorf, *Les sciences humaines et la pensée occidentale* (Paris: Payot, 1967), 2:461.

[25]*Chronica* (1531), 120v-21r; *Chronica* (1536), 156v, 157v, 158v.

[26]"ingedenck, das den billich yederman hasset, den yederman förchten müss," ibid. (1531), 121v; (1536), 158v. Aristotle (*Historia Animalium* 6.6 and 9.34, 44) and Pliny (*Natural History* 10.4) tell these stories of eagles and their young. Cited by John Boswell, *The Kindness of Strangers. The Abandonment of Children in Western Europe from Late Antiquity to the Renaissance* (New York: Pantheon, 1988), 24-85.

[27]Ibid. (1531), 121v-22r; (1536), 158v-159r.

[28]For the influence of Erasmus' *Adages* on Franck, see Rudolf Kommoss, *Sebastian Franck und Erasmus von Rotterdam* (Berlin: E. Ebering, 1934), 31-33; Franck's independence from Erasmus is affirmed on 90-91.

many in one kingdom, which princes especially repudiate."[29] Franck repeated with evident pleasure the story of how the cranes of Cilicia eluded the eagles of the Taurus by filling their bills with stones so that their cries would not betray them. In the years after the Peasants' War such a story had an obvious moral, but Franck was careful to leave himself a defense. At any time he could retreat and claim that he was only repeating a story about birds. As with his *Paradoxa,* his translations, and his collection of aphorisms (the *Sprichwörter*), Franck worked by indirection, leaving himself loopholes and escapes. But usually his intention was all too clear, as when he finally found something praiseworthy in the eagle: "At least he is no drunkard and by no means wanton or unchaste, regardless of how rapacious he is. In this respect our nobles far surpass the [emblems on] their coats of arms."[30] If only some of the nobles would just imitate the eagle on their banners, instead of raping and defiling maidens and married women.

Christians, Franck insisted, had to live by higher standards than the bestial and heathen models of lions, bears, and eagles. The only conquest of which one could be genuinely proud was the conquest of oneself, so that one might withstand the temptations of good luck and wealth, which otherwise led noble and rich men into folly and self-destruction. It was the pressure of fortune and wealth that sent the ruling class to its destruction: "The bigger the lord the bigger the fool" ("Je grösser herr je grösser thor"). No wonder it was said that "the faces of all pious princes could be engraved on one ring."[31] It was obvious to Franck that the "Christian" rulers of the earth had made fatal concessions to this world; as a moralist and theologian Franck was hardly creating a realistic politics, but his views were taken with great seriousness. So offensive was his *Chronica,* and especially the "Vorred vom Adler" ("Preface on the Eagle"), that religiously tolerant Strasbourg sent Franck into exile after its publication in 1531. The council of Strasbourg may also have been reacting to a complaint from Erasmus that Franck had libelously called him a heretic, but it seems likely that the main reason was that Franck "vigorously insults the [Holy] Roman Empire," as the councillors put it in their edict of December 18, 1531.[32] Fully three years before the Strasbourg council decided to force all Anabaptists into exile, it was clear

---

[29]"villeicht darumb, das diesen gefellt Democracia, das ist gleiche herrschaft viler in einem reich, dem die Fürsten besonder abhold siend," *Chronica* (1531), 121r; (1536), 158v.

[30]Ibid. (1531), 122r; (1536), 159r: "ist doch das züloben, das er keyn sauffer ist, und gar nicht geil noch unkeüsch, wie rabgiering er sunst immer ist. In dem übertreffen unsere Adler weit ir wappen."

[31]Ibid. (1531), 123r; (1536), 160r (misprinted as 140): "Aller frommen fürsten angesicht möchten auff einen ring gestochen werden."

[32]Manfred Krebs and Hans Georg Rott, eds., *Elsaß, I. Teil, Stadt Straßburg 1522-1532,* Quellen zur Geschichte der Täufer 7, and Quellen und Forschungen zur Reformationsgeschichte 16 (Gütersloh: Gerd Mohn, 1959), no. 262, pp. 342-43; no. 286, pp. 358-59. My thanks to Professor James Kittelson for this reference.

enough that Franck represented a different sort of threat.[33] Martin Bucer, Johann Cochlaeus, and Martin Frecht of Ulm kept up a campaign against him that was only partially theological in origin. As Franck noted, the clergy, when embarrassed by his account of their excesses, were quick to accuse him of "tarnishing the imperial majesty, of sternly rebuking the eagle and offending their sensitive ears so that they would have me guilty of high treason."[34] Four years later, in Ulm, the preface was still causing Franck so much trouble that he finally had to leave in 1539. The "Vorred vom Adler" even reached the attention of the highest imperial authorities. In November of 1531 King Ferdinand complained to his brother Charles V about the *Chronica* and demanded a tightened censorship.[35]

Franck's attack on the eagle and on the godless princes and nobles whom the eagle represented could lead a hasty reader to conclude that Franck had no use for nobles of any sort, but such a conclusion would be careless. Very early on in his *Chronica* he had written of the origins of true nobility and in doing so had made an important distinction. Nobles arose, he claimed, in the aftermath of Nineveh, because the pious people of God needed protection from the wicked:

> Therefore a pious, just, and wise man (who went before the others in virtue like a light in the darkness and excelled the untamed rabble in understanding and virtue) was chosen to decide all wars, to control the mighty, and to distribute the common property. Back then a nobleman was one who was far ahead of the others in virtue, so that it was a common saying among them: Virtue makes [one] noble.[36]

Such a description of true nobility, of course, fed Franck's purpose of discrediting the nobility of his own day, but we would be wrong in thinking that the equation of virtue and nobility was always part of a subversive strategy. In fact, as Ellery Schalk has recently pointed out, the equation of nobility and virtue was one generated in the Middle Ages and kept alive in the sixteenth

---

[33]On Strasbourg's attitudes toward toleration and exile, see Henry George Krahn, "An Analysis of the Conflict Between the Clergy of the Reformed Church and the Leaders of the Anabaptist Movement in Strasbourg, 1525-1534" (Ph.D. Dissertation, University of Washington, 1969), 366-95 and 448-75.

[34]*Chronica* (1536), 142r.

[35]Eberhard Teufel, *'Landräumig': Sebastian Franck, ein Wanderer an Donau, Rhein und Neckar* (Neustadt an der Aisch: Degener, 1954), 34-57, esp. 39.

[36]*Chronica* (1531), 12v; (1536), 15r: "darum ward ein fromm, gerecht, weiss man, der mit tugend wie ein liecht in der finsternis den andern vorgieng und weit übertraff mit verstandt unnd tugendt dem unzempten pöfel vorzugehen erwölt, allen krieg zü entscheiden, die verwaltigten handzuhaben und das gemein güt auszuteilen. Dazumal was ein edler der vor andern in tugenten merklich er war wie ein sprichwort bei in was. Tugend macht edel. . . ." For the use of the theory of the golden age, see Philip L. Kintner, "Studies in the Historical Writings of Sebastian Franck (1499-1542)" (Ph.D. Dissertation, Yale University, 1957), 71-107.

century by the nobles themselves.[37] They were proud to think that their rank did not depend on birth alone but on their valor, honesty, magnanimity, and wisdom as well. Franck would only add to this description that true nobility could not rest on birth at all. It was as uninheritable as such other spiritual qualities as faith and sin. Nobility of the conventional sort, dependent upon wealth, birth, and the subjection of others, was a heathen remnant that Christians should have eradicated. "In sum, to be noble by birth and to elevate one's name on high is a piece of heathendom, and that is why the nobility of our day are almost all heathens," Franck wrote.[38] No wonder the rulers of this world, from Jacob Sturm in Strasbourg to King Ferdinand himself, were incensed. The trouble was that Franck's notions of nobility were based on more than simply a Franciscan ideal of poverty, condemned by the church from the fourteenth century onwards. They were based in the zoology, theology, and ethics of his day. Owing to the savagery with which the mighty pursued such views, however, Franck's was not a popular or comfortable position, at least not if one wanted to express oneself in print.

It is understandable, therefore, that Franck had no immediate or obvious successor in Germany. About forty years later, however, another reckless scholar undertook to criticize the nobility. We may remember that like Franck, the famous poet Nicodemus Frischlin (1547-1590) of Tübingen had a turbulent career, which ended when he was forty-three in a fatal attempt to escape imprisonment at Hohenurach, where Duke Ludwig of Württemberg had locked him up. Despite his many scholarly controversies, especially with Martin Crusius, how many remember that his big mistake, again like Franck before him, was to criticize the German nobility? In 1578 he delivered a lecture on Virgil's *Bucolics* and *Georgics,* which he was foolish (or brave) enough to publish as *Oratio de vita rustica (Oration of the Rural Life)* in 1580.[39] In thinking about Virgil's idealized portraits of country living, Frischlin realized that the delights of the herdsman or the farmer depended on being far from the corruption of city, court, and battlefield. These were, in fact,

---

[37]Ellery Schalk, *From Valor to Pedigree. Ideas of Nobility in France in the Sixteenth and Seventeenth Centuries* (Princeton: Princeton University Press, 1986); cf. Davis Bitton, *The French Nobility in Crisis, 1560* (Stanford: Stanford University Press, 1969); Arlette Jouanna, *L'idée de race en France au xvie siècle,* 3 vols. (Paris: H. Champion, 1976).

[38]*Chronica* (1531), 13r; (1536), 15v.

[39]David Friedrich Strauss, *Leben und Schriften des Dichters und Philologen Nicodemus Frischlin. Ein Beitrag zur deutschen Culturgeschichte in der zweiten Hälfte des sechzehnten Jahrhunderts* (Frankfurt, 1856), 174. Cf. Gustav Bebermeyer, *Tübingen Dichter-Humanisten: Bebel, Frischlin, Flayder* (Tübingen: H. Laupp, 1927), which adds little to Strauss's thorough account of the dispute over the nobility. For a critique of Strauss's account see Samuel Millard Wheelis, "Nicodemus Frischlin: Comedian and Humanist" (Ph.D. Dissertation, University of California, Berkeley, 1968). On the political and rhetorical thinking of Frischlin, see David E. Price, "Nicodemus Frischlin and Sixteenth-Century Drama" (Ph.D. Dissertation, Yale University, 1985), esp. 110, 113-119, 162-166. On the *Oratio de vita rustica* see Klaus Schreiner, "Frischlins 'Oration vom Landleben' und ihre Folgen," *Attempto* (Tübingen) 43/44 (1972): 122-35.

the sources of wickedness depicted by Virgil, but when Frischlin tried to discuss their application to his day, he found himself attacking not just politics, war, and urban sophistication, but also warriors and politicians, and specifically the nobles:

> Compare now this praise of peasants with the life of our so-called noblemen, and decide for yourself which of the two is more pious, more holy, more just, more reasonable, and more noble. For where do we hear more gruesome blasphemies in our day than among the nobles? Those who would appear the most pious exalt the pope, but not because they regard the papist religion so highly; rather it's because they respect much more the high honor, dignity, and position (and the fancy cuisine) of the lordly cathedral canons.[40]

But noble treatment of the peasants was even worse. Frischlin called the lords cannibals (*Leutfresser, Centauri*) and blasted them for punishing innocent tenant farmers with death for no good reason at all. "And who has ever heard of accusing, or of an executioner ever punishing, such a one for any crime?" Frischlin added.[41] If accused of atrocities by anyone from a lower estate, the nobles banded together in a conspiracy to defend one another. Reflecting on the refusal of the nobility to accept men with high academic degrees as their equals, Frischlin burst out,

> Now what kind of pride is it when they consider no one noble unless he can display the rusty old pictures or coats of arms of his ancestors and recite by heart his descent from his four grandparents? Here is the source of that contempt for the most learned persons, whom the least learned and coarsest squire thinks he far surpasses; and since they are puffed up and swollen with this amazing fantasy about their descent, they demand to sit down on benches everywhere, to be given precedence in all things; and in court and chancery we are supposed to be appreciative of their grace and fall at their feet.[42]

Scripture said that the devil was a fountain and father of vanity and pride, and nobles proved that on this account they were his sons. "If these days behavior and vices made one a peasant, then by eternal truth there would be nothing more boorish (*Bäurischer*), nothing coarser than these folk who would like to be squires and noblemen."[43] Add to that their disloyalty toward superiors, and one would have to admit that peasants often showed more fidelity.

---

[40]Strauss, *Leben und Schriften*, 178-179. Throughout my account I am ignoring Frischlin's later alterations, made in an attempt to soften his impact. Strauss notes many of the alterations in detail.

[41]Ibid., 179.   [42]Ibid., 180.

Aware that he had gone over the brink, Frischlin tried belatedly to backtrack, claiming that he did not mean to condemn all noblemen indiscriminately. "For I do know some (*etlich*) among them who fear God, hold piety in high regard, respect their princes, love justice, and honor those people who are more learned or more talented than they are, relying not on their own nobility but on their discipline, virtue, and understanding."[44] Such noblemen, although few in number (*quamlibet numero exigui*), had no need to take offense at his writing, Frischlin protested. He was attacking "only the cyclops and gross oppressors, the noble centaurs and monsters, the noble gangs and agitators; so that I might wish that a second Hercules appear, such as Emperor Maximilian I and his kind, to root them out."[45]

Turning to the remaining virtues of the peasants, Frischlin praised their moderation in contrast to "our sweating, belching courtiers who stuff themselves like fattened oxen." Peasants were free, he said, from avarice, ambition, and envy, again in sharp contrast to the life at court.[46]

Bethinking himself again, Frischlin conceded that his idealized peasants were all drawn from antiquity. Nowadays there were no more plowmen like Curius Dentatus or Cincinnatus, and rural life had become as greedy and luxury-loving as life in any town. Why, a conscientious prince now worked harder than three thousand peasants together.[47]

The poet must have known that his speech was indiscreet, but he could not have guessed what an uproar it would provoke in its printed form, especially once it was translated by his enemies into German. He narrowly escaped assassination, and soon the assembled knighthood of Swabia registered their complaint to Duke Ludwig of Württemberg. In 1581 the knights of Franconia and the knights of the Wetterau and the Upper Rhine brought similar charges, complaining that Frischlin had slandered them *in genere,* aiming at "a peasant government, or even a Turkish government; hoping for confusion of the spiritual and secular estates; intending *in summa* the destruction of the common, good old peaceful German system."[48] They claimed that Frischlin wanted to set those of high and low estate at each others' throats and to provoke a rebellion: "Take careful note of this," they urged. At first Duke Ludwig paid little attention to the exaggerations of the knights, and Frischlin must have enjoyed reminding him that "if anyone in Switzerland tries to elevate himself above others on account of his nobility, [he finds that] his nobility is worth no more than a piece of cow shit."[49] The charges of Frischlin's fomenting another peasants' war did not die down, however; by August of 1581, Landgraf Wilhelm V of Hesse wrote to Ludwig

---

[43]Ibid., 181.   [44]Ibid., 182.   [45]Ibid., 182.

[46]Ibid., 182-83.   [47]Ibid., 184.   [48]Ibid., 208.

[49]Ibid., 210, a letter dated July 16, 1581: "Wenn sich bei den Schweizern Einer seines Adels wegen über die Andern erheben wollt, so gelt sein Adel nicht mehr denn ein Kühdreck."

to say that his nobles too were upset by Frischlin's oration, reminding him also that nobles were crucial to social order. Ludwig should not permit, through negligence, a repetition of the Poor Conrad rebellion of 1514, the Bundschuh conspiracy, or the great war of 1525.[50] It is clear enough that the nobles of Germany were touchy to the point of paranoia. Two generations after the revolution of 1525, their fears represent one of its most lasting results. In fact it is the disproportionate outrage and uproar of the German lesser nobility that prompt me to contend that they must have been experiencing a crisis of legitimacy in the late sixteenth century.[51] I cannot imagine that a confident, clearly legitimate class would have reacted to the Latin poetry of a rhetoric professor with such rabid ferocity. What made matters worse was that after triggering an avalanche of protest, Frischlin was not one to retire in all humility. By 1582 he had lost his position in Tübingen; he then moved to Carniola to run a school. By 1584 he was back in Germany, as unrepentant as ever. His published apology of 1585 did him little good, for by now he had lost favor at the court of Württemberg.[52] In 1587 he went into exile again, prompting him in 1590 to write a dangerously foolish attack on Ludwig's councillors. Now he had really gone too far; he was arrested in Mainz and transported to Hohenurach, where he died six months later in an attempted escape.

Such outward events register one kind of reaction to Frischlin's critique of the nobility, but there was an intellectual reaction as well. In the fall of 1581, the Saxon Marcus Wagner published an attack on Frischlin entitled *Von des Adels Ankunfft, oder Spiegel,* to which Frischlin replied in Latin in

---

[50]Ibid., 216

[51]This provides further evidence for an important thesis of Winfried Schulze, who has sought to show that after 1525 German peasants developed a surprising ability to sue their own lords: *Bäuerlicher Widerstand und feudale Herrschaft in der frühen Neuzeit* (Stuttgart: Fromann-Holzboog, 1980); idem., *Deutsche Geschichte im 16. Jahrhundert* (Frankfurt: Suhrkump, 1987), 33 and 297. On the general question of crises of the German nobility, see Peter Uwe Hohendahl and Paul Michael Lützeler, eds., *Legitimationskrisen des deutschen Adels: 1200-1900* (Stuttgart: Metzler, 1979). The masses of recent research on the German nobility and on the other elites of the sixteenth and seventeenth centuries have been expertly surveyed in Hans Hubert Hofmann and Günther Franz, eds., *Deutsche Führungsschichten in der Neuzeit: Eine Zwischenbilanz,* Büdinger Vorträge 1978 (Boppard am Rhein: Boldt, 1980), especially in the pieces by Volker Press, "Führungsgruppen in der deutschen Gesellschaft im Übergang zur Neuzeit (um 1500)," 29-77; Rudolf Johannes Kunisch, "Die deutschen Führungsschichten im Zeitalter des Absolutismus," 111-41.

[52]Nicodemus Frischlin, *Entschuldigung und endtlicher bestendige Erklärung Doctoris Nicodemi Frischlini gestellt an den löblichen Adel, Teutscher Nation. In wölcher lautter dargethon würdt, dass er in seiner Oratione de vita rustica (wie auch in andern seiner Schrifften) den löblichen Adel anzutasten, zu verkleinern, oder zuschmähen niemalen bedacht gewesen* (Tübingen, 1585).

December of the same year.[53] Already in this work we can see that the defense of the nobility depended not on assertions of their legal claims but upon claims of their virtue. This was even truer of the remarkable and massive work published by Cyriacus Spangenberg in two volumes in 1591 and 1594, the *Adels Spiegel*.[54] Well known to theologians and church historians as a defender of Flacius Illyricus's notion of original sin, Spangenberg is much less well known as a historian and defender of the German nobility.[55] Actually Spangenberg's *Adels Spiegel* conducted two campaigns at once. He hoped to show that God had ordained only three estates, the well-known *Nährstand*, *Wehrstand*, and *Lehrstand;* but he shifted the medieval categories, as Luther had before him, to mean the three estates of marriage, ruling, and preaching.[56] On this reckoning a person could enjoy membership in two or even in all three estates at once, but "whoever doesn't fit into one of these three estates is not in a godly estate and cannot truly be sure of God's grace or blessing."[57] Who was not in a godly estate? Mainly the clergy of the Roman church, to whom Spangenberg devoted Book XII of the first part of his work.

The second campaign was of secular interest. Spangenberg declared openly that he was moved to write by the irresponsible attacks of none other than Sebastian Franck (in his "Vorred vom Adler") and Nicodemus Frischlin (in

[53]The full title of Wagner's book was *Von des Adels Ankunfft, oder Spiegel, sammt zweien ritterlichen, adelichen Geschlechtern, als zur Tugend Anreitzung . . . , kurtzer Auszug aus vielen Antiquitäten, Chronicis etc. . . . , Darin: Kurtze einfeltige bewrische Verantwortung auff das lesterliche, unnütze und fladdergeisterische Geschmeis und Gewesch eines queckenden Fröschleins* (Magdeburg, 1581). For Frischlin's reply, see Strauss, *Leben und Schriften*, 230-35.

[54]The full title: *Adels Spiegel. Historischer Ausführlicher Bericht Was Adel sey und heisse, Woher er komme, Wie mancherley er sey, Und was denselben ziere und erhalte, und hingegen verstelle und schwäche. Desgleichen von allen Göttlichen, Geistlichen und weltlichen Standen auff Erden. . . .* (Schmalkalden, 1591, 1594).

[55]For a brief life of Spangenberg and a list of his works, see Heinrich Rembe, *M. Cyriacus Spangenbergs 'Formularbüchlein der alten Adamssprache,' mit Lebensbeschreibung Spangenbergs und einem Verzeichnis seiner Werke* (Dresden, 1887); for Spangenberg's place in the religious controversies of his day, see Robert Kolb, "God, Faith and the Devil: Popular Lutheran Treatments of the First Commandment in the Era of the Book of Concord," *Fides et Historia* 15 (1982): 71-89; and Kolb, "The Flacian Rejection of the Concordia. Prophetic Style and Action in the German Late Reformation," *Archiv für Reformationsgeschichte* 73 (1982): 196-217; Kolb has also written about one small aspect of the *Adels Spiegel*: "'A Beautiful, Delightful Jewel': Cyriakus Spangenberg's Plan for the Sixteenth-Century Noble's Library," *Journal of Library History* 14 (1979): 129-47. A hundred years ago Johannes Janssen used the *Adels Spiegel* extensively to illuminate (uncritically) the condition of the German nobility: *Geschichte des deutschen Volkes seit dem Ausgang des Mittlealters,* expanded and ed. by Ludwig Pastor, vol. 8 (Freiburg i. Br.: Herder, 1903), 232-47.

[56]On the shifting doctrine of the estates, see Winfried Schulze, "Vom Gemeinnutz zum Eigennutz. Über den Normenwandel in der ständischen Gesellschaft der frühen Neuzeit," *Historische Zeitschrift* 243 (1986): 591-626. On Luther's transformation of the traditional terms of social analysis, see Thomas A. Brady, "Luther's Social Teaching and the Social Order of His Age," *Michigan Germanic Studies* 10 (1984): 270-90; and idem, "Luther and Society," *Luther Jahrbuch* 52 (1985): 197-212; note also the comments on Brady's theses by Geoffrey Elton (ibid., 213-19) and Mark U. Edwards (ibid., 220-24).

[57]*Adels Spiegel* I: 1r-4r; the quotation is on 2r.

his *Oratio de vita rustica*). These were serious matters, and Spangenberg did not stoop to the scurrilous language of Marcus Wagner. Instead he tried to build an overpowering case for the German nobility as a wise, godly, virtuous, and necessary part of German society. The *Adels Spiegel* is so large, however, that in a restricted space I can give only an impression of its method and contents. Spangenberg was well aware that he had been compendious, claiming at the outset, "It won't be easy to say anything more about the nobility that I haven't already written in this work."[58] Before examining his argument in detail, it would be well to have a rough idea of all the subjects he included. Each volume was divided into thirteen books focusing on the following topics:

Part I

Book 1:   on God's Order and the Three Estates.

Book 2:   on the origin and meaning of *Adel*.

Bartolus thought there were three kinds of nobility, namely:

Book 3:   the spiritual nobility (Christians as the goodliest knight-hood);

Book 4:   the natural nobility (on the natural, i.e. inherited, superiority some have in beauty, strength, intelligence);

Book 5:   the political, external, secular nobility

a. obtained by birth, or

b. by merit, or

c. bought, stolen, or obtained by cunning.

Of this last category of political nobility, one must consider

Book 6:   (related to a. above) the hereditary nobility of all nations, alphabetically from the Arabs and Assyrians to the Turks and Hungarians, and more especially,

Book 7:   (related to a. above) the German nobility, alphabetically from Bavarians and Burgundians to Thuringians and Vandals.

Book 8:   (related to b. above) on nobility granted for merit.

Book 9:   (related to c. above) on nobility obtained by force, money, or fraud.

---

[58]Ibid., "Vorrede," iiii v.

Book 10: on the grades and ranks of the political nobility (from emperors and kings down to poor, one-horse nobles).

Book 11: on the knights and lesser nobles.

Book 12: on ecclesiastical orders and ranks.

Book 13: on noble women from all the world.

Part II

Book 1: a return to the meaning of *Adel* with special reference to the eagle (a refutation of Franck).

Book 2: on the origin of nobility (also a refutation of Franck).

Book 3: that the noble estate is good.

Book 4: that nobility is ancient (and that antiquity makes it better).

Book 5: that virtue is the fifth (and crucial) mark of the nobility.

The following kinds of virtue get special treatment:

Book 6: piety (fifty-four chapters, mainly on heroic Protestant noblemen);

Book 7: founding schools, churches, libraries, and hospitals;

Book 8: love of the fatherland (in praise of the Roman virtues of *veritas, magnanimitas, aequitas, epieikeia, clementia, humanitas*);

Book 9: proper relations (*justitia*) with others (with friends, wife, children, servants, preachers, rulers, Jews, the dead);

Book 10: noble personal virtues (*prudentia, temperantia, fortitudo*).

All of these virtues find illustration in the sixth mark of nobility:

Book 11: great deeds of the nobles (learned nobles, war heroes, noble inventions).

And the seventh outward mark of nobility is:

Book 12: on the offices, coats of arms, titles, privileges, and freedoms of the nobility.

But the whole institution would crumble if nobles did not pay attention to:

Book 13: those things that weaken, besmirch, and corrupt true nobility.

As one can tell from just this extended summary of the table of contents, the *Adels Spiegel* was not merely an occasional piece; Spangenberg said in his preface that he had been working on it for over forty years. He noted as well that the Frischlin affair of 1581 had been brought to his attention by several junkers but that he had refrained from writing a heated but useless polemic.[59] We can also tell at a glance that Spangenberg's defense of the nobility was not the sort to gladden every noble's heart. It was, after all, an outspokenly Lutheran account; but more than that, it was a defense so openly couched in terms of the virtue, merit, and heroic deeds of the nobility that any nobleman who hoped to rest comfortably on the merits and virtue of his ancestors was bound to feel restless. Indeed, although Spangenberg recognized the value of descent from an honorable lineage, he saw little merit in birth alone. He thought the very word *Adel,* probably stemmed from "*hat Heil* (*habens salutem*), and *edel* was always used to describe things that were better than others. Noble children, if badly brought up, were noble in name only, and instead of honor they earned shame:

> For when the children of the nobility fail to behave nobly and honorably, it is no honor for them that they have laudable forefathers; instead it is all the more shame that, being descended from such fine, honorable, and upright parents, they have become such undutiful, rude monsters. Then their parents' good name helps them but little, and really no more than it would help a cripple or a blind man that his father was smart, or a beggar that his father was rich, or a sick, weak, diseased person that his parents were sturdy and healthy . . . .[60]

Actually Spangenberg did not mean by this that each generation had to earn its own nobility. Inheritance and noble descent were worth a good deal. But he did mean that no nobleman should be proud of his descent alone.

Spangenberg was clearly not in sympathy with efforts to accentuate the importance of pedigree. Refusing to take a position on the vexing question of how many noble generations a nobleman should be able to demonstrate, Spangenberg merely noted the conflicting arguments for thirty-two, sixteen, fourteen, eight, or four noble ancestors, and then reminded his readers of Plato's point that even kings had peasants in their lineage. He also noted the fact that although bastards generally had no honor, God could raise up the lowliest to positions of highest honor, as in the cases of Hercules, Alexander the Great, Theseus, Romulus, and many others.[61] One should in any event not push such inquiries to absurd lengths, he thought, "because there is no plant, regardless of how green and beautiful it is, that doesn't have an ugly little root."[62]

[59]Ibid., "Vorrede," iiii r.   [60]Ibid., 1:46v.   [61]Ibid., 1:46v, 45v.   [62]Ibid., 1:46v.

In angry rejection of Sebastian Franck's portrait of the nobles, Spangenberg insisted that nobles were not just a good, but a necessary good. Everyone would rather be subject to noblemen than to commoners, as the aphorism had it: "Woe to those peasants who are subject to another peasant."[63] Princes made a fatal mistake if they let their knights die out in order to seize their lands and thus support ever higher levels of waste and luxury, banqueting and masquerades. Without a strong nobility, kingdoms fell prey to *"Herr Omnes"* (Sir Everyman), as had threatened to happen in 1525.[64] Franck was wrong to think that nobility began as late as Nimrod, the mighty hunter, for by then the world was already 1,800 years old and well accustomed to aristocracy. And Franck was downright blasphemous to suggest that all rule was a profane and human convention, for Christ himself was a nobleman, descended from princes and kings.[65] In his depiction of the eagle it was easiest to see how distorted Franck's views were, Spangenberg said, and it is noteworthy that he took Franck's exercise in ethology seriously enough to provide a point-by-point rebuttal, dealing with the eagle's name, his eyes, beak, nest, flight, drinking and eating, his "child-rearing," and his social relations. He even claimed that eagles could be tamed (according to Aelian and Pliny), that an eagle's claws were given by God not for wanton depredations but for God's purposes, and that when an eagle threw out all but one of his young, it was simply because he could not rear all of them properly. To Franck's charge that the Jews had recognized the eagle as an unclean animal, Spangenberg responded that the true meaning of this judgment was that God was teaching the Jews to condemn robbery, to reject the proud, and to spurn false teaching.[66]

This would appear to concede at least some points to Franck, but Spangenberg went even further in other respects. Despite his amazing and voluminous efforts to memorialize the heroic, learned, and virtuous members of the nobility, Spangenberg had to admit that some things did corrupt them and bring them into ill repute. From the table of contents of his two volumes, one can see that Spangenberg concentrated his critical remarks in the very last book of all, perhaps in an effort to minimize them. If so, it was a rhetorical and strategic mistake, for he had too much to say on the subject. Book 13 of Part II actually runs from fol. 339v to 487r – 296 large pages – and what he said was damaging in a practical sense even if it was theoretically consistent with all the talk of virtue that had come before. First Spangenberg dealt with apparent causes of noble corruption and decline, heatedly denying that poverty,

---

[63]Ibid., 2:16v: "Erbarme sich Gott dessen, Über welchen ein Bauer herrschet . . . Wehe denen Bawren, die einem andern Bawren unterworffen sein müssen."

[64]Ibid., 2:20v.

[65]Ibid., 2:11v. This was, of course, an ancient German theme, going back even to the *Heiland*.

[66]Ibid., 2:8v-11r.

undeserved contempt, or wicked gossip could truly harm a nobleman. Nor could the mere accidents of losing a battle in war or having one's children turn out badly. Even marriage to a commoner could not rob one of noble rank, even if it did mean that one's children would be excluded from tournaments for lack of uniformly noble ancestors on both sides. Similarly, living in a town, attending a university, or assuming judicial office were no real bars to noble status, regardless of what some ignorant and boorish nobles might think. What of trade? Could a nobleman descend to being a merchant? Here Spangenberg agreed with the fifteenth-century tournament regulations (and incidentally with the Italian jurists, as well as with Reinhard Graf zu Solms and Martin Luther) that trade defiled because it pulled men down into monopolies, greed, and a general striving for profits, to say nothing of how messy certain trades were.[67]

Echoing the bucolic and "georgic" tradition, Spangenberg also agreed that nobles could easily be corrupted by their lords – by the debt, usury, drunkenness, and rioting common at court – for in the end the only real harm a nobleman could suffer was to fall into vice. One of his favorite sources, André Tiraqueau, had put it succinctly when he claimed that without virtue, noble status was nothing.[68] The trouble was that men found it all too easy to fall prey to their animal lusts, becoming *Unmenschen,* no better than wolves, dogs, foxes, lions, deer, asses, birds, or swine. The tyrant who had lost all sense of human kindness could hardly be called noble.

The causes of such corruption were everywhere to be seen. First, of course, was human nature, which had been corrupt ever since the Fall, but bad child rearing was an equally potent cause. As a devout believer in marriage (and the author of a huge *Ehespiegel [Mirror of Marriage]*), Spangenberg had long held that parents needed to care for their children intelligently and piously. Mothers, even noble mothers, needed to nurse their own babies.[69] Noble youths were also tempted into vice by bad company, bad examples, and through their own moral laziness. The results were a general loathing of nobles in various parts of Europe and occasionally their elimination, as in Switzerland or in the Spanish Armada of 1588, which Spangenberg curiously regarded chiefly as a catastrophe for the Spanish nobility. Who could blame the common man for hating noblemen who despised God's Word, cursed freely, and fell into sacrilege, adultery, whoring, incest, and the protection of notorious criminals? The common man called such nobles wolves. "The older a man, the worse he is; the worse he is, the more noble" ("Quanto senior, tanto peior: quanto peior, tanto nobilior.")[70]

---

[67]Ibid., 2:347r-v.

[68]Ibid., 2:348r; for Tiraqueau's views see Schalk, *From Valor to Pedigree*, 51-53.

[69]*Adels Spiegel* 1:52v; 2:135r-137r, 353r, 400r. On Spangenbergs's *Ehespiegel,* see Thomas Miller, "'Mirror for Marriage': Lutheran Views of Marriage and the Family, 1520-1600," Ph.D. Dissertation, University of Virginia, 1981.

The root of such bestial behavior was godlessness. Many nobles, he admitted, had no Christian faith and little Christian knowledge. Most nobles refused to believe the simple words of Christ, doubting their pastors and placing more hope in their high birth than in Christ. They easily fell prey to desperation, magical uses of scripture (*falsa fiducia*), and a vast array of superstitions. Some even went over to full apostasy, becoming Papists, Turks, or Jews. As for blasphemy, Spangenberg conceded what everyone knew: the nobles were by far the worst. They joked about the devil, scurrilously doubted the existence of the soul or the torments of hell, and turned foolishly to black magic.[71] Noblemen often appeared to think that religious differences were of no real consequence. Their religion was a faithless Epicureanism whose creed was "Tranquility and Pleasant Times" ("*nur gute Tage und Ruhe*"). Spangenberg had begun his mighty encyclopedia with the avowed aim of refuting Franck and Frischlin, but it was all coming unglued for him:

> Now nothing bars lords and nobles from heaven but their damnable, stinking, fleshly pride, so that they think too well of themselves to have to learn anything godly, and their shameful contempt for the Word, for preaching and the preacher's office, and their outward self-satisfaction in which they live for days and years, refusing to subject themselves to the Word, to be instructed and punished by it. So it is that lords and squires are rare beasts in heaven, and they have no one to blame but themselves and their stubborn, prideful, and unrepentant hearts.[72]

Nobles were generally so faithless and uncivil that, as Luther said, for every nobleman who is kind to his neighbor you would find one hundred who are not. To gather together all the truly Christian nobles would not require a very large castle, Spangenberg added sarcastically with words that recall Franck's aphorism about the ring inscribed with the faces of all the pious nobles. Warming to his task, Spangenberg dramatically imagined that someone might protest that he was unfairly condemning a whole class. Such an objection ran the risk of contradicting the Holy Spirit, he noted, because Paul had written, "Not many noblemen are called" (I Cor. 1:26).[73] Most nobles, Spangenberg was sad to say, had complete contempt for church discipline and the sacraments, using them only for earthly purposes of friendship. Nobles frequently ignored the Eucharist, church weddings, and open confession of sins, preferring to dance on Sundays. They were likely to persecute any pastor brave enough to criticize them.[74]

---

[70]*Adels Spiegel*, 2:357r.   [71]Ibid., 2:359r-384v.   [72]Ibid., 2:385v.

[73]Ibid., 2: 385v-386r: "Nicht viel edele sind beruffen."

[74]Ibid., 2:391v-399r, including several intriguing examples of tension between noblemen and pastors.

Turning to the nobles' worldly transgressions, Spangenberg continued to release a pent-up litany of complaint. Nothing in Franck or Frischlin was worse than the portrait he painted of tyrannous, merciless, negligent, generally corrupt, and lazy lords; of reckless oppressors who drove their peasants to rebel; of faithless, disloyal, and quarrelsome *frondeurs*; of ungrateful traitors to prince and fatherland; of coarse, drunken gluttons and wanton lechers, adulterers and whoremongers; of envious, ambitious, greedy usurers and pompous builders of idiotic palaces, all erected at the expense of the suffering poor. The list goes on for chapter after chapter.

Just short of complete and deliberate disaster, Spangenberg collected himself and pointed out that where he disagreed with Franck was in the general assessment of nobility. While Franck had held that nobility had vicious and unworthy origins, Spangenberg hoped to salvage his position by reminding his readers that almost two thousand pages earlier he had documented the honorable origins of aristocracy. Even though it was true, as Franck claimed, that nobles were strangers in heaven (or literally venison in heaven, "Wildprat im Himmel"),[75] this was not the fault of the whole aristocracy, but only of individuals. Even though Franck's aphorism rang true – "The greater the lord the greater the fool" (*Je grösser Herr je grösser Narr*) – that did not mean that all lords were fools. Snatching at straws, Spangenberg even quibbled with Franck's exaggerated claim that nobles knew only one thing, namely, how to ride horses.[76] His was a desperate effort to save the genus of nobility after admitting that most specific examples were hopeless sinks of godless corruption. Considering the forces of religious and social unrest present in Germany during the late sixteenth century, Spangenberg staked his confidence on a social class whose members were worthless. It was a remarkable performance and a surprising conclusion to an enormous heap of erudition.

If these were the sentiments of a self-proclaimed defender of the nobles, no wonder the squirelings of Swabia had reacted in such terror and outrage at the bucolic but barbed critique of Frischlin. It is time now to attempt a few more general remarks on where this leaves us with regard to Otto Brunner's theme. For starters, we will surely be unable to agree with him that it was only in the late eighteenth century that nobles, at least in Austria,

---

[75]The phrase was well known: "wer weisz das nicht, das ein furst wiltprett im himel ist?" See Jacob Grimm and Wilhelm Grimm, *Deutsches Wörterbuch,* ed. Ludwig Sütterlin (Leipzig: S. Hirzel, 1960), col. 53. This proverbial critique of the ruling class existed in sixteenth-century England, too. John Northbrooke's *Treatise Against Dicing, Dancing, Plays and Interludes* (ca. 1577) invokes it: "I pray God the olde proverbe be not found true, that gentlemen and riche men are venison in Heaven (that is), very rare and daintie to have them come thither." Morris P. Tilley, *A Dictionary of the Proverbs in England in the Sixteenth and Seventeenth Centuries* (Ann Arbor: University of Michigan Press, 1950), 557, no. P 593.

[76]*Adels Spiegel,* 2:480r-481r.

began to feel the need to justify their existence.[77] We can certainly recognize now that even without the resources of a fully revolutionary ideology, the teachings of Aesop and Virgil, of zoology and bucolic verse had a critical capacity we should not overlook. When we take account of just how touchy and defensive the German nobles were regarding their legitimacy, moreover, we obtain a new perspective on two features of the German nobility that seem most distinctly new in the late sixteenth century: the drive among nobles to obtain a specifically noble education, on the one hand, and their growing zeal for purity of blood on the other.

We know – and Brunner's book made the point clear even if that were all we knew – that the nobles of the seventeenth century were often learned. The works of Norbert Elias have underscored the role of the court in creating more polished expectations.[78] Recently Norbert Conrads has given us a full account of one of the ways this became so, through his excellent history of the knights' academies in the sixteenth and seventeenth centuries.[79] One of Conrad's points is that the chivalric schools were much more than war colleges or riding schools; they had general educational purposes. Founded by a variety of German princes, and starting with Duke Frederick I of Württemberg's Collegium Illustre at Tübingen in 1594, these academies aimed at realizing the ideals of François de la Noue and Antoine de Pluvinel, who hoped for a moral and intellectual renewal of the nobility.[80] Conrads does a remarkable job of demonstrating the ideals of the princely founders, but he seems to leave open the question of why they became popular among noblemen whose fathers had previously shown a sensible skepticism regarding the plans of princes. The works of historians such as J. H. Hexter and Notker Hammerstein have demonstrated the growing aristocratic drive for education, to be sure, but they have not, I think, adequately explained the curious content of the first noble curricula or the form of academic life attempted

---

[77]*Adeliges Landleben,* 329; see also the article "Herrschaft" in *Geschichtliche Grundbegriffe. Historisches Lexikon zur politischsozialen Sprache in Deutschland,* vol. 3 (Stuttgart: E. Klett 1982), 1-102, here at 51, 98.

[78]Norbert Elias, *The Civilizing Process,* 2 vols. with distinct titles: 1, *The History of Manners;* 2, *Power and Civility,* trans. Edmund Jephcott (New York: Unzen, 1978, 1982); idem, *The Court Society,* trans. Edmund Jephcott (New York: Pantheon, 1983). For a general orientation see Jean-Pierre Labatut, *Les noblesses européennes de la fin du xve siècle à la fin du xviiie siècle* (Paris: Presses Universitaires de France, 1978), 160-76.

[79]Norbert Conrads, *Ritterakademien der frühen Neuzeit. Bildung als Standesprivileg im 16. und 17. Jahrhundert* (Göttingen: Vandenhoeck und Ruprecht, 1982).

[80]On the complicated legal efforts to rethink and redefine noble privileges, see Klaus Bleeck and Jörn Garber, "Nobilitas: Standes- und Privilegienlegitimation in deutschen Adelstheorien des 16. und 17. Jahrhunderts," *Daphnis* 11 (1982): 49-114.

in the first knights' academies.[81] In Tübingen the goal of moral improvement was so explicit that at first the young aristocrats were expected to live up to the standards of the former Franciscan cloister that housed them, going to evening prayers "just as mutatis mutandis a short while ago in the monasteries" ("quales in Monasteriis breves mutatis mutandis"). Duke Frederick's original plans indeed included enforcing an extraordinary level of moral rigor. Cursing, drinking, and whoring were to have special punishments; the young aristocrats were to walk *in processione* to church, attending services as early as 4:00 or 5:00 in the morning. The rector of the University of Tübingen opined in 1592 that "through too many and too harsh statutes . . . the youths would be more beaten about the head and terrorized" than given any good reason to join the Collegium.[82]

So what can we suppose made this and the other *Ritterakademien* (knights' academies) attractive? An answer lies, I think, in the fact that at Tübingen the curriculum was gradually separated from that of the university just as the student body slowly shifted, so that by 1609 only noble sons from the Holy Roman Empire of the German Nation (including Scandinavia and Hungary) were allowed to attend. From 1601 on, the Collegium had four professors: two for law, one for politics and history, and one for modern languages. It seems possible, considering the kinds of criticism leveled at the German nobility throughout the sixteenth century, that aristocratic sons were sent to Tübingen's Collegium Illustre and to the other chivalric academies in order to learn to live up to the high standards they had long claimed for themselves. Crucial to the academies' success, I think, was their exclusiveness and their creation of a cloistered world of noble attainments and virtues.[83] Without the sixteenth-century crisis of legitimation of the German nobles, such institutions might not have been very attractive. It is at least a line of inquiry worth pursuing.

The other major change with which the German nobility redefined itself in the sixteenth century was a growing emphasis upon noble blood. Of course, descent from a noble family had long been one of the marks of the old nobility, but it was apparently the cathedral chapters of the fourteenth century and the tournament societies of the fifteenth century that began the process of inquiring closely into the noble birth of all four grandparents. By the mid-sixteenth or the early seventeenth century, an authenticated proof

---

[81]J. H. Hexter, "The Education of the Aristocracy in the Renaissance," in his *Reappraisals in History* (London: Longmans, 1961), 45-71; Notker Hammerstein, "'Großer fürtrefflicher Leute Kinder': Fürstenerziehung zwischen Humanismus und Reformation," in *Renaissance – Reformation: Gegensätze und Gemeinsamkeiten*, ed. August Buck (Wiesbaden: O. Harrassowitz, 1984), 265-85; idem, "Prinzenerziehung im landgräflichen Hessen-Darmstadt," *Hessisches Jahrbuch für Landesgeschichte* 33 (1983): 193-237.

[82]Conrads, *Ritterakademien*, 108.

[83]See Schalk, *From Valor to Pedigree*, 174-201, for this argument in French costume.

of noble ancestry (*Ahnenprobe*) had become the crucial qualification for membership in the knighthood, as Heinz Reif has pointed out for Westphalia.[84] By
the mid-seventeenth century the knights of Westphalia and elsewhere were
demanding proof of sixteen noble ancestors and approval of such claims not
just by two investigators but by the whole body of knights. This was a level
of purity intended to keep out the patricians (*Erbmänner*) of Münster. But it
also far exceeded imperial requirements, with the result that many imperial
knights and princes failed to qualify for membership in the territorial nobility
of Westphalia.[85] The process by which the nobility there became a tight-knit
caste of blood is visible in the fact that the knighthood in 1495 and 1554
still comprised all those families who performed knight service. But with
the first *Privilegium Patriae* of 1570, the territorial estate of the Westphalian
nobility was redefined as those who passed the *Ahnenprobe* and possessed a
Westphalian fief (a *landtagfähiges Rittergut*).[86] It may be, as Reif and others
have assumed, that this shift to the *Ahnenprobe* was a sheer piece of calculation
to exclude urban patricians and princely favorites, but the emphasis on purity
of blood was not just a local feature of German life. It was also for example,
a prominent feature of Spanish social theory, in which purity of blood
(*limpieza de sangre*) became the new weapon by which old Christians excluded
the newly converted Jews from all public and ecclesiastical offices. In Spain,
religious distinctions shifted over rather swiftly to a clearly racial prejudice
in the sixteenth century, and the Spanish Inquisition became the enforcer
not just of religious orthodoxy but of racial purity.[87] Pressed by a new group
of rivals for honors and offices, many of whom they saw as aristocrats of
questionable credentials, the men of "pure blood" moved with decision and
terror against the *conversos,* those whose ancestors were Jewish.

The rhetoric of blood became common in France as well, but here there
was no religious element in the emerging form of racial consciousness, if we
may call it that.[88] It may be, as Schalk has argued, that the French nobility
moved more resolutely after 1590 to a "realistic" assessment of what made

[84]Heinz Reif, *Westfälischer Adel, 1770-1860. Vom Herrschaftsstand zur regionalen Elite* (Göttingen:
Vandenhoeck und Ruprecht, 1979), 34-37.

[85]Ibid., 35-36.   [86]Ibid., 57.

[87]A. A. Sicroff, *Les controverses des statuts de pureté de sang en Espagne du XVe xviie siècle* (Paris:
Didier, 1960); Léon Poliakov, *Histoire de l'antisémitisme de Mahomet aux Marranes* (Paris: Calmann-Lévy,
1961), 226; Henry Kamen, *The Spanish Inquisition* (New York: NAL, 1965), 121-39; Pierre
Chaunu, *L'Espagne de Charles Quint* (Paris: Sociétée d'édition d'enseignement supérieur, 1973),
2:469-525.

[88]André Devyver argues for the use of "racism" in his massive work, *Le sang épuré. Les
Préjugés de race chez les gentilshommes français de l'Ancien Régime (1560-1720)* (Brussels: Éditions
de L'Université de Bruxelles, 1973), 52 100-108; Ellery Schalk argues for the redefinition of
the French nobility from one of virtue and birth to one of birth alone in the years after 1594
(*From Valor to Pedigree*), but he does not call this new theory of nobility racism; see also Arlette
Jouanna, *L'idée de race,* who points out that around 1600 it was commonly thought that acquired
traits were inheritable, which makes race an extremely fluid concept; and most recently Harold

them noble – namely, birth – and in the process dispensed with some of the extravagant language of the sixteenth century that held that nobles were noble because of their virtue and valor, and only incidentally because of their birth.[89] But the nobles were never entirely comfortable with the unadorned legal claim to nobility through simple right of inheritance. Indeed, well on into the eighteenth century the French nobles claimed to be virtuous because of the good breeding and good example of their parents. It is an exaggeration to say that virtue and birth had grown apart, even if they had become separable. Even so, it seems impossible to deny that from abut 1570 onwards, French nobles came to emphasize their descent from the Frankish conquerors of Gaul, a Germanic myth that has fascinated many commentators and illustrates the rise of a kind of racial theory, even if not in a form we would call racism.[90] Surely we should recognize that despite its concern with blood and race, this style of thought, with its concern for marital legitimacy, was still far from the biological racism of our century. Three or four hundred years ago it was not only a question for nobles of who one's ancestors were, but of when and how they had joined the nobility.

Despite important differences among the Spanish, French, and German examples, the growth of the language of pedigree and of blood did signal a common reaction. In each of the cases, defenders of the old felt threatened: by the pretensions of a state that claimed the right to enfranchise or ennoble at will and to replace older families with newer ones; by urban patricians or office-holding nobles who pressed ever harder for inclusion in the noble ranks; and by those who claimed that some new attainment, whether it be virtue or education or conversion to Christianity, should entitle them to a more general equality. The appeal to birth had this obvious advantage: it could not be invented or ascribed, at least not if fraudulent documents could be exposed and if adoption was not an acceptable substitute for childbearing. Here it needs to be said that much work remains to be done. We have as yet no history of the *Ahnenprobe,* with its increasingly skeptical investigative method. It may be that we need a new approach to the heightened importance of legitimacy and the increasing fear of dishonor apparent in the *Ahnenprobe* as well. And there may be hitherto unsuspected connections between these noble anxieties and the eighteenth-century guild moralism of the German town, a moralism that would exclude a man from guild membership if he

Ellis, "Genealogy, History and Aristocratic Reaction in Early 18th-Century France: The Case of Henri de Boulainvilliers," *Journal of Modern History* 58 (1986): 414-51, who argues against the applicability of "racism" and for "genealogical consciousness."

[89]Schalk, *From Valor to Pedigree,* 115-44, 202-22.

[90]Erwin Hölze, *Die Idee einer altgermanischen Freiheit vor Montesquieu* (Munich: R. Oldenbourg, 1925); Jacques Barzun, *The French Race. Theories of Its Origins and Their Social and Political Implications Prior to the Revolution* (New York: Columbia University Press, 1932); Devyver, *Le sang épuré*; Ellis, "Genealogy, History, and Aristocratic Reaction."

could not prove that his four grandparents were all upstanding and of legitimate birth.[91] We have, moreover, no proper history of adoption. In particular, it would be worth learning how a European culture steeped in Roman law successfully avoided or reinterpreted the Roman law of adoption.[92]

My general point is this. Under attack even from their friends for their immorality, the German nobles retreated into pride of blood, an exclusiveness of race that was reinforced by the chivalric education of the *Ritterakademie*. This late-sixteenth-century process enabled the nobility to surmount a crisis of legitimacy without having to stoop to vulgar argument, and it also laid the foundations for such eighteenth-century defenses of high noble rank as that of Johann Stephan Pütter. In 1795 the Göttingen jurist published a treatise on the German nobility that argued that the two ranks of high and low nobility (the *Grafen- und Herrenstand* as opposed to the *Ritterstand*) were, and always had been, radically separate in blood and genealogy: *"zwei ganz verschiedene Gebuhrtsstände."*[93] Along with its merits as a virtuoso denial of the servile origins of the ministerials, Pütter's tract is chiefly memorable for its constant insistence on birth, blood, and genealogy as the crucial determinants of true nobility, quite irrespective of ennoblements and honors passed out promiscuously by imperial authority.[94] It was an argument that could not have been made in the sixteenth century but one that made sense in the wake of the crisis to which I hope to have drawn attention. At the very least we will have to recognize that even in the generations after 1525, *Herrschaft* was controversial;[95] claims to noble legitimacy were constantly under scrutiny, sometimes by outspoken opponents of aristocracy but more often by writers who contented themselves with curiously georgical reminders of the Virgilian *impius miles*.

[91]See Mack Walker, *German Home Towns. Community, State, and General Estate, 1648-1871* (Ithaca: Cornell University Press, 1971), 73-107. The German sense of honor has a painful history connected to these matters as well.

[92]Jack Goody provides an introduction or sketch of the problem in *The Development of the Family and Marriage in Europe* (Cambridge: Cambridge University Press, 1983), arguing cynically that the change from ancient Roman practice was prompted by the needs of the early Church to acquire property by inheriting from those who died without offspring, 48-102. John Boswell usefully redirects attention to the history of Western attitudes towards children in *The Kindness of Strangers*.

[93]Johann Stephen Pütter, *Über den Unterschied der Stände, besonders des hohen und niederen Adels in Teutschland. Zur Grundlage einer Abhandlung von Missheiraten Teutscher Fürsten und Grafen* (Göttingen, 1795; reprinted Meisenheim/Glan: Scriptor, 1979), 83-86, 89.

[94]For the controvery surrounding the right of princes to create new nobles, see Bleeck and Garber, "Nobilitas," 85-99.

[95]At this point I agree with David W. Sabean, *Power in the Blood, Popular Culture and Village Discourse in Early Modern Germany* (Cambridge: Cambridge University Press, 1984), 22-27; see also Winfried Schulze, "Peasant Resistance in Sixteenth- and Seventeenth-Century Germany in a European Context," in Peter Blickle, et al., *Religion, Politics and Social Protest. Three Studies on Early Modern Germany* (London: Allen and Unwin, 1984) 61-98; and Peter Blickle, *Deutsche Untertanen. Ein Widerspruch* (Munich: C. H. Beck, 1981).

The Social Role of Seventeenth-Century German Territorial States

Richard L. Gawthrop

This essay explores new ways to conceptualize the social impact of seventeenth-century German territorial states. Were they agents of modernization or mere exploiters of a society whose relative backwardness they did little to change? In thus attempting to get beyond the debate over the concept of "absolutism," the author draws on such themes as confessionalization, the "Second Reformation," the effects of the Thirty Years' War on statebuilding, and the actual effectiveness of the "police ordinances" decreed by the central authorities.

IN ATTEMPTING TO RECONSTRUCT the development of the state in early modern Germany, historians have traditionally assumed that the decisive turning point toward strong, "absolute" state authority took place in the seventeenth century. That century, redefined here as the period extending from the outbreak of the Thirty Years' War in 1618 to the conclusion of the wars against Louis XIV in 1714, has been associated with the alleged superseding of the weak, loosely structured Holy Roman Empire by a group of newly powerful, centralized territorial princedoms as the leading political force in central Europe. Contributing to the impression of a fundamental break in continuity at this time was the unprecedentedly calamitous Thirty Years' War, which has been plausibly regarded as *the* social and political crisis to which princely absolutism was the necessary response. That the Peace of Westphalia (1648) and laws passed by the *Reichstag* in the 1650s conferred formal sovereignty and additional new constitutional powers on the princes has lent further weight to this view. To many, perhaps, the decisive confirmation of the accuracy of this scenario was the sudden increase in the military power of Brandenburg-Prussia during the reign of the Great Elector (1640-1688). Historians of all ideological persuasions have ritualistically singled out that prince's agreement with the Brandenburg estates in 1653, which permitted him to levy direct taxes for five years, as constituting the very foundation for Hohenzollern absolutism and subsequent Prussian state power.[1]

---

[1] For a compelling critique of the tendency to exaggerate the significance of the 1653 agreement, see William W. Hagen, "Seventeenth-Century Crisis in Brandenburg: The Thirty Years' War, The Destabilization of Serfdom, and the Rise of Absolutism," *American Historical Review* 94 (1989): 302-35.

244

One of the problems with this conceptualization of the role of the seventeenth-century German state inherited from the Prussian Historical School of the late nineteenth century has been the tendency to make a certain interpretation of Prussian developments prototypical for the German lands as a whole. Another more fundamental distortion has been the inclination to telescope much of the change in the nature of the German state that occurred in the early modern period, to place it in the seventeenth century, and to attribute it to the effects of the Thirty Years' War. One obvious consequence of this way of thinking has been to minimize the significance of state-building efforts in the prewar period. Gerald Strauss's *Law, Resistance, and the State* has demonstrated the success of sixteenth-century princes in establishing the legal and administrative framework within which the stronger, postmedieval political authority developed.[2] As Strauss and others have also shown, the growth in power signified by the promulgation – and partial enforcement – of uniformly applicable territorial law was further enhanced by each prince's de facto or de jure assumption of leadership over the post-Reformation church in his territory, be it Catholic, Lutheran, or Reformed.[3] This new mandate gave the state a considerable amount of control over the educational and welfare activities of the territorial church at a time when the competing confessions were seeking to impose a stricter moral discipline and a standardized religious culture on their members.[4] It also provided a most potent ideological justification for the across-the-board expansion of princely power occurring at that time.

The drive toward legal and religious uniformity that so benefited sixteenth-century German princes was occasioned in no small measure by the socially destabilizing effects of the economic expansion, population growth, and inflation characteristic of that age.[5] Though the princes' growing pretensions were repeatedly and often vehemently contested by the estates, nearly every group in society at some point demanded the intervention of the territorial state in order to help secure a position perceived to be threatened by socioeconomic

[2]Gerald Strauss, *Law, Resistance, and the State in Sixteenth-Century Germany* (Princeton: Princeton University Press, 1986).

[3]For a concise statement of the significance of this process of "confessionalization" for the development of the sixteenth-century territorial state, see Heinz Schilling, "Between the Territorial State and Urban Liberty: Lutheranism and Calvinism in the County of Lippe," in *The German People and the Reformation,* ed. R. Po-chia Hsia (Ithaca: Cornell University Press, 1988), 266. For an extended treatment see his *Konfessionskonflikt und Staatsbildung: Eine Fallstudie über das Verhältnis von religiösem und sozialem Wandel in der Frühneuzeit am Beispiel der Grafschaft Lippe* (Gütersloh: Gerd Mohn, 1981).

[4]For a brief treatment of this theme, see Richard Gawthrop and Gerald Strauss, "Protestantism and Literacy in Early Modern Germany," *Past and Present,* 104 (August 1984): 31-43.

[5]This is certainly the premise informing the study by William J. Wright, *Capitalism, the State, and the Lutheran Reformation: Sixteenth-Century Hesse* (Athens: Ohio University Press, 1988).

change.[6] By responding to these needs and playing off different classes of the urban and rural communities against each other, sixteenth-century German princedoms were able to establish their administrative presence in the towns and villages.[7]

Thus, in addition to decreeing new statutory law and issuing "police ordinances" intended to regulate the behavior of their subjects, these territorial states were able to build up an often substantial, if largely informal, power base by developing working relationships with such groups as urban patriciates, the peasant elite that controlled the large farms in each village, and various factions of the nobility.[8] The possibilities inherent in this situation were made manifest by the accomplishments of a series of formidable princes who ruled in the late sixteenth century: Elector August of Saxony, who so successfully promoted economic growth in his lands; Duke Frederick I of Württemberg, whose bold schemes and power to intimidate his estates found no parallel among his seventeenth-century successors; and, of course, Duke/Elector Maximilian I of Bavaria, whose state-building efforts enabled him to play such a decisive military role in the early years of the Thirty Years' War.

The traditional emphasis on the decisive importance of the seventeenth century in the history of German statebuilding, besides minimizing the significance of the preceding era, has also tended to project characteristics of regimes from subsequent eras back onto the seventeenth-century state. The result has been a perception of the latter as a kind of Leviathan, able to dominate the rest of society and impel it along the road toward "rationalization." This long-accepted image does not conform to empirical reality. Just as was the case in its relations with the sixteenth-century state, the traditional corporate order in the German lands clearly survived the often-stated aim of the seventeenth-century authorities to reduce or eliminate its privileges and immunities in order to create a society capable of responding uniformly to state initiatives and directives.[9] A key factor in blocking the attempt at a leveling of society made by seventeenth-century states was the ability of the territorial estates to maintain their monopoly of office holding at the local

---

[6]Strauss, *Law, Resistance, and the State,* 161-62.

[7]For a sense of the new ability of the territorial states to interfere in the affairs of German towns, see Heinz Schilling, "The European Crisis of the 1590s: The Situation in the German Towns," in *The European Crisis of the 1590s,* ed. Peter Clark (London: George Allen and Unwin, 1985), 147-50. For the increase in the power of a small patrimonial state over its villages during this period of time, see Thomas Willard Robisheaux, *Rural Society and the Search for Order in Early Modern Germany* (Cambridge: Cambridge University Press, 1989), 175-94.

[8]For the relationship between an urban patriciate and a princely regime, see Susan C. Karant-Nunn, *Zwickau in Transition, 1500-1547: The Reformation as an Agent of Change* (Columbus: Ohio State University Press, 1987).

[9]This conclusion applies equally to France during the reign of Louis XIV. For a thorough discussion of the relationship between the monarchy and provincial society in seventeenth-century France, see William Bein, *Absolutism and Society in Seventeenth-Century France: State Power and Provincial Aristocracy in Languedoc* (Cambridge: Cambridge University Press, 1985).

level. In this capacity, notables representing the interests of traditional society continued to collect taxes for the princely regimes and to perform other, mostly judicial, tasks on the state's behalf.

Though the social composition and day-to-day workings of seventeenth-century German bureaucratic structures have scarcely been investigated at all, those historians who should know them best invariably comment on the dependence of the bureaucracies on the established corporate order – and not just in the small patrimonial states but in Saxony, Bavaria, and the Habsburg lands as well.[10] Even Brandenburg-Prussia must be included in this category, moreover, for until the reign of Frederick William I (1713-1740), the functionaries of the War Commissariat generally confined their activities to collecting taxes (with local help) and coordinating the (infrequent) passings of royal armies through the districts in their charge.[11] A case study of one section of East Prussia indicates, for example, that the commissars visited the towns only occasionally and that political control in the municipalities remained securely in the hands of the local elite.[12]

It is thus not surprising that, in the so-called age of absolutism, the territorial estates were able to retain important political power. Only in a few cases were the estates completely and permanently excluded from the highest levels of state decision making. In some of the larger polities, the estates were able either to resist absolutism completely (Mecklenburg) or to regain their customary position after a period of absolutist rule (Württemberg). Even in the more typical cases where the estates had lost ground compared to their position in the sixteenth century, executive committees representing the estates played important advisory roles (Saxony, Hesse, Bavaria).[13]

The wave of seventeenth-century absolutism, then, was on the whole resistible. This was especially true in Germany because there, as historians in recent years have emphasized, the empire did not wither away after 1648. On the contrary, the imperial government, especially its judiciary, provided an elaborate system of checks and balances that limited the princes' ability

[10]Robisheaux, *Rural Society and the Search for Order*, 178-79, 232; Richard Dietrich, "Merkantilismus und Städtewesen in Kursachsen," in *Städtewesen und Merkantilismus in Mitteleuropa*, ed. Volker Press (Cologne and Vienna: Böhle, 1983), 259; Rudolf Schlögl, *Bauern, Krieg und Staat: Oberbayerische Bauernwirtschaft und frühmoderner Staat im 17. Jahrhundert* (Göttingen: Vandenhoeck and Ruprecht, 1988), 214; R. J. W. Evans, *The Making of the Habsburg Monarchy, 1550-1700: An Interpretation* (Oxford: Oxford University Press, 1979), 146-51.

[11]Anything much more than this was beyond the capacity of the seventeenth-century bureaucracy in Brandenburg-Prussia. For the Great Elector's failure to reform the guild system, see Gustav Schmoller, "Das brandenburgisch-preussische Innungswesen," in *Umrisse und Untersuchungen zur Verfassungs-, Verwaltungs- und Wirtschaftsgeschichte besonders des preussischen Staates im 17. und 18. Jahrhundert* (Leipzig, 1898), 348-52.

[12]Hannelore Juhr, *Die Verwaltung des Hauptamtes Brandenburg/Ostpreussen von 1713 bis 1751* (Berlin: Inaug. Diss., Free University of Berlin, 1967), 118-26.

[13]F. L. Carsten, *Princes and Parlements in Germany: From the Fifteenth to the Eighteenth Century* (Oxford: Oxford University Press, 1959), 183-85, 233, 239-40, 414-15, 437.

to abrogate unilaterally the constitutionally guaranteed liberties of their subjects.[14] After his thorough investigation of early modern Lippe, where all of these constraints on princely power were in evidence, Gerhard Benecke questioned "whether in fact an age of absolutism ever existed for this territory."[15] This judgment could be applied to many other territories as well.

From an administrative and even, to a large extent, from a constitutional standpoint, therefore, it seems justifiable to emphasize the element of continuity between most of the seventeenth-century German states and their sixteenth-century predecessors. Except for cases such as Brandenburg-Prussia, where the sense of dramatic change was mainly the result of an unusually weak sixteenth-century regime rather than the revolutionary nature of its postwar successor, the seventeenth-century territorial state seems, from the perspective developed so far, to be basically a restored, consolidated version of the prewar German princedom. But is this the whole story? Is there anything fundamentally valid about the initial historiographical intuition that this period constituted a major turning point? Or, at least, were there certain aspects of seventeenth-century princely rule that modified German society in ways that contributed to the eventual emergence of the more highly bureaucratized regimes of the eighteenth century? It is these latter possibilities that the rest of this essay will explore.

Perhaps it is the case that the lasting impact of the seventeenth-century territorial states stemmed from the greater "modernity" of their economic policies. Indeed, historians have traditionally regarded this period as constituting the beginning of an age of state intervention in the economy carried out in accordance with mercantilist theoretical principles. They identify the origins of this movement with the states' allegedly dynamic response to the catastrophic economic conditions created by the Thirty Years' War. They further point to the simultaneous founding of the German mercantilist school of thought, usually known as "cameralism," by J. J. Becher in the 1670s and 1680s. Becher's call for the establishment within the state bureaucracy of a separate "commercial college" charged with aggressively promoting trade and manufacturing in the Habsburg lands inspired bureaucrats throughout the empire to attempt to establish such colleges in their own territories.[16] Becher's proposals to the Viennese court also embodied a new spirit that had appeared

[14]For a classic description of this system, see Mack Walker, *German Home Towns: Community, State, and General Estate, 1648-1871* (Ithaca: Cornell University Press, 1971), 11-13. On the ability of peasant communities to use the imperial judiciary to protect their rights, see Winfried Schulze, "Peasant Resistance in Sixteenth- and Seventeenth-Century Germany in a European Context," in *Religion, Politics and Social Protest: Three Studies on Early Modern Germany,* ed. Kaspar von Greyerz (London, Boston: George Allen and Unwin, 1984), 61-88.

[15]Gerhard Benecke, *Society and Politics in Germany, 1550-1750* (London: Routledge and Kegan Paul, 1974), 377.

[16]Ingomar Bog, "Mercantilism in Germany," in *Revisions in Mercantilism,* ed. D. C. Coleman (London: Methuen, 1969), 175-77.

before 1700 in many German state bureaucracies. As Marc Raeff's comparative study of sixteenth-century and post-1648 police ordinances concludes, the late seventeenth-century legislation was based on a much more rationalistic and pragmatic approach to problem solving and assumed a much broader mandate for state-directed economic transformation than did the sixteenth-century ordinances.[17]

In practice, however, this new spirit was not to bear much fruit until well into the eighteenth century. With respect to the efforts of German states to assist economic reconstruction after the Thirty Years' War, it is true that governments in southern, central, and especially northwestern Germany acted decisively in the immediate postwar period to prevent the nobility from buying out abandoned peasant holdings and thereby depriving the state of its tax base.[18] In protecting the peasantry from expropriation, the states were not, however, doing anything they had not already done many times in the course of the sixteenth century, though these protection operations were admittedly on a larger scale. The same was true of the economic measures taken by the various states to assist recovery in the countryside: inducing furnishing peasants with building materials, forgiving debts and unpaid taxes, and offering short-term tax relief. The purpose of these initiatives was to promote rapid resettlement of the land and a restoration of the prewar relationship between the state and the peasant communities.[19] To achieve these objectives, especially in light of the postwar labor shortage that gave the peasantry substantial bargaining leverage,[20] it would have been counter-productive for the princely authorities to have adopted radically innovative strategies, even if they had possessed bureaucracies capable of putting them into effect. Thus seventeenth-century German states did not, like their eighteenth-century counterparts, seek to increase productivity by introducing new crops and farming techniques; nor did they try to change the mentality of the peasantry, as later states did, by a more concerted effort to spread literacy among the rural populace.[21]

---

[17]Marc Raeff, *The Well-Ordered Police State: Social and Institutional Change through Law in the Germanies and Russia, 1600-1800* (New Haven: Yale University Press, 1983), 169-79.

[18]Henry Kamen, "The Social and Economic Consequences of the Thirty Years' War," *Past and Present*, 39 (1968): 56; Schlögl, *Bauern, Krieg und Staat*, 88-90.

[19]Robisheaux, *Rural Society and the Search for Order*, 228, 237-38; Schlögl, *Bauern, Krieg und Staat*, 85, 90-96.

[20]For an important reminder of how this market factor operated even in the East Elbian territories, see Hagen, "Seventeenth-Century Crisis in Brandenburg," 315-20, 327-329.

[21]A comparison between the school ordinances of the seventeenth with those of the eighteenth century reveals that in the former century there were relatively few ordinances that pertained to the school of an entire territory, whereas such comprehensive statutes were common in the eighteenth century. This pattern suggests that the latter century, like the sixteenth century, was a period in which territorial governments sought to carry out systematic pedagogical campaigns designed to produce a cultural change in the population at large. See Richard L.

Despite cameralist ambitions, moreover, the bureaucracies' attempts to stimulate trade and industrial development were also inhibited by a similar reluctance, or inability, to sponsor a major restructuring of the urban economy. In this area, the opposition of vested corporate interests, especially the guilds, was a difficult obstacle to overcome. Whereas for the countryside the Thirty Years' War, with its attendant famine and plague, eased the prewar crisis of overpopulation and enabled a strong postwar recovery to be achieved in many areas with surprising speed,[22] for most German towns and cities the same circumstances brought about a permanent loss of prosperity. Competition from cheap manufactured goods produced in the countryside or imported from abroad, depletion of capital from inflation and heavy taxation, loss of distant markets due to wartime disruption of trade, and weaker postwar demand closer to home all reduced many hitherto complex urban economies to being mere district market centers.[23]

The guilds in these communities responded to this limitation on available opportunity by tenaciously holding on to whatever privileges they possessed. Costly, distracting law suits were frequently resorted to, fought over such issues as preventing non-guild members from practicing the craft, resisting the introduction of new production techniques, and preserving the guilds' right to limit the size of each producer's enterprise. The guilds also became much more exclusive in their membership; since only masters' sons could now hope to achieve master status, the large numbers of journeymen formed a permanently underemployed, poorly motivated, and alienated element within the urban communities.[24]

Gawthrop, "Literacy Drives in Preindustrial Germany, 1500-1800" in *National Literacy Campaigns in Historical and Comparative Perspective,* ed. Robert F. Arnove and Harvey J. Graff (New York: Plenum Press, 1987), 19-48. For a compilation of the texts of Lutheran school ordinances from the sixteenth to the eighteenth centuries, see Reinhold Vormbaum, ed., *Die evangelischen Schulordnungen,* 3 vols. (Gütersloh, 1858-1864).

[22]Though not the traditional view, this assertion of a revival of the agrarian sector in the middle decades of the seventeenth century has been made in recent studies by Robisheaux and Schlögl. How general this phenomenon was and how it can be reconciled to the very high levels of destitution reported in postwar Germany should become clear with more research in the social history of the time.

[23]The current consensus seems to be that, although the German urban economy was undergoing significant structural change in the prewar period, the cities and towns still seemed capable of adjusting creatively to the changing circumstances. It was the negative factors unleashed by the war and the trade depression of the 1620s, taken together, that proved debilitating in so many cases. See Heinz Schilling, "The European Crisis of the 1590s: The Situation in the German Towns," 138-46; Rudolf Vierhaus, *Germany in the Age of Absolutism* (Cambridge: Cambridge University Press, 1988), 2-3.

[24]Karlheinz Blaschke, "Grundzüge der sächsischen Stadtgeschichte im 17. und 18. Jahrhundert," in *Die Städt Mitteleuropas im 17. und 18. Jahrhundert,* ed. Wilhelm Rausch (Linz/Donau: Österreichischer Arbeitskreis für Stadtgeschichtsforschung, 1981), 176; Carl Hinrichs, *Preussentum und Pietismus* (Göttingen: Vandenhoeck and Ruprecht, 1971), 335.

Yet the territorial states did very little to try to rectify these negative features of postwar German towns. The long-standing institution of the guild so permeated urban life that drastic measures against them were almost unthinkable for a seventeenth-century regime. For one thing, the guilds, as corporations, were protected by imperial law;[25] for another, they, like many other traditional bodies, performed important social and administrative services for the territorial state, including the collection of taxes.[26] Abolishing the guilds would also have eliminated much of the basis for the legal and economic separation of town from country, a deeply embedded feature of premodern German society.

From the point of view of nineteenth-century liberalism, razing this ancient barrier would have had the desirable economic effect of unleashing market forces being held in check by the system of monopolies run by the guilds. Seventeenth-century policy makers, however, if they even considered such a step, would have recoiled from the resulting social destabilization. It would have also occurred to them that the states' method of collecting excise taxes on the transit traffic passing through town gates depended on the preservation of the town-country dichotomy.[27] Furthermore, at least in the Bavarian case, Maximilian I had appropriated certain of the most lucrative economic rights of the towns in order to create highly profitable state monopolies.[28] Hence the territorial states were themselves inextricably enmeshed in the status quo and had strong fiscal reasons for not challenging the guilds' rights. In some cases, princely governments even went so far as to devise mercantilist legislation, such as banning the importation of certain products, for the specific purpose of helping the guilds survive.[29]

Prevented for these reasons from disturbing the existing economic order in the towns, the territorial princes sought to promote trade and industry on the margins of the guild-controlled economy. Despite formally affirming guild monopoly privileges, the princes, like their sixteenth-century predecessors, often tolerated and even actively favored the growth of beer brewing and other artisanal activities in the countryside, especially on their own domain

[25]The Peace of Westphalia, while conferring sovereignty on the princes, also guaranteed the rights of corporate institutions if they were a part of the territorial constitution, as guild rights invariably were. See Carol M. Rose, "Empire and Territories at the End of the Old Reich," in *The Old Reich: Essays on Germany Political Institutions, 1495-1806*, ed. James A. Vann and Steven Rowan (Brussels: Les Editions de la Librairie Encyclopédique, 1974), 66-68.

[26]Wilhelm Treue, "Wirtschafts- und Sozialgeschichte vom 16. bis zum 18. Jahrhundert," in Bruno Gebhardt, *Handbuch der deutschen Geschichte*, ed. Herbert Grundmann, 8th ed., vol. 2 (Stuttgart: Union Deutsche Verlagsgesellschaft, 1955), 381-82.

[27]Blaschke, "Grundzüge der sächsischen Stadtgeschichte," 178-79.

[28]Wilhelm Störmer, "Wirtschaft und Bürgertum in den altbayerischen Städten unter dem zunehmenden absolutistischen Einfluss des Landesfürsten," in Rausch, ed., *Die Städte Mitteleuropas*, 241-42.

[29]Treue, "Wirtschafts- und Sozialgeschichte," 380-81.

lands. Another, more novel strategy was to encourage the development of industries not included in the existing guild system, notably those making luxury goods or products needed by the military. Foreign entrepreneurs were frequently recruited through privileges and concessions to run these businesses, which in most cases could not operate without princely protection.[30]

A few rulers took this type of strategy a step further by seeking to use state power to give these new industries (and some existing ones) a better chance to grow by selling their goods on the world market. Thus Karl Ludwig, elector of the Palatinate, refounded Mannheim in 1652, hoping that it would become the Amsterdam of the Rhine. Another Calvinist prince, the Great Elector of Brandenburg-Prussia, had a similar vision of emulating the Dutch by establishing a seaborne and colonial trade based on the Baltic ports of his realm.[31]

Such efforts faced an uphill struggle in the late seventeenth century. If these policies were pursued too vigorously, the indigenous corporate groups would combine to resist them. Mannheim's special status, for example, was keenly resented, and it eventually lost its unique privileges after Karl Ludwig's death.[32] When Duke Eberhard III of Württemberg sought funding for an ambitious economic development program to help bolster state revenues in the aftermath of the Thirty Years' War, the estates refused to vote the necessary taxes.[33] The dependence on immigrants for many of these schemes was also a source of weakness, for the high-profile presence of foreigners not only aroused the opposition of the guilds but could also produce ecclesiastical complications. In Catholic and most Lutheran states, the established churches refused to permit the settling of immigrants who did not adhere to the same confession as that of the territorial church.[34]

Even when these obstacles were overcome and the right entrepreneur found, the chances of survival for the state-sponsored businesses were not very great. In the case of the Great Elector's overseas plans, the Dutch were not flattered by his attempts at imitation, and in the long run they were successful in frustrating his maritime ambitions. A much more common

[30]Volker Press, "Merkantilismus und die Städte," in Press, ed., *Städtewesen und Merkantilismus,* 8-9.

[31]Volker Sellin, *Die Finanzpolitik Karl Ludwigs von der Pfalz: Staatswirtschaft im Wiederaufbau nach dem Dreissigjährigen Krieg* (Stuttgart: Klett-Cotta, 1978), 205-206; Hugo Rachel, "Der Merkantilismus in Brandenburg-Preussen," *Forschungen zur brandenburgischen und preussischen Geschichte* 40 (1928): 225-26.

[32]Sellin, *Die Finanzpolitik Karl Ludwigs,* 208-209.

[33]James Allen Vann, *The Making of a State: Württemberg, 1593-1793* (Ithaca: Cornell University Press, 1984), 107-109.

[34]For Bavaria, see Schlögl, *Bauern, Krieg und Staat,* 88; for Württemberg, where the estates, in alliance with the Lutheran church, prevented the government form admitting Huguenot refugees until 1699, see Wilhelm Söll, "Die staatliche Wirtschaftspolitik in Württemberg im 17. und 18. Jahrhundert" (Inaug. Diss., University of Tübingen, 1934), 86.

problem facing these enterprises was that state budgetary constraints often meant that from the outset they were undercapitalized; in addition to this, demands of the court and army frequently burdened them with excessive taxation. In short, most of these state-initiated ventures failed because of a willingness to allow short-term requirements for more state revenue to override the longer-range economic interests of the state.[35]

This "fiscalist" orientation, already present in territorial administrations, was greatly strengthened during the period of protracted war from 1672 to 1714. Indicative of its impact on economic development was the fate of those "commercial colleges" established on Becher's Austrian model. Fiscalist opposition within the bureaucracies led to the failure of all the colleges founded before 1700, including Becher's. Only after 1740 did the commercial colleges become numerous, long-lasting, and productively innovative.[36]

Motivated by this all-pervasive fiscalism, the bureaucracies of the seventeenth-century territorial states worked far harder at exploiting traditional corporate society for ever-greater revenues than at transforming its fundamental nature. This fact in itself is not without significance, however, because of the scale of the exploitation involved. During the Thirty Years' War, to cover their operating expenses the Swedish and imperial army commanders levied extremely heavy taxes on the German people, and they were quickly imitated by the German princes themselves.[37] By the 1640s it was clear that the peasantry in particular could bear much heavier tax burdens than had been assumed possible during the prewar era. Once made, this discovery was not forgotten, even with the coming of a short-lived peace in 1648. During the interwar interlude, to be sure, tax levels were reduced by the small, patrimonial princes, as were the levies paid to the empire by the imperial cities.[38] But in the larger states, with their heavy debt burdens and continuing military commitments, tax rates either stayed roughly the same in nominal terms or, as in the case of the Palatinate and Brandenburg-Prussia, rose still higher.[39] This latter trend became the norm once more with the resumption of almost continuous warfare in the 1670s. The scope of the resulting permanent gain in state revenues is illustrated by the Bavarian case, in which the nominal rate of

----

[35]For specific examples in the case of Württemberg, see Söll, *Die staatliche Wirtschaftspolitik,* 49-60, 77-81.

[36]Bog, "Mercantilism in Germany," 178-80.

[37]For the scope and impact of Wallenstein's taxation on Hohenlohe, see Robisheaux, *Rural Society and the Search for Order,* 109-110; for a discussion of Swedish war taxation in Germany, see Michael Roberts, *The Swedish Imperial Experience, 1560-1718* (Cambridge: Cambridge University Press, 1979), 52-53.

[38]Robisheaux, *Rural Society and the Search for Order,* 238; Christopher Friedrichs, *Urban Society in an Age of War: Nördlingen, 1580-1720* (Princeton: Princeton University Press, 1979), 293-94.

[39]Sellin, *Die Finanzpolitik Karl Ludwigs,* 207; Hagen, "Seventeenth-Century Crisis in Brandenburg," 321.

direct taxation on the peasantry in 1700 was three-and-one-half times that levied on average during the decade 1611-1620. Since except for the 1620s and 1690s this period was a time of deflation, the real value of this tax increase was even higher.[40]

In theory, such extraordinary growth in the resources of the public sector would enable the territorial states, through their spending policies, to exert a major influence on the evolution of seventeenth-century German society.[41] Since expenditures on the army and court made up the overwhelming bulk of princely outlays, to understand the social impact of seventeenth-century German princedoms it is necessary to examine the effects on society of these two types of state spending.

During this period a major priority for many princes was the creation of a standing army, partly because of political necessity and partly because of the prestige and *gloire* it would bring to a princes' name. Although military expenditure added weight to the prince's political pretensions, from the point of view of the traditional society the money spent on maintaining the army brought proportionately little benefit. To be sure, foreign subsidies covered some of the costs, some members of the native nobility found employment in the princely force, and in some cases the army's need for uniforms and other supplies stimulated select sectors of the local economy.

Typically, however, within the officer corps the majority of the regimental commanders were mercenary adventurers with no organic connection to their employer's territorial society.[42] The positive economic impact of the military establishment was limited, moreover, by the long-term absence from the territory of most of the troops owing to the almost nonstop character of late seventeenth- and early eighteenth-century wars. While this absence spared the home front the social strains of hosting garrisons, it also meant that in contradistinction to, say, eighteenth-century Prussia, most of the military supplies procured by the commanders as well as the goods and services purchased by the common soldiers were supplied by foreign enterprises. It is not surprising that the estates generally resented having to pay for such forces and that their recalcitrance on this issue was sometimes the impetus

[40]Schlögl, *Bauern, Krieg und Staat,* 260-61. In Württemberg, tax rates in the late seventeenth century were four times what they had been in 1618. Wolfgang von Hippel, "Bevölkerung und Wirtschaft im Zeitalter des Dreissigjährigen Krieges: Das Beispiel Württemberg," *Zeitschrift für historische Forschung* 5 (1978): 444.

[41]Niels Steensgaard, "The Seventeenth-Century Crisis," in *The General Crisis of the Seventeenth Century,* ed. Geoffrey Parker and Lesley M. Smith (London: Routledge and Kegan Paul, 1978), 37-42.

[42]For the best account of the organization of seventeenth-century central European armies, see Fritz Redlich, *The German Military Enterpriser and His Work Force: A Study in European Economic and Social History,* 2 vols. (Wiesbaden: Steiner, 1964-1965).

behind a prince's decision to exclude the estates from his inner councils and govern in an "absolutist" manner.[43]

While the weight of these relatively unfruitful military expenditures within the state budget varied from territory to territory, in almost every princedom a substantial proportion of the princely revenues was spent on the court. Magnificent palaces for the princes and stately residences for the court nobility, sumptuous clothes and decorations, elaborate ceremonies and lavish entertainments all were intended to enhance a ruler's "representation" of himself and his dynasty. In a century that was even more status conscious than its predecessors, presiding over the most elegant court, with the highest ranking nobility in attendance, was the most tangible and visible way for a ruler to demonstrate his rank and authority.[44]

Representation was intended as a means of bolstering the prince's prestige within the aristocratic society of Europe, but it had important social and economic impacts within the prince's own territory as well. The court, far more than the military, offered opportunities for the industrious and ambitious. Although some luxury articles and individual artists were imported from abroad, the concentration at court of high culture and high fashion provided employment for large numbers of skilled artisans, masons, architects, painters, actors, and musicians.[45] The newly rich also gravitated to the courts in hopes of receiving a grant of nobility, by purchase if necessary.[46] The centers of the action, the so-called "residence cities" (*Residenzstädte*) of the princes, grew rapidly during the seventeenth century, outstripping in size and cultural influence other territorial cities that had rivaled or surpassed them in the sixteenth century.[47] The presence of the court and its great economic impact on the *Residenzstadt* naturally affected the tone of social relations in that city; the patriciate devoted their energies to securing favor at and benefits from the court, adopting the courtly culture in the process and thereby separating

[43]For an account of such a confrontation in Württemberg in 1698-1699, see Vann, *The Making of a State,* 164-70. Carsten makes the point, however, that standing armies and the preservation of a reasonably strong political role for the estates could coexist. See his *Princes and Parliaments in Germany,* 438.

[44]On the relationship between theatricality and display, on the one hand, and princely power, on the other, see James Van Horn Melton, "From Image to Word: Cultural Reform and the Rise of Literate Culture in Eighteenth-Century Austria," *Journal of Modern History* 58 (1986): 98.

[45]For a discussion of the economic impact of the court on a *Residenzstadt,* see Edith Ennen, "Mitteleuropäische Städte im 17. und 18. Jahrhundert," in Rausch, ed., *Die Städte Mitteleuropas,* 15-18.

[46]Gerhard Benecke, "Ennoblement and Privilege in Early Modern Germany," *History* 56 (1971): 360-65.

[47]Rudolf Vierhaus, "Höfe und höfische Gesellschaft in Deutschland im 17. und 18. Jahrhundert," in *Absolutismus,* ed. Ernst Hinrichs (Frankfurt/Main: Suhrkamp, 1986), 122-23.

themselves still further from their urban subjects.[48] Their counterparts in the outlying towns imitated them in this respect as much as possible, with similar consequences for their communities.

The most important – and sometimes most desperate – suppliants for princely largesse were, however, the territorial nobility. With the fall of grain prices after 1630, the real value of feudal ground rents, usually paid in kind, fell steadily, while the labor shortage created by the Thirty Years' War raised the level of wages that had to be paid to workers on the nobles' domain lands. Moreover, west of the Elbe, as we have seen, the states prevented their territorial nobility from compensating for declining income by buying up devastated or deserted peasant farms. Even east of the Elbe, in Brandenburg-Prussia the tax demands successfully imposed on the peasantry by the state meant that, despite the legal authority late seventeenth-century Junkers possessed over their serfs, they could not increase their share of the surplus that could be extracted from the peasants.[49]

Under these circumstances, the only way a large group of noble families could avoid a steep downward slide on the socioeconomic ladder was to receive an office, officership, or pension from the ruler. Officeholders gained wealth from their position not so much from its salary but from the opportunities it offered them to claim their share of the taxes collected from the population at large, since there was invariably a substantial difference between that sum and the revenue actually received by the central treasury.[50] In return, these recipients of princely favor – by no means always or even usually members of the same families who were at the top of territorial society in the sixteenth century[51] – put their talents, local influence, or merely the lustre of their names at the disposal of their prince.

The most apparent consequence, then, of the manifold expansion in the seventeenth-century territorial state's ability to squeeze funds out of its subjects was this operation for recycling income to the nobility. It is no wonder that this period in the history of central Europe is so frequently described as a

[48]For the case of Koblenz, see Etienne François, *Koblenz im 18. Jahrhundert: Zur Sozial-und Bevölkerungsstruktur einer deutschen Residenzstadt* (Göttingen:Vandenhoeck and Ruprecht, 1982), 195-98.

[49]Hagen, "Seventeenth-Century Crisis in Brandenburg," 326, 330.

[50]Peter Blickle, "Untertanen in der Frühneuzeit: Zur Rekonstruktion der politischen Kultur und der sozialen Wirklichkeit Deutschlands im 17. Jahrhundert," *Vierteljahrschrift für Sozial-und Wirtschaftsgeschichte* 70 (1983): 511-12. For a detailed analysis of how monarchy and provincial estates shared tax revenues in seventeenth-century France, see Beik, *Absolutism and Society*, 245-78.

[51]For the turnover in the top ranks of the nobility in the Habsburg lands in the early-to-mid-seventeenth century, see Evans, *The Making of the Habsburg Monarchy*, 93-94. For the same phenomenon in Brandenburg, see Peter-Michael Hahn, "Landesstaat und Ständetum im Kurfürstentum Brandenburg während des 16. und 17. Jahrhunderts," in *Ständetum und Staatsbildung in Brandenburg-Preussen: Ergebnisse einer internationalen Fachtagung*, ed. Peter Baumgart (Berlin: de Gruyter, 1983), 62-65.

time of "refeudalization," or that Perry Anderson was moved to define absolutism as a "redeployed and recharged apparatus of feudal domination."[52] Indeed, what must have lain at the root of the perception of the seventeenth-century state as a momentous novelty was its ability to project a great deal more power than its immediate predecessor, even though that increase in power was based on intensified utilization, through the institution of the court, of the same basic techniques of personal rule that prevailed in the sixteenth century.

Yet however strong the continuity between the seventeenth-century German territorial state and earlier forms of social and political organization may have been, there is also a connection, largely indirect, between it and the emergence of modern capitalism and the nation-state. The effects of rampant fiscalism on the people from whom the taxes were collected in the long run undermined the social basis of the ancien régime itself. The type of basically traditional state that still prevailed in sixteenth- and seventeenth-century Germany rested on a typically premodern society, i.e. one that was segmented into semiautonomous social groupings, each of which largely took care of its own affairs and required only a modest amount of coordination and protection from the central government.[53] In early modern Germany, two key institutions of this sort were the town community (an association of guilds) and the peasant commune, and it was their long-term viability that was significantly diminished by the policies of the seventeenth-century states.

This was especially the case in the larger territorial states, where the fiscal pressure was greatest. But even in the imperial city of Nördlingen, as Christopher Friedrichs has shown, the heavy (imperial) taxation of the late seventeenth century so crippled the guild structure that in the eighteenth century the town's economy, and ultimately its government, became dominated by putting-out capitalist entrepreneurs.[54] A corresponding decline in the strength of the peasant commune during the seventeenth century has also been noted, though not adequately investigated, by historians.[55]

Yet there are some clues as to what was going on in the countryside. In a pioneering study of rural Bavaria, Rudolf Schlögl has discovered evidence of increased social insecurity in the villages in the second half of the seventeenth century. For the first time, peasants with substantial landholdings sought in large numbers to confirm their property rights by receiving notarial documents from the electoral government rather than relying on oral agreements within

[52]Perry Anderson, *Lineages of the Absolutist State* (London: New Left Books, 1974), 18.

[53]For an illuminating discussion of the traditional state, see Anthony Giddens, *The Nation-State and Violence: Volume Two of a Contemporary Critique of Historical Materialism* (Berkeley: University of California Press, 1987), 35-82.

[54]Friedrichs, *Urban Society in an Age of War,* 295-96.

[55]Blickle, "Untertanen in der Frühneuzeit," 507-17.

the peasant community. Given the present state of knowledge, one can only speculate that the upheavals caused by the Thirty Years' War severely disrupted the social solidarity of many villages and that the burdens of postwar taxation perpetuated an atmosphere of tension and conflict. In any case, the consequences of such dependence on the state by the village elite were profound. The documents in question gave the bureaucracy a great deal of hitherto hard-to-secure information about the wealth and landholdings of the peasantry. The new reliance on written records also gave the better-off peasants a strong incentive to become literate and thereby culturally differentiated from the rest of the village.[56]

Another critical impact of the tax surge of the seventeenth century on the countryside was the monetarization of the village economy, as all of its members now had to make substantial tax payments to the state in cash. In thereby promoting the integration of central Europe's villages into the market economy, the seventeenth-century territorial states prepared the way for the dramatic social changes of the eighteenth century, when the pace of the market economy quickened and rapid population growth greatly increased the numbers of cottagers and landless laborers in the rural communities.

Depending in part on local economic factors and in part on the extent of state exploitation, there were two types of rural society that emerged in eighteenth-century Germany. As Thomas Robisheaux points out, in areas where the peasants with substantial landholdings continued to dominate a functioning village commune, urban entrepreneurs were unable to organize proto-industrial operations. While these communities thus preserved their traditional character (and the peasant elite became wealthy selling cash crops to the urban market at steadily increasing prices), the negative consequence of this situation was a large-scale emigration of the poorer inhabitants out of such villages.[57] In other regions, where perhaps because of heavier taxation the communes had lost their former authority, rural industry blossomed in the eighteenth century, further cutting into the economic position of the guild-controlled manufacturing sector and further diminishing the legal and cultural barriers between town and countryside.[58]

As these processes of social disintegration gained momentum, the ability of traditional institutions in town and countryside to exercise social control in the customary manner declined. Hence the need for a new political system

[56]Schlögl, *Bauern, Krieg und Staat,* 290-91, 365-66.

[57]Robisheaux, *Rural Society and the Search for Order,* 254-55. In East Elbian areas, of course, the bulk of the profits from sales of agricultural products went to the Junker landlords. Another important difference was that, except for Silesia, these regions were still relatively underpopulated and in fact served, along with the America colonies, as destination points for colonists from the overcrowded lands in western Germany.

[58]For a discussion of the origins of "proto-industry" in the German lands, see Peter Kriedte et al., *Industrialization Before Industrialization,* trans. Beate Schempp (Cambridge: Cambridge University Press, 1981), 12-25.

that would compensate for the perceived lack of order in society by imposing tighter social discipline through bureaucratic and pedagogical means. When such regimes became the norm in central Europe by the middle of the eighteenth century, the era of courtly absolutism had come to a close because the new states, such as Frederician Prussia, had the greater power.

The Contributors

The Contributors

Thomas A. Brady, Jr.

Thomas A. Brady was for many years professor of history at the University of Oregon; he is now at the University of California at Berkeley. His first book, *Ruling Class, Regime, and Reformation at Strasbourg, 1520-1555* (1978), has become a model of the new social history as applied to the urban Reformation. His second book, *Turning Swiss: Cities and Empire, 1450-1550* (1985), received the German Studies Association Book Prize. Brady is also the author of numerous articles and of several dozen historiographically rich book reviews. He has served as president of the Society for Reformation Research. As a Guggenheim Fellow during 1988-1989, he wrote a biography of the Strasbourg educator Jakob Sturm, which is forthcoming.

Miriam Usher Chrisman

Miriam Usher Chrisman received her Ph.D. in history from Yale University in 1962 and went on to a distinguished teaching career at the University of Massachusetts at Amherst, becoming full professor in 1972 and professor emerita in 1988. She has served as president of the American Society for Reformation Research, vice-president of the Sixteenth Century Studies Conference, American editor of the *Archive for Reformation History,* and as a member of the editorial board of *Church History.* Her book *Strasbourg and the Reform* (1967) established her as one of the pioneers in the field of the urban Reformation. Her later books include *Lay Culture, Learned Culture: Books and Social Change in Strasbourg 1480-1599* (1982) and *Bibliography of Strasbourg Imprints* (1982), along with many articles and other works. In her honor, the Society for Reformation Research created the biennial Miriam U. Chrisman Travel Fellowship. Professor Chrisman is currently working on a book on lay pamphlets in the sixteenth century.

Mark U. Edwards, Jr.

Mark U. Edwards, Jr. is professor of the history of Christianity at the Divinity School of Harvard University, which he joined in 1987 after serving as professor of history at Purdue University. He has been an officer or council member in the Society for Reformation Research, the American Society of Church History, and the Sixteenth Century Studies Conference. He is currently the chair of the Continuation Committee for the Eighth International Luther Congress, scheduled to meet in Saint Paul, Minnesota, in August 1993. Edwards is author of *Luther's Last Battles: Politics and*

261

Polemics, 1531-1546 (1983); *Luther: A Reformer for the Churches* (with George Tavard, 1983); *Luther and the False Brethren* (1975); and many articles on Luther and the German Reformation. He is now working on the presentation of Luther and Luther's theology in the vernacular press of the sixteenth century.

Andrew C. Fix

Andrew C. Fix received his Ph.D. in 1984 from Indiana University in Bloomington, where he was a student of Gerald Strauss. He has been Assistant Professor of History at Lafayette College in Easton, Pennsylvania, since 1985. He has received grants from the National Endowment for the Humanities, the Fulbright Foundation, the Woodrow Wilson Foundation, and the Newberry Library Renaissance Center. He has published several articles on intellectual life in seventeenth-century Holland and his book, *Prophecy and Reason: The Dutch Collegiants in the Early Enlightenment* was published by Princeton University Press in 1991. One of the themes of his research in the influence of Radical Reformation religious ideas on the growth of seventeenth-century philosophical rationalism.

Richard L. Gawthrop

Richard Gawthrop received his Ph.D. in 1984 from Indiana University, where he was a student of Professor Strauss. His thesis "'For the Good of Thy Neighbor': Pietism and the Making of Eighteenth-Century Prussia," explored the connections between religion and statebuilding in early modern Germany. The thesis was awarded the Esther Kinsley Dissertation Prize by the Indiana University Graduate School in 1984. Gawthrop has received grants from the German Academic Exchange Service and he has taught at Northwest Missouri State University and the University of South Carolina, where he is currently assistant professor of history. His publications include *Literacy Drives in Preindustrial Germany, 1500-1800" in National Literacy Campaigns in Historical and Comparative Perspective,* ed. Robert F. Arnove and Harvey Graff (1987), and "Protestantism and Literacy in Early Modern Germany," coauthored with Gerald Strauss, in *Past and Present* 104 (August 1984). He currently has a book forthcoming from Cambridge University Press dealing with Lutheranism, statebuilding, and society in seventeenth- and eighteenth-century Germany.

Hans J. Hillerbrand

Hans J. Hillerbrand received his Ph.D. from the University of Erlangen in 1957 in the field of intellectual history. He taught at Duke University, the City University of New York, and Southern Methodist University before becoming professor of religion and history at Duke in 1988. Hillerbrand has served as dean of the graduate school at the City University of New York and as provost/vice president of academic affairs at Southern Methodist University, as well as president of the American Society for Reformation Research. He has served on the boards of the American Society for Church History, the Renaissance Society of America, and the Center for Reformation Research, and on the editorial boards of the *Journal of the History of Ideas,* the *Mennonite Quarterly Review,* the *Journal for Medieval and Renaissance Studies,* and the *Archive for Reformation History.* His major publications include *A Bibliography of Anabaptism* (1962), *A Fellowship of Discontent* (1967), *Christendom Divided* (1971), and *The World of the Reformation* (1973), along with many other books and articles. Dr. Hillerbrand is currently Professor of Religious Studies at Duke University and is working on "Germany 1517-1531: An Essay on Religion and Society." He is senior editor of a forthcoming multivolume Encyclopedia of the Reformation.

Susan C. Karant-Nunn

Susan C. Karant-Nunn received her Ph.D. in 1971 from Indiana University in Bloomington, where she was a student of Gerald Strauss. She is currently professor of history at Portland State University, where in 1982 she was awarded the fourth annual Branford P. Miller Award for Faculty Excellence. She has held fellowships from the International Research and Exchanges Board and the American Association of University Women, and travel grants from The American Council of Learned Societies, the American Philosophical Society, and the National Endowment for the Humanities. Her publications include *Luther's Pastors: The Reformation in the Ernestine Countryside* (1979) and *Zwickau in Transition, 1500-1547: The Reformation as an Agent of Change* (1987). She has written several articles on the effects of the Lutheran Reformation on women, and she is currently writing a book on the silver-mining communities of the Saxon Erzgebirge and their reception of the Reformation.

H. C. Erik Midelfort

H. C. Erik Midelfort received his Ph.D. from Yale University in 1970 and began teaching as an assistant professor at the University of Virginia that same year. In 1972 he became an associate professor and in 1987 a full professor at Virginia. Professor Midelfort has received fellowships from the National Endowment for the Humanities and from the John Simon Guggenheim Memorial Foundation, among others. His publications include *Witch Hunting in Southwest Germany 1562-1648* (1972) and over twenty articles on the history of witchcraft, peasants, madness, the insanity defense, Foucault, the social history of the Reformation, and other topics. He is especially interested in the social history of the Reformation era, including the social history of ideas in Germany and the connections between ideas, society, and politics. His current research is on madness in sixteenth-century Germany.

Heiko A. Oberman

Dr. Heiko A. Oberman is director of the Center for Late Medieval and Reformation Studies at the University of Arizona. He has also taught at the University of Tübingen and Harvard University. He is a fellow of the Medieval Academy of America, corresponding fellow of the British Academy, and correspondent of the Royal Netherlands Academy. He is the author of many important books in late medieval and Reformation studies, including *The Harvest of Medieval Theology, Forerunners of the Reformation, Masters of the Reformation, The Roots of Anti-Semitism in the Age of Renaissance and Reformation,* and *Luther: Man Between God and the Devil.* In 1985 he received the Historischer Sachbuchpreis for the German edition of his biography of Luther. Oberman is by general consent one of the most important scholars of Reformation history in the world today.

R. Po-chia Hsia

R. Po-chia Hsia is professor of history at New York University. He received his Ph.D. in 1982 from Yale University and has been awarded grants from the American Council of Learned Societies, the National Endowment for the Humanities, and the John Simon Guggenheim Memorial Foundation. His publications include *Society and Religion in Münster 1535-1618* (1984), *The Myth of Ritual Murder: Jews and Magic in Reformation Germany* (1988), and *Social Discipline in the Reformation: Central Europe 1550-1750* (1989). In addition, he was editor of *The German People and the Reformation* (1988). Hsia is currently working on a history of Jewish communities in early modern central europe and has forthcoming *Trent 1475: Story of a Trial.* He is presently a Fellow at The Woodrow Wilson International Center for Scholars.

Heinz Schilling

Dr. Heinz Schilling studied German literature, philosophy, and history at the Universities of Cologne and Freiburg before receiving his doctorate at Freiburg in 1971 with a thesis on the influence of Dutch Calvinist refugees in Germany and England during the sixteenth and seventeenth centuries. He taught at the University of Bielefield and the University of Osnabrück before being appointed to the chair of modern history at Justus-Liebig University in Giessen in 1982. Professor Schilling's research interests include the social and ecclesiastical history of towns and territories in northwest Germany during the early modern period, early modern Dutch history, and the social and intellectual history of Calvinism and Calvinist communities in Germany and northwest Europe. His major publications include *Niederlandische Exulanten im 16. Jahrhundert* (1972), *Konfessionskonflikt und Staatsbildung* (1981), *Burgerliche Eliten in den Niederlanden und in Nordwest Deutschland* (1985), and *Aufbruch und Krise: Deutsche Geschichte von 1517 bis 1648* (1988), among many other works. Professor Schilling is a member of the Work Group for Comparative Urban History at the University of Münster and a member of the board of directors of the German Society for Reformation Research. He is currently preparing a book on the social and intellectual history of Calvinist presbyteries from the sixteenth to the eighteenth centuries.

Hans-Christoph Rublack

Hans-Christoph Rublack has been professor of modern history at Tübingen University since 1978. At Tübingen he has participated in the Special Research Group for the Late Middle Ages and Reformation, heading the research team on cities. He is the managing editor of the *Literature Review* of the *Archive for Reformation History*, and in his own work has become one of the leading authorities on the Reformation in the cities. Among his many publications are *Die Einführung der Reformation in Konstanz* (1971); *Gescheiterte Reformation. Frühreformatorische und protestantische Bewegungen in süd- und westdeutschen geistlichen Residenzen* (1978); and *Eine bürgerliche Reformation: Nördlingen* (1982). He is currently working on the problem of Lutheranism in early modern society.

Merry E. Wiesner

Merry E. Wiesner received the Ph.D. from University of Wisconsin at Madison. She is associate professor of history at the University of Wisconsin at Milwaukee, is an authority on women's history in Reformation Germany. Her 1986 book, *Working Women in Renaissance Germany,* examined the social economic and ideological changes that affected the lives of working women in that period. She has also published *Women in the Sixteenth Century: A Bibliography* (1983) and *Discovering the Western Past: A Look at the Evidence* (with Julius Ruff and Bruce Wheeler, 1988), as well as numerous articles. She has received grants from the American Council of Learned Societies, the Deutscher Akademischer Austauschdienst, the Fulbright Foundation, and the American Association of University Women, among others. She is currently completing a book on women and gender in early modern Europe, which will be published by Cambridge University Press.

Index